FOURTH EDITION

D0037507

Women and Men

Cultural Constructs of Gender

Nancy Bonvillain
Simon's Rock College of Bard

PEARSON

Prentice
Hall

Upper Saddle River, New Jersey 07458

Library of Congress Cataloging-in-Publication Data

Bonvillain, Nancy.
  Women and men : cultural constructs of gender / Nancy Bonvillain.— 4th ed.
    p. cm.
  Includes bibliographical references and index.
  ISBN 0-13-111476-X
  1. Sex role—Cross-cultural studies. I. Title.
  GN479.65.B66 2008
  305.3—dc22

                                                    2006023977

Publisher: Nancy Roberts
Editorial Assistant: Lee Peterson
Full Service Production Liaison:
  Joanne Hakim
Senior Marketing Manager:
  Marissa Feliberty
Manufacturing Buyer: Ben Smith
Cover Art Director: Jayne Conte
Cover Design: Bruce Kenselaar
Cover Illustration: Jose Ortega,
  Stock Illustration Source
Director, Image Resource Center:
  Melinda Patelli

Manager, Cover Visual Research &
  Permissions: Karen Sanatar
Manager, Rights and Permissions:
  Zina Arabia
Manager, Visual Research: Beth Brenzel
Photo Coordinator: Debbie Latronica
Full-Service Project Management:
  Shiny Rajesh/Integra Software Services
Composition: Integra Software Services
Printer/Binder: RR Donnelley &
  Sons Company

Credits and acknowledgments borrowed from other sources and reproduced, with
permission, in this textbook appear on appropriate page within text (or on page 366).

Pearson Education LTD., London
Pearson Education Singapore, Pte. Ltd
Pearson Education, Canada, Ltd
Pearson Education–Japan
Pearson Education Australia PTY,
  Limited

Pearson Education North Asia Ltd
Pearson Educación de Mexico,
  S.A. de C.V.
Pearson Education Malaysia, Pte. Ltd
Pearson Education, Upper Saddle River,
  New Jersey

10 9 8 7 6 5 4 3 2
ISBN 0-13-111476-X

Contents

Preface

This book aims to present a synthesis of a wide range of ethnographic and historical data concerning the roles of women and men in different kinds of societies. It focuses on both material conditions and ideological valuations that affect and reflect cultural models of gender.

The fourth edition of *Women and Men: Cultural Constructs of Gender* contains new sections in several chapters, along with updated economic and social statistical data pertaining to the United States and to global trends as well as expanded discussions of a number of topics interspersed throughout the book. These additions are detailed in the chapter descriptions below.

PART I: THE IMPACT OF MATERIAL CONDITIONS ON GENDER ROLES

Chapter 1 considers the notion of gender as a social construct. It discusses interrelationships of gender and other aspects of culture (economy, social and political organization, and religion), which form the basis for the presentation of data and theory in subsequent chapters. Two new sections are included. The first, "Gender and Evolution," discusses theories of the interplay of features of gender with both biological and social evolutionary patterns. The second new section, "Women in Prehistory," presents data regarding the role of women in prehistoric societies in an attempt to make women's lives visible through the archaeological record.

Chapter 2 considers gender roles and relations in several societies whose economic base is centered on foraging. Comparison is made between the Ju/'hoansi (ju-TWAN-si) in Namibia and Botswana and the Inuit and Inupiat of Arctic Canada and Alaska.

Gender roles in pastoral and farming societies are discussed in Chapter 3. The chapter begins with a new section, "The Origins of Farming," that discusses theories about women's contribution to the development of farming techniques in the Middle East and in North America. Then a number of societies are considered, including nomadic pastoral societies of the American Plains, mixed pastoral and farming societies (the Navajo, Nuer, and Luo), and horticultural societies such as the Iroquois of North America, the Yanomamo and Jivaro of the Amazon, and the Igbo of Nigeria.

In Chapter 4 is a discussion of gender roles in stratified societies, concentrating on peoples of the Canadian Pacific coast (the Haida and Tlingit), the Kpelle of Liberia, the Mpondo of the Transkei, and the Tonga of Polynesia. Interrelationship between increased stratification and gender inequality is demonstrated to varying degrees in these societies.

The existence of marked gender inequality in agricultural states is discussed in Chapter 5, exemplified by the Incan society of Peru and the modern states of India and China. Chapter 6 analyzes the historical development of industrialization in the United States in terms of its use of and impact on gender inequalities in preexisting societies. Utilization of women's labor in early industrialization and the subsequent marginalization of women in advanced industrial nations are discussed. Statistics on employment, income, poverty rates, and other social and economic data are updated from the U.S. Bureau of the Census and the Department of Labor for the early twenty-first century. Finally, Chapter 7 reviews processes of global economic development and demonstrates their effect on women's and men's roles and relationships. The chapter also includes current data compiled by the United Nations on economic, social, and political patterns worldwide.

PART II: IDEOLOGICAL CONSTRAINTS ON GENDER CONSTRUCTS

Chapter 8 examines several worldwide issues concerning the interrelationships among gender, health, and survival. It also contains a new, detailed discussion of a third gender, a social category existing in many native cultures of North America that was distinct from the genders of woman and man. In addition, women's so-called reproductive illnesses—namely, premenstrual syndrome (PMS) and menopausal disorders—are discussed as examples of societal attitudes that label women's normal biological functions as illnesses requiring control and correction. Chapter 8 includes two new sections: "Hormones and Behavior" and "Gender and Aging." It also contains a section on "Female Genital Mutilation," previously located in Chapter 9, "Gender and Religion."

The function of religious beliefs and practices in justifying and reinforcing gender roles and relations is the focus of Chapter 9. It includes a discussion of religion and homosexuality, examining religious proscriptions against and prescriptions for sexual relations between members of the same sex. And, finally, the chapter includes a review of some tendencies within the women's spirituality movement.

Chapter 10 considers evidence of the role of language in maintaining and reproducing societal gender relations. It begins with an examination of English and English speakers and then proceeds with discussion of language in a variety of cultures. Data are derived from Japanese, Javanese, Malagasy (Madagascar), Kuna (Panama), and Mohawk (Native North America), with French, German, and Spanish briefly noted.

Finally, Chapter 11 summarizes the main arguments presented in our analyses of gender roles and relations. It also examines the impact of historical forces of change on gender models. The chapter concludes with a discussion of ideological barriers to changing beliefs and attitudes of gender but, in the end, stresses the possibility of individual and societal transformation.

I wish to thank Nancy Roberts, publisher, for her continued advice and encouragement throughout the preparation of this new edition. I also wish to thank Shiny Rajesh of Integra Software Services, India, for her suggestions and her diligence in overseeing the final production process. Appreciation and thanks go to Amanda Lee and Allison Newton, students at Simon's Rock College of Bard for their initiative and hard work in researching sources for some data updates. I also wish to thank several anonymous reviewers whose comments were the stimulus for some of the new sections.

Nancy Bonvillain

PART I

The Impact of Material Conditions on Gender Roles

Chapters in Part I deal with the ways that material conditions affect the allocation of roles performed by men and women. Among the most important societal roles are those entailed in economic production. Access to and control over subsistence resources are instrumental in determining an individual's status in household and community. Status within the household is reflected in individuals' rights to autonomy and in their ability to make decisions affecting themselves and others. Status in the community is expressed through public participation in discussion, decision making, and leadership. The roles people are permitted to perform determine or at least influence the positive or negative cultural value accorded to each person.

The data and analyses presented in Part I are organized around the intersecting perspectives of economic modes of production and systems of political integration. Although a given culture may make use of several economic strategies, each society has a predominant economic mode that organizes not only subsistence activities but also the nature of structural relations among groups of people. These structural relations have consequences for the dynamics of daily interpersonal behavior as well. Gender is a basic criterion for the assignment of economic work in most cultures and is therefore deeply entwined in a society's mode of production.

Systems of political integration are also fundamental in organizing society both on the macrolevel of social functioning and on the microlevel of personal activity. Whether men and women are permitted full participation in their household and community or whether one group is given structural advantages of prestige and power is a significant factor in the valuation of women and men.

Each chapter in Part I focuses on cultures that exemplify the ways modes of production and systems of political integration affect gender roles and gender models. Chapter 2 is concerned with egalitarian foraging societies. It principally contrasts the Ju/'hoansi of Botswana and Namibia and the Inuit and Inupiat of Arctic Canada and Alaska. Among the traditional Ju/'hoansi, both men and women have access to and control over resources. Their economic equality is reflected in the fact that gender equality is both the ideal and the norm. In contrast, among the Inuit and Inupiat, men have significantly greater control over resources than do women. In these societies, men's control over resources is translated into dominance over women in certain key social and familial arenas.

Chapter 3 analyzes data from pastoral and horticultural societies. In general, access to resources is again shown to be a determining factor in women's and men's rights and status. Where men control production, such as among the Yanomamo of Venezuela and the peoples of the Great Plains of North America, men's dominance over women develops. In contrast, where both women and men have control over resources and over their own behavior, as among the Iroquois of northeastern North America, gender equality is maintained.

In Chapter 4, material concerning stratified societies indicates that as social and political structures become more hierarchically ordered, gender is often used as a basis for the differentiation and **segmentation** of social rights. Gender becomes enmeshed in competition over resources and for control of the means of dominating others. Societies with relatively weak systems of political integration (for example, the Haida of the Pacific coast of Canada) tend to be characterized by greater equality between men and women, whereas those with marked political hierarchies (for example, the Kpelle of Liberia) tend to legitimate male dominance. The example of Tonga in the South Pacific demonstrates that as chiefdoms are transformed into states, gender inequality emerges as an organizing principle of social ordering and control.

The connection between social and political hierarchies and gender inequality intensifies in state societies. Chapter 5 takes up this issue, beginning with the Incan state, whose development was cut short by Spanish conquest in the sixteenth century. The dynamics of state and gender are further studied in India and China, two agricultural states with systems of intense patriarchal control and severe restrictions on and devaluation of women.

Chapter 6 analyzes interconnections between the development of industrial production and gender models in the United States. It demonstrates interrelationships among economic mode, allocation of roles, control over resources, and the subsequent status and rights of men and women. The chapter also shows how the ideology of male dominance is used both to exploit women's labor and to create competition between women and men. Although this competition results in direct disadvantages for women, it can be detrimental to the interests of the majority of men as well.

Chapter 7 reviews global economic development programs in Latin America, Africa, India, Asia, and the Pacific. Research demonstrates that rather than being gender-neutral, development strategies often primarily benefit men, whereas women experience a decline in their economic and social status. Socialist nations have attempted to establish gender equality but have generally failed because they have principally concentrated on economic participation and ignored the social and ideological features of women's subordination.

Summary List of Cultures

Name	Location	Mode of Production	Kinship System
Ju/'hoansi (ju-TWAN-si)	Botswana and Namibia	Foraging	Bilateral
Inuit (IN-u-it)	Arctic Alaska and Canada	Foraging	Bilateral
Montagnais (mon-tan-NYAY)	Labrador	Foraging	Bilateral
Naskapi (nas-KAP-i)	Labrador	Foraging	Bilateral
Navajo (NAV-a-ho)	U.S. Southwest	Horticulture (maize, beans), sheepherding	Matrilineal
Nuer (NEW-er)	Sudan	Cattle herding, horticulture (millet, maize)	Patrilineal
Luo (LU-o)	Kenya	Cattle herding, horticulture (millet)	Patrilineal
Huron (HU-ron)	Ontario	Horticulture (corn, beans, squash), foraging	Matrilineal
Iroquois (IR-o-kwoy)	New York	Horticulture (corn, beans, squash), foraging	Matrilineal
Yanomamo (ya-na-MA-mo)	Brazil and Venezuela	Horticulture (manioc), hunting, fishing	Patrilineal
Jivaro (HE-va-ro)	Peru	Horticulture (manioc, sweet potatoes), hunting, fishing	Patrilineal
Igbo (I-bo)	Nigeria	Horticulture (yams, manioc, maize)	Double descent
Haida (HAI-da)	British Columbia	Foraging	Matrilineal
Tlingit (TLING-git)	British Columbia	Foraging	Matrilineal
Kpelle (PEL-le)	Liberia	Horticulture (rice, manioc)	Patrilineal
Mpondo (PON-do)	South Africa	Cattle herding, horticulture	Patrilineal
Tonga (TONG-ga)	South Pacific	Horticulture (yams), fishing	Patrilineal
Inca (ING-ka)	Peru	Agriculture (maize, potatoes, beans)	Parallel descent

CHAPTER 1

Prologue

People in every culture maintain and transmit ideas about the roles that women and men perform, the rights they have in relation to each other, and the values associated with their activities. Taken together, these ideas comprise culturally shared and accepted models of gender. They are all social constructs, developed and sustained specifically within each culture. Gender constructs obviously make use of sexual differences between males and females, but they are not constrained in a predetermined manner by these sexual differences. If they were, roles performed and values attached to women's and men's behavior would be identical in all societies. This clearly is not the case. Variation in activities and attitudes is well attested throughout the world. Although some pattern of gender differentiation exists in all cultures, the degree of separation and the rigidity of boundaries vary. We examine the content of gender constructs and attempt to understand and explain similarities and differences across cultures.

Because gender is a social category, it has a social interpretation and valuation. Gender is a primary aspect of one's personal and social identity. This identification begins in one's earliest socialization through the ways that a baby is handled, treated, and spoken to. Childhood learning teaches individuals the appropriate behavior expected by others and molds one's personality to conform to cultural **norms**. Through assignment of roles and evaluation of worthiness, girls and boys acquire their gender identities. They learn skills and attitudes that render them functioning members of their community. Females and males are born, but women and men are products of enculturation.

Behavior and **ideology** are intertwined in the development of humans as social beings. Therefore, in addition to our focus on people's activities, we attend to the expressed and hidden ideological messages about women's and men's place in their families and communities and about their social value. These messages are often symbolized in religious beliefs and practices. They are conveyed as well in subtle ways through language by words and expressions that label men and women or describe their activities. Social constructs of gender are also transmitted in daily interactions between men and women in their families, local communities, and wider social arenas. Rights to make decisions, to speak, and/or to participate in activities are manifestations of cultural valuations and privileges allocated to people.

We compare behaviors, attitudes, and symbols of gender in many diverse societies to gain an understanding of the range of meanings assigned to gender. In the course of this endeavor, we explore theories about the origins and maintenance of gender differentiation and of its interpretation.

Although each culture is unique, certain general patterns of social life tend to be manifest in various types of societies. Numerous possible approaches are available in classifying cultures. In this book, we follow two intersecting perspectives. One classifies societies according to their mode of **subsistence** or economic production. Mode of production is everywhere a fundamental feature of societal organization. People employ a range of strategies in obtaining their food and producing goods. These include **foraging**, **pastoralism**, **horticulture**, **agriculture**, and industrial production. Variations in modes of production are interrelated with differences in other aspects of culture. Peoples who rely on foraging for food differ considerably from those who rely on horticulture, pastoralism, or agriculture. All of these groups differ markedly from modern industrial nations. The organization of production in each type of culture has an impact on economic, political, and social activities. Rights to participate in these activities are often constrained by cultural models of gender. Therefore, classifying cultures according to their predominant mode of production is a useful analytic approach in investigating the ways that gender concepts and behaviors are organized.

A second perspective we follow is the differentiation of societies according to the type of political system that integrates and mediates members of the group. Political organization is a key feature of societal functioning. It has significant implications for the development and maintenance of other aspects of social life. For instance, participation in political structures is often constrained by gender. The ideological constructs used to legitimate political systems are usually consistent with general societal concepts that include, subsume, or imply gender models.

Political systems are frequently labeled by the terms *band, tribe, chiefdom,* and *state.* Although societies may or may not fit neatly into analytic categories such as these, the classification is useful as a tool in differentiating cultures.

Band societies are small, loosely organized groups of people that tend to be politically autonomous and function with minimal leadership. **Tribes** are larger configurations uniting, with varying degrees of cohesion, numerous local communities within a recognized, named group. They have some form of leadership that may be limited to the level of villages or may combine villages in networks of decision making, social control, and cooperative action. **Chiefdoms** have more established patterns of leadership and succession of leaders. These leaders, or "chiefs," represent their kin groups and localities. They generally have more influence over members of their groups than tribal leaders do and play a more direct role in organizing economic production and distribution or exchange of goods. However, they are still accountable to the wishes and interests of their constituents. **States** are more highly organized and centralized political units. They are characterized by centrally controlled and administered systems of government, typically including a police and/or military force, and groups of functionaries who collect tribute or taxes, oversee economic exchanges, establish legislative procedures, and regulate social controls.

It is important to stress that use of the terms *band, tribe, chiefdom,* and *state* does *not* imply an evolutionary progression of societal types. Under certain historical conditions, a specific society of a given type may be transformed into one of another type. However, such change is an instance of dynamic processes basic to all societies. It is not indicative of social progress.

It is also important to stress that the chapter organization presented in this book does not imply that all societies of given economic or political systems are identical. To exemplify this point briefly, societies of the North Pacific coast of North America (that is, Haidas and Tlingits of British Columbia) had economies based on foraging and social systems based on stratification. Their cultures contrasted with the more common patterns of association between foraging and egalitarian sociopolitical systems and between social stratification and farming or pastoral economies.

Gender constructs are influenced by economic modes and by forms of political organization. Of course, generalizations about patterns of gender-linked behavior and values are difficult to establish with complete reliability. However, tendencies toward the development and maintenance of different kinds of gender relations and ideological constructs are manifest in different kinds of societal types. We examine these interrelationships throughout the book.

Gender relations can be characterized on a continuum from full equality to the complete domination of members of one gender by members of the other. The notion of gender equality itself is not so easily specified. We use the term **gender equality** to refer to a constellation of behaviors, attitudes, and rights that support the **autonomy** of both women and men. Women and men may have different economic, social, and political roles, but the valuation and rewards given to them are roughly similar. In such systems, all people have access to equal rights, prestige, ability to make decisions for themselves and others, and autonomy in their households and communities. In contrast, **gender inequality** refers to denial of autonomy and equal rights to one group of people based on their gender. Gender equality is more likely to exist in foraging band societies where all individuals make important contributions to subsistence and where hierarchical leadership is absent or minimal. In contrast, gender inequality tends to be most marked in complex state societies where economic specialization obtains and where social and political stratification affects the allocation of differential rights and privileges along several dimensions, especially including class and gender. In complex multiclass or multiethnic societies, models of gender may differ as well among classes or racial and/or ethnic groups. Other types of societies (namely, tribes and chiefdoms) seem to be most variable and least amenable to generalizing about gender. Therefore, examination of specific cultural formations and historical circumstances unique to each group is necessary to reveal complexities of beliefs and practices related to gender. Only careful analyses of both cross-cultural and local behaviors can help us understand the meaning of gender.

One universal manifestation of gender identity is the external marking of differentiation in several obvious behaviors. For example, women and men may wear different kinds of clothing or ornaments. They may fashion their hair in different styles, perhaps with distinction in length of hair and manner of adornment. Use of body decorations or tatoos may distinguish the genders. In addition to these external physical markings, most cultures make use of two sets of personal names, one appropriate for females and one appropriate for males.

Other kinds of differentiating behaviors are more subtle and less conscious but just as powerful in identifying oneself as a man or woman. One's social presentation includes dynamics of walking, sitting, and general body posture. Speech styles employed by women or men are also often distinct. These may consist of variations in pronunciation and choice of vocabulary or grammatical constructions. Features of nonverbal communication such as use of gestures, smiling, eye contact, and touch may be differentially employed.

Gender constructs obviously pertain to and affect the kinds of roles that people fulfill. These roles may include economic, social, political, and religious activities. In all societies, some form of division of labor by gender determines, or at least influences, the range of daily work that an individual carries out. Work naturally depends on the economic mode of production that forms the basis of a culture's subsistence. Men's and women's work is often complementary, both contributing to the maintenance of their household by providing food, shelter, clothing, and necessary equipment.

Gender categorization may have begun in concert with an economic division of labor (Leibowitz, 1975, 1983). Inferences from data concerning nonhuman primate behavior and traditional foraging societies whose cultural patterns are well documented led Lila Leibowitz (1983) to postulate that a division of labor and gender categorization was unnecessary when human ancestors engaged in "unspecified and undifferentiated" production (p. 123). However, when technological innovations eventually "led to the development of a number of different productive processes, divisions of labor became practicable" (p. 124).

The division of labor took the form it did—that is, based on gender—because of restrictions on movement of women necessitated by their reproductive roles. Pregnancy and childbearing limit women's ability to travel during significant periods of their lives. Years spent nursing babies and young children also restrict a mother's ability to leave settlements unless she takes her child with her. Reproduction does not absolutely negate possibilities of women's activities away from home bases, but it does make travel more burdensome and also more dangerous to a mother's and child's survival. Women's reproductive activities, then, influence the assignment of other types of roles to them and contrastively assign complementary roles to men. In all traditional cultures, women assume the care of infants and young children. Presumably as an extension of these duties, women generally perform other caretaker activities that exceed the biological necessities of birthing and nursing. These include preparing family meals and caring for sick, disabled, or aged individuals within the household.

In foraging societies, gathering of wild plants, fruits, and nuts tends to be the work of women. Women in many foraging groups also hunt small animals. These are duties compatible with a home-based lifestyle. In contrast, men generally assume economic roles that include travel away from home settlements. Such activities may require a man's absence all day or over a period of days, weeks, or even months. Hunting and trading with other groups are typically the work of men in foraging societies.

In addition to considerations of energy and mobility, foraging societies may assign home-based activities to women and external hunting and traveling to men because of the need to protect women against possibilities of accidents and deaths that might occur away from local settlements (Friedl, 1975). Because the survival and continuity of a community depends on the successful reproductive life of women, it is rational to protect them from unnecessary danger.

The basic division of labor is an efficient allocation of human resources and energy in cultures where different kinds of labor require different outputs of energy and strength and where biological reproductive activities engage women for significant periods of their lives. Therefore, if such a division of labor accounts for the origin of gender differentiation, it can be seen as a rational effect of reproductive differences. Furthermore, it is most efficient to teach people skills they are going to use during most of their lives. Skills needed to recognize and utilize edible plants, roots, herbs, and fruits or to track, locate, and kill animals require many years of careful instruction, observation of adults engaged in these activities, and practice in fulfilling the tasks. Because subsistence activities of a community include a wide range of behaviors, it is presumably difficult for any one individual to learn all of them well. Therefore, some basis of specialization is efficient and provides for the survival of all. Because reproductive responsibilities restrict women's mobility, it is rational to assign home-based duties to them and to teach men to engage in pursuits outside of local settlements.

Although this model of differentiation seems sensible enough, several cautions must be added. The gender division of labor is often not as rigid as is described and taken for granted by anthropologists or other observers. Restrictions on doing work generally assigned to the other gender are often ignored by people in actual practice. Behavior is frequently flexible even when people overtly claim to engage in separated tasks. It is often the case that people report their actions in more idealized terms than is consistently revealed by their behavior. Anthropologists, too, tend to report normative rules rather than the complexity of real choices.

Another caution concerns the existence of cooperative labor that includes both men and women within a community. For example, communal hunting might involve adults of both genders; farming might also engage both women and men.

It is critically important to recognize that cultural forms arise in specific conditions and are changeable when those conditions no longer prevail. That is, although gender differentiation may have arisen in the assignment of distinct kinds of work to women and men because of different reproductive functions and the energy and mobility requirements of different activities, when productive work was historically transformed and could be performed equally well by both women and men, the actual economic necessities of a division of labor according to gender lost its rational imperative. Its maintenance in societies therefore needs to be explained in other than purely economic terms. This is where additional factors can be seen to support and perpetuate an economic form that fulfills functions that are more than economic in the narrow sense.

One such factor is the social organization of households coexisting with economic divisions of labor. All societies structure households on the basis of families, although family composition and household organization vary in different types of societies. Family structures, and the existence of family itself, are social, not biological, institutions. As with all cultural forms, they originated and are organized to fulfill social needs. Kathleen Gough (1975) defines *family* as a "married couple or other group of adult kinfolk who cooperate economically and in the upbringing of children, and all or most of whom share a common dwelling" (p. 52). The marriage bond is a socially recognized union that validates an economic and social relationship between a woman and man and between their kin groups. It also confirms a link between a man and his wife's children, establishing what Gough calls "social fatherhood" (p. 53).

Economic cooperation both rationalizes and sustains family units. Because social cohesion within communities is based on stability of households, which is based on fulfillment of complementary economic pursuits by members, the gender division of labor is used as a convenient method of organizing household production even after it is no longer of purely economic necessity.

Although a gender division of labor ensures fulfillment of economic needs of families, it may be structured to endow men or women with either equal or disproportionate control over resources. In some societies, such as the Ju/'hoansi of Botswana and Namibia, women's and men's contributions and control are viewed as equal and sustain gender equality. In others, such as the Inuit of Arctic Canada, men's labor contributes more direct survival necessities than does women's labor. Unequal productive pursuits validate men's domination of their wives in part by rendering women more dependent on men. In contrast, among the Ju/'hoansi, women and men are equally dependent on each other's labor.

Regulation of sexuality and rules of incest are another universal characteristic of families. These rules ensure both stability within families and maintenance of bonds between families, thus contributing to community cohesion. Interfamilial bonds are themselves often cemented by economic exchanges based on gender divisions of labor. In some societies, ritualized exchanges between families prior to marriages or during marriage ceremonies symbolize economic cooperation. For example, among Mohawks (Amerindians of northeastern North America), marriage rituals began with the presentation of gifts of corn by a woman to her intended husband's mother, who then reciprocated with gifts of deer meat. In traditional Mohawk (and other Iroquoian) economies, women were responsible for food production, based primarily on corn, whereas men provided their households with animal meat and fish.

Families also function universally as vehicles for socialization of children into expected roles and goals. Children learn what is appropriate by observation of adults and by overt instruction and practice of skills they will assume as adult women and men. Moreover, and perhaps of even greater importance, children learn gender through observation of social relations between their parents or among all adults in their households. They learn whether men and women have equal rights to speak, to contribute to discussion, and to make decisions. They also deduce social rights through ways that conflicts are resolved. Finally, girls and boys learn whether they can expect emotional and economic support from their natal kin groups once they reach adulthood and form their own marriages.

Social structures and the organization of families and households are interrelated with other aspects of culture. As we have seen, they comprise the basic functional economic units of a community. They may also have political functions as units within which decisions are made, conflicts are resolved, and social control is exercised. Gender distinctions may be reflected in these political features of households if men and women do not have equal rights to participate in decision making, if spousal conflicts are usually resolved to favor one party, or if social controls are disproportionately applied. For instance, an important reflection of gender valuation in a society is acted out within families through attitudes toward premarital or extramarital sexual activity. When freedoms or limitations are applied equally, gender equality is made manifest. In contrast, when a double standard affects women and men, inequality is overtly displayed.

In societies where households join together in larger decision-making or political units, gender differentiation can be evidenced by choice of household representatives. Rights to speak for one's household and to be recognized as a leader can in turn be manipulated within the household itself to justify and legitimate domination of other family members.

In many cultures, households also perform religious functions. They are often the locus of ritual activity. **Rites of passage** may be organized and enacted on the basis of family units, with or without participation of larger community groups. Gender distinctions may be reflected in rights to plan and officiate on such occasions. In addition, the specific content of these ceremonies may significantly differ depending on the gender of a ritual's focal participants. For instance, verbal instruction of boys and girls at puberty rites or of women and men in marriage ceremonies may contain similar or contrasting messages about their respective roles and valuation.

To understand the meaning of gender and ways that it is culturally manifested, economic, social, political, and religious features of culture need to be examined. A cross-cultural view allows us to determine the conditions under which particular forms develop and are maintained. Through this method, we can ascertain the societal and cultural functions that gender constructs fulfill. We can also document the interrelationships between societal change and gender. That is, we can see whether change in economic, social, and political formations affects gender constructs and whether ideological change in gender constructs affects other aspects of culture.

This preliminary discussion of gender leads us to confront an issue that is frequently raised—namely, the postulated universality of some degree of gender stratification and **male dominance** (see Friedl, 1975; Rosaldo, 1974). The notion of **stratification** refers to unequal access to social prestige and power available to and assumed by certain members of a society. It may be linked to unequal access to resources, goods, and political power. These inequalities may be evidenced by deference shown to those of high status, by social or material rewards given to them, and/or by power they are able to exert over others' actions. Although gender stratification is often stated as a given by anthropologists and other researchers, it is typically more presumed than investigated. It is certainly obvious that differences exist across cultures in the degree of **hierarchy** and in the ways it is manifested. But an important and necessary question remains: Are there (or more probably, were there) genuinely egalitarian societies? This is a complex question, for several reasons. One is the long history of male bias in reporting behavior and beliefs existing in non-Western cultures (Leacock, 1981; Rohrlich-Leavitt, Sykes, and Weatherford, 1975). Explorers, missionaries, soldiers, and travelers in early periods of European colonization of the Americas, Africa, Asia, and the Pacific were almost exclusively men who interpreted the cultures of native peoples through their own **ethnocentric** worldviews. Later observers, including anthropologists, economists, and historians, also were predominantly men. Notwithstanding their supposed objectivity, they brought with them, as all people do, biases and frames of reference dominant in their own cultures. They interpreted men's activities as more important than those of women because of their ideological beliefs about men's importance. They usually asked for men's opinions, partly because it was difficult for a foreign man to spend a great deal of time interacting with women, but also partly because these male investigators considered men's opinions to be more significant than women's opinions. It is well to be reminded of the admonition made by Joseph Lafitau (1724/1974), a French observer of Native American cultures, who commented that "authors who have written on the customs of the [Native] Americans [concerning the rights and status of women] have formed their conceptions, in this as in everything else, on European ideas and practices" (p. 344).

In addition to the inherent problem of obtaining a truly objective view of another culture, colonial contact often swiftly and dramatically altered traditional gender relations by transforming many aspects of the indigenous cultures of colonized peoples (Etienne and Leacock, 1980; Gailey, 1987; Leacock, 1981; Wolf, 1982). Economic roles were radically changed in response to trade. Emphases on external trade rather than household production and consumption undermined women's contributions and enhanced male control over resources. European traders typically ignored native female traders and refused to deal with them (for example, on the North American Pacific coast and in West Africa). Transformation of modes of economic production has an impact on allocation of productive roles. It may result in shifts in economic contributions to household subsistence or standards of living made by women and men. Relations of complementarity or dependence may be altered, with concomitant changes in the ability of one party to influence or control others' actions.

Changes in economies were often accompanied by rapid realignments of indigenous political formations in accord with the demands of colonizers. Europeans helped solidify local male power, again often ignoring female leaders and decision makers (for example, the Iroquois clan mothers and female African chiefs and warriors). Innovations in political organization can lead to restructuring of societal relations, both in communities and within individual households. Participation in decision making, leadership, and social networks can be broadened or restricted. Changes in traditional **polities** after European colonization usually led to enhanced public prestige of men, which was in turn translated into greater control over their localities and families.

Through economic and political policies of colonizers, traditional lifeways were quickly undermined and transformed in keeping with European norms. These transformed societies were then characterized as "traditional." Gender relations resulting from economic and political change therefore could be interpreted to justify theories of universal male dominance.

In all societies, ideological constructs support and perpetuate social, economic, and political modes. For example, religion often provides explanations and justifications for existing social relations. Religious belief sanctions status and roles of women and men within their households and communities. It explains and provides divine origins for personal freedoms or restrictions, for differences in the prestige or power of men and women, and for the rights and obligations that they have. Myths of creation may give greater or lesser prominence to male or female deities, justifying the social value of human women and men (Sanday, 1981). Religious practice also affects gender by allowing or restricting men's and women's ability to function as ritual practitioners. Barring women from ritualist activities blocks them from achieving a respected social status and receiving social prestige. This tendency is especially marked in state societies with highly organized priesthoods where the priesthood is linked to political power. However, even in such societies, women often experience direct connections with spiritual beings and powers through dreams, visions, and other forms of personal contact. But gender distinctions remain in the private or public validation of religious experience.

Another powerful manifestation of the ideology of gender is conveyed nonconsciously through forms and uses of language and communication. Differences in men's and women's speech are overt and covert displays of gender. Rights to speak, to introduce or control topics of conversation, and to have others respond positively to one's contributions are all symbolic reflections of a person's social rights. They are also reinforcements of the same system of social differentiation. The content of language itself may reflect and reinforce cultural constructs of gender by the way people and their activities are named or described. Language can be used either to enhance social status of people viewed positively or to trivialize, restrict, and demean members of negatively valued groups.

Ideological constructs thus reflect, legitimate, and reinforce underlying social relations. Through transmission of widely accepted models, people are encouraged to internalize and act out their appropriate roles. Cultural values and social encouragements not only mold people's behavior but, more important, contribute to forming their attitudes about themselves and their relations to others. In societies where gender equality exists, both women and men are encouraged to act autonomously, to value themselves, and to relate to others as equals. In contrast, where male dominance pervades economic, political, and social structures, entrenched ideological constructs teach men to disvalue women and to assume rights to control women's activity. Women in these cultures learn to disvalue themselves and to acquiesce to male domination. The mechanisms through which these attitudes and behaviors are achieved are quite complex. They are both conscious and nonconscious. Indeed, the fact that cultural models are in part acquired and transmitted nonconsciously contributes to the power of their influence over people. Because gender models are often conveyed nonconsciously, individuals are not aware of their origin or even of their content. These constructs, then, are not questioned. Instead, they are automatically accepted and followed, leading to their further entrenchment and dissemination.

Before proceeding with the data and analyses central to this text, let us consider critical questions that have emerged in the field of anthropology about the origins of human behavior and human cultural patterns. Some of these questions bear directly on issues of gender. As anthropologists have attempted to understand human culture, in both contemporary and prior societies, they have proposed theories about the origins and development of human practices and attitudes. In this endeavor, they have sometimes looked to the evolutionary and archaeological records to explore questions of origins of gendered roles and behaviors. But what can we learn about our earliest hominid ancestors? And what data can we use to develop models of hominid and human behavior?

On the basis of DNA evidence, biological anthropologists suggest that the ancestors of humans and nonhuman primates such as chimpanzees and gorillas diverged some 5 or 6 million years ago (Zihlman, 1986, pp. 85–86). A complex series of adaptations deriving from climatic changes in southern and eastern Africa led to species differentiation and the exploitation of distinct ecological zones. Fossil evidence indicates that the hominid ancestors of modern humans (the Australopithecines) were established by about 3.5 million years ago. These creatures were small by modern standards but were markedly different from other primates, principally because they had undergone structural skeletal and mechanical changes that enabled them to walk upright. Among the critical interrelated adaptations were changes in the structure of the knee allowing it to lock to support an extended leg, development of an arch in the foot to support body weight and shift balance from heel to toe in walking, and repositioning of the spine and pelvis to support upright posture.

Another issue in hominid evolution is the skeletal features distinguishing males and females. Nonhuman primate species vary in their degree of sexual dimorphism. In some species, there are relatively slight differences in height, weight, and structural features; in others, the differences are marked. A general decline in sexual dimorphism in human evolution came about because of the dual factors of decreases in male body size and increases in female stature (Hager, 1991, p. 48). The significant contrasts in the size and shape of the female and male pelvis, a critical factor in human evolution, began about 2 million years ago. This adaptation was interrelated with the enlargement of the brain. As cognitive complexity increased, presumably to process information and solve problems, the brain itself increased in size. This growth eventually posed dangers to pregnant females because an infant's head would be too large to pass through the pelvic opening without endangering the mother's life. Adaptive changes in the size and positioning of the female pelvis responded to these dangers, allowing for safe births. But human babies also had to undergo adaptive processes: They are born relatively undeveloped as compared to other mammals and even other primates in terms of muscular coordination, so they are dependent on adult caregivers for extended periods of time. This dependency had critical consequences for the development of social bonds, especially between mother and child but extending to other family and community members as well.

Although scientists have learned much about the physical structure of early hominids, researchers know very little about the lifestyle of our earliest hominid ancestors. The first direct reflection of cultural patterns comes from about 2 million years ago. By that time, there is evidence of the manufacture and use of stone tools. Although there is controversy about the uses of these earliest tools, they are often found in association with animal bones (McBrearty and Moniz, 1991, p. 72). At some sites, bones are found having cut marks made by stone tools. In addition, stone hammers may have been used to break or smash bones, possibly to extract the marrow.

The association of tools and animal bones has led some researchers to propose theories emphasizing the significance of meat-eating and therefore of hunting in the development of human culture. By implication, this thesis privileges males as the catalysts and major agents of human cultural advances. However, one of the assumptions needing but lacking clear evidence is whether or not meat eaten by early hominids was obtained by hunting. Nonhuman primates and presumably some early hominid groups obtained meat by scavenging as often as by hunting. Both techniques were probably in use, with no clear-cut evidence distinguishing the methods in the archaeological record.

Still, despite a lack of supporting data, a wide array of behaviors has been postulated as stemming from a dietary emphasis on hunting. Because males are assumed to have been the primary hunters in early hominid groups, they are also assumed to have been the inventors of tools and weapons, artifacts considered to be the hallmarks of humanity, differentiating us from other primates. And from these assumptions, models of early hominid groups have been suggested, representing males as active and inventive, using their intelligence and skills to provide food for themselves and others. In contrast, females are represented as passive recipients of meat provided by males but leading a relatively sedentary lifestyle, remaining at home bases to care for their offspring and either sick or elderly members of the group.

This model of "Man the Hunter" is a modern manifestation of assumptions that first became popularized through the works of Charles Darwin in the mid—to-late nineteenth century. However, they need to be contextualized historically as embedded in a particular cultural constellation of practices and attitudes of nineteenth-century Europe. When twentieth-century anthropologists revisited questions of human cultural origins, they again privileged Man the Hunter as the key to human development differentiating us from other primates. As Linda Fedigan (1986) summarized, these models posited hunting as the

> catalyst for all of the technological, social, and intellectual achievements of human beings. Just a short list of traits believed to have resulted from hunting would include: bipedalism, elaborate toolkits, development of language, appreciation of beauty, male aggressiveness and pleasure in killing, division of labor, the nuclear monogamous family, loss of female estrus, the invention of incest taboos, and bonding between males. Furthermore, [it was argued] that the killing of animals with tools dominated human history for such a long time that it became the shaping force of the human psyche for all time, even when men no longer hunt for a living. (pp. 32–33)

Significantly, it is male behavior (that is, hunting) that becomes the "catalyst" underlying and promoting human inventiveness and achievement. Female behavior, in contrast, becomes passive and secondary. In this model, males are the shapers of human culture, supplying women and children with necessary resources. (Zihlman, 1981, p. 75)

Despite the seeming logic of these models, they are based on several questionable or even faulty assumptions. First, hominid species evolved about 2 million years before evidence of stone tool use. Although it has been suggested that bipedalism was an adaptation to the need to see over tall savanna grasses in order to spot prey animals and throw simple weapons at them, this assumption is contradicted by the fact that structural changes allowing bipedalism evolved many millennia before stone tools were being made. According to Margaret Ehrenberg (1989, p. 42), bipedalism more likely developed in response to the fact that early hominid mothers had to carry their infants because the infants were unable to cling to their mothers, as was the prior primate pattern. Infants' inability to cling resulted both from the hominid loss of body hair, leaving the baby nothing to cling to, and from changes in the foot and toes that did not permit gripping.

In addition, tools made of stone were not necessarily the first kind of tools that hominids invented. Other types of tools made from plant fibers might as likely have been used at earlier stages of development. Because of their nonpermanence, however, they disintegrated within a relatively short period of time and did not become part of the fossil or archaeological record. Other types of tools have therefore been absent from theories about human cultural origins. Indeed, some researchers have suggested that the earliest tools were artifacts used to dig for plants because gathering preceded hunting as a strategy for resource exploitation (p. 46). Furthermore, early inventions probably focused on containers and devices to hold foods obtained in gathering expeditions and to carry infants and young children. Carrying devices, especially, were likely to have been invented by females because, in keeping with universal primate behavior, mothers and other females were the primary caregivers of children. Knowledge of their production would also have been transmitted by females.

In addition, assumptions about the importance of meat-eating in the diet of early hominids are not supported by clear-cut evidence. Early hominid teeth were adapted for an omnivorous diet, and the relative percentages of plants, seeds, and meat eaten cannot be determined (Fedigan, 1986, p. 52). Evidence of meat-eating is found in its association with stone tools, but evidence of plants or seeds in the diet would not be preserved because of the nonpermanence of both the foods and the wooden or fiber tools used to process or transport them. As compared to nonhuman primates, hominids had relatively smaller front teeth while their back teeth were larger and flatter, indicating an adaptation to chewing fibrous foods. In addition, the size of male and female hominid canine teeth was similar, contrasting with the nonhuman primate pattern in which the canines of males are typically much larger than those of females (p. 51), perhaps indicating decreased emphasis on dominance and aggression in males.

Furthermore, although we may find evidence of the association of stone tools with animal bones, we do not know all of the uses to which early hominids put this equipment. The earliest examples of tools have been characterized as "scrapers" or "choppers," but there is no clear indication of their actual function. The kind of wear patterns on some of them indicates that they were used for a number of different functions, such as processing meat, plants, and hides, but many may have been used for multiple purposes (Ehrenberg, 1989, p. 46; McBrearty and Moniz, 1991, p. 76).

An additional feature of the Man the Hunter construct is its stress on male dominance behavior. Hominid males and their human descendents are seen as protectors of dependent females and children. But this model too is impossible to verify. While male dominance is a feature of many, but not all, nonhuman primate groups, its role in human evolution is unknown. Some researchers, especially those within the field of sociobiology, emphasize the importance of dominant males in selecting mates and therefore in transmitting their genes to future generations. But other theorists question the centrality of dominance in mate selection. Zihlman (1981), for example, notes that in most species, it is the sex investing the greatest amount of energy and time in offspring that chooses mates and therefore has the greatest influence on gene flow (p. 88). Given this assumption, a reasonable question presents itself: What kind of mate would a female favor if she were looking forward to years of caregiving for dependent children? Zihlman has suggested that such females would select mates who are "sociable" and "willing to share food and protect them and their offspring" (p. 91). Smuts (2001) cites comparative evidence from nonhuman primate studies indicating that females mate with males who are cooperative and nonaggressive. Data from observational research also indicate that female chimpanzees do not mate with males who act aggressively (Ehrenberg, 1989, p. 49). Such evidence leads Ehrenberg to conclude that hominid females probably preferred sociable and friendly males. Furthermore, Lancaster and Whitten (1993) agree that sharing is both a behavior and an attitude that distinguishes human beings from all other primates. Through sharing and cooperation, people forge bonds of mutual interdependence. These ethics are the foundations of human families and community life.

During periods of early human evolution, female roles combined reproduction, economic pursuits, and social responsibilities. Males also gathered plant foods, at first primarily for themselves, following the primate pattern. Gradually, traits of sharing and cooperation were favored as females selected mates and established pair bonds. Males' emotional investment in their children consequently increased (Zihlman, 1981, p. 93). Indeed, rather than hunting providing the template for human society, hunting patterns were built on behaviors developed in gathering and sharing plant resources.

Although we do not know how social roles developed in the evolutionary or prehistoric past, some researchers have suggested theories that account for the development of the role of fathers in social interaction with their children. Some theories stress that male involvement with children developed from men's roles in hunting and sharing the meat with women and their children (Lancaster, 1983; Mackey, 1985). Other theories emphasize the evolutionary trends toward greater dependency of infants and young children due to larger brain size and the consequent need for birth earlier in the developmental process (Hewlett, 1991; Smuts, 1985). Hewlett suggests that the critical factor in the evolution of the role of fathers was the particular kind of male-female relationship that developed in the early stages of human evolution. As social bonds among our earliest hominid ancestors (the Australopithecines) were created and strengthened between a male-female pair, associated with ongoing and consistent sexual relations, males formed bonds with the offspring of the females with whom they mated. Males provided meat and offered protection, primarily to their female mate, but their offspring benefited indirectly from the male's investment in the female (Hewlett, 1991, p. 160). During later periods of evolution, transmission of cultural knowledge based on experience became another feature of fathers' involvement with their children.

It seems, then, that the model of Man the Hunter cannot be supported by existing evidence. First, the model implies that while males contributed actively by hunting and supplying meat, females were mainly sedentary caregivers and suppliers of plant foods; through procuring meat, males established bonds of dependency with females who relied on them for primary economic support. A critical problem with this model of human origins is that it finds no supporting comparative evidence either from nonhuman primate groups or from known contemporary or recent foraging societies. In most nonhuman primate groups, the primary social bond is between mother and children from infancy through adolescence. Males may or may not be present in the group and usually have positions of dominance, sometimes (but not always) acting as leaders and decision makers for group movements. Male and female pairing is usually temporary but does not include provisioning of supplies from one partner to the other. Indeed, even mothers do not bring plant foods to their infants, although they do of course nurse each child for several years. All animals in a primate group, except those too old, sick, or injured, are on the move, searching for food, building nests or other sleeping areas, and socializing.

The diet of most nonhuman primates overwhelmingly consists of plants, fruits, seeds, and nuts. Animal protein is obtained mostly by eating insects. Some chimpanzee groups have been observed killing and eating small monkeys or other animals, but this source of protein forms a relatively minor part of their intake.

Observation of toolmaking and tool-using behavior in nonhuman primates suggests a greater likelihood of female involvement than of male involvement. For instance, more frequently than males, female chimpanzees at Gombe in Tanzania modify twigs to extract termites from tree trunks and branches, transporting their "tools" for use to other locations. Female chimpanzees observed in Guinea and Ivory Coast are more likely than males to use stone hammers to extract nuts from shells. Females in these groups also transport nuts and stone hammers for reuse, creating "archaeological sites" (McBrearty and Moniz, 1991, p. 76).

Chimpanzee males are more often observed killing animals and distributing their meat. However, in contrast to models of human behavior, males are more likely to share meat with their mothers and siblings rather than with sexual partners (Linton, 1971).

If we consider comparative evidence from known foraging societies, it is clear that women are hardly sedentary, passive group members; instead, they are active and productive, contributing food resources and manufactured goods to their households and communities. Although there is often an idealized division of labor based on gender, actual work roles tend to be flexible in response to available resources and the circumstance of which people able to procure them. Chapter 2 deals extensively with the behaviors and attitudes found among foraging peoples, but suffice it to say here that the model of Man the Hunter is easily balanced by that of "Woman the Gatherer" in the economies and social life of foraging societies.

If one looks to known foraging societies for suggestions about the diet of early hominid groups (and of course there are problems with extrapolating too closely), except where the environment constrains plant growth, such as in the Arctic, foraging diets emphasize plant foods rather than meat. In any case, we cannot know whether early hominids obtained most of their meat from hunting or from scavenging. Hunting differs from scavenging in that hunting is a planned, cooperative behavior requiring communication and coordination of activities. In addition, in most known foraging societies, women as well as men participate in some hunting. Women may independently fish and catch small animals, and they may participate along with men in large animal drives. We obviously do not know the proportion of male and female labor in any particular activity among hominid groups.

Finally, it is always important to take care not to impose contemporary attitudes and constructs on hominid ancestors living hundreds of thousands, if not millions, of years ago. The model of Man the Hunter as the primary actor in human origins and as the primary agent of cultural innovation and progress needs to be recognized as a projection backwards into history and prehistory stemming from contemporary constructs of gender.

As Fedigan (1986) concludes, models of human origins are "symbolic statements about and prescriptions for human nature" (p. 61). Indeed, they tell us more about the theorists' assumptions, perspectives, and attitudes about gender than they do about the evolutionary record.

WOMEN IN PREHISTORY

Archaeologists have begun to approach issues of gender as they investigate societies of the past. These endeavors raise questions about the kinds of materials that can give clues about men's and women's roles in prehistoric societies and about their relative status. Among the key questions are these: "How and in what ways do people make and use material culture in establishing, producing, changing, or challenging gender relations, gender ideologies, gender roles? What kinds of 'marked' and/or 'bounded' contexts might obtain and how might these provide clues to the heightening/ebbing dynamics of gender?" (Conkey and Gero, 1991, p. 10). In order to begin answering these questions, archaeologists investigate settlement patterns, household structure, and associations of artifacts with dwellings, workspaces, and burials.

Archaeologists deal with the examination of material culture, the artifacts remaining from past peoples. They have developed techniques for classifying these artifacts, and they are now developing theories to "see the archaeological evidence of gender operating in past societies"; a key necessity is to "move from men's and women's artifacts to interpretations about the role gender played in the structure of life in past societies, whether at the level of the household, community, or region"(Scott, 1994, p. 5).

Through these studies, researchers attempt to "find" gender in the past. Problems arise, however, in the interpretation of material remains and their associations. Archeologists need both to ascertain the linkage between artifacts and people and to develop theories about gender ideology and relations, the latter a task of some difficulty. But as Conkey and Gero (1991) conclude, when archaeologists inquire "into the social dynamics of the everyday activities of prehistoric life," they need to be mindful of the fact that these activities, in the past and present, are gendered (p. 15). Many of the traditional research questions posed by archaeologists need to be rethought through the lens of gender, including "trade, craft specialization, state formation, status, alliances, households, divisions of labor, architecture, imagery, ritual" (p. 17). Through examining the artifacts indicative of these behaviors or concepts and "adopting gender as an explicit conceptual and analytical category . . . women are brought into view as active producers, innovators and conceptualizers of the very material world by which we know the past" (p. 23).

It should be added that the focus on gender not only reveals women's work and contributions; the point is that in the usual "nongendered" examination of the past, men were assumed to be the major contributors and innovators in their societies. That is, men's place in their communities has never been questioned; it is women's lives that have often been rendered invisible.

So where in the archaeological record can researchers look to find evidence of either similarities or differences in the lives of women and men? Burial sites and skeletal remains can be examined to ascertain how women and men were treated, not only at the time of their funerals and burials but during their lives as well. Grave goods buried with the dead may indicate the kinds of work people did. Of course, grave goods may or may not be found depending on the permanence or nonpermanence of the materials from which they were made. For example, stone or metal tools and weapons buried with men might remain for millennia, whereas fiber baskets or unfired clay pottery buried with women might disintegrate much more quickly. In addition, differences in status and wealth may be reflected in the number and quality of goods buried with the dead. But it is not always clear how to interpret the array of grave goods. Does their presence reflect status of the individual or that person's family? Was the displayed wealth obtained through personal achievement or through family inheritance? Did men and women achieve or obtain wealth by the same means?

Skeletal remains can also be examined to ascertain differences in the lives of women and men. For example, clues about diet can be found in the mineral content of bones, revealing whether men and women ate the same kinds of foods or whether certain foods were reserved for one gender or the other. Bones can also shows signs of malnutrition, revealing whether women or men were differentially valued as evidenced by their relative nutritional status. Dietary facts can also be reflected in patterns of wear on teeth because the kind of chewing necessary for different foods leaves distinct patterns of abrasion.

Examination of burials and skeletal remains from archaeological sites can provide clues about the division of labor and its consequences among peoples for whom there are no written records. For example, study of the ancestors of the Chumash of California, residing near the present-day city of Santa Barbara, indicates that in an early period of Chumash culture from about 3500 to 1200 B.C., the gender division of labor was relatively flexible. Evidence to support this conclusion comes from examination of grave goods buried with the deceased. There was no differentiation in either the type or the quantity of associated goods. Both men and women were likely to be buried with grinding tools and basketry, items later associated with women's work. Similarly, both women and men were likely to be buried with arrowheads and fishhooks, equipment later associated with men's tasks (Hollimon, 1991, p. 463).

Examination of skeletons reveals the kinds of trauma and illness experienced during life. In particular, the appearance of arthritis or degenerative joint disease is suggestive of a person's activities and stresses. In the middle period of Chumash culture history, women's knees and spines developed more severe arthritis than those of men while men's shoulders, elbows, and hands were more vulnerable to arthritis (p. 465). Presumably the differences reflect distinct economic pursuits: women used digging sticks and grinding implements to obtain and process plant resources while men's work consisted primarily of hunting and fishing. During later periods, after about A.D. 1150, the differences in degenerative joint disease of women and men diminished, probably reflecting a decline in distinct economic tasks. A gender division of labor was replaced by craft specializations that were open to both women and men.

In addition, study of the pathology of teeth indicates that women in early Chumash prehistoric periods had higher rates of tooth decay than did men, probably reflecting their greater consumption of plant foods high in carbohydrates. In contrast, men's diets included more protein because of their access to meat and fish. Later, as the gender division of labor became less significant, and as the economic emphasis on fishing increased, women's and men's diets and access to protein converged (p. 465).

Disease rates among the Chumash varied in different periods. Throughout prehistoric times, women and men were equally likely to be victims of infectious diseases, yet it was men who were more likely to have severe infections in the earlier periods while women were more likely to have severe infections in the late period (p. 466). These data suggest a gradual decline in women's nutritional status at the same time as there was a gradual improvement for men. Finally, skeletal evidence indicates that men were more likely than women to suffer head injuries, presumably resulting from raids or other types of conflict and violence.

Patterns of wear on teeth may also reveal craft specializations. For example, a study of indigenous farmers living in California around 2000—to 1000 B.C. revealed that some women, but no men, had an unusual pattern of wear on their teeth, interpreted as resulting from "holding or pulling fibrous materials with the teeth, such as in basketmaking" (Ehrenberg, 1989, p. 29). From these data, researchers can draw two conclusions: first, that women, but not men, were basketmakers; and second, that only some women specialized in this craft, presumably supplying others with these items in systems of barter or trade.

Additional clues about craft specialization can be sought in comparative evidence from historically documented societies who are the descendents of groups in prehistory. These data can give clues about work sites. For example, if it is known or presumed that women were potters or that men were weavers, one can gain insights into work and possibly socializing patterns if one finds areas within a dwelling or separate sites where craft items were produced or stored.

Much of the archaeological record is found in housing sites. As Joan Gero (1991) surmises, it is ironic, given the absence of women's presence in discussions of prehistory, that "women can be expected to be most visible and active precisely in the contexts that archaeologists are most likely to excavate: on house floors, at base camps and in village sites where women would congregate to carry out their work" (p. 169). Now, basing theories on this assumption, researchers can examine the tools found in the sites associated with work. Through this examination, women's lives become more visible; it is likely that if women did the work, they made the tools that rendered their work more efficient and productive. After all, this is the same type of assumption that links men as creators of hunting tools and weapons.

Examination of housing styles and sizes may also suggest particular patterns of residence and marriage. Some researchers have suggested that round houses are associated with **polygamous** marriages (marriage between one man and two or more women or between one woman and two or more men) while rectangular houses are found more often with **monogamous** marriage (marriage between one man and one woman) (Gero, 1991, pp. 34–35). And in polygynous households, if co-wives are sisters, the entire family is more likely to live within the same large house, although each sister generally has separate quarters with her own hearth. If co-wives are not related, each wife is likely to have her own dwelling (Chase, 1991, pp. 151–152). Similarly, societies in which couples reside with the husband's family after marriage usually prefer small houses, whereas societies in which couples reside with the wife's family usually prefer large family dwellings (pp. 34–35).

Researchers can also make inferences about gender ideologies by examining the artworks produced by prehistoric peoples. The earliest known works of art date to about 30,000 to 40,000 years ago in Africa and Europe and to about 30,000 to 50,000 years ago in Australia (Peregrine, 2003). Most of these are paintings in caves or on rocks. The most famous European examples come from caves in southern France and northern Spain. There, people used paints to depict animals and hunting gear. Because of the association between the animals and the weapons, anthropologists believe that the paintings were intended to bring about a successful hunt. Perhaps people believed that by drawing pictures of animals being hunted, they were increasing the likelihood of a successful outcome. Although this is a reasonable hypothesis, it is impossible to know what people living 30,000 or 40,000 years ago believed or intended by their actions. But theories associating the art with a particular subsistence strategy—that is, hunting—privilege the roles of men, both as providers of food and as presumptive makers of art.

Cave paintings and rock paintings of animals dating to about the same time as those in Europe have also been discovered in Africa. Even older examples have been found in Australia. Some of the Australian examples include outline and stick-figure drawings of animals and human beings as well as stenciled outlines of human hands. It is possible that these paintings and etchings, as well as those found in Europe and Africa, may be reflections of images connecting the artists to the spirit world and to experiences of spiritual power obtained through prayer, trance, and shamanic performances. Again, we will never know what these drawings and etchings meant to the people who created them, but we do know that modern Aboriginal Australians intend their paintings and drawings to represent spirit beings alive in the Dreaming, a primordial time when the world was being formed (Hume, 2000). These spirits arose from inside the earth and then crossed the Australian continent, performing works and creating features of the landscape as they went. They also created human beings and taught the people important elements of their culture and beliefs.

In addition, ancient stone sculptures have been discovered in Europe, dating to about 30,000 years ago. These sculptures, referred to by researchers as Venus figurines, are thought to represent pregnant women with enlarged breasts and hips. As in the case of cave or rock paintings, there are several theories that attempt to explain the meaning of the carvings (Peregrine, 2003, p. 15). Some researchers suggest that they were fertility objects, intended through principles of imitative magic to promote human reproduction. Others suggest that they were meant as erotic representations of women. And still others analyze them as self-portraits made by women to depict their own bodies (McDermott, 1996). All of these views focus on the disproportionate size of the breasts and hips of the sculpted figurines. By emphasizing secondary sexual characteristics, the figurines could be representations of fertility or of erotic sexual pleasure. Male figurines with enlarged penises have also been found in Europe and elsewhere. These date from the earliest farming communities and may, along with female symbols, be representations of generative impulses and powers (Gimbutas, 1982).

But as is true for so much of the archaeological record, interpretations of art often tell us more about the interpreters than they do about the original artists. For example, in a study of sculptures, carved altars, and ritual instruments discovered at a prehistoric site in present-day Serbia, Russell Handsman (1991) challenges the standard notion that men "were the artists, and that women were one of the objects of their art" (p. 333). Furthermore, he questions the idea that "a prehistoric art about women will always be about their reproductive, procreative function. In this by now familiar and oppressive story, women are doubly encompassed by the customary male gaze that limits their purposive roles to birth and childrearing and sees their sexuality only as an expression of the means to guarantee the survival of the group. Through this gaze, representational art as it is both made and interpreted is used to control women and empower men" (p. 334).

What, then, can we learn about gender and power from the archaeological record at particular sites? In his study of Lepenski Vir, Handsman proposes several theories based on housing sites and burial sites. He traces changes in status from a basically egalitarian society to one in which particular **patrilineages** (kinship groups tracing descent through men) began to accumulate greater power as reflected in the size of houses, the appearance of monumental statues representing male lineage leaders, and grave goods associated with the deceased. Handsman interprets the placement of large stone carvings of human heads of the dominant lineages as "a visually compelling materialization of an ideology of ancestral clan" (p. 348). He also considers the placement and content of graves to be indicative of both status and gender relations. During earlier phases, elder men and women were treated in similar ways. Their graves contained about equal amounts of goods, and their bones were as likely to be reburied in large communal sacred repositories. Later, however, younger males became dominant, as reflected in their more elaborate burials. In addition, earlier communal workplaces were replaced by configurations that separated the spheres of women and men (p. 354). But in what Handsman interprets as a process of resistance to the deterioration of their status, women's workspaces began to contain statues and carvings very different in style and material from those that celebrated male lineages. Women's art objects, as well as their utilitarian tools, were made of bone and boar's tusk while men's tools were made of deer antler. And women decorated their work with curved and wavy patterns unlike the linear representations on men's work (p. 355).

Through investigation of the archaeological record, researchers asking questions about women's and men's lives can uncover the ways in which gender ideologies influenced material production and social organization in societies of the past. Their findings and theories can also inform our understanding of gender relations and gender constructs in the present.

PLAN OF THE BOOK

In subsequent chapters, we investigate gender roles and relationships in a variety of cultures throughout the world. We examine as well the ideological constructs that sustain, legitimate, and reinforce gender-linked behavior. The impact of historical change is ascertained to understand the circumstances under which social and cultural forms develop and are maintained. A historical view also helps us understand the ways in which cultural models can be transformed.

Part I, containing Chapters 2 through 7, is organized around modes of economic production and political organization. Chapter 2 discusses gender in egalitarian foraging societies. Special focus is given to a comparison of the Ju/'hoansi of Botswana and Namibia and the Inuit of Arctic Canada. These two groups differ in their allocation of value to men's and women's roles. Gender equality exists among the Ju/'hoansi, whereas male domination in key areas of life prevails among the Inuit. This contrast is explained on the basis of differential control over resources.

Chapter 3 presents data on gender roles in societies whose subsistence economies are based on foraging, pastoralism, and/or farming. Patterns of gender in these societies are quite variable. Some, such as the Iroquois of the North American Eastern Woodlands, were characterized by gender equality; others—for example, Plains tribes of the North American West and the Yanomamo of the South American Amazon—displayed marked male dominance. Differences in the division of labor, control over resources, warfare, and historical conditions all affected gender relations.

In Chapter 4, we discuss gender relations in several societies characterized by marked social stratification. In general, increased social and political stratification inherent in these societies tends to affect gender relations. Male prerogatives in political leadership often are reflected in unequal models of gender and are translated into restrictions on women's behavior. Stratified societies (often called *chiefdoms*) in Polynesia, Africa, and the North American Pacific coast are examined.

Chapter 5 investigates economic and political conditions in agricultural state societies that historically and currently affect gender roles. Social stratification characteristic of states restricts people's rights in terms of their autonomy, access to prestige, and participation in society. As we demonstrate, gender is often intertwined with other indexes of stratification. Agricultural states are exemplified by the Inca of pre-Columbian Peru and by the peoples in India and China.

Gender constructs in industrial economies are the topic of Chapter 6. The historical development of industrialization in the United States is analyzed in terms of its use of and impact on gender inequalities in preexisting societies. Utilization of women's labor in early industrialization and marginalization of women in the advanced industrial economy are discussed. Examination of gender roles and relations includes issues of labor participation, social and legal rights, and ideological supports for models of gender.

Chapter 7 reviews global economic development programs in Latin America, Africa, India, Asia, and the Pacific, examining the ways in which such programs have differential effects on men and women. Most research demonstrates that, rather than being gender-neutral, development programs have often contributed to a deteroriation in women's status. The chapter concludes with presentation of social and economic data compiled by the United Nations Division for the Advancement of Women.

Following these analyses focusing on different types of societies, Part II deals directly with issues related to the ideological manifestations and rationalizations of gender. Chapter 8 takes up topics concerned with the implications of beliefs about gender and the body. It begins with consideration of the crucial distinction between gender and biological sex, exemplified in part by the existence of a third gender in some societies. Notions about life cycle and biological processes, health status, and nutrition are investigated in a worldwide survey. We analyze these beliefs and conditions as they reflect societal attitudes toward the genders. Women's and men's rights to function as health care practitioners are also examined.

Chapter 9 discusses the function of religious beliefs and practices in justifying and reinforcing gender constructs. Chapter 10 provides evidence of the role of language in transmitting and reproducing societal gender relations through the linguistic expression of entrenched cultural symbols of gender. An important emphasis throughout the book is that to understand gender relations and valuations, we must pay special attention to the organization of economic and political functions. Work, rights, and power all interact in complex ways in contributing to the roles that women and men perform and to their status in households, communities, and societies. Equally significant in understanding gender relations are the ideological constructs that develop and become instrumental in sustaining, legitimizing, and transmitting models of gender. People's behavior is constrained both by what they are allowed to do and by what they are guided to think. Our task is to analyze and understand how structural and ideological components interact to produce and reproduce women and men, their relations, and the social orders in which they live.

REFERENCES

CHASE, SABRINA. 1991. "Polygyny, Architecture and Meaning." In *Engendering Archaeology: Women and Prehistory* (ed. Margaret Conkey and Joan Gero). Cambridge: Basil Blackwell, pp. 150–158.

CONKEY, MARGARET, and JOAN GERO. 1991 "Tensions, pluralities, and engendering archaeology: An introduction to women and prehistory." In *Engendering Archaeology: Women and Prehistory* (ed. Margaret Conkey and Joan Gero). Cambridge: Basil Blackwell, pp. 3–30.

EHRENBERG, MARGARET. 1989. *Women in Prehistory.* Norman: University of Oklahoma Press.

ETIENNE, MONA, AND E. LEACOCK (eds.). 1980. *Women and Colonization.* New York: Praeger.

FEDIGAN, LINDA. 1986. "The Changing Role of Women in Models of Human Evolution." *Annual Review of Anthropology,* 15: 25–66.

FRIEDL, ERNESTINE. 1975. *Women and Men.* New York: Holt, Rinehart & Winston.

GAILEY, CHRISTINE. 1987. "Evolutionary perspectives on gender hierarchy." In *Analyzing Gender* (ed. Beth B. Hess and Myra Marx Ferree). Newbury Park, CA: Sage, pp. 32–67.

GERO, JOAN. 1991 "Genderlithics: Women's roles in stone tool production." In *Engendering Archaeology: Women and Prehistory* (ed. Margaret Conkey and Joan Gero). Cambridge: Basil Blackwell, pp. 163–193.

GIMBUTAS, MARIJA. 1982. *Goddesses and Gods of Old Europe 6500–3500 B.C.* Berkeley: University of California Press.

GOUGH, KATHLEEN. 1975. "The origin of the family." In *Toward an Anthropology of Women* (ed. Rayna R. Reiter). New York: Monthly Review Press, pp. 51–76.

HAGER, LORI. 1991. "The evidence for sex differences in the hominid fossil record." In *The Archaeology of Gender* (ed. Dale Walde and Noreen Willows). Calgary: University of Calgary, Archaeological Association, pp. 46–49.

HANDSMAN, RUSSELL. 1991. "Whose art was found at Lepenski Vir? Gender relations and power in archaeology." In *Engendering Archaeology: Women and Prehistory* (ed. Margaret Conkey and Joan Gero). Cambridge: Basil Blackwell, pp. 329–365.

HEWLETT, BARRY. 1991. *Intimate Fathers: The Nature and Context of Aka Pygmy Paternal Infant Care.* Ann Arbor: University of Michigan Press.

HOLLIMON, SANDRA. 1991. "Health consequences of divisions of labor among the Chumash Indians of Southern California." In *Engendering Archaeology: Women and Prehistory* (ed. Margaret Conkey and Joan Gero). Cambridge: Basil Blackwell, pp. 462–469.

HUME, LYNNE. 2000. "The Dreaming in Contemporary Aboriginal Australia." In *Indigenous Religion* (ed. Graham Harvey). London: Cassell, pp. 125–138.

LAFITAU, JOSEPH. 1974. *Customs of the American Indians.* Toronto: Champlain Society. (Original work published 1724)

LANCASTER, JANE. 1983. "Evolutionary perspectives on sex differences in the higher primates." In *Gender and the Life Course* (ed. Alice Rossi). Hawthorne, New York: Aldine.

LANCASTER, JANE, AND PHILIP WHITTEN. 1993. "Sharing in human evolution." In *Anthropology: Contemporary Perspectives*, 7th ed. (ed. Phillip Whitten and David E. K. Hunter). New York: HarperCollins, pp. 70–74.

LEACOCK, ELEANOR. 1981. *Myths of Male Dominance.* New York: Monthly Review Press.

LEIBOWITZ, LILA. 1975.. "Perspectives on the evolution of sex differences." In *Toward an Anthropology of Women* (ed. Rayna R. Reiter). New York: Monthly Review Press, pp. 20–35.

———. 1983. "Origins of the sexual division of labor." In *Woman's Nature: Rationalizations of Inequality* (ed. Marian Lowe and Ruth Hubbard). Elmsford, NY: Pergamon, pp. 123–147.

LINTON, SALLY. 1971. "Woman the gatherer: Male bias in anthropology." In *Women in Perspective: A Guide for Cross-Cultural Studies* (ed. Sue-Ellen Jacobs). Urbana: University of Illinois Press, pp. 9–21.

MACKEY, WADE C. 1985. *Fathering Behaviors: The Dynamics of the Man-Child Bond.* New York: Plenum.

MCBREARTY, SALLY, AND MARC MONIZ. 1991. "Prostitutes or providers? Hunting, tool use, and sex roles in early *Homo.*" In *The Archaeology of Gender* (ed. Dale Walde and Noreen Willows). Calgary: University of Calgary, Archaeological Association, pp. 71–82.

MCDERMOTT, LEROY. 1996. "Self representation in female figurines." *Current Anthropology*, 37: 227–275.

PEREGRINE, PETER. 2003. *World Prehistory: Two Million Years of Human Life.* Upper Saddle River, NJ: Prentice-Hall.

ROHRLICH-LEAVITT, RUBY, BARBARA SYKES, AND ELIZABETH WEATHERFORD. 1975. "Aboriginal woman: Male and female anthropological perspectives." In *Toward an Anthropology of Women* (ed. Rayna R. Reiter). New York: Monthly Review Press, pp. 110–126.

ROSALDO, MICHELLE. 1974. "Women, culture and society: A theoretical overview." In *Women, Culture and Society* (ed. Michelle Rosaldo and Louise Lamphere). Stanford, CA: Stanford University Press, pp. 17–42.

SANDAY, PEGGY. 1981. *Female Power and Male Dominance.* New York: Cambridge University Press.

SCOTT, ELIZABETH. 1994. "Through the lens of gender: Archaeology, inequality, and those 'of little note.'" In *Those of Little Note: Gender, Race, and Class in Historical Archaeology* (ed. Elizabeth M. Scott). Tucson: University of Arizona Press, pp. 3–24.

SMUTS, BARBARA. 1985. *Sex and Friendship in Baboons.* Hawthorne, NY: Aldine.

———. 2001. "What Are Friends For?" In *Anthropology: Contemporary Perspectives* (ed. Phillip Whitten). Needham Heights, MA: Allyn & Bacon, pp. 49–55.

WOLF, ERIC. 1982. *Europe and the People without History.* Berkeley: University of California Press.

ZIHLMAN, ADRIENNE. 1981. "Women as shapers of human adaptation." In *Woman the Gatherer* (ed. Frances Dahlberg). New Haven: Yale University Press, pp. 75–120.

———. 1986. "Women as shapers of human adaptation." In *Woman the Gatherer* (ed. Frances Dahlberg). New Haven: Yale University Press, pp. 75–120.

CHAPTER 2

Egalitarian Foraging Societies

People in earliest human societies engaged in essentially similar subsistence strategies founded on collecting resources from their local environments. Foragers gathered naturally growing plants, fruits, nuts, and roots. They hunted animals and birds, caught fish, and collected birds' eggs and insects. Such endeavors provided people with necessary foods over the course of tens of thousands of years before the invention of farming techniques. Beginning approximately ten thousand years ago, societies based on farming developed in several areas of the world and gradually either absorbed or pushed out groups of foragers. In the past five hundred years, imperial and later industrial states have accelerated processes of economic transformation so that today few, if any, societies remain with a subsistence based exclusively on foraging.

Examination of the cultures of foraging societies provides insights about the dynamics of gender relations in earliest human groups. It allows us to ascertain the conditions that lead to establishment and maintenance of women's and men's roles. Furthermore, recent well-documented changes in economies of foragers provide evidence of the ways that gender constructs may be transformed.

TRADITIONAL FORAGING SOCIETIES

Because foragers depend totally on the natural environment for their subsistence, they are, more than any other peoples, influenced by environmental constraints. (Note that we use the ethnographic present tense in discussing traditional cultures, although most of the practices of these groups are no longer maintained.) Several environmental constraints directly affect composition of households and principles of descent and family organization. In general, foragers live in small settlements, dispersed over a large territory. Community size is obviously constrained by needs to adjust populations to limits imposed by the availability of natural resources. Foragers tend to be nomadic, shifting their camps to be close to seasonally available vegetation and water sources and/or to follow migrations of wild animals.

Settlements are composed of groups of families related bilaterally. **Bilateral kinship** systems provide flexibility in living arrangements because they allow individuals to make most efficient use of scarce resources by choosing among the widest possible range of people to reside with. Norms of locality are generally diffuse, although some foraging groups seem to prefer **virilocal** or **uxorilocal residence**. Approximately 60 percent of foraging band societies tend to live virilocally, whereas 16 to 17 percent prefer uxorilocal residence. The remaining 15 to 17 percent are bilocal, choosing location with the family of either spouse (Gough, 1975).

People in most foraging societies live in **monogamous**, nuclear households. Family size is limited among foragers because of requirements not to exceed carrying capacities of local environments. In addition, a nomadic lifestyle provides a further constraint on families. Because infants and young children need to be carried when traveling, it is obviously best to manage the spacing of births. In addition, because of the lack of grains and animal milk available as foods for babies in foraging societies, mothers nurse their children for as long as three or four years. Therefore, closely spaced children have a low chance of survival. Frequent pregnancies and deliveries impact negatively on health and long-term survival of mothers as well.

The small size of foraging communities, resulting from natural constraints, is associated with a lack of structured leadership. These groups generally are loosely organized as bands. They live in locally autonomous camps without any form of overtly institutionalized political structure. Cohesive functions, such as leadership and mechanisms of social control, are acted out within communities on a relatively informal basis.

Economies among foragers are based on division of labor by gender. As a general pattern, women are responsible for gathering wild vegetation and frequently participate in hunting small animals and birds. Men provide their families with animal meat and fish. Complementarity of subsistence pursuits allocated by gender is rational given women's reproductive roles (see chapter 1 for a discussion of this correlation).

In many foraging bands, women's and men's interdependent contributions to their households are reflected in equality of social relations and social status. However, among others, male dominance is apparent. We now turn to a comparison of two foraging cultures, the Ju/'hoansi (ju-TWAN-si) of southern Africa and the Inuit (IN-u-it) of the North American Arctic, to ascertain the conditions under which gender equality is maintained, contrasted with the dynamics through which male dominance develops. We end the chapter with a discussion of historical transformations in gender relations in a third group, the Montagnais-Naskapi of Labrador.

The Ju/'hoansi of Botswana and Namibia

The Ju/'hoansi, a San-speaking people of Botswana and Namibia, exemplify a foraging band in which equality between women and men is manifested in many cultural practices and beliefs. (Note that throughout this text, the name

Ju/'hoansi has replaced the term *!Kung* by which these people have formerly been known in the anthropological literature. *Ju/'hoansi* is the name that the people themselves use for their group. It means "real people" in their language.) The following discussion focuses primarily on people known as the Dobe Ju/'hoansi (Lee, 1982, 1984; Shostak, 1983), a group of approximately four hundred who live in the Kalahari Desert. The Dobe area covers 3,000 square miles of semidesert terrain where changes in rainfall divide the year into dry and rainy seasons.

Water is the most critical scarce resource in the Kalahari, and its availability determines settlement size and location. There are ten permanent water holes in the Dobe area, each said to be "owned" by a principal resident group. Ownership, however, does not imply exclusive rights, although it may result in accrual of status by those who "own." Rights to water supplies are granted by owners to anyone who can claim a kinship relationship by either birth or marriage to any member of the resident group.

During the dry season, camps are located near permanent water holes. They generally consist of from eight to fifteen huts, housing in all approximately twenty to fifty people. Rainy season settlements, located near seasonal and secondary water sources, are variable in size, ranging from three to twenty huts (Lee, 1984). Each camp has a core group of residents, usually siblings or cousins, who form the basis of affiliation of other members. Lee's survey of core groups of twelve camps revealed that considerations of gender played no part in their organization: four core groups consisted of a sister and brother, two of two sisters and a brother, one of two brothers and a sister, four of two

Gender equality characterizes the culture of the Ju/'hoansi of southern Africa.

sisters, and one of two brothers. Other residents were related bilaterally or through marriage to some member of the core group. Camp composition is flexible but not random. If numerical imbalances between males and females develop and persist, some families shift residence to another camp. The Ju/'hoansi are also sensitive to what Lee refers to as a "dependency ratio"— that is, if the number of children in a camp becomes too large and thus creates substantial burdens for adult caretakers, some families move to other settlements.

Subsistence activities are allocated by a gender division of labor, although assignment of tasks is not rigid. In general, women collect natural vegetation, including more than a hundred edible varieties of plants, roots, fruits, and nuts. In all, vegetable foods account for approximately 70 percent of the Ju/'hoansi diet. Mongongo nuts are among the most prized foods and are available year-round from trees growing near water holes. According to Lee's calculations based on extensive observation of subsistence activities, Ju/'hoansi women spend twelve or thirteen hours per week in foraging. They are able to collect enough mongongo nuts in a two-hour period to feed one person for ten days, amassing and carrying a load weighing 30 to 50 pounds.

Men also engage in gathering wild foods, although their allocation of time and energy to this endeavor is much less than that of women. Men provide approximately 20 percent of gathered foods (Lee, 1982), but their primary subsistence task is hunting. Small animals are tracked and hunted by individual men, but larger animals are usually pursued by groups of men from a camp. Lee (1984) estimates that Ju/'hoansi men spend 21 or 22 hours per week in subsistence activities.

Disparities between women and men in time allotted to food collecting are equalized by differences in other kinds of labor because women are more often engaged in food preparation and other household duties. Lee estimates an average workweek for Ju/'hoansi men and women as shown in Table 2.1.

Although men expend more time and energy in subsistence work than women do, their contribution to total caloric intake is less. Resources obtained by men in hunting and gathering amount to approximately 44 percent, compared to women's contribution of 56 percent, obtained primarily from gathering (Lee, 1982). Women's greater productivity despite less time expended results

TABLE 2.1 **Estimate of Overall Work Effort in Hours per Week**

	Subsistence Work	Toolmaking and Fixing	Housework	Total Workweek
Men	21.6	7.5	15.4	44.5
Women	12.6	5.1	22.4	40.1
Average (both sexes)	17.1	6.3	18.9	42.3

SOURCE: From The Dobe Ju/'Hoansi 3d edition by Lee. 2002. Reprinted with permission of Wadsworth, a division of Thomson Learning: *www.thomsonrights.com*.

from the fact that men's success rate in hunting is appreciably lower than women's success rate in food collecting. On average, men kill one animal for every four days of hunting.

Meat is a highly valued food, although it accounts for only 30 percent of the Ju/'hoansi's annual diet. Its value is derived from several factors. First, meat provides the most concentrated source of protein and calories. The nutritive content of meat is obviously important to people who expend a great deal of energy in their daily activities. Second, given the relatively low rate of success in hunting, meat is a scarce resource, which may contribute to its desirability. Third, and perhaps most important, is the fact that meat has great "social value" (Lee, 1984, p. 45). Whereas plant products are usually consumed within a gatherer's household, meat is distributed throughout an entire camp. Indeed, meat from an especially large animal may be given to residents of other camps as well. Sharing of meat makes its acquisition socially visible and prominent in a way that household consumption of plant resources does not.

Successful hunting leads to feasting and occasions for the social display of proper etiquette in distributing portions to kin and neighbors. According to Lee (1984):

> Distribution is done with great care, according to a set of rules, arranging and rear-ranging the pieces for up to an hour so that each recipient will get the right proportion. Successful distributions are remembered with pleasure for weeks afterwards, while improper meat distributions can be the cause of bitter wrangling among close relatives. (p. 45)

Men's labor, then, contributes more than calories or taste. It results in a focal activity that binds a community together in reciprocal exchanges of a valued product. It also becomes ritualized through the etiquette of distribution.

Despite the social importance of hunting, neither individual man nor men as a group are able to translate their achievement into dominance in their society. The Ju/'hoansi adhere to two practices that function as leveling mechanisms. One is the fact that a killed animal is said to be "owned" not by the hunter who caught it but rather by the person who owns the arrow that killed it. Arrows are given to hunters through gift exchanges called *hxaro*. In *hxaro* presentations, people exchange material goods such as tools, utensils, hunting gear, and decorative objects. An individual can give a present to any-one and thereby establish a relationship based on an eventual reciprocal gift to the original donor. Such relationships become permanent over time. When a man goes hunting, he may have arrows that he himself has made and others given to him by one of his *hxaro* partners. People establish *hxaro* relationships without regard to gender so that the giver of arrows and thus the "owner" of an animal may be a woman or man. Prestige accrues to the owner because it is this individual who supervises the distribution of meat.

A second leveling mechanism is the practice of "insulting the meat." To set the stage for this ritualized behavior, a successful hunter does not immediately bring his kill into camp. Instead, he leaves it a distance outside and returns alone. Then, as a Ju/'hoansi hunter recounted (Lee, 1984):

> My elder kinsman asks: "Well, what did you see today?" I reply: "I didn't see anything." I am sitting there with my head in my hands but my kinsman comes back to me and says: "What do you mean you haven't killed anything? Can't you see that I'm dying of hunger?" "Well, there might be something out there. I just might have scratched its elbow." Then you say, as he smiles, "Why don't we go out in the morning and have a look." And so we two and others will bring home the meat together the next day. (p. 49)

When the group arrives at the site, they proceed to make derogatory comments about the animal and voice annoyance at the hunter for bothering to take them to such a scanty kill. The hunter is expected to join in insulting the meat and ridiculing himself.

The Ju/'hoansi are well aware of the purpose of these social rituals. An elder hunter explained:

> When a young man kills much meat, he comes to think of himself as a chief or a big man, and he thinks of the rest of us as his servants or inferiors. We can't accept this. We refuse one who boasts, for someday his pride will make him kill somebody. So we always speak of his meat as worthless. In this way we cool his heart and make him gentle. (p. 49)

Leadership among the Ju/'hoansi is quite amorphous. Individuals can gain respect and influence because of their abilities and cooperative personality. Success in subsistence activities contributes to one's prestige, but it cannot be used to render other people socially dependent or subservient.

Despite the generally egalitarian nature of Ju/'hoansi society, most leaders and camp spokespersons are men. Although women and men participate in group discussions and decision making, men's contributions are more frequent. According to Lee (1982), men's talk in discussions involving both genders amounts to about two-thirds of the total.

Ju/'hoansi marriage practices convey mixed messages about gender relations. First marriages are usually arranged by parents without consulting the couple involved. In some cases, a man who is interested in marrying a particular woman may ask his mother to approach the woman's family with a proposal (Shostak, 1976, 1983). Although Ju/'hoansi social norms clearly support the notion of equality of women and men, age differences between spouses typical of first marriages may bestow some authority to husbands. In the traditional pattern, girls generally marry when they reach the ages of 12 to 16. Their husbands are somewhat older, usually between 18 and 25 (Lee, 1984). Parents of a daughter are most likely to agree to a marriage for her if the prospective husband is a successful hunter. Because of the fact that many years of training and experience are needed to become established as a hunter, men cannot marry at as young an age as women. But because seniority confers prestige in Ju/'hoansi society, the greater age, experience, and maturity of husbands may make wives socially, if not personally, subordinate.

Although the younger age of a wife may lead to a difference in status between spouses, initial postmarital residence with wives' natal households provides women with emotional support. Couples typically remain with a wife's kin for a minimum of three to five years and later switch to virilocal residence, although they may continue to live uxorilocally (Lee, 1982). In either case, the fact that a young woman remains near her own kin during the formative years of her marital relationship helps her assert her rights and establish her autonomy.

Marriage rituals among the Ju/'hoansi contain elements that symbolize tensions between spouses. When the day of marriage arrives, the bride often voices loud protests, sometimes physically fighting against her mother's efforts to lead her to the hut that has been built for the couple and in which her husband waits. The following description of a bride's reaction was given by a Ju/'hoansi woman discussing her daughter's impending wedding (Lee, 1984):

> She will be crying and refusing and she will be kicking and screaming against us. With some girls it is necessary to carry them bodily to the hut on the back of one of the women. But all the while we are talking to her and saying: "This is the man we have given you to; he is our man and a good man; he won't hurt you, and we, your relatives, will be right here with you in the village." (pp. 77–78)

Evidently some brides are not convinced and instead run away from their husbands. Marjorie Shostak's (1983) biography of a Ju/'hoansi woman, Nisa, recounts such an experience. When Nisa initially learned that negotiations were under way for her marriage to a man named Tashay, she felt that "my heart didn't agree" (p. 151). On the day of her wedding, she escaped into the bush and had to be chased and caught by her relatives. Nisa recalled:

> They came and brought me back. Then they laid me down inside the hut. I cried and cried. People told me "A man is not something that kills you; he is someone who marries you. He kills animals and gives you things to eat. Even tomorrow, while you are crying, Tashay may kill an animal. But when he returns, he won't give you any meat; only he will eat. Why are you so afraid of your husband and what are you crying about?" (p. 154)

Over the next several weeks, Nisa repeatedly ran away from her husband, returning to her parents' hut. She finally accustomed herself to married life and consented to stay with her husband.

If a Ju/'hoansi woman persists in objecting to her marriage, the union is usually terminated. Nearly half of first marriages end in divorce, mostly on the wife's initiative (Lee, 1984). In contrast, later marriages, which are negotiated directly by the couple concerned, have a high chance of success.

Women's ritualized resistance to marriage symbolizes a variety of attitudes. It obviously reflects a woman's independence and insistence on claiming her autonomy. But it also acts out a fear of losing independence. If such a fear is dramatized, it must reflect some element of reality—namely, that a wife is vulnerable to assertions of her husband's authority. It seems reasonable to assume that if it never happens that wives are subordinate to husbands, they would not develop a ritual enacting their refusal to be subordinated.

Nearly all Ju/'hoansi marriages are monogamous, although both **polygyny** (a man marries more than one woman) and **polyandry** (a woman marries more than one man) are possible. The Ju/'hoansi consider polyandry to be an unusual form. In Lee's data, only one such union was attested. Significantly, it involved people of advanced age, well past their childbearing years. Of the seven cases of polygyny noted, all husbands were well-known healers, a specialty conferring great social prestige on the practitioner. Indeed, five of the seven polygynists were among the most powerful Dobe healers. According to Lee, many Ju/'hoansi men would like to have more than one wife, but women strenuously object to such unions. Women's opposition successfully squelches nearly all polygynous arrangements.

Gender equality is reflected in attitudes toward sexuality before, during, and outside marriage. Premarital sexual experience is the norm for both girls and boys and carries no stigma even if it leads to pregnancy. Of course, the young age of a girl at her wedding tends to lessen the chances of pregnancy before marriage. In fact, because the average age for the onset of menses is between 16 and 17 years, most girls marry before they reach puberty (Shostak, 1983). In any case, it is significant that a girl's sexual behavior is viewed in the same light as that of a boy.

Upon marriage, sexual intercourse depends on the full willingness of both the wife and the husband. Experiences of Nisa and her husband evidently conform to a fairly typical pattern in which newlywed couples often do not have sexual relations for weeks or months after marriage. Because first marriages are arranged by parents, a couple may not know each other well, and a young wife may be reluctant to have sex with a man she considers a stranger. In addition, because brides are frequently only in their early teens, they may resent the new domestic and familial roles they are expected to assume. As Nisa explained, "We began to live together but I ran away again and again. A part of my heart kept thinking, 'How come I'm a child and have taken a husband?'" (p. 155).

Extramarital affairs are evidently common on the part of both husbands and wives. Lee (1984) estimates that in approximately one-third of all marriages, either (or both) spouse has sexual relations with another person. Discretion is advised because fights can arise if a husband or wife discovers that his or her spouse is having an affair. However, gender parity is reflected in the fact that the social and interpersonal costs are equal for errant wives or husbands.

A further manifestation of the lack of male dominance is that physical violence against women in the form of wife beating and rape is rare. The latter in fact is often reported to be entirely absent (Marshall, 1976). The former, although it occurs occasionally, is socially condemned. Relatives and neighbors of the victim quickly intervene and put an end to beatings.

Taken as a whole, Ju/'hoansi society overtly validates equality of women and men. This norm is not just spoken; it is enacted through people's lives. The social system gives equal weight to women's and men's rights, to their autonomy, and to their role as productive and respected members of their communities. The system of leadership, as amorphous as it is, is open to any able individual. Both men and women can aspire to become ritual and healing specialists. Significantly, societal attitudes toward sexuality and toward people's rights in marriage are uniform regardless of a person's gender.

The Ju/'hoansi culture of equality is supported by subsistence activities of women and men, both of whom make vital contributions to their households. Although their economic roles are normatively different, there is actual flexibility in an individual's behavior. Gathering may be women's main subsistence work, but they also notice animal tracks in the bush and convey this information to men who then act on it; hunting may be men's main work, but they gather wild vegetation as well. Women's caretaking activities are regularly shared by men. Although mothers have primary responsibility for child care, especially of infants, fathers also routinely attend to their children.

Group norms stress the importance of cooperation in sharing information and the rights of all to join in making decisions. Boastful, aggressive behavior by anyone is strongly condemned. People who display such traits are ridiculed and severely criticized.

The constellation of behaviors and attitudes that Ju/'hoansi culture prefers supports equality and autonomy for its members regardless of gender or of any other principle of social categorization. A contrast with another foraging society can shed light on the critical aspects of Ju/'hoansi life that validate gender equality. We turn now to such a contrast, focusing on Inuit and Inupiat peoples of Arctic North America.

The Inuit and Inupiat of Arctic North America

Unlike the environment in which the Ju/'hoansi live, Arctic regions of Canada and the United States present inhabitants with enormous difficulties. Resources are scarce, and weather conditions often make subsistence activities hazardous. Inuit (IN-u-it) and Inupiat (i-NU-pi-at) living along the Arctic coast depend primarily on sea mammals, fish, and birds for their sustenance. People living in interior regions rely on caribou in addition to fish and birds. Because large animals found in coastal and inland regions are migratory, their annual numbers are subject to changes in migratory patterns. In addition, factors of breeding and disease in the animal population affect the availability of resources. Therefore, people who depend on animals for subsistence have a precarious lifestyle because they are unable to predict or control their supply. Learning to endure harsh weather and occasional periods of deprivation is thus an essential aspect of life for all Arctic peoples. Survival in the Arctic demands a highly ingenious and sophisticated technology, especially for hunting and for making clothing. But even with the most suitable equipment, the ablest hunter is apt to fail.

An Inupiat family's life traditionally revolved around hunting sea mammals such as whales and seals.

As a result of environmental and resource constraints, settlements are small. They vary somewhat in size depending on seasonal subsistence activities. Among coastal people, the largest settlements occur in winter during the annual seal-hunting period. These camps are typically inhabited by no more than forty or fifty people. Inland groups tend to congregate in late autumn in preparation for collective caribou drives. This period is also the time for making and repairing clothing, so essential to survival in Arctic winters. As spring approaches, people begin to disperse, setting up smaller camps usually consisting of from two to several **nuclear families**. Families may reside together on the basis of bilateral kin relationships. However, there is a marked preference for **patrilineal** affiliation. Camps therefore tend to consist of families of a father and son(s), of brothers, or of male cousins.

Residence patterns are presumably generated by the gender division of labor that allocates primary food-collecting responsibility to men. Because men often depend on each other in group hunting, it is rational for related men to live together and to cooperate in their activities.

Economic roles of Arctic men and women are often described by anthropologists as rigidly defined and separated, but references to actual behavior imply some flexibility. Some researchers do explicitly state the possibility of adjustments in activities. According to Graburn (1969), writing of the central Canadian Inuit:

> The household was a social and economic unit maintained by an adult man and woman, usually husband and wife. Both were essential for successful existence in the Arctic and the numerous tasks of living were about evenly divided between

men and women. Thus the main division of labor was by sex, although Eskimo adults never hesitated to cross roles when this was warranted. (p. 58)

And in the Alaska, both women and men are taught skills necessary for hunting and surviving in the arctic. Women often accompany men in whaling crews, paddle boats, lead dog teams, and track animals (Bodenhorn 1993, pp. 184–185). Their knowledge of the land and sea is respected and sought by hunters.

In general, though, hunting and fishing are considered men's work while women engage in food preparation and gathering available foods such as berries, algae, and birds' eggs. Women are also responsible for child care and for sewing. The latter task includes making clothing, boots, boat covers, and containers (Boas, 1888/1964). Cooperative labor involving men and women occurs in inland communities during caribou drives. Fishing is also done by both women and men. Among coastal groups, women often engage in hunting, fishing, and catching birds found near their settlements (Damas, 1984; D'Anglure, 1984; Graburn, 1969). In some communities, each individual makes the tools and utensils that she or he uses; in others, men are the primary producers of equipment (D'Anglure, 1984; Lantis, 1984).

Among some Arctic peoples, daughters may be trained by their fathers to become hunters. If a father especially prefers his daughter or if he has no son, a daughter may accompany her father on hunting expeditions and learn all the requisite skills (D'Anglure, 1984). Inuit ideally want at least one son and one daughter to fulfill complementary responsibilities, but if a family lacks children of each sex, one child may be trained in tasks usually associated with the other gender in addition to their own gender-linked activities. Such individuals are valued as spouses because they have a double set of subsistence skills. In Alaska, families sometimes adopt children to balance the size and gender composition of their households (Bodenhorn, 1988, p. 14).

Collective labor among men is especially important in coastal communities. Seal and walrus are often hunted in open seas by groups of men. Although seal hunting through ice requires an individual man to wait near a breathing hole for a seal to appear, several men may leave camp together and disperse to breathing holes in the same vicinity so that when one man harpoons a seal, the others can come quickly to help him pull the animal onto the ice. In addition to advantages in efficiency and increased chances of success accruing from collective labor, men traveling and working together are able to aid each other in case of accidents, a not uncommon occurrence.

Many coastal communities, particularly those in Alaska, rely on collective whale hunting. Whaling crews work under the direction of a leader, called an *umialik*. A leader owns the boat and equipment used in whaling. He recruits a crew, usually but not exclusively from among relatives. Men who work together in a whaling crew form a cohesive social group. Their solidarity creates relationships that are second only to ties with their families (Spencer, 1984).

An *umialik*'s wealth as an owner of boats and gear gives him social prestige. *Umialiks* compete with each other and attempt to amass more wealth by recruiting and retaining the best workers. An *umialik* has authority over his crew and makes decisions concerning whaling expeditions. Although his economic position enhances his social status in the community, his authority does not extend beyond the sphere of production.

An *umialik*'s wife also has prestige in camp as a result both of her link to her husband and of her own contributions to the cooperative effort. She is responsible for sewing new sets of clothing that must be worn by the whaling crew and for making or repairing sealskin covers for their boat. If many men are in the crew, an *umialik*'s wife engages other women to help make clothing (Blackman, 1989).

The importance of whaling is symbolized by the rituals associated with it. Hunters must abide by many taboos before departing on whaling expeditions, including abstaining from sexual activity and refraining from eating certain foods or building cooking fires. Once the men are out on the hunt, the *umialak*'s wife must "move slowly, think peaceful thoughts and act generously" (Bodenhorn, 1993, p. 192). These actions attract the whales and persuade them to give themselves up to be caught. Recognition of a woman's role was expressed by a skilled Alaskan hunter who said, "I am not a great hunter, my wife is" (Bodenhorn, 1988, p. 5). When a crew returns with a whale, the *umialik*'s wife, dressed in her best clothing, greets the whale, offers it fresh water from a special wooden pot, and thanks it for allowing itself to be caught; later she gives her husband water from the same pot. Then the *umialik* distributes specific portions of whale meat, blubber, and oil to members of his crew. Each man subdivides his portion and allocates it among his kin in a set sequence (Blackman, 1989, pp. 204–205; Spencer, 1984, p. 330). Any man or woman in the community who contributed labor or equipment to the collective effort also gets a share of meat (Bodenhorn, 1988, p. 6).

In interior Alaska where caribou hunting entails collective labor, an especially skilled and successful hunter is also called *umialik* and occupies a status similar to the organizer of coastal whaling crews. His authority is transient and applies only to economic activities that he coordinates (Hall, 1984).

Each Inuit camp has a "leader" who is generally the eldest active man in the group, often the father or older brother through whom other families are related. Leaders have some degree of influence over decisions affecting the entire group, such as when to relocate camp or to engage in collective hunting. However, they have no power to control others. Graburn (1969) notes that the Inuit language, significantly, has no word meaning "obey" but only *maliktuk* ("he follows") and *nalaktuk* ("he listens to") (p. 59).

Distribution of food is an important social process in Arctic communities. Distribution is managed by the "acquirer" of meat (D'Anglure, 1984). If the kill resulted from individual hunting, the acquirer is the man who killed the animal. In collective seal or walrus hunting, the acquirer is the man who first harpooned the animal. In other cases, a man becomes an acquirer by discovering an animal's location—for example, a bear in its den or on the open ice.

Whales, walrus, and seal are butchered into specific sections and allotted according to defined rules. For example, after one hunt, seal meat was distributed in the following manner: the head, eyes, forelimbs, thoracic vertebrae, and heart were given to women; the cervical and lumbar vertebrae were given to men; the hunter who killed the animals received the ribs, sternum, and attached meat; the lumbar meat went to all the men in the hunting party; and the sacral and caudal vertebrae and hind flippers were cooked in broth and eaten by all (Graburn, 1969, p. 69). Whales were also butchered and their meat distributed according to formal procedures. In Alaska, the whaling captain directs the butchering and then allocates shares of meat. The hunter who killed the animal receives the hide. He and other members of the crew and any man or woman who contributed labor or equipment to the communal effort are entitled to meat. The captain generally receives extra shares, but these are later distributed at public gatherings and ceremonials, not consumed by his household. Once the meat destined for sharing has been cut from the whale, any woman in the community is entitled to carve away what she wants (Bodenhorn, 1988, pp. 6–7).

Children learn the etiquette of food distribution, not only as observers but as distributors as well. A first kill of an animal or bird by an adolescent boy or girl is marked socially and ritually. The girl or boy cuts up the kill and gives the first and best piece to the woman who served as midwife at her or his birth. The midwife then takes over and completes the distribution, all the while praising the accomplishments of her *angusiaq,* or the "person she had made" (D'Anglure, 1984, pp. 490–491).

In the western Arctic, among both coastal and inland groups, societal emphases on men's activities and male solidarity are reflected in the existence of a "men's house," or *kashim,* in each settlement. Although *kashims* appear throughout the region, their organization and functioning vary in different areas. Among the Nunivak of Nunivak Island in the Bering Sea, men and young boys reside in the *kashim.* Women live in separate households with their daughters and very young sons. Women bring meals to their husbands in the *kashim* but generally do not remain there long. Husbands visit their wives at night and occasionally spend time in the family household during the day. A man's possessions are stored in his wife's house, except for hunting and ritual gear that must be kept away from women and children (Lantis, 1984).

Residential separation of women and men among the Nunivak is correlated with a greater degree of rigidity of gender-linked tasks than is the case in central Arctic regions. Gender-appropriate subsistence activities are not only acknowledged and followed but are also marked ritually. For example, ceremonies are performed when a boy kills his first bird or a girl gathers grass. Separation but complementarity in economic tasks of men and women is also ritualized in Nunivak practices preceding a marriage. As a proposal of marriage, a young man offers fur pelts to the mother of the woman he wishes to marry, bringing enough fur for the mother to make her daughter a parka. If the young woman agrees to the union, she brings food to the man in the *kashim.* These practices symbolize the separation but reciprocity and interdependence implicit in divisions of labor by gender.

Kashims also exist in Alaskan communities, but their functions differ from the northerly Nunivak. Among coastal Alaskans, *kashims* are places for men to socialize, but a man resides with his wife and family (Spencer, 1984). In interior Alaska, they function as ceremonial houses for an entire community. In addition, women and men eat their main daily meals together in the *kashim* (Hall, 1984).

Marriages among Arctic peoples are generally not marked with a formal ritual. A couple decides to marry and simply takes up residence together. They then are socially recognized as married. Most marriages are monogamous, but both polygyny and polyandry are possible. The former, although infrequent, is more common than the latter. Among some groups, plural unions are formed by marriage between a man and two sisters or a woman and two brothers. In other areas, plural marriages never involve siblings (Lantis, 1984; Spencer, 1984).

Among central Arctic groups, although marriage is not ritualized, betrothal is formalized and arranged by parents. Negotiations are often concluded at the time of a child's birth or during early childhood. Child betrothal seems to be correlated with the incidence of sex imbalances in a community resulting from female infanticide. In the central Arctic where child betrothal was formerly common, female infanticide was also practiced, perhaps as recently as 1940 (Damas, 1984). According to Balikci (1984), a father made the decision concerning his daughter's fate immediately after her birth. Occurrence of female infanticide is reflected in population statistics for central Inuit. Among the Netsilik, for example, Rasmussen (1931) noted a numerical preponderance of males in 1923, recording a Netsilik population of 150 males and 109 females. If one assumes an equal number of male and female births, approximately one-third of the girls may have been victims of infanticide.

Given lowered numbers of available women in central Arctic communities, infant betrothal can be interpreted as an attempt by parents of a boy to ensure a wife for their son. However, this strategy does not actually lead to future stability. Although a couple may marry, there is no assurance that they will remain together. Divorce is quite common and can be initiated by either a wife or husband.

Some anthropologists rationalize female infanticide as a reflection of the need to limit population growth given dire survival circumstances and the fact that men perform primary subsistence activities. According to this theory, whereas men as hunters are essential to survival of a family and community, women are expendable. However, this argument presents a number of problems. Among the groups in the central Arctic who practiced female infanticide, gender roles are not as rigid as in the west where the practice seems to have been rare. Central Inuit women engage with men in cooperative hunting during caribou drives. They also independently catch birds and fish. In addition to these direct subsistence pursuits, a woman's labor in making and repairing clothing is essential to the survival of her entire family. In the Arctic environment, warm clothing and watertight boots are paramount necessities. Without them, a hunter would quickly freeze and die. Women's skills in sewing and repairing clothing are socially recognized. Just as a successful hunter is desired as a potential husband, so an expert sewer is a valued wife (Briggs, 1974). It is therefore not true that women's labor is expendable or socially invisible.

Furthermore, female infanticide does not solve societal problems for central Arctic communities. Indeed, it actually creates discord within settlements because it results in gender imbalances that then lead to competition and conflict among men over available women. For example, Netsilik men often attempt to steal a wife from another man, sometimes killing the husband in the process (Balikci, 1984). Husbands are always on the alert against the possibility that another man may try to convince his wife to leave him. Such suspicions result in a husband's jealousy and accusations against his wife and other men. Fighting between men and murder are not uncommon. Retaliatory beating of wives is even more frequent.

Given the social outcomes of female infanticide, it does not seem to solve urgent problems. Although it is true that it helps reduce population growth, female infanticide has tremendous social, not to mention personal, costs. It leads to conflicts among men and to excuses for violence against women. Community cohesion, presumably a societal imperative, is thus undermined by conditions resulting from female infanticide.

Because infanticide among the Inuit was practiced almost exclusively against females, except in cases of physical deformity resulting in a male infant's death, it cannot be interpreted solely as an attempt to limit population. The occurrence of this practice must have additional roots. It was likely a reflection of male dominance that existed in Inuit society. Male dominance was not uniform among Arctic peoples, nor was it as extreme as in other cultures, but it was a feature of gender relations in the region. It was demonstrated in several behaviors and values. One manifestation was the occurrence of violence against women. As already discussed, husbands might beat their wives in retaliation for real or imagined adultery. Beatings also arose in conflicts derived from other sources and tensions. In addition, rape was not uncommon.

The practice of spouse exchange in some arctic communities raises the question of male dominance as well. Spouse exchange was a means through which bonds between unrelated men could be formed. For example, among coastal North Alaskans, an *umialik* could recruit and retain whaling crew members by allowing the men to have sexual relations with his wife. Once a relationship of this sort was established, social bonds among men were perpetuated. These bonds were transmitted to children of the people involved so that they, too, had a recognized social relationship (Spencer, 1984, p. 331). Further to the west among Inuit of St. Lawrence Island, men who were trading partners granted sexual access to each other's wives as a means of establishing and strengthening economic and social ties. Spouse exchange was not aimed at sexual gratification but rather was a feature of economic production, cementing alliances and cooperative networks between men

(Schweitzer, 1989, p. 30). According to Peter Schweitzer (1989), the ethnographic and historical record is ambiguous regarding the degree to which women had choices in the matter. Although ideally the practice required the consent of wives, "there are cases of coercion" (p. 30).

Spouse exchange occurs among central Arctic peoples too. Among the Netsilik, it could be initiated by either a husband or a wife. In some cases, resulting social bonds between men were permanent. However, these ties were just as likely to end as a result of "jealousy, bitterness and hatred" between the two men (Balikci, 1984, p. 425).

Spouse exchange reflects a male orientation to the extent that women are manipulated by men to further their own social and economic goals. Women's noted lack of resistance to spouse exchange may also indicate their realization that opposition is futile or their fear that they may be beaten if they were to protest. And, as Schweitzer (1989) points out, recorded observations may be biased because they do not "even pose the question of female actors" (p. 30).

Although some degree of male dominance exists among Arctic peoples, it is tempered by several practices. First, while residence patterns tend to favor patrilateral bonds, couples typically begin married life residing with the wife's kin. They may remain there until several children are born and the marriage is assumed to be stable. Uxorilocal residence aids a woman in establishing a cooperative relationship with her husband. Given a couple's proximity to the wife's kin, a husband who may be inclined to abuse his wife is unlikely to persist. In cases of excessive conflict, divorce is an option.

Second, attitudes toward premarital sexuality are equally permissive concerning girls and boys. Although there is some pressure for an unwed mother to marry the father of her child, it is not intense. Little, if any, stigma is associated with her condition.

Third, flexibility in subsistence activities also lessens tendencies for male dominance because it publicly recognizes the fact that tasks can be performed equally well by either women or men. Women's participation in hunting and fishing demonstrates their productive contributions to their households. For their part, men freely participate in child-care responsibilities. Fathers are attentive, affectionate, and playful with their sons and daughters.

Fourth, decision making tends to involve people who are directly concerned in the focal activity. Men make decisions regarding their tasks; women do likewise. However, decisions involving movements of settlements are more often made by men because camps tend to relocate in keeping with availability of animal resources. Because men are more directly involved in securing these resources than women are, their opinions carry most weight.

Fifth, ritual activity tied to economic endeavors symbolizes the "gendered interdependence" (Bodenhorn, 1993, p. 198) that is pervasive in Inuit worldview and ethics. Finally, absence of warfare in Arctic communities may contribute to limiting male dominance. Without much intercommunity violence, the kind of warrior ideologies that often enhance men's prestige at the expense of women have not developed among Arctic peoples.

In sum, then, Arctic cultures manifest tendencies toward male dominance, but they also contain support for egalitarian gender relations. Autonomy for all individuals is an underlying value. Women are able to establish their rights on the basis of substantial and essential contributions to their households. They generally control their labor and make decisions regarding their activities. However, men are able to translate their more direct control over resources into some degree of dominance over their wives. Although a wife's labor is essential for her husband's survival, a husband's position as direct supplier of food gives him a socially recognized prominence.

According to Peggy Sanday (1981), male dominance often occurs in societies living in environmental conditions that produce stress because of difficulties of survival. When these conditions are combined with subsistence based on men's hunting of large animals, male dominance is even more likely. Sanday suggests that hunting large animals places a psychological focus on risk and control that results in prestige for those who take the risks and attempt to exercise the control. Sanday's suggestion seems to be borne out by data from the Arctic. Because men take substantial life-threatening risks in their subsistence activities and may be seen as directly controlling the likelihood of community survival in a harsh and unyielding environment, they are endowed with social power to an extent that women are not. Perhaps the rewards for fulfilling their economic duties include not only their own survival but also dominance over their wives.

Comparing the Ju/'hoansi and Inuit

Comparisons of data concerning the Ju/'hoansi and the Inuit make apparent a number of basic similarities. Both of these small nomadic bands are organized around bilaterally related kin groups. Economic roles are defined according to gender, but flexibility and overlap are also attested. The productive labor of both women and men, essential for survival, is socially recognized and rewarded. Formal political structures and formalized leadership are absent. Settlements are politically and economically autonomous.

In Ju/'hoansi and Inuit society, marriages are usually monogamous, although polygyny and polyandry are infrequent possibilities. Initial postmarital residence is uxorilocal, providing a young wife with support from her kin until children are born and her marriage becomes stable. Divorce, though, is common, particularly in early years of marriage, and can be initiated by either spouse. Fathers in both cultures take an active role in child care and are affectionate and playful with their children. In general, attitudes toward premarital sexuality are permissive concerning the behavior of both girls and boys. And, although adultery is criticized, punishments are not as severe as found elsewhere.

Despite these similarities in the cultures of Ju/'hoansi and Inuit peoples, important differences also exist that help us understand the conditions under which egalitarian gender relations are maintained and, conversely, some of the conditions that promote male dominance.

Environmental constraints are much more imposing in the Arctic than in the semidesert homeland of the Ju/'hoansi. Whereas the Ju/'hoansi have enough variety of foods available on a changing seasonal basis to ensure a relatively secure resource base, the Inuit face threats of deprivation and actual starvation in a harsh and dangerous environment. Arctic peoples attempt to gain some control over their environment by enactment of numerous rituals, prayers, and taboos that precede, accompany, and end many subsistence activities and daily routines. These practices are especially important in regard to hunting. A successful hunter therefore is not only a skilled worker but a powerful ritualist as well.

In contrast to the Ju/'hoansi (and most other foraging peoples), for whom annual caloric intake consists mainly of plant products, the Inuit diet is based almost exclusively on meat and fish. Because these resources are supplied primarily by men, male labor is seen as more directly producing conditions for survival. Women's contributions, although substantial and essential, are seen as adjunctive. Such a situation contrasts with that of Ju/'hoansi economies. Ju/'hoansi hunters may be respected and socially rewarded, but Ju/'hoansi women are also recognized for contributing and controlling the major food supply.

An emphasis on male labor among the Inuit leads to preferences for virilocal residence and for camp affiliation based on kinship bonds among men. Collective male labor is essential for many economic pursuits, especially among coastal peoples engaged in hunting seal, walrus, and whales. In some groups, such as those along the Alaskan coast, male labor is organized by *umialiks* who further gain wealth and social prestige because of their ownership of means of production—namely, whaling boats and gear.

Economic distinctions between men and women are symbolized by some Arctic peoples through the *kashims* that spatially separate the genders. *Kashims* are not taboo to women (as "men's houses" are in some cultures), but for several Arctic societies they visibly manifest a distinction between women and men. Men and women tend to socialize separately. The division of labor that requires men to leave their camps for individual or collective hunting results in another basis for physical separation of men and women and for primary social interactions with members of one's own gender.

In contrast to the Inuit, physical and social separation of women and men is relatively absent among the Ju/'hoansi. Conversational and interactional groupings form casually without regard to gender. Just as their economies are based on nearly equal work efforts and contributions, daily encounters manifest equality and autonomy of all participants.

Although men's prominence in Arctic subsistence is translated into some degree of dominance over women, gender inequality cannot be explained solely by referring to economic contributions. There are certainly many societies where the major share of production is carried out by people with little social power (for example, economies using slave labor are extreme forms of this type). We therefore have to look further into the conditions under which men pursue their economic roles. The Arctic environment presents constraints unlike most other regions. A man's efforts, no matter how skilled and fearless the hunter, are likely to result in failure. Risks to his survival are encountered daily. If his boat capsizes, he will drown in frigid waters; he may fall on ice, break his leg, and freeze to death; an animal he tracks, such as a bear, may turn and kill him. These possibilities must result in a hunter's apprehension, to say the least. In contexts of real dangers, compounded with the likelihood of failure rather than routine success, hunters make every effort to establish some control over their situation. Their religious beliefs revolve around the necessity of ritualized precautions, taboos, and prayers to forestall disaster. But stress and tension result nevertheless.

People living in the Arctic may conceptualize their existence as dependent on men's ability to control and extract resources in situations of danger where violent acts against animals are the only hope for human survival. The supernatural realm is also viewed as dangerous. For people to succeed, they must combat hostile spiritual beings and forces that attempt to thwart human plans and render human actions futile. In this context, those people—namely, men—who take the greatest risks and whose successes are therefore most noteworthy are rewarded with social prestige. But they are additionally rewarded by being allowed to translate their subsistence achievements into personal dominance over women, who are normatively seen as not taking the same kind of direct physical risks on a daily basis. In a society where interpersonal aggression is supposedly condemned, where cooperative, friendly, and hospitable behavior is strongly preferred, men are permitted to sometimes act violently toward women. Male aggression is permitted despite other norms that stress nonaggressive behavior and endow all individuals with recognized social rights. Although male dominance among Inuit peoples is certainly much weaker than displayed in many other cultures, it is nevertheless real and manifested in both symbolic and actual behavior.

This summary should not lead one to ignore the fact that Inuit women also function autonomously and are expected to develop as independent and self-reliant individuals, as are all Inuit people (Briggs, 1982). Conflicting norms and values are commonly held in all societies so that among Arctic peoples, women's autonomy coexists with men's social dominance.

TRANSFORMATION OF FORAGING SOCIETIES

Neither the Ju/'hoansi nor Inuit live today the way their parents and grandparents did. Contact with members of other societies has led to fundamental changes in native economies and social relations. In some cases, these contacts were benign or mutually advantageous. In others, however, **indigenous peoples** have been dominated by invaders and colonizers. The contexts of intercultural contact therefore are relevant to understanding the direction of change and the choices facing peoples under pressure.

Economic and political changes experienced by the Ju/'hoansi and Inuit have had significant impacts on gender roles, relationships between women and men, and cultural evaluation of the genders. Examination of these dynamic processes that alter behavior and ideology help us understand how gender comes to have the meaning it has.

The Ju/'hoansi

Ju/'hoansi society has been affected by introduction of modern technology, involvement in wage work by large segments of the population, and incorporation into national states that first surrounded and now have engulfed Ju/'hoansi territory. These changes occurred over a relatively short time. As Lee comments (1984):

> If our work had begun in 1983 instead of 1963, we would not have seen daily hunting with poisoned arrows, full-time gathering of the rich mongongo harvest, and weekly healing dances in which powerful healers spiritually defended the Ju/'hoansi against illness and misfortune. Today, bow-and-arrow hunting has almost ceased, cultivated grains are now the staples of the diet, and penicillin, not "num" [traditional healing power], is the main defense against illness. Livestock, cash reserves, and material wealth have replaced social relationships as the main source of security for the Ju/'hoansi. Game meat, once freely given, is now bought and sold. (p. ix)

Economic changes began for some Ju/'hoansi people in the early twentieth century. At that time, people of European descent, called Boers, came to the area from South Africa. Boers appropriated land from the San and then hired natives as laborers to tend their herds and work in their fields. The fact that Boers relied on native labor did not stop them from imposing segregationist policies on the San (Guenther, 1976).

The San suffered increased discrimination after the 1950s, when a new wave of immigrants of British descent entered San territory from South Africa. Settlers established large cattle-herding operations and hired African laborers. They tended not to hire the San but rather members of other African groups, principally Herero and Tswana, who were themselves traditional cattle herders. These peoples are speakers of Bantu languages and have cultures vastly different from that of the Ju/'hoansi. They live in sedentary villages and practice a mixed economy based on pastoralism and farming. Herero and Tswana herders began to expand their settlements into Ju/'hoansi territory in the 1920s, gradually encroaching on Ju/'hoansi resources and contributing to transformations in Ju/'hoansi economies.

During the first half of the twentieth century, the Ju/'hoansi were not much affected by all of these newcomers, so that even as recently as the 1960s, most Ju/'hoansi followed a foraging subsistence mode. But increases in the numbers of Herero have since combined with new waves of immigration by Tswana pastoralists (Lee, 1984). Expansion of villages and herding areas of both the Herero and Tswana have brought the Ju/'hoansi into their sphere of influence. Policies of the national governments of Botswana and Namibia have also affected Ju/'hoansi life. Shortly after Botswana's independence in 1966 from colonial status under the control of Great Britain, the central government introduced programs for educational and economic development in rural areas, including the Kalahari region. Two schools were opened in the 1970s. The government proceeded with several development projects, such as marketing of Ju/'hoansi crafts, improvement of wells, and expansion of agriculture and stock raising. Technological innovations include mechanical wells and steel plows. In addition to changes in material conditions, schools and missionary activities help foster ideological changes compatible with economic development imposed by ruling authorities and governments.

Although the independence of Botswana has resulted in eradicating many discriminatory features of colonial society dominated by whites, the Ju/'hoansi still suffer in ethnic conflicts with other African peoples. The Ju/'hoansi (and the San as a whole) are among the poorest groups in Botswana. They and their culture are denigrated by the more prosperous, numerous, and powerful African peoples such as the Tswana (Guenther, 1976).

The Ju/'hoansi living in Namibia were affected by policies of the government of South Africa that illegally occupied and controlled Namibia until its independence in 1990. During the war for independence, the South African government established sedentary camps for native people, including the Ju/'hoansi. In the 1980s, many Ju/'hoansi were recruited into the South African army to fight against the Namibian independence forces led by SWAPO (SouthWest Africa People's Organization). Ju/'hoansi soldiers and their families were settled on rural army bases. These bases often became scenes of violence, brought on by overcrowding and easy access to alcohol and firearms (Lee, 1984; Lee and Hurlich, 1982).

Beginning in the 1960s, the majority of Ju/'hoansi in Botswana and Namibia became involved in pastoral and farming activities, first as laborers for Herero and Tswana villagers and more recently as owners of their own herds and fields. Economic changes in Ju/'hoansi life have directly affected gender roles and the contributions women and men make to their households. As we have seen, traditional foraging activities involved both genders in productive work under the worker's own control. Even though hunting conferred social prestige on men, women's labor was also socially visible and acknowledged. But this way of life has been fundamentally altered. Most Ju/'hoansi today live in sedentary villages where subsistence is based on farming and herding. These pursuits are carried out primarily by men, whereas women's work consists mainly of domestic caretaking tasks in addition to occasional foraging for wild foods (Draper, 1975).

Three important factors leading to transformation of gender relations among the Ju/'hoansi are associated with changes in economic activities. First, in the traditional context, men and women contributed roughly equal amounts of labor time to subsistence, but in modern villages, men's contributions are much greater, in terms of both the amount of labor expended and the quantity of food produced. Second, whereas traditional Ju/'hoansi women and men had individual control over their use and distribution of resources, this control is now vested primarily in men because they are the owners of herds and fields. Although women remain workers for their households, they have become subsidiary. Finally, the division of labor by gender that was previously idealized but not necessarily practiced has become more rigid. Working with livestock is a male domain, as is the heavy labor involved in clearing fields for planting, erecting fences, and harvesting crops. Perhaps because women's work has declined in visible social value, men are extremely reluctant to carry out any tasks identified as "women's work."

As a consequence of economic changes, settlement patterns and the flow of daily life have been fundamentally altered in ways that also impact on gender constructs. Villages now consist of permanent houses spaced at greater distances from each other rather than the casual shelters previously built in the bush. Because the new structures are larger and more permanent, women must expend time and labor on their upkeep. Mud walls and floors have to be periodically cleaned and resurfaced. Family possessions also require cleaning and repair. In addition, greater effort is needed to prepare and cook the current dietary staples of grain foods than was needed to prepare plants gathered in the wild. The time required for fulfilling responsibilities of cooking and other domestic tasks means that women spend more of their daily life indoors and apart from other villagers. According to Draper's (1975) contrast of Ju/'hoansi nomadic and settled life, "the work of [village] women is more specialized, time-consuming and homebound" (p. 102).

Even when Ju/'hoansi women engage in foraging activities, they tend to do so for shorter periods of time and to remain closer to their settlements than was true of traditional women. In contrast to decreasing mobility for women, men have become more mobile. They regularly leave their villages for substantial periods of time, engaging in herding, farming, and trading with other peoples. In addition, many Ju/'hoansi men are now employed for wages in nearby towns and even as far away as the gold mines in South Africa.

In modern Ju/'hoansi villages, men and women occupy separate social spheres as a result of separation of their subsistence roles and daily tasks. This situation contrasts with that of traditional Ju/'hoansi camps that Draper (1975) described:

> Observing the way people group themselves during leisure hours in a Ju/'hoansi camp gives one a feeling for the tone of informal heterosexual interaction. Men and women (children too) sit together in small clusters—talking, joking, cracking and eating nuts, passing around tobacco. Individuals pass among these groups without causing a rift in ambiance, without attracting attention. In general, the sexes mix freely and unselfconsciously without the diffidence one might expect to see if they thought they were in some way intruding. (p. 93)

Notions of private ownership of property by individuals have become incorporated into Ju/'hoansi ethics. Goats and cattle in Ju/'hoansi herds are owned separately by men. Houses are also said to be "owned" by the male head of household. Particular men who have amassed greater material wealth than others are even said to be "owners" of a village. Because property that constitutes wealth is identified more with men than with women, men are endowed with status on the basis of their ownership of material goods. Furthermore, men's status results from their own activities, whereas women are increasingly identified in terms of their husbands.

Social prestige also accrues to men because of their involvement with other peoples and cultures. Men often interact with nearby Herero and Tswana people for whom they work as herders or with whom they trade. Ju/'hoansi men are frequently bilingual and often serve as intermediaries in bringing technological innovations into Ju/'hoansi communities. Women are usually barred from intercultural activities, in part because of domestic responsibilities that limit their mobility and in part because of patriarchal attitudes of Herero and Tswana men that generally demean and restrict women. Behaviors and values associated with male dominance characteristic of Herero and Tswana culture have undoubtedly contributed to changing gender constructs among the Ju/'hoansi. Because the Ju/'hoansi think of the Herero and Tswana as higher in status and wealth than themselves, they are influenced by Herero and Tswana ideologies as well as by their economies. Ju/'hoansi men are impressed by these newcomers' ability to contract polygynous marriages and generally to control their wives and families. Ju/'hoansi women are not so impressed. When Draper (1975) asked a Ju/'hoansi woman, aged 50, "Who do you think has the better life—a Ju/'hoansi woman or a Herero woman?" the Ju/'hoansi speaker answered:

> The Ju/'hoansi women are better off. Among the Herero if a man is angry with his wife he can put her in their house, bolt the door and beat her. No one can get in to separate them. They only hear her screams. When we Ju/'hoansi fight, other people get in between. (p. 109)

In sum, an egalitarian society has been transformed into one in which hierarchies are in the process of being established. Societal differentiation is now based on wealth and work. Gender roles and relations have been affected by both factors. Because work roles are now rigidly defined and assigned according to gender and only some kinds of labor lead to possibilities of accumulating wealth, those people who engage in wealth-producing work have more prestige than those who do not. This hierarchical system distinguishes among men in terms of their individual material standing. But it also rewards men socially as a group, separating them from the work and worth of women.

The Inuit

Turning from the desert to the Arctic, we find that processes of change resulting from trade and contact with colonizers have affected indigenous Inuit culture. Inuit peoples in regions along the Atlantic and Hudson Bay coasts were contacted by European explorers as early as the seventeenth century. Many of these expeditions were searching for ocean routes to the west but instead met Arctic peoples dispersed throughout a vast territory. European traders and missionaries soon followed the explorers. The Hudson's Bay Company was established in 1670 and immediately began to trade for furs with Inuit people. Fox, mink, bear, and wolf pelts were especially desired. Overland exploration by adventurers and traders commenced in the late 1700s, heading westward from Hudson Bay. Merchants brought European goods to inland Inuit in exchange for furs (Neatby, 1984).

In the following century, whaling enterprises from New England contacted peoples in the east along the Atlantic coast and in the west along the Pacific coast of Alaska. By the early years of the nineteenth century, many Inuit groups were quite familiar with the annual appearance of whaling and trading ships along the coasts. Inuit people, both men and women, boarded ships in order to trade animal skins and meat for whatever goods sailors possessed. Natives particularly desired metalware, including iron pots, nails, and knives (Graburn, 1969).

The late 1800s and early 1900s witnessed the most intense whaling throughout the Arctic (Neatby, 1984; Spencer, 1984). Crews on whaling ships traded with Inuit people on an independent basis. Although natives wanted to acquire European goods, they had to endure cheating as well as other abuses from traders and sailors. In the words of Bernhard Hantzsch (1977), a German observer writing in 1911:

> The whaling crews treated the natives in shameless fashion, betraying the men with a little tobacco and the women with "Branntwein." The poor Eskimos yielded themselves to degrading influences not from badness of character, but from frivolity, good-humoured compliance and heathenish ignorance. (pp. 98–99)

Inuit men evidently attempted to extract trade goods from sailors and traders by exploiting sexual services of their own wives, much the way they might do in spouse exchange relationships in their native communities. According to W. Chappell's narrative written in 1817:

> Several brought their wives on board the ship, and, in return for a tin spoon or a pot, compelled them, nothing loath, to receive our salutations. Nay, one man plainly intimated, that if I wished to hold a private conversation with his lady, he would have no objection to her visiting this cabin, provided I rewarded him with an axe. (quoted in Graburn, 1969, p. 98)

Inuit men assumed a right to control and exploit their wives' sexual behavior. However, the fact that wives did not have rights to control their own sexuality is indicated in an excerpt from Finlayson's journal of 1830: "The men of Chimo would prostitute their women for gain very gladly with us, yet they are highly offended if their women commit a fault without their knowledge" (quoted in Graburn, 1969, p. 98).

In the late 1800s, whaling companies hired native crews to supplement Anglo workers. They preferred to hire men, but when their need for crews exceeded the local supply of Inuit men, they hired women as well (Blackman, 1989).

The importance of whaling as a source of income and trade goods was replaced in the early twentieth century by emphases on trapping animals for furs destined for markets in Canada, the United States, and Europe. Expansion of trading throughout the nineteenth and early twentieth centuries directly and indirectly transformed Inuit economies. To obtain desired manufactured goods, men had to engage in trapping animals for furs wanted by traders. Trapping and trading endeavors caused a shift away from subsistence hunting. At first, such a change in emphasis was slight, but trapping gradually became a focal activity, whereas hunting steadily declined in importance. As a consequence of spending less time hunting, some food had to be obtained through trade. This led in turn to an even greater dependence on trapping to amass furs needed to barter for the expanding quantities of goods desired.

Trading emphasized economic roles of Inuit men in several ways. First, the status of men who engaged in trade was enhanced because trading resulted in accumulation of valued manufactured goods. Access to and control of material wealth increased men's prestige. Second, the majority of trade goods obtained by Inuit were items related to men's work. Fishing nets, metal fishhooks, guns, and ammunition were among the most valued objects (Graburn, 1969). Later, in the twentieth century, new trade items in men's domain were added, including steel traps, modern boats, and outboard motors.

As Arctic economies were transformed to focus on trapping, a gradual shift occurred in settlement patterns. At first, native men hunted and trapped animals in local territories and transported furs to dealers at trading posts. Gradually, though, whole families began to congregate closer to the posts as the people became more dependent on material goods and foods that they received in exchange for furs. Small, dispersed, temporary camps became less common as larger, more concentrated, settled towns took shape. These towns sprang up in numerous locales where trading posts had initially been established. Eventually, in the twentieth century, Canadian and U.S. authorities helped accelerate relocation by establishing administrative offices, schools, and nursing stations in settled villages. These burgeoning centers attracted Inuit from outlying camps because of goods available and services provided. Contributing to change in Arctic villages, missionaries set up churches in attempts to convert natives to Christianity and impose Western ideological values.

Adoption of trapping also led to men's increased absence from their home communities. Men had to spend much time checking their trapping lines spread out over many miles of terrain at long distances from settlements. Their absence from households created an additional incentive for the rest of the family to settle in towns where other similar households were congregated.

Changes in Inuit culture took place in attitudes toward ownership. Trapping lines and the animals they snared were considered individual property. Animal pelts, particularly fox, mink, wolf, and bear, remained outside the traditional system of reciprocal exchange that had always bound members of Inuit camps into cohesive economic and residential units. Because inspecting trapping lines and retrieving animals were accomplished individually rather than collectively, cooperation in economic activities was no longer necessary. In fact, men came to believe that group efforts and the resulting responsibility each member felt toward others might interfere with one's own ability to amass greater wealth. In the old days, the prestige of an *umialik* depended on his ability to muster a crew and retain their loyalty and labor, but in the trapping business, a man succeeds as well on his own. A decline in group cooperation eventually led to the fact that even meat from sea mammals and caribou was no longer exchanged between families.

As a further consequence of trapping, emphases on individual property and accumulation of wealth often resulted in heightened status of young men who were successful trappers. In time, this led to a decline in the traditional authority of elder leaders of camps and even of fathers over sons. Relocation into permanent towns also helped erode a senior leader's authority. Because towns were settled by people from numerous families previously unknown to each other, no one individual was recognized as a leader.

Inuit living in towns had social contacts with many more people than had been the norm in previous years. They associated with others on the basis of friendships and personal interests rather than solely on the basis of kinship. In fact, possibilities of choosing one's friends and alliances were factors in attracting people to town life. For some Inuit men, especially the Netsilik, who commonly practiced female infanticide and had difficulties finding wives in their own communities, larger settlements consisting of people from disparate regions provided opportunities for contracting marriages with women from other groups (Mary-Rousseliere, 1984).

Since World War II, the pace of change throughout the Artic has accelerated. Towns are larger due to consolidation of neighboring communities, influx of people from distant camps, and natural population increases. Towns also provide industrial and service sector jobs attracting a larger population. Exploration for oil, particularly in Alaska, and its expropriation by transnational corporations have created numerous jobs as well as stimulating immigration of thousands of nonnatives to the region.

Wage work is available to some Inuit women and men in a variety of gender-linked occupations. Men are typically employed in construction, mining, building maintenance, and work at Canadian and U.S. military bases. Seasonal jobs loading and unloading ships and work as trappers and guides also are available. Women find employment in service occupations and as nurses' aides, teachers, and school aides. Both men and women also gain income from skilled craftwork, including sculpture, painting, and basketry. Some Inuit artisans are able to obtain prestige and a good income from these pursuits. However, despite the array of occupations, relatively few jobs are actually available. Most of these are seasonal or temporary. Therefore, annual income levels are extremely low (Chance, 1984). Such conditions necessitate some continued reliance on traditional subsistence activities to survive.

Political innovations have gradually been incorporated into Inuit communities. As towns grew and their populations became more diversified, and as the traditional authority of elders eroded, new forms of leadership and decision making were adopted. Government authorities from Canada and the United States played an active part in setting up local councils to act as intermediaries between native communities and federal bureaucracies. Graburn (1969) describes formation of one such council in the town of Sugluk in northern Quebec:

> Soon after the Northern Service officer arrived in 1958, he suggested the formation of a community council made up of an elected headman and two assistants. Monthly meetings were organized for *all interested men*. (p. 212; emphasis added)

Local bodies of this sort had little if any real power and were not given much attention by the majority of Inuit communities. However, they publicly emphasized men's participation in decision-making and administrative functions.

In the late 1960s, political organizations developed spontaneously in native communities in Alaska to deal primarily with native land claims. For example, the Arctic Slope Native Association, founded in 1966, became instrumental in negotiations with the U.S. government, leading to the Alaska Native Claims Settlement Act of 1971 that spelled out agreements concerning land rights and royalties from oil resources. Both women and men are actively involved in many local political organizations, and both hold administrative positions, although the top leadership is most often monopolized by men (Ager, 1980; Blackman, 1989).

In addition to influences stemming from economic and political transformations in the Arctic, new ideological constructs were introduced and widely disseminated by missionaries and teachers beginning in the nineteenth century. Imposition of Western values had various effects on Inuit gender. Some practices that were particularly demeaning to women were eliminated. Most important among these were eradication of female infanticide, polygyny, and spouse exchange. However, missionaries also preached against some Inuit norms that gave personal freedoms to both women and men, including permissive attitudes toward premarital sexuality and rights of spouses to divorce their mates. Missionaries affected Inuit marital relationships by sanctioning rights of husbands as authorities over their wives and obligations of wives to defer to husbands. These attitudes were latent in traditional Inuit culture but were given added emphasis by church teachings that essentially perpetuated and possibly strengthened male-dominated family systems.

Relevant to a discussion of both traditional and modern norms concerning marriage, Graburn's (1969) study of Sugluk in Arctic Quebec indicates that a large number of people have never married. This trend contrasts with aboriginal Inuit camps in which all (or nearly all) adults married. Today, young women especially are choosing not to marry. Several factors may contribute to their decisions. In some specific cases detailed by Graburn, widowers denied their daughters permission to marry because they wanted the daughters to continue fulfilling domestic tasks in their own households. Some widows similarly blocked their daughters' marriages to retain their companionship.

In addition, economic independence influences young women's choices not to marry. Women who are employed in wage work as service workers, school aides, or craftspeople earn their own money and can support themselves. Unmarried mothers can also live independently because they obtain financial support from the Canadian government in the form of aid to mothers with dependent children. Finally, widows receive government pensions that allow them to be self-sufficient.

A third compelling factor is likely present as an influence in women's decisions not to marry. Women are possibly resisting the kind of control and violence in marital relationships to which their mothers and grandmothers were sometimes subjected.

Documentation of both change and continuity in gender roles and relationships over the past century is provided by a narrative of the life of Sadie Brower Neakok, an Inupiaq woman living in Barrow, Alaska (Blackman, 1989). Neakok, born in 1916, is the daughter of an Anglo man and an Inupiat woman. Her mother, Asianggataq, lived as much as possible according to traditional modes and values. She was a skilled hunter of seal and caribou, had a large dog team, and led whaling crews on boats owned by her husband. Asianggataq also followed her own inclinations when it came to moving out to seasonal hunting camps while the rest of her family remained in Barrow. She cooked and ate her own native foods even though her husband hired an Anglo cook to prepare meals for him and their ten children.

Asianggataq was hardly the stereotype of a subordinated woman. Perhaps one reason for her independence and self-sufficiency stems from the fact that she was raised by an elder brother who taught her to hunt and fish, taking her along as his aide on hunting trips.

When Asianggataq had her own children, she taught all her sons and daughters to hunt and fish. Later, in the early years of Sadie Neakok's own marriage, she and her husband continued to follow traditional subsistence activities. The couple taught these skills to their sons and daughters as well. Neakok explained:

> As far back as I can remember, in the old tradition, women were out there on the ice with the men. They could go out and hunt with the menfolk; they would cook for them, or sew, or tend to their men's needs out there. But we are shying off from that today. There's not very many women who would go out and stay out there, but Nate [Neakok's husband] gives our girls a chance to be out there. (pp. 215–216)

As in the past, whaling continues to be important for subsistence in native Alaska. A successful whaling season in May and June provides an entire community with food for many months. Whaling has now become a focus of Inupiat identity through continuation of cultural traditions associated with it. Neakok described women's contributions to these activities:

> Being a whaler's wife is just as much work as preparing to go out with a crew. Once your crew members are named, you have to see that they all have warm

clothing. New clothing is made every year because it's tradition. You started sewing in March if you knew who was going to be in your crew.

If you want a good skin on your husband's boat, you have to hire several women to sew together six or seven ugruk hides with waterproof seams and stretch them over a frame. The skins have to be replaced every year. . . .

Then all the time the crew is out there, you fill all of their requests for food, and if their clothing needs mending or cleaning, you do it. (pp. 209, 211)

After detailing the work of women in helping to butcher and distribute whale meat to the community after a successful catch, Neakok concluded:

When you're a whaling captain's wife, your part is just as important as the men's because you're entrusted with keeping your husband's crewmen out there comfortable and fed. You're in charge of all of their care. It's an exciting event when your crew gets a whale, a lot of work, but when all the women's work of feeding the whole town is done, then you feel like you have shared in the whale catch. (p. 216)

Neakok's narrative indicates changes in attitudes toward marriage. Child betrothal was still common when Sadie was young, but the practice has since been abandoned by most Inupiat. Neakok noted changes in attitudes and behavior, from common acceptance by young people of arrangements that their parents had made to desires to seek their own mates. "As we grew older we saw how that type of marriage as arranged by parents failed." Her comments further indicate difficulties people experience in adopting social and interpersonal changes even when they prefer them: she explained that "it was strange, but we had to live through it, when people realized that they didn't love each other and lived all these years and finally separated, went their own way" (p. 46).

Later, after Neakok returned from college in Fairbanks and became a magistrate in Barrow, she revised the standard marriage vows to "make it a little more personal" by adding "a little advice to the newly married couple," a practice consistent with traditional native customs. Neakok further noted that the nuptial question "'Wilt thou obey?' was deleted out of the marriage ceremony, because women were beginning to feel that they were equal to their husbands" (p. 197).

It would be erroneous to consider Neakok's life typical of Inupiat women. Her advanced education prepared her for professional work as a teacher, social worker, and magistrate, obviously setting her apart from most other women and men in her community. However, in many ways her attitudes toward herself and others were consistent with traditional Inupiat norms. Neakok and her husband, who was not educated, developed a closely cooperative and respectful relationship giving each their autonomy. No doubt much of Neakok's sense of self-assurance came from her opportunities for education and professional achievement, encouraged particularly by her father. But her independence and self-sufficiency were also valued traits instilled by her Inupiat mother's example.

Neakok's narrative demonstrates that constructs of gender are not simple or simplistic. Male dominance, to the extent it existed in traditional

Inupiat culture, was not total and did not thoroughly suppress women's wills. As economic conditions have changed and as both women and men can participate in socially valued productive work, women can widen their areas of autonomy. Women, like Neakok, can also shake off the combined ideological pressure of traditional Inupiat customs and Western social and religious teachings that impose patriarchal beliefs, symbolized, for example, in the standard marriage vows that Neakok altered.

The Montagnais-Naskapi of Labrador

For some indigenous peoples, understanding of transformations of gender relations can be facilitated by examining documents from earliest historical periods of contact. We turn now to data concerning the Montagnais-Naskapi (mon-tan-NYAY/nas-KAP-i), a foraging society of eastern Labrador, for a discussion of dynamics of change in gender roles. Data from the seventeenth century are available from journals of French Jesuit missionaries who worked among the Montagnais-Naskapi. Statements made by Jesuits and inferences from their documents clearly indicate social conditions prevalent in traditional native communities. They demonstrate as well deliberate attempts made by missionaries to alter gender relations. Many of these attempts at directed change were eventually effective. Examination of data concerning the Montagnais-Naskapi is important because it illustrates processes of societal transformation that presumably occurred in many other cultures, although the specific motives and methods employed by agents of change may be less well documented elsewhere.

Eleanor Leacock's (1981) review of Jesuit material and comparison with modern Montagnais-Naskapi communities demonstrate that rapid shifts can occur in roles and values allocated to women and men. Leacock contends that prior to the period of European colonization, Montagnais-Naskapi were loosely organized into egalitarian bands based on a foraging subsistence. Status hierarchies stemming from social or economic differences were entirely absent. A division of labor was idealized by the Montagnais-Naskapi, allocating hunting to men and gathering, domestic tasks, and child care to women. However, in actual practice, this division of responsibilities was ignored. Women often accompanied their fathers or husbands in hunting; men spontaneously attended to their children and cooked meals if the need arose. The Jesuit priest most knowledgeable about Montagnais-Naskapi, Paul LeJeune, commented that husbands and wives got along well together because of the "order which they maintain in their occupations, . . . the women know what they are to do, and the men also; and one never meddles with the work of the other" (Thwaites, 1906, vol. 5, p. 133; hereafter *JR*). In other words, each person had autonomy in his or her behavior with rights to make decisions concerning personal activities.

Matters affecting an entire household were discussed by all concerned with no hint of domination from any particular individual. In a cogent explanation of difficulties that Western observers have in analyzing egalitarian societies like the Montagnais-Naskapi, Leacock (1981) remarks:

> What is hard to grasp about the structure of the egalitarian band is that leadership as we conceive it is not merely "weak" or "incipient," as is commonly stated, but irrelevant. Personal autonomy was concomitant with the direct dependence of each individual on the group as a whole. Decision making in this context calls for concepts other than ours of leader and led, dominant and deferent, no matter how loosely these are seen to apply. (pp. 138–139)

Decision making among the Montagnais-Naskapi did not depend on leaders or authorities but rather on opinions and wishes of all participants, both men and women. Because women played an active role in reaching household or camp decisions, the Jesuits may possibly have exaggerated the power of women. For example, Father Vimont noted, "The choice of plans, of undertakings, of journeys, of winterings, lies in nearly every instance in the hands of the housewife" (*JR*, vol. 68, p. 93). LeJeune commented:

> The women have great power here. A man may promise you something, and if he does not keep his promise, he thinks he is sufficiently excused when he tells you that his wife did not wish to do it. (*JR*, vol. 5, p. 181)

Even more telling was LeJeune's retort to a native man: "I told him then that he was not the master, and that in France, women do not rule their husbands."

It is mistaken to accept as accurate some of the descriptions of women's absolute power over their husbands just as it would be to believe that men controlled their wives. Jesuits' statements reflect their inability to understand truly egalitarian relations between the genders. Because Montagnais-Naskapi women were clearly not subservient to their husbands, missionaries assumed that men were dominated by their wives. And in the genuine equality existing between the genders, the Jesuits saw women's exhorbitant powers.

Missionaries sought to change Montagnais-Naskapi life to "civilize" the natives and render them amenable to religious conversion. Among cultural mores they attacked were the freedom to divorce, acceptance (without condoning) of occasional extramarital sexuality, and existence of polygyny. On the first matter, LeJeune wrote:

> The young people do not think that they can persevere in the state of matrimony with a bad wife or a bad husband. They wish to be free and to be able to divorce the consort if they do not love each other. (*JR*, vol. 16, p. 41)

LeJeune lectured a native man about the evil of marital infidelity:

> I told him that it was not honorable for a woman to love any one else except her husband, and that this evil being among them, he himself was not sure that his son, who was there present, was his son. (*JR*, vol. 6, p. 255)

But the native responded, "Thou hast no sense. You French people love only your own children; but we all love all the children of our tribe."

Finally, LeJeune found resistance by women to his stance against polygyny:

> Since I have been preaching among them that a man should not have more than one wife, I have not been well received by the women; for, since they are more numerous than the men, if a man can only marry one of them, the others will have to suffer. Therefore this doctrine is not according to their liking. (*JR*, vol. 12, p. 165)

In addition to attempting to eradicate Montagnais-Naskapi customs dealing with relations between spouses, Jesuits hoped to reorient household organization to conform to patriarchal nuclear family units considered by them to be a mark of civilization. Changes in household composition entailed breaking up **extended family** households that were the traditional norm. Such a change was especially deleterious to women for two reasons. First, aboriginal postmarital residence patterns showed preference for uxorilocal affiliation (Leacock, 1981). Perhaps it was because of uxorilocal residence that women had rights to make decisions concerning movement of camps. In any case, uxorilocal residence gave women the support of their kin, not only in daily activities but especially in times of conflict with their husbands.

Secondly, nuclear family households eventually came to be established in conjunction with fundamental economic changes that transformed a society of self-sufficient foragers into one of trappers and traders locked into a market economy. By the middle of the seventeenth century, the Montagnais-Naskapi were already engaged in trapping furs destined for trading posts in Quebec. Initial involvement was slight, but eventually, as natives became dependent on European manufactured goods, they spent more time and energy in trapping and trading. These activities were the work of men. Women's responsibilities came to be primarily focused on domestic tasks and support labor in preparing furs for market. Shifts to nuclear family households tended to isolate women and render them even more economically dependent on their husbands.

Men's authority began to emerge as economic relations were transformed. In accordance with native constructs, people who carry out activities have rights to make decisions directly affecting those activities. As men assumed most productive roles and as women's work became peripheral, women's role in decision making declined.

Despite considerable pressures exerted directly by missionaries and indirectly by traders, Montagnais-Naskapi society still retains basic egalitarian ethics. Leacock's fieldwork in the 1950s among these peoples in Labrador and Quebec recorded patterns of gender equality, continuing flexibility in subsistence activities, and fundamental respect for all individuals' rights to autonomy.

Leacock's documentation also reveals historical processes that influence social relations. Economic and ideological pressures exerted on indigenous peoples by agents of colonization have contributed to societal transformations and have specifically affected values and behaviors associated with gender. These are worldwide processes. We proceed next to analyzing gender constructs and their transformation in tribal societies where we see that dynamics and directions of change are often similar despite underlying differences in native cultures.

Summary

Comparisons of data concerning the Ju/'hoansi and Inuit indicate similarities and differences in the ways that gender roles and relations can be structured in foraging societies. Traditional economic modes in the two cultures required substantial contributions from both women and men. The labor of all people was socially recognized and socially rewarded.

Both Ju/'hoansi and Inuit society view men and women as autonomous. Their individual rights to participate in decision making and participation in family and community life were well respected. Attitudes toward marriage, divorce, and sexuality indicated that women and men were expected to follow similar norms.

Although the Ju/'hoansi and Inuit consider women and men to be equals, important differences exist between the two societies. Male dominance was manifested among the Inuit in incidences of men's violence against women, occasionally taking the form of female infanticide, wife beating, and rape. The tendency for male dominance in Inuit society can perhaps be explained by the fact that the people depend directly on men's labor to provide food in a harsh, dangerous environment.

Transformations of the cultures of the Ju/'hoansi, the Inuit, and the Montagnais-Naskapi have resulted in the introduction or legitimation of some degrees of male dominance in all three societies. Women's roles were restricted and marginalized as the people's economies were altered under direct and indirect pressures to adapt to colonizing forces. In the case of the Inuit and the Montagnais-Naskapi, these forces were unleashed by European traders and missionaries. Among the Ju/'hoansi, the Tswana and Herero began the processes of change toward male dominance. Recent European and South African agents have had similar impacts on Ju/'hoansi society. Gains in social status for men have been coupled with a decline in independence and equality for women.

References

Ager, Lynn. 1980. "The economic role of women in Alaskan Eskimo society." In *A World of Women* (ed. Erika Bourguignon). New York: Praeger, pp. 305–317.

Balikci, Asen. 1984. "Netsilik." In *Arctic*, vol. 5 of *Handbook of North American Indians* (hereafter *HNAI*). Washington, D.C.: Smithsonian Institution Press, pp. 415–430.

Blackman, Margaret. 1989. *Sadie Brower Neakok: An Inupiaq Woman*. Seattle: University of Washington Press.

BOAS, FRANZ. 1964. *The Central Eskimo*. Lincoln: University of Nebraska Press. (Original work published 1888)

BODENHORN, BARBARA. 1988. "Whales, souls, children, and other things that are 'good to share': Core metaphors in a contemporary whaling society." *Cambridge Anthropology*, 13 (1): 1–19.

———. 1993. "Gendered spaces, public places: Public and private revisited on the North Slope of Alaska." In *Landscape: Politics and Perspectives* (ed. Barbara Bender). Providence: Berg, pp. 169–203.

BRIGGS, JEAN. 1974. "Eskimo women: Makers of men." In *Many Sisters: Women in Cross-Cultural Perspective* (ed. Carolyn S. Matthiason). New York: Free Press, pp. 261–304.

———. 1982. *Never in Anger: Portrait of an Eskimo Family*. Cambridge: Harvard University Press.

CHANCE, NORMAN. 1984. "Alaskan Eskimo modernization." In *Arctic*, vol. 5 of *HNAI*, pp. 646–656.

DAMAS, DAVID. 1984. "Copper Eskimo." In *Arctic*, vol. 5 of *HNAI*, pp. 397–414.

D'ANGLURE, BERNARD SALADIN. 1984. "Inuit of Quebec." In *Arctic*, vol. 5 of *HNAI*, pp. 476–507.

DRAPER, PATRICIA. 1975. "!Kung women: Contrasts in sexual egalitarianism in foraging and sedentary contexts." In *Toward an Anthropology of Women* (ed. Rayna R. Reiter). New York: Monthly Review Press, pp. 77–109.

GOUGH, KATHLEEN. 1975. "The origin of the family." In *Toward an Anthropology of Women* (ed. Rayna R. Reiter). New York: Monthly Review Press, pp. 51–76.

GRABURN, NELSON. 1969. *Eskimos without Igloos: Social and Economic Development in Sugluk*. Boston: Little, Brown.

GUENTHER, MATHIAS. 1976. "From hunters to squatters: Social and cultural change among the Farm San of Ghanzi, Botswana." In *Kalahari Hunter-Gatherers* (ed. Richard B. Lee and Irven DeVore). Cambridge, MA: Harvard University Press, pp. 120–133.

HALL, EDWIN. 1984. "Interior North Alaskan Eskimo." In *Arctic*, vol. 5 of *HNAI*, pp. 338–346.

HANTZSCH, BERNARD. 1977. *My Life among the Eskimos: Baffinland Journeys in the Years 1909–1911* (ed. Leslie H. Neatby). Mawdsley Memoir series 3. Saskatoon: University of Saskatchewan Press.

LANTIS, MARGARET. 1984. "Nunivak Eskimo." In *Arctic*, vol. 5 of *HNAI*, pp. 209–223.

LEACOCK, ELEANOR. 1981. *Myths of Male Dominance*. New York: Monthly Review Press.

LEE, RICHARD. 1982. "Politics, sexual and non-sexual, in an egalitarian society." In *Politics and History in Band Societies* (eds. Eleanor B. Leacock and Richard B. Lee). New York: Cambridge University Press, pp. 37–60.

———. 1984. *The Dobe !Kung*. New York: Holt, Rinehart & Winston.

LEE, RICHARD, AND SUSAN HURLICH. 1982. "From foragers to fighters: South Africa's militarization of the Namibian San." In *Politics and History in Band Societies* (ed. Eleanor B. Leacock and Richard B. Lee). New York: Cambridge University Press, pp. 327–345.

MARSHALL, LORNA. 1976. *The !Kung of Nyae Nyae*. Cambridge, MA: Harvard University Press.

MARY-ROUSSELIERE, GUY. 1984. "Iglulik." In *Arctic*, vol. 5 of *HNAI*, pp. 431–446.

NEATBY, L. H. 1984. "Exploration and history of the Canadian Arctic." In *Arctic*, vol. 5 of *HNAI*, pp. 377–390.

RASMUSSEN, KNUD. 1931. *The Netsilik Eskimos: Social Life and Spiritual Culture*. Report of the Fifth Thule Expedition 1921–1924, vol. 8 (1–2). Copenhagen.

SANDAY, PEGGY. 1981. *Female Power and Male Dominance*. New York: Cambridge University Press.

SCHWEITZER, PETER. 1989. "Spouse exchange in northeast Siberia: On kinship and sexual relations and their transformation." In *Kinship, Social Change and Evolution* (ed. Andre Gingrich et al.). Vienna Contributions to Ethnology and Anthropology no. 5. Horn Wien: Berger & Sohne, pp. 17–38.

SHOSTAK, MARJORIE. 1976. "A !Kung woman's memories of childhood." In *Kalahari Hunter-Gatherers* (ed. Richard B. Lee and Irven. DeVore). Cambridge, MA: Harvard University Press, pp. 246–277.

———. 1983. *Nisa: The Life and Words of a !Kung Woman*. New York: Vintage.

SPENCER, ROBERT. 1984. "North Alaska Coast Eskimo." In *Arctic*, vol. 5 of *HNAI*, pp. 320–337.

THWAITES, REUBEN (ed.). 1906. *Jesuit Relations and Allied Documents 1610–1791 [JR]*. Cleveland: Burroughs, 73 vols.

CHAPTER 3

Pastoral and Horticultural Societies

The societies discussed in this chapter encompass a wide range of economic modes and political organizations. They include groups whose subsistence is based on farming and/or pastoralism, both often supplemented by foraging. Some of these societies are informally organized groupings of autonomous bands; others are complexly integrated tribes. Given this diversity, their social relationships cannot be neatly summarized or generalized. In some, egalitarian principles are characteristic of relations among all members, whereas in others, people in various social categories are hierarchically stratified. Where stratification prevails, gender may be used as one of the ways to segment society.

We examine gender constructs in several cultures, chosen to exemplify a range of economic and political modes and of gender relations characteristic of them. Historical processes and contacts have transformed pastoral and horticultural societies, often affecting the roles and valuations of women and men.

THE ORIGINS OF FARMING

Techniques of farming were first developed about 10,000 B.C. in a region of Southwest Asia known as the Fertile Crescent, fed by the waters of the Tigris and Euphrates Rivers in what are now the modern countries of Iran, Iraq, Syria, and Turkey. At that time, the region's climate was gradually drying, prompting people to concentrate their settlements and activities near rivers, where plant resources remained plentiful. Over time, people learned to control their supplies of food by observing the patterns of growth of plants, enabling the people to eventually learn to plant their own crops. The earliest crops were wheat and barley. Once farming proved productive, more people settled in the region and learned the new techniques. Others acquired the skills and moved to outlying areas, gradually spreading farming knowledge to other communities. By 6000 B.C., farming was well established in the region. Over the following millennia, similar processes led to the independent emergence of farming in several other regions of the world, including the Indus Valley of Pakistan, the Yellow River Valley of China, the Nile Valley of Egypt, the fertile valleys of central and southern Mexico, and the Andean region of South America.

Archaeologists have proposed a variety of explanations for the origin of farming. Some suggest that the increasingly concentrated population exceeded the capacity of the fertile regions to sustain a foraging existence, while at the same time declines in wild vegetation discouraged people from dispersing into surrounding environments (Binford, 1971; Flannery, 1973). Another theory suggests that some people within foraging societies began to accumulate surpluses of storable foods to sponsor feasts and thereby raise their social status. As their desire for larger surpluses grew, they began to control and augment their accumulation of foods by protecting and then producing their own crops (Bender, 1978). These theories are not mutually exclusive. Several factors operating together may have led to the beginnings of plant and animal domestication.

It is not possible to know for certain how people first developed techniques that controlled the growth of plants, but it is likely that because women were responsible for tasks that involved foraging for plants, they were keenly observant about plant behavior (Ehrenberg, 1989, p. 77). Given this context, it is therefore likely that women invented early farming practices; certainly they contributed a great deal to agricultural development. Ehrenberg suggests that the shift to farming was a gradual process based on accumulating observations by women whose economic tasks centered on gathering wild plants. Women observed the conditions of soil, water, and sunlight that benefited plant growth and noticed that when plant seeds fell to the ground, new plants would grow the following year (p. 84).

Another insight about the development of farming comes from Bruce Smith (1987), elaborated by Patty Jo Watson and Mary Kennedy (1991). Smith outlines a series of stages in the development of horticulture in the Northeastern Woodlands of North America:

a. Beginning about 6,500 years ago, the activities and settlements of foraging peoples disturbed the existing flora and fauna to the extent that new plant populations gained the opportunity to colonize new locations.

b. Humans contributed to this process by favoring foods that had big seeds and thin seed coats. They either ignored or removed other species of plants.

c. Foraging peoples intensified this process by actively encouraging the growth of useful species and harvesting them through a system of managed gardens. Surplus foods were stored for winter use.

d. People began to deliberately plant seeds of the useful species.

e. By about 3,500 years ago, people's activities led to the emergence of clearly domesticated plant species.

Interpreting this sequence, Watson and Kennedy (1991) suggest that women were primarily responsible for the development of the deliberate processes that led to farming. Their assumption is based on a number of inter-related premises. First, in all known foraging societies, it is women who are the principal gatherers of plant resources. They therefore were most likely to notice the growth cycles of plants and the conditions under which plants prosper. Given these observations, they were most likely to develop methods of increasing plant growth and eventually of controlling their growth through purposeful acts. Women were probably also the major agents in the initial stage leading to plant domestication because it was they who likely were responsible for creating the conditions that disturbed existing plant growth by performing tasks such as food processing activities and building houses, storage facilities, drying racks, earth ovens, and hearths (p. 262).

Although archaeologists cannot know exactly how farming originated, researchers are more certain about the consequences of food production. Because people developed the ability to control the growth of crops, to plant more crops, and to harvest, preserve, and store greater surpluses, thus leading to greater security in food resources, populations were able to increase. In addition, people became more sedentary, not needing to change their locations periodically in order to avail themselves of wild resources. Reliance on grains also allowed women to nurse their babies for shorter periods of time because young children could be given cereals to eat. And fertility levels rose with the decline in lactation, leading to greater increases in population size and greater crowding of population centers, intensifying the need for increased food production through farming.

Another consequence of food production was a general decline in health (Diamond, 1995). Studies of the bones and teeth of early farming communities indicated signs of malnutrition, probably resulting from an overdependence on only a few sources of food rather than the more typical varied range of the foraging diet. And diseases spread more rapidly among sedentary farming people.

In addition, permanent settlements made possible by farming permitted people to accumulate an increasing number and variety of material possessions. Many significant cultural developments took place after sedentary settlements became the norm. Among these was the invention of pottery, first discovered in Southwest Asia in the same regions as the earliest development of farming. Clay pots were first put to use for storing cereals or cooking plant foods, presumably by women (Ehrenberg, 1989, p. 88).

Pottery is everywhere associated with sedentary settlements. Clay pots have many advantages as storage containers and cooking vessels; pots are more secure, watertight, and heat-resistant than baskets made from fibers. Furthermore, food can be heated to much higher temperatures when cooked in a ceramic vessel, so a broader range of foods could be processed and made edible, supplying people with a wider and more nutritious diet. However, pottery has the disadvantage of being breakable and therefore are not reliable or practical for nomadic peoples. In addition, the weight of clay pots would add to the burden of carrying possessions from place to place.

Once people learned the methods involved in firing clay into durable ceramics, advances in technique, style, and artistic embellishment developed rapidly. These techniques were then applied to the creation of other utensils and objects. For example, in South Asia (the present sites of India and Pakistan) by 6000 B.C. people were making clay containers, human and animal figurines, ovens, nails, bangles, rattles, and pendants (Wright, 1991, p. 206).

Archaeologists can also discover the ways in which pottery production was organized by examining spatial configurations such as vats, storage and preparation areas, firing areas, rotary devices, platforms, and benches (Wright, 1991, p. 210). At the South Asian site of Mehrgarh, for example, evidence indicates that production began and expanded within the household. Indeed, pottery-making remained associated with dwellings even after large-scale production intensified in the context of intercommunity trade. Because women are usually assumed to be associated with production within households, it is reasonable to propose that women were heavily if not exclusively involved in pottery production (p. 212).

When anthropologists study known farming societies, they discover that the labor necessary for the farming tasks of preparing fields, planting, weeding, and harvesting are variously distributed in different societies. Generally, in horticultural societies in which farmers use simple technology consisting of hoes or digging sticks, women dominate production, and in agricultural societies in which farmers use plows and other heavy equipment, men do most of the farmwork.

At some point in the past, a general shift took place in the work roles in some farming communities. While women continued to be the primary producers in societies practicing simple farming techniques using hoes and digging sticks, men became the major farmworkers when plows and carts became widely employed. Archaeologists suggest that in the Near East these changes began about 5,000 years ago in what is called the later Neolithic period, spreading quickly throughout the region and into Europe (Ehrenberg, 1989, p. 100). Plows and carts aided farming in conjunction with the use of domesticated animals, particularly cattle and horses, as draft animals. Earlier, people had kept some domesticated animals but relied on hunting as well; presumably hunting and animal husbandry tasks were assigned mostly to men. Keeping larger stocks of domesticated animals provided several important economic advantages, supplying meat and especially milk from cows as a dietary staple and providing animal power to pull plows and ease the heavy work of turning over the earth to ready it for planting. People in the Near East and in Europe also began to domesticate sheep, utilizing their milk, meat, and wool.

The use of plows to aid in farming actually intensified the input of labor in production, although the amount of yield per acre increased substantially. Plowing also meant that land that might not have been arable using a simpler hoe technology became available for growing crops. As a consequence, larger populations could be sustained. But, while societies as a whole benefited from the productive revolutions begun by the discovery of farming techniques, women as a group tended to lose status and rights as technology and production intensified and their work shifted from direct food production to subsidiary tasks. One of the consequences of this change was a strengthening of bonds among male kin through principles of patrilineal descent and inheritance. In addition, men gained control or ownership, either as individuals or as members of patrikin groups, of most domesticated animals and arable land.

PASTORAL ECONOMIES

Native Peoples of the Plains of North America

We begin with the complex cultures of the western Plains of North America. Little is known of many of these groups prior to European colonization. During the millennia before Europeans arrived in North America, native peoples living in the western Plains had developed two different types of subsistence strategies. Most were nomadic foragers, dependent primarily on wild vegetation and small animals for their food. They occasionally hunted large animals, particularly buffalo migrating across the northern Plains. Foraging peoples lived in dispersed, autonomous camps. It is these groups, and others who joined them after the turn of the eighteenth century, whose cultures we discuss here. A different subsistence mode emerged among some people, such as the Mandans and Arikaras, who lived along the Missouri and Mississippi Rivers. These people were horticulturalists, settled in small sedentary villages.

Beginning in the seventeenth century, European colonization in North America led directly and indirectly to a series of dramatic transformations in economic modes that supported Plains peoples. These changes affected sociopolitical organization as well as gender roles, relations, and ideological evaluation.

Settlement patterns in the Plains were altered, particularly in the eighteenth and nineteenth centuries. Warfare between Europeans and native people over land and resources and among native people over resources and access to trade quickly resulted in massive dislocations of indigenous communities. Many nations in eastern regions of North America attempted to extricate themselves from impending disaster by fleeing westward. As they did so, they infringed on territories occupied by other groups. In some cases, warfare expanded to these new regions as people competed over available lands. In others, western people continued the process of dislocation, moving further west and in turn entering territories of disparate groups.

Relocations and cultural transformations affected many different native nations. Some had previously been sedentary horticulturalists—for example, Cheyennes, Crows, and Lakotas. Others, such as Comanches, Kiowas, and Blackfeet, had been nomadic foragers. In all cases, adaptation to Plains ecosystems and to conditions wrought by European contact resulted in the development of cultural similarities despite the diversity of antecedents among Plains societies.

As a result of relocations, native peoples found themselves adapting to new ecological conditions and consequently revolutionized their subsistence activities. The Plains region attracted many groups for several reasons. First, because the area was originally sparsely populated, newcomers did not have to compete for resources. Paucity of population in the Plains was due to the fact that resources were not abundant there and neighboring areas to the east and west offered more economic advantages. Given the relative availability of land and lack of pressure on resources typical of most of native North America prior to European colonization, it had previously been unnecessary for people to attempt to utilize the Plains ecosystem intensively. Therefore, when groups began to move onto the Plains in the seventeenth and eighteenth centuries, they found few competitors. Second, with the advent of Europeans in North America came new animals—namely, horses—that allowed people to exploit resources fully in the Plains.

Adoption of a pastoral economy based on acquisition of horses not only affected subsistence, however. In a relatively short time, it transformed political structures and social relationships as well. Foraging and farming economies were transformed into modes focused on hunting and pastoralism, using horses as a means for success in hunting and as a measure of wealth.

Direct evidence of gender relations obtaining in precontact Plains cultures is lacking. However, inferences derived from the kinds of gender constructs generally found in similar cultures elsewhere are presumably applicable. As we discussed in chapter 2, foraging peoples living in small, dispersed camps tend to maintain basically egalitarian social systems. This generalization probably applied to groups of foragers occupying lands in or near the Plains region. Plains economies were organized by a division of labor based on gender. As is common among foragers, men were responsible for hunting while women were engaged in gathering wild vegetation and in domestic tasks and child care. This allocation of work created interdependent households consisting of women and men who provided their families with basic supplies through their productive labor.

Economic innovations and reorientations resulting from conditions initiated by Europeans dramatically altered the egalitarian nature of Plains societies and created hierarchical social orders. Gender differences became incorporated into these stratified systems.

The two most critical elements in the new economic order were expansion of trade and adoption of horses. Use of horses allowed Plains cultures to exploit their resources more effectively, particularly herds of buffalo that migrated in the region and gathered in enormous numbers in summertime. Men on horseback could pursue animals at greater distances from local camps, make swift assaults on and retreats from the herds, and bring back large amounts of meat and hides using their horses to haul heavy loads.

People's desire to exploit resources to the fullest was not derived so much from motivations within Plains cultures as it was driven by needs developing from contact with Europeans. As elsewhere in North America, and for that matter throughout the world, indigenous peoples in the Plains became enmeshed in trade to obtain manufactured goods. To acquire these items, natives had to supply European traders with animal skins—in this case, with hides from buffalo, deer, and moose. Demand for hides compelled native hunters to slaughter animals by the hundreds rather than limiting their kill to subsistence and survival needs. Although large kills of buffalo had occurred prior to European contact, involvement in the fur trade expanded and accelerated this practice.

The labor of both genders was crucial to expansion of trade in the Plains. However, men and women served in different capacities. Men were directly involved in trade networks. They traveled to trading posts and dealt with merchants, exchanging the hides they brought for manufactured goods. Men also were largely responsible for procuring the hides. They organized themselves into communal hunting groups, recruiting members from their camps. In summertime when buffalo coalesced into huge herds, men from many Plains bands joined together to attack the animals.

Women's labor was also essential to Plains trade. In addition to helping butcher animals and transport meat and hides to camp, women were responsible for tanning hides and preparing them for market. Although women's and men's tasks were complementary, a critical difference lay in the kind of control exerted over their activities. Men were generally independent producers. They organized and controlled their own hunting and trading expeditions. Furthermore, they directly benefited from their labor in two ways. First, they exchanged the hides for manufactured articles that in turn helped them achieve subsequent success. The most desired items were guns, ammunition, and iron knives and other metal tools and weapons.

Second, through trade, men were able to amass the wealth that came to be the measurement of social prestige. Wealth was symbolized by goods and particularly by the numbers of horses a man owned. Many groups were able to amass large numbers of horses. For example, the Crows, a northern Plains tribe rich in horses, were estimated to have had as many as ten thousand horses for a populace of four hundred households in the early nineteenth century (Mishkin, 1940). Among the southwestern Plains tribes, the Comanches had the most horses. With a population of approximately two thousand, Comanches owned fifteen thousand horses in 1867. Horses were sometimes received in trade but were more often obtained through raiding other native communities. Men achieved prestige and status from their exploits as raiders, successfully stealing upon a village and absconding with horses. Economic transformations, specifically the acquisition of horses and involvement in Euro-American trade, thus affected military actions and increased the region's instability. But many men prospered in this context by engaging in warfare and raising their status and power.

In contrast to men's autonomy in directing their own labor, women's work in expansion of trade was organized and controlled largely by others— namely, men. First as daughters and then as wives, women labored in tanning hides of buffalo, deer, and moose obtained by their fathers and husbands (Jablow, 1950). Women became engaged as necessary but adjunct workers in a trade economy.

Allocation of tasks based on gender and the differential control over one's work led to a number of critical transformations in familial and social relations, all of which undermined women's autonomy. Marriage patterns were adapted to fulfill needs stemming from the new economic mode. An individual man could kill buffalo by the score and even by the hundreds, but their hides were worthless unless tanned and rendered marketable. One woman, however, could not prepare such a large number of hides in a timely manner. Therefore, men attempted to contract marriages with more than one woman to supply themselves with additional workers (Jablow, 1950; Lewis, 1942). The more wives a man had, the more women's labor he controlled. His wives provided him with additional children, whose labor he also managed. Sons helped in hunting and raiding, and daughters aided their mothers in tanning hides. Polygyny among Plains cultures was therefore not so much a feature of social structure as it was of the mode of economic production.

As women's skills were used to procure commodities in trade, women themselves became commodities in exchanges between men. Patterns of bridewealth developed in which a man exchanged his daughters for horses given by a prospective husband. The horses were symbols of wealth that compensated a father for loss of his daughter's labor. Essentially, the husband traded horses for the right to benefit from his wife's work.

Concomitant with the development of polygyny, the age at which women and men married became markedly different. Prior to the period of expanding involvement in trade, women married in their late teens to men in their early 20s. But afterward, girls were married when they were as young as 13, although men usually did not marry until they reached their 30s (Lewis, 1942). Girls were productive workers at a very early age, trained from childhood to help their mothers in tanning and sewing. In contrast, it took many years for a man to prove himself an able hunter and amass the number of horses needed for bridewealth. The substantial age difference between a husband and wife was especially significant in the Plains, where seniority was an important component in status and authority. Therefore, age and gender combined to enhance husbands' rights and undermine wives' autonomy.

Men's dominance in their households was solidified by increased emphasis on **patrilocal residence**. Preferences for affiliation with a husband's family combined with strengthening bonds between fathers and sons and among brothers and male cousins. Patrilocal residence deprived women of the support of their own kin groups for daily companionship and for aid in the event of conflict with their husbands.

As in all cultures, Plains people were socialized to fulfill roles that they assumed as adults. In addition to demarcating a division of labor, Plains gender constructs developed notions of differences between women and men as social and human beings. Men were expected to be adventurous, independent, and competitive. In contrast, women were taught to be obedient and industrious. Not only were values associated with women's behavior conveyed through verbal messages, but they were also reinforced through physical control over women. Violence against women in the form of beatings was commonly used as punishment against daughters and wives who were disobedient or lazy. But it also functioned as a warning to others to adhere to rules of propriety.

Plains cultures contained a double standard of sexual behavior. Men's sexual exploits were condoned, but premarital or extramarital sexual activity by women was strongly condemned. Because a daughter was considered valuable for her ability to produce wealth and to be exchanged for wealth to a prospective husband, male dominance was reflected in requirements for girls' chastity before marriage and for women's fidelity to their husbands. Transgressions were severely punished by beatings, disfigurement, and sexual assaults (Hoebel, 1960).

Men's prominence was manifested in political institutions in Plains society. Tribal polities developed in the Plains as an outgrowth of collective hunting efforts. As a response to needs to amass large numbers of buffalo hides destined for trade, formerly disparate bands united to exploit available resources most efficiently. At the same time, political leadership emerged to plan and direct economic activities. Councils of elders and "chiefs" assumed prominent positions. These men achieved their status by successes in hunting, trading, and warfare. During most of the year, their authority was based on personal influence, but in the period of summer communal hunts, they wielded actual power. For example, they organized police forces of men who patrolled camps and ensured that no hunter leave to hunt on his own. Because a single hunter attacking buffalo could potentially frighten away an entire herd, it was necessary to control the actions of every individual to guarantee communal success.

Men's status was additionally enhanced by their success as warriors. Intensification of warfare, particularly in the form of raiding, was an outgrowth of competition in trade. As the system of social differentiation based on wealth developed, men attempted to accumulate property. Their status became symbolized through the medium of horses, which in turn could be used to acquire more wealth. As already noted, horses were frequently obtained in surprise raids against other native villages. This practice obviously put a premium on a man's military prowess. In addition, by the middle of the nineteenth century, warriors' skills were needed for survival against inroads of American settlers and the armies that accompanied them. Men's actions in defense became increasingly necessary for protecting communities just as their involvement in trade had become the means for enhanced material standards of living experienced by their households.

In spite of patterns of male dominance that developed in Plains cultures by the nineteenth century, individual women were able to rise to prominence. Women were admired for their expertise in tanning and for their artistry in sewing and embroidery (Lowie, 1954). These skills, which were socially approved, functioned to raise a woman's value as a wife. Women could also be admired for achievement in hunting and warfare. Most women, of course, did not participate in these activities, but those few who did were respected for their success (Ewers, 1955; Hungry Wolf, 1980; Linderman, 1972). Such women were praised for their ability to function in male roles. In most Plains societies, religious beliefs and symbolism included significant female deities whose spiritual gifts and powers were used to benefit humankind. Both female and male deities taught people how to live and were sought for their aid in times of personal and communal affliction.

Within a century of intensive contact between Plains cultures and European traders and colonial authorities, previously egalitarian native societies developed stratified socioeconomic systems based on accumulation of private property. Wealth became a medium not only of exchange but of measurement of status. Men competed with each other in amassing and displaying wealth, symbolized directly by numbers of horses. Men needed women's labor as well as their own to succeed. But a woman's status was derivative, based first on that of her father and later of her husband. Rarely did women achieve recognition on their own. The economic system that took hold in Plains cultures led to social benefits for men and social costs to women. In a short period, however, material advantages offered by new productive modes disappeared when territorial and political expansion of the United States and Canada created chaos for native people in the region.

MIXED PASTORAL AND FARMING ECONOMIES

In other areas of the world, some societies have combined pastoral and farming modes of subsistence. Two distinct groups provide examples of such cultures and demonstrate contrasts in gender roles and relations. The Navajo of the American Southwest exemplify a society where gender constructs validate equality of women and men, whereas the Nuer, a Nilotic people of the Sudan, typify a society with male dominance. Experiences of a third group, the Luo of Kenya and Tanzania, provide evidence of effects on gender of historical changes among Nilotic cultures.

The Navajo of Southwestern North America

Navajo (NA-va-ho) culture has undergone a series of economic and social transformations in the last five or six centuries. Prior to their migration into the Southwest sometime after A.D. 1000, the Navajo were nomadic foragers living in small camps in semidesert regions of the West. Once arriving in the Southwest in what is now Arizona and New Mexico, they adopted economic modes from neighboring peoples, the most important of whom were the

A Navajo homestead typically consisted of several dwellings inhabited by matrilineally related families.

Hopi and other Puebloan sedentary horticulturalists. Navajos borrowed farming techniques from Hopis, adopting maize cultivation for their subsistence.

Social systems indigenous to the Hopi were also incorporated into Navajo culture. Due to the Hopi example, **matrilineal** clans developed among the Navajo and controlled the allocation of land for farming. **Matrilocal residence** became the preferred pattern, uniting extended families in a collective residential area.

The next wave of extensive change occurred in the middle of the nineteenth century. After the United States defeated Mexico in the Mexican-American War and annexed former Mexican territories in the Southwest, the U.S. army was sent on a brutal campaign to "pacify" native tribes in the region. Soldiers killed hundreds of Navajos and then rounded up approximately eight thousand Navajo men, women, and children and imprisoned them in Bosque Redondo, a fort in New Mexico, from 1864 until 1868 (White, 1983). When the Navajo were released, they were given sheep to add to their own stocks in the hope that these animals would provide food to sustain the people and wool to sell for additional income.

After 1868, Navajo economy became somewhat stabilized for little more than half a century. Then, in the 1930s, U.S. government policies again undermined Navajo subsistence by imposing drastic reductions in the number of stock allowed for each household in a mismanaged attempt to conserve the semidesert land on which the Navajo lived (Weiss, 1984; White, 1983). Since then, reliance on pastoralism and farming has declined in most areas of the Navajo Reservation, and wage work has increased.

Each of the economic transformations just outlined led to changes in social relations. Gender constructs have consequently been affected. Although little is directly known of gender roles among the Navajo prior to the adoption of farming, their previous foraging economy was presumably based on a division of labor typical of such groups, that is, men engaged in hunting and women primarily in gathering and domestic tasks. Once horticulture was adopted, both women and men worked in farming, although men spent more time in this activity. Women's work consisted of farming, gathering wild vegetation, fulfilling domestic tasks, and caring for children.

Control of land was vested in matrilineal clans that allocated their territory to extended family units, or *outfits*, as they have been called (Kluckhohn and Leighton, 1962). Preferences for matrilocality were strong. An outfit therefore was typically composed of several dwellings inhabited by matrilineally related families. Outfits consisted of an elder woman, her husband, their daughters and families, and their unmarried sons. Unmarried men worked land alloted to their mothers, whereas married men farmed on land controlled by their wives' families.

After the Navajos' release from Bosque Redondo, sheepherding combined with horticulture in economic importance. Sheep were individually owned by both women and men. When a man married, he brought with him the sheep he had inherited from his parents or had acquired through barter or purchase. A husband's animals were combined with those belonging to his wife and other members of her outfit. All residents of a unit were individual owners of sheep, but resources were pooled into a common herd that was managed collectively. Herds were tended by any member of the outfit, including youngsters, who also had rights to own animals.

In the context of Navajo economic pursuits, gender constructs essentially validated the equality and autonomy of women and men. Although a division of labor based on gender was idealized, actual behavior was little constrained by it. Men and women worked in farming and sheepherding. Domestic tasks were usually performed by women, but men engaged in food preparation when necessary. Child care, too, was primarily a concern of women, but men also attended to their children's needs and gave them a great deal of emotional support.

Private ownership of herds that elsewhere has often led to gender stratification (for example, among nineteenth-century Plains cultures and the modern Ju/'hoansi) did not create an imbalance between Navajo men and women. Among the Navajo, both women and men are independent owners of sheep and retain their distinctive control regardless of age or marital status. Even though accumulation of wealth and ranking according to wealth became important components in the Navajo social order, gender was never a segmenting factor in the system because men and women could amass and control their own property.

Relationships among people living together in an outfit were informed by the importance of kinship ties, particularly those with one's mother and her kin. In Navajo worldview, mother and child are "bound together by the most intense, the most diffuse and the most enduring solidarity to be found in Navajo culture" (Witherspoon, 1975, p. 15). A father's relatives were also significant but secondary.

Mothers and daughters formed the closest grouping because these women were united not only by kinship but also by stability of residence. Sons never lost their rights to return to their mothers' or sisters' households, but their link to the outfit was not as tight because they shifted location after marriage. A husband lived with his wife's outfit, contributing his labor and benefiting from the labor of others. However, if a woman died before her husband, the latter might or might not remain with his wife's outfit. A man's age at the time of his wife's death and the number and ages of their children were decisive factors. Young men with no children typically returned to their mothers; elderly men with adult daughters in the outfit likely remained.

The position of sons-in-law was somewhat tenuous, particularly in early years of marriage. Divorce in these years was not uncommon and could be initiated by either spouse. An economic reflection of the uncertain stability of marriages was the fact that when a husband moved to his wife's outfit, he brought only a token number of his sheep with him. Once the marriage became more secure, he gradually brought more sheep until all his animals had been transferred. An etiquette of social avoidance between a son-in-law and his wife's mother made his behavior circumspect. However, as years of marriage lengthened, bonds between a son-in-law and others in the outfit solidified.

Despite recognized differences among residents of an outfit, every individual had rights to his or her independence and autonomy. Although elder women who headed lineages had some greater influence in making decisions that affected the collective group, everyone contributed to discussion, and no one had coercive powers.

During most of the history of Navajo people, links among outfits were based on matrilineal clanship. Community cohesion beyond the kin group was weak or absent among these widely dispersed units. However, intensive contact with U.S. government authorities led to the development of political entities that now unify localities to some extent. Men tend to function as representatives of their households in public contexts. Two contributing factors explain this gender preference. First, as elsewhere, U.S. officials sought male representatives, ignoring prominent women. Second, functioning as a public leader of one's household was a logical substitution for men's prior roles as raiders and protectors of their families. These traditional activities were eliminated after the Navajos' release from Bosque Redondo because a condition of their release was agreement to refrain from armed conflict.

The underlying egalitarian nature of Navajo society remained strong despite economic and political changes experienced in the nineteenth century. Gender roles were differentiated in some endeavors, but overlap was also characteristic of actual behavior. Interdependence of members of an outfit was combined with the fundamental independence and autonomy of every individual. Balance between women and men was enacted on a daily basis in the work people performed and in the quality of their social interactions. Conflict within households was minimal; violence among family members was especially rare.

Attitudes toward sexuality were permissive. Premarital sexual experience was the norm for both boys and girls. Although adultery was not condoned, repercussions in the form of conflict or divorce were similar regardless of the offender's gender. Most marriages were monogamous, although polygyny was possible. When it occurred, it most often took the form of a man married to sisters. This pattern did not disturb the basic preference for matrilocal residence because sisters remained with their mothers' outfits.

Although egalitarian gender relations among the Navajo have persisted, recent economic transformations have altered productive roles and contributions of women and men to their households. Household composition itself has changed in many areas of the Navajo Reservation. In some communities, matrilocal extended families remain the center of outfits. In other areas, **neolocal** nuclear family households have become the norm. To a large extent, differences in household composition are correlated with subsistence modes. Families who continue to focus on sheepherding and farming tend to live in traditional outfits; those engaged in wage work tend to split off into nuclear units.

Available jobs on or near the reservation are gender linked. Men's work includes construction, building maintenance, railroad and highway repair, mining, and forestry. Women are most often employed in the service sector or as school aides and factory operatives. Many of the available jobs are tempo rary, especially those held by women. Women's work also is compensated at lower wages than men's salaries. Factors of job instability and low wages combine to decrease women's comparative productivity relative to that of men (Hamamsy, 1979; Weiss, 1984).

As matrilocal extended residential units split up and as women's opportunities for outside employment narrow, women become increasingly isolated in nuclear households. Furthermore, work in households that had previously been shared by spouses falls predominantly if not exclusively to women (Hamamsy, 1979).

The stock reduction program initiated by the U.S. government in the 1930s had a strongly detrimental effect on the Navajo economy. The program required Navajo households to surrender as much as half of their sheep. Sheep provided Navajos with wool that was sold to local traders to purchase food, clothing, and equipment. Loss of half of a household's stock forced people to find other means of income and support. Navajos' involvement in wage work consequently increased. Although all members of a household collectively suffered economic decline, a differential impact was experienced by many women who relied on supplies of wool to produce rugs for sale (Weiss, 1984). Women's work in the hand manufacture of rugs has also been negatively affected by market shifts away from skilled handwork to cheaper, imitative factory-produced rugs.

Traditional Navajo ethics of individual ownership of property and control over the products of one's labor have worked to benefit men and harm women's position in their households. Wages earned are predominantly held and disbursed by the earner. Because men tend to contribute more income than women do, they have come to have greater influence in economic decisions. Women have become vulnerable to financial insecurity. Their position in households is peripheral rather than central. According to Hamamsy's (1979) study of social and economic change among the Navajo:

> The poorest women are generally the middle-aged and old women who have no male providers. Under traditional conditions these women would be well off; they might be managers of large extended family units, or at least respected female relatives with secure positions within the family group. (p. 83)

Although recent economic and political changes have created some degree of imbalance between men and women, it would be erroneous to conclude that male dominance has developed. Women's autonomy is respected, and their rights have not been undermined, even though their relative economic contributions have declined. A principal reason for the continuing strength of women's and men's rights rests in underlying social and religious ideologies that have not been seriously eroded. These ideologies stress the importance of balance and harmony between the genders and the equal contributions of both women and men to maintain their households, communities, and indeed the universe as it is conceived.

Navajo culture can be instructively compared to that of many African peoples who also rely on a mixed economy of pastoralism and farming. But among these groups, patterns in the division of labor and in control over resources differ considerably from the balanced egalitarianism of the Navajo and in contrast have led to the development of male dominance. Of course, the degree of male dominance varies throughout the region, but it is a characteristic of all these societies.

The Nuer of Sudan

The Nuer (NEW-er), living in southeastern Sudan below the Sahara Desert, provide an example of a tribal culture that sanctions male dominance. Nuer reside in villages along the Nile River and its tributaries. They are a grouping of at least ten separate tribes whose total population exceeds 300,000. Each tribe is identified by its own name and elicits strong allegiance from members, but there is no sense of Nuer unity as a whole.

Nuer subsistence modes combine cattle herding and horticulture. However, despite the substantial contribution of grains to their diet, Nuer ideology stresses the dependence of people on their cattle. Cattle are an important source of food for the Nuer. Although meat is seldom eaten except when an animal dies a natural death, cows' milk provides daily nutrition. Other products derived from cattle are also utilized, including blood that is taken as a drink or added to food, skins and bones that are made into various utensils, and dung used as fuel for fires and as plaster for the walls of huts (Evans-Pritchard, 1940).

An economic division of labor rigidly allocates tasks to men and women. Herding of cattle is the job of men and boys who have undergone ritual initiation into adulthood, usually at the approximate age of 15. In addition to caring for cattle, men's productive roles include fishing in the many streams and rivers in the region. Fish constitute an important year-round food source. Men also engage in some hunting, although it adds little to Nuer diets.

Women, girls, and uninitiated boys are not permitted to take cattle to grazing lands. Instead, they are responsible for milking the animals, a task performed twice a day. Women also tend gardens, principally growing millet and maize. And, as elsewhere, women are responsible for child care and domestic tasks, including food preparation and upkeep of living quarters (Evans-Pritchard, 1951).

Nuer settlement patterns change seasonally in response to the amount of rainfall and consequent variation in river levels and water supplies. During the dry season, people concentrate in large villages around streams providing permanent water sources. In the rainy season when lands are completely flooded from rains and the overrun of rivers, people shift location to higher ground and settle in small camps of between fifty and two hundred residents.

Village composition is ideally organized around **patrilineal kin**. Such preference is consistent with a social system based on patrilineal clans and a strongly developed system of **lineages**. Villages are composed of extended family homesteads consisting of a cattle barn and several huts. Huts are inhabited by women, girls, and uninitiated boys. Older boys and men reside in cattle barns. Physical separation thus segments families in terms of gender and age, the two most critical features of Nuer social order. Furthermore, locational association of men with cattle reflects their economic interdependence and also reinforces an ideological bond that Nuer believe exists between cattle and men. This bond is enacted through assigning men responsibility for herding and tending cattle. It is also significantly demonstrated in the practice of boys' taking a personal name derived from an attribute or name of their favorite animal (Evans-Pritchard, 1940).

Homesteads consist of families united by kinship and marriage. Marriages are legitimated through payment of bridewealth in cattle from a husband's kin to that of a wife. Of the cattle received as bridewealth, half is distributed among the bride's father's male kin and half among her mother's male kin (Gough, 1971). Bridewealth, then, is given by and to men as owners and distributors of cattle. Although the Nuer kinship system favors patrilineal descent, relationships traced through both men and women are recognized in the practice of dividing bridewealth between the lineages of both parents of a bride.

Initially after marriage, a wife remains in her own kin's compound, although she takes up residence in a separate hut where her husband visits. After the birth of a first child, a husband moves in with his wife. They continue to live in the wife's compound until their child is weaned, whereupon the family relocates to the husband's family compound (Evans-Pritchard, 1951).

The gradual shift from wife's to husband's residential area reflects Nuer attitudes toward marital stability. During the early years of marriage, a union is considered unstable. The security of marriage that is felt to deepen after the birth of a child is symbolized by a husband's residence in his wife's hut. The final move to the husband's compound is made a few years later when the child is more mature and its survival is more secure (Evans-Pritchard, 1945).

Most Nuer marriages are monogamous, although polygyny is possible and desired by men. In polygynous homesteads, each wife has a separate hut for herself and her children.

Although residential patterns demonstrate a preference toward affiliation among men, initial years of uxorilocality provide a young wife with emotional security while her marriage is stabilized. However, a wife's family does not necessarily support her if she has conflict with her husband. Because a husband's family has given cattle as bridewealth to the wife's kin, her family is usually reluctant to see the marriage fail. If a couple separates, the receivers of bridewealth must return the cattle. They therefore often pressure their kinswoman to remain with her husband unless she has been severely mistreated.

Despite the normative preference for patrilocality, matrilocal residence is not uncommon; according to Kathleen Gough's (1971) review of settlement lists compiled by Evans-Pritchard for the Nuer, fewer than half of the men surveyed lived in their fathers' villages.

Nuer attitudes toward premarital sexuality are somewhat ambivalent. Although such behavior is not fully condoned, it is considered natural. If an unmarried woman becomes pregnant, the father of the child is expected to marry her. Evidently no lasting stigma is attached to the woman or child in these cases.

Cultural values about adultery are expressed differently by Nuer men and women. Men believe that a husband's extramarital affairs are normal, although adultery should not become public knowledge. They believe, however, that a wife should not engage in such behavior. In contrast, women do not condemn other women who are adulterers. Socially sanctioned repercussions in the event of adultery vary depending on the gender of the errant spouse. A husband's extramarital sexual behavior is not punished unless the woman also is married. If a man, married or not, is found to be having an affair with a married woman, he must give compensation to the woman's husband in the form of payment in cattle. Two conditions might obviate this necessity. If the woman's husband is impotent, no compensation need be given to him. If the adulterous relationship produces a female child and the offending man can prove he is indeed the father, again he need not compensate the woman's husband.

Because the lover of another man's wife has to pay compensation to the husband, adultery on the part of a wife leads to more serious social and economic consequences than a husband's adultery, unless his lover is also married—that is, somebody's wife. However, a husband cannot claim his wife's adultery as a proper grounds for divorce. If he divorces her because of it, her kinsmen are not obligated to return the bridewealth they received when she married.

Nuer patrilineages have several functions in addition to determining kinship relations. They are named groupings, usually taking their name from a founder or most influential (that is, wealthiest) elder. They tend to become associated with a particular territory, although they do not own land as such. Lineages also act through elders and other leaders to settle disputes among members. The authority of such men derives from their age and their wealth in cattle. Although patrilineal descent is ideally traced through men, it is sometimes traced through women. This option is chosen especially in cases of incorporation of foreign people, notably from the neighboring Dinka tribe. In addition, people wishing to manipulate social relationships to substantiate claims to dominant or wealthy kin groups may trace descent through women in prominent lineages (Gough, 1971).

Importance of descent and continuity of patrilineages is demonstrated in two practices concerning marriage. If a married man dies without sons, one of his younger brothers marries the deceased's wife, but children of the new couple are considered heirs of the first husband (Evans-Pritchard, 1951). Nuer "ghost marriage" thus permits an elder brother to provide continuity fictively for his patrilineage even after his own death. Because seniority in a lineage is an important criterion for determining relative social status, allowing descent to follow from an elder sibling is a strategic practice.

Another marital option is possible in cases where a lineage has not produced a male heir. In that event, a woman in the lineage can take the fictive role of "husband" and be married to another woman. The woman who becomes a "husband" is usually barren, and therefore the option of tracing descent through her is not possible. The "wife" has sexual relations with a chosen man, but her children belong to the "husband's" lineage rather than to that of their biological father. According to Evans-Pritchard (1951), such marriages are "by no means uncommon" (p. 108).

In marriages between women, the woman who acts as "husband" is transformed into a legal man. As a "man," she can receive bridewealth given in marriages for her kinswomen, and she can inherit cattle from her father. Similarly, as a "husband," she can be compensated with cattle if her "wife" has an adulterous affair without her consent.

Nuer practices of marriage between women and "ghost marriage" both function to create fictive fatherhood to secure the continuity of patrilineages. These marital options demonstrate the difficulties faced in strong lineage systems based on patrilineal descent. Because it is women who bear children, the link between a father and his heirs is indirect. Patrilineal groups must recruit women through marriage to bear children belonging to the patrilineage or patriclan. In contrast, because children in matrilineal systems automatically belong to their mothers' kin group, the source of one's inheritance is clearly identifiable regardless of whether the mother is married or not. The Nuer are somewhat unusual in the overt institutionalized manipulation of marriage practices that they have developed to deal with the problem of continuity in patrilineal societies.

According to Evans-Pritchard (1951), Nuer "family life is remarkably harmonious on the surface" (p. 133). However, this statement must be contextualized, both within Nuer culture and within Evans-Pritchard's own discussion of the matter. He claims that at least one underpinning for harmony in Nuer family life is "the unchallenged authority of the husband in the home. A woman must obey her husband." One must ask, then, from whose point of view is family life so "harmonious"? It is clear throughout Evans-Pritchard's writings that his principal informants are Nuer men. He cares little for women's opinions, and when they are given, it seems that they are obtained secondhand from men.

In the same discussion of families, Evans-Pritchard (1951, p. 133) notes the "latent hostility between husband and wife," reflected in men's overt statements that after a man has several children, he often "secretly wishes his wife to die." Evidently men do not want to die and leave a widow because they are jealous of her future lovers and husbands. They worry that another man will profit from their cattle or mistreat their children. As far as women's sentiments are concerned, Evans-Pritchard comments, "Men say also that women wish for their husband's death." Women's motivation for this sentiment is not recorded.

Male dominance among the Nuer is demonstrated in attitudes and behaviors that give greater social value to men than to women. Several practices separate the genders in ways that mark men as special or powerful. Physical residence in separate areas of a family compound indicates gender segmentation. The meaning of such separation is underscored by the association between men and cattle. Much of a man's life is concerned directly and indirectly with cattle, the most treasured possessions of the Nuer and the embodiment of their wealth. Men literally live with cattle, they name themselves after cattle, and they alone can herd, clean, and care for these animals.

Initiation of boys into adulthood distinguishes them from uninitiated boys and women. Rites of initiation include scarring of horizontal cuts across a boy's forehead. This physical sign has a critical social function, symbolically marking the distinctiveness of men. Afterward, a boy is permitted to reside with men and to tend cattle.

Men's and women's relationship to cattle is a significant reflection of ideological value accorded to the genders. In the context of Nuer subsistence, women's work with cattle is directly productive because they are responsible for milking the cows. But it is men who are symbolically linked to cattle and who perform the socially prestigious work associated with their care and survival. And it is men who are the owners of cattle; they make decisions concerning their use and distribution; they employ cattle in exchanges for marriage, as payment of debts, and on ceremonial occasions.

Attitudes toward sexuality indicate conflict between women's and men's views of behavior. Whereas men condemn a wife's adultery, women do not. Such differences in reactions indicate what is probably a widespread, if not universal, tendency—that cultural constructions are not homogenous. Culture—that is, life—is not experienced the same way for all members of a given society. People differentiated on the basis of gender, class, and race do not receive identical social, economic, and/or political rewards. Distinctions among individuals are not manifested only in public contexts but also within the context of familial and interpersonal relationships. Therefore, "harmonious family life" to a member who is endowed with rights and authority may be a stressful and demeaning existence for others. In many cases, of course, those individuals who have few rights give little voice to their own dissatisfaction. In fact, they may overtly express acceptance of their lot, as did the few Nuer women whom Evans-Pritchard (1951) actually queried on the subject. He explains women's positive attitudes on the basis of the fact that Nuer men do not abuse their wives without "just cause." That is, so long as a wife fulfills her obligations, she is not mistreated. Men known as wife beaters receive a "most shameful" reputation, disparaged as men who prefer fighting with women to fighting with men. Although severe mistreatment is socially legitimate grounds for a wife to seek a divorce, women are socialized to be deferential and obedient. Their acceptance of the rules of family life does not necessarily attest to its inherent satisfaction for them but rather to the success of their socialization.

Nuer culture, then, demonstrates the complexity of ideological constructs in organizing social value. Ability to exert control over publicly proclaimed cultural beliefs is a manifestation of generalized social rights. Ideological value is both a reflection of daily life and a reinforcement of expected behavior. It is translated into control over other members of one's household, over distribution of resources, and over positions of public and ritual leadership within one's community. In all of these domains, Nuer men exert dominance. Based on their control of economic and political modes, they are able to manipulate ideological concepts giving them social rights. Their social prestige is in turn used to justify and solidify their economic and political control. Through complex social and ideological processes, Nuer men are able to assume prominence, whereas women are relegated to subsidiary roles and secondary status.

The Luo of Kenya

Data from another East African culture provide evidence of the multiple ways that gender relations can be affected as social transformations become incorporated. The Luo, a tribal people currently residing in Kenya, were formerly inhabitants of the southern Sudan and developed a culture resembling that of the Nuer and other Nilotic peoples in the region. Luo subsistence was based on a mixture of cattle herding and farming, although like the Nuer, cattle pastoralism dominated their activities and their ideology. Sometime after A.D.1400, Luo emigrated from Sudan as a response to several factors, including population growth and overcrowding of land, increases in cattle herds and pressure on grazing land, and disputes within communities resulting from conflicts over land (Okeyo, 1980). The search for additional pastureland and water led to emigrations from the area.

The Joluo, a division of Luo peoples, eventually settled in Kenya and Tanzania in the fifteenth or sixteenth century. Although pastoralism remained central to Luo subsistence until 1800, it declined in importance thereafter due in part to losses of cattle from epidemics. Agriculture then came to dominate Luo economy. Shifts to farming led to some enhancement of women's rights because women were largely responsible for cultivating crops.

Land for farming and grazing was held by kinship groups organized into patrilineages. Lineages allocated land for use to men within the group. Land use rights were then allotted by men to their wives and sons. Therefore, men received land rights by membership in patrilineages, whereas women obtained land through marriage. But once a woman received land for use, she controlled production and distribution of crops resulting from her labor. Although women had no rights to take or allot land to others, they had control over land use under their domain within their husbands' acreage.

The basic economic unit of husband and wife was essentially cooperative. Homesteads consisted of extended families in accordance with patrilocal residence patterns. Men and their sons and/or brothers formed local residence groups, consistent with principles of patrilineal descent. In polygynous marriages, each wife resided separately with her children and was, in effect, the head of her household, although her husband was the head of the larger family unit.

Despite male control over kinship relations, preferences for patrilocal residence, and inheritance of land use rights through men, Luo women had some degree of independence and autonomy because of their substantial contribution to household subsistence and their control over distribution of crops. Their rights to land and the social recognition of their productive labor in supporting heirs to patrilineages gave women a more important social position than experienced by women of pastoral peoples such as the Nuer.

However, women's rights to land and the autonomy that followed have since been undermined by changes in Luo economy in colonial and postcolonial periods. In 1899, the British government extended its colonization of Kenyan peoples to the Luo. The British eventually formulated policies of so-called land reform aimed at consolidating holdings of individuals that previously had been scattered in different locations. Traditional patterns of landholding through which individuals held use rights in various parcels permitted people to obtain land in different ecological zones, thus enabling them to plant a variety of crops. However, because this system ended in fragmenting an individual's holdings, it was seen as inefficient by British authorities. In keeping with European ideals, landholdings were not only solidified but were also registered in the names of male heads of households. Consolidation and registration of land had the dual effect of undermining the corporate nature of lineages and the rights of women to land.

In addition, during the first half of the twentieth century, British colonial authorities imposed hut taxes that had to be paid in cash. For men as heads of households to secure money for taxes, they often had to engage in wage work requiring their absence from local communities. Although taxation was a financial burden, subsequent economic changes enhanced men's status. First, men who became involved in a cash economy obtained prestigious goods derived from European sources. Second, men who remained in their traditional villages were able to exercise control over land as individuals rather than through corporate lineages. As a result of the combination of individual ownership of land and the necessity of obtaining cash for goods and taxes, much Luo land has been taken out of domestic production and is now utilized for production of cash crops for export. This shift in land use has further benefited men who own the land and receive payment for produce.

Economic policies initiated by the British subsequently were adopted by the Kenyan government following independence in 1960. These policies continued the registration and individuation of land ownership and thus continued shifts away from women's ability to contribute to socially recognized production. As land is increasingly controlled by men, men's contribution to household survival has become central. In contrast, women remain engaged in production oriented to sustaining themselves and their children. But their ability to manage their resources has been undermined both by governmental actions and by Luo men who use land resources to produce cash income.

Registration of land has favored male ownership to a nearly exclusive extent. According to a survey conducted by Achola Okeyo in 1974, 91.1 percent of women farmed land registered in the name of a male relative (or relatives), usually a husband, son, or combination of husband and son. A real danger for women in the current system is that a man who controls the land may decide to sell some or all of it to obtain cash needed to pay taxes or purchase goods. Such decisions have the effect of rendering women even more dependent on their husbands or sons for their own survival, again undermining their autonomy and social value.

In sum, then, processes deriving from internal cultural transformations in the nineteenth century initially focused Luo economy on farming and enhanced the independence and status of women. Economic changes instituted by colonial authorities and followed by indigenous governments have shifted control over production, land use, and decisions concerning family subsistence almost exclusively to men. In this context, the flexibility of traditional patterns has been undermined and women's status has become precarious.

HORTICULTURAL ECONOMIES

Societies whose economies are based on horticulture obtain most of their food from farming, but foraging may supply some portion of their diet as well. As in societies utilizing other subsistence modes, women and men in some horticultural groups are considered equals, whereas in others, male dominance is normative. We examine contrasting societies to highlight the dynamics of both forms. Iroquoian cultures of native North America and the Yanomamo (ya-na-MA-mo) and other Amazonian peoples of native South America provide data for such a comparison. Finally, we end the chapter with a discussion of the West African Igbo (I-bo) to consider the importance of marketing in the development of gender roles and constructs.

The Huron and Iroquois of Northeastern North America

Iroquoian (ir-o-KWOY-an) societies principally included two native confederations inhabiting the northeastern Woodlands of North America in what are now New York State and Ontario, Canada. These groups were the Huron of Ontario and the five Iroquois (IR-o-kwoy) Nations of New York, including Mohawks, Oneidas, Onondagas, Cayugas, and Senecas. The Huron and Iroquois developed cultures essentially similar in most respects and are discussed as a composite example. Information concerning Iroquoian society comes from earliest periods of contact between natives and Europeans. Much of it is derived from writings of French Jesuit missionaries who worked among the Huron and Iroquois in the seventeenth and eighteenth centuries (Thwaites, 1906; noted as *JR* in the text). Later observers have recorded

Communal Iroquois longhouses were home to several nuclear families belonging to the same clan.

Iroquoian culture as well. These two sources of historical documentation provide data on traditional Iroquoian culture and also allow us to understand how economic and political changes following European colonization affected indigenous gender constructs.

In general, traditional Iroquoian norms sanctioned equality and autonomy of women and men. All people had rights to make decisions concerning their activities. No individual had rights to impose their will on others. As we demonstrate, these interactional principles formed the essence of Iroquoian culture and affected behavior in all societal domains.

Iroquoian peoples lived in concentrated villages of varying sizes. Small settlements contained one or two hundred residents; large villages had populations of more than a thousand. People lived in large communal dwellings called *longhouses*. These houses were built near one another and formed a residential area surrounded by wooden palisades to keep out intruders. Fields for farming lay outside the settlements.

Iroquoian economies were based on horticulture centered on production of maize, beans, and squash. When new fields were needed, they were prepared for planting by men through slash-and-burn techniques. All other farmwork, including planting and tending crops, was performed by women. Women also did most of the harvesting, although men occasionally helped in this activity. In addition to farmwork, women gathered wild foods, including a wide assortment of fruits, nuts, and roots. Finally, they were responsible for domestic tasks and child care. Men's subsistence roles included hunting and fishing to supplement the basic plant diet. Trading with other native peoples for animal skins and utilitarian and luxury articles was also the work of men (*JR*, vol. 15, p. 155).

The division of labor among Iroquoians therefore separated tasks of women and men. Each contributed resources and goods through their labor. Men and women in a household performed complementary tasks, all necessary for the functioning and survival of the group. Contributions of both women and men were highly valued. Their work was socially recognized and rewarded.

Household organization coalesced around matrilineal clans that formed the basis of Iroquoian kinship. Clans owned longhouses in which their members lived. Because matrilocality was the preferred residence pattern, a house typically consisted of an elder woman, her husband, their daughters and daughters' families, and the couple's unmarried sons. Each nuclear group had its own quarters in the house, separated from others' quarters by bark partitions.

Iroquoian behaviors and attitudes related to sexuality and marriage were critical reflections of the independence and autonomy of women and men. People freely chose to engage in sexual relationships and to form marriages. No individual had rights to control others in any coercive manner. According to Gabriel Lalemant, a Jesuit priest writing in 1645 of Huron attitudes toward marriage:

> In the closest of their marriages, and those which they consider most comfortable to reason, the faith that they pledge each other is nothing more than a

> conditional promise to live together so long as each shall continue to render the services that they mutually expect from each other, and shall not in any way wound the affection that they owe each other. If this fail, divorce is considered reasonable on the part of the injured one, although the other party who has given occasion for it is blamed. (*JR*, vol. 28, pp. 51–53)

Marriages were monogamous. There are two references in eighteenth-century accounts of the Seneca (one of the five Iroquois Nations) of the possibility of polyandry, but the practice, if it existed, was extremely unusual (Charlevoix, 1721/1761; Lafitau, 1724/1974). Parents sometimes took a hand in arranging marriages for their sons and daughters, but unions did not proceed without consent from the young people involved. In most cases, a marriage was contracted by the couple themselves.

Iroquoian attitudes toward sexuality were permissive. Premarital sexual activity was the norm. Extramarital affairs seem to have been quite common, if one can judge from the Jesuits' complaints about such behavior. Although adultery was met with negative public opinion, no penalties resulted to any party. Indeed, according to Joseph Lafitau (1724/1974), an eighteenth-century observer, "among the Iroquois, I must confess that the women, being more in the position of mistresses [of the household] fear an outburst less" (p. 352).

Divorce was evidently fairly common in the early years of marriage. It could be initiated by either spouse. As years passed, however, unions were strengthened and less likely to dissolve.

Violence against women in the form of wife beating or rape was unheard-of. In the words of Gabriel Sagard (1632/1939), a seventeenth-century French missionary, the Iroquois believed in "leaving all to the wishes of the woman" in sexual matters (p. 125). The Iroquois themselves recognized the difference between their attitudes and those of Europeans. In 1722, Mohawk residents of a Catholic mission near Montreal wrote to the French governor of Canada asking for removal of a French garrison posted near the mission:

> Our fields and our cabins, which are left open, and—what is of more importance—our wives and our daughters, are not safe with the French soldiers. Our young men . . . follow the bad examples before their eyes; and a thousand vices that were formerly unknown amongst us have unfortunately been introduced. (*JR*, vol. 67, p. 73)

Even as late as 1779, James Clinton, an American general who led a military campaign to destroy Iroquois villages in New York, wrote in a letter to his confederates, "Bad as these savages are, they never violate the chastity of any woman, their prisoner. It would be well to take measures to prevent a stain upon our army" (quoted in Hewitt, 1933, p. 483).

Women's importance to their lineage and community was manifested in attitudes toward children. According to François Du Peron, a Jesuit priest writing on the seventeenth-century Huron, "they rejoice more in the birth of a daughter than of a son, for the sake of the multiplication of the country's inhabitants" (*JR*, vol. 15, pp. 181–183). But all children were desired. Much attention and indulgence were shown to them by women and men in their households and communities (*JR*, vol. 52; Sagard, 1632/1939).

A symbolic expression of emphasis on women's procreative roles was enacted in practices concerning payment of fines in cases of murder. To forestall blood feuds between families that might occur in such circumstances, relatives of a murderer were obliged to give a set number of presents to the victim's family. The number of presents, usually in the form of wampum belts, was based on the gender of murderer and victim. A man's life was valued at ten belts, whereas a woman's was set at twenty. According to a Jesuit missionary, Paul Ragueneau, greater reparation was given for a woman's life because "women cannot so easily defend themselves, and, moreover, as it is they who people the country, their lives should be more valuable to the public" (*JR*, vol. 33, p. 243). The system of tribute or fines required that when a man killed another man, his family offered twenty belts, ten for the life of the victim and ten for the murderer's, because by committing murder an individual forfeited his or her own standing in the community and thus rendered his or her own life without social value. If a man killed a woman, his kin gave thirty belts, ten for his life and twenty for the victim's. If a woman committed murder, her family gave thirty belts to kin of a male victim and forty to a female victim's family.

Iroquoian women's prestige was strengthened through many features of their roles within clans. Senior women of matrilineages composing each clan had responsibility for overseeing domestic tasks performed in their households and for allocating farmland to their kinswomen (Lafitau, 1724/1974). Senior women, often referred to as "matrons" or "clan mothers" in the literature, were socially prominent and achieved their status due to combinations of merit, intelligence, and desired social attributes such as cooperativeness, generosity, and good nature.

Not only were women responsible for food production, but they also controlled distribution of both the food that they produced and the resources and goods contributed by their husbands and sons. In fact, their control over resources was a crucial factor in Iroquoian women's status in their households and communities (Bonvillain, 1980; Brown, 1975). In addition to allotting food for daily consumption, women collected and distributed supplies for public feasts and ceremonial occasions (Lafitau, 1724/1974).

A final example of women's control over resources was their duty to dispense food, typically in the form of dried cornbread, to men setting out on hunting, trading, or warring expeditions. Indeed, if a woman was opposed to her husband or son joining a group of warriors, she could withhold the expected supplies, thereby symbolically signaling her opposition. Men usually complied with their wives' or mothers' wishes in these matters.

Literature on Iroquoian societies written in the nineteenth and early twentieth centuries often described them as examples of "matriarchy" (Beauchamp, 1900; Carr, 1883; and others). Such an appellation is inaccurate. A **matriarchy** would, by definition, be a society in which women dominated sociopolitical life to the exclusion of men, a mirror image of **patriarchy**. There is no evidence that matriarchies existed among any people and certainly no evidence that Iroquoian societies were matriarchal. However, two reasons perhaps account for nineteenth-century Euro-American descriptions of Iroquoian culture labeling it as such. First, postulation of a stage of so-called matriarchy was a feature of theories of social evolution popular at the time. These theories began with the claim that ancient peoples had originally lived in undifferentiated "hordes" but had gradually organized themselves into lineages and clans. These kinship groupings were initially based on matrilineal descent because people recognized the obvious biological link between mother and child. Later, people shifted to reckoning descent on the basis of patrilineal principles when men asserted their economic and political control of society. Early stages of matriarchy were thus overthrown by patriarchy. Data from Iroquoian cultures were interpreted to fit into such schemes of progression. In fact, Iroquoian data were often used to argue for the validity of the theory, providing a living example of an earlier stage of social evolution (Engels, 1884/1972; Morgan, 1877).

A second explanation for the misinterpretation of Iroquoian practices lies in the inability of writers steeped in Euro-American hierarchical cultures to appreciate a genuinely egalitarian system. Because existence of hierarchy and power of one group over another were taken as givens, and because men clearly did not exert control over women in Iroquoian societies, Euro-American observers assumed that women controlled men.

The societal domain in which observers and scholars saw most evidence of women's power was in Iroquoian politics. It certainly was true that Iroquoian women held positions of public trust and respect and their opinions were critical in formulation of public policy, but it is a mistake to view women's roles as entailing control to the exclusion of men. The Iroquois polity was in all cases open to contributions by both men and women.

The five Iroquois Nations (Mohawk, Oneida, Onondaga, Cayuga, and Seneca) formed a confederacy or league whose purpose was to establish peace among themselves and to join together when necessary to defend against external enemies. On the whole, these goals were achieved, although internal conflicts were not unknown. Councils were established on three geopolitical levels to discuss matters and negotiate consensus. Councils functioned in local villages for all residents, on the tribal level for each separate nation in its principal village, and in a central meeting place for the united confederacy attended by representatives from all five nations. Issues were discussed and debated first in localities, next in tribal meetings, and lastly at confederacy councils. Tribal and confederacy councils were concerned with national and international issues such as negotiations with foreign groups (native and later European), trade, and warfare. On a local level these matters were also discussed, as were such community affairs as visits of prominent guests, village ceremonials, or other communal events.

National and confederacy councils were attended by chiefs who represented their clans. Chiefs were chosen by "clan mothers" from among kinsmen well respected by their relatives and communities as a whole. Each chief had assistants or advisers. These people, men and women, advised the chief concerning community opinion on important matters.

People were organized in their localities into what might be termed "caucuses" to discuss matters of moment. Women had their own councils to debate issues and form their consensus, chiefs and elders had their meetings, and young men (sometimes referred to as "warriors") held separate meetings. Members of each group met among themselves to discuss relevant matters and arrive at a unified opinion. Opinions of local communities were then voiced at tribal and confederacy councils. Lafitau (1974) describes the process as follows:

> The women are always the first to deliberate . . . on private or community matters. They hold their councils apart and, as a result of their decisions, advise the chiefs on matters on the mat, so that the latter may deliberate on them in their turn. The chiefs, on this advice, bring together the old people [probably referring to elder men] of their clan and, if the matter which they are treating concerns the common welfare, they all gather together in the general Council of the Nation. The warriors also have their council apart for matters within their competence but all the individual councils are subordinate to that of the Old People which is the superior council, as it were. (p. 295)

In each caucus, individuals voiced their opinions and discussed together to arrive at a consensus. At tribal and confederacy councils, each group had spokespeople who presented its unified opinion. Chiefs delegated one of their number to speak for them; women and young men appointed representatives who made their opinions publicly known. These representatives were often specially chosen among prominent men, but in some cases, a woman or a warrior was the selected delegate.

Chiefs and advisers were ideally installed in office for life, but if their behavior was deemed incompatible with local interests, if they became arrogant or refused to heed people's opinions, they were demoted on the advice of their clan mothers, who first gave them three reprimands and warnings. Father Dablon, a Jesuit missionary writing of the Mohawks in 1671, described one such demotion:

> They degraded her from her noble rank, in an assembly of the village notables; and deprived her of the name and title of Oiander—that is, a person of quality. This is a dignity which they highly esteem, which she had inherited from her ancestors, and deserved by her own intelligence, prudence and discreet conduct. At the same time, too, they installed another woman in her place. Women of this rank are much respected; they hold councils, and the Elders decide no important affair without their advice. (*JR*, vol. 54, p. 281)

Although clan mothers played publicly prominent roles in selecting, installing, and demoting clan chiefs and advisers, they were sensitive to community opinion. The men they chose as chiefs were individuals who were well respected by members of their clans; when they demoted an officeholder, they were responsive to negative public sentiments. In other words, clan mothers' actions were in no way dictatorial or based on narrow self-interest but rather were consistent with Iroquoian ethics of community interdependence and consensus.

In sum, activities in traditional Iroquoian societies were not dominated by women or by men. All people made important, socially valued contributions and had ultimate control over their own behavior.

Iroquoian societies experienced massive contact with Europeans beginning in the sixteenth century. Two periods of transformation of Iroquoian culture can be identified. In both, native economic and political life was altered, with concomitant changes in gender constructs. The first period of contact was highlighted by development of an economy focused on trade with Europeans. Trade commenced in the early seventeenth century and continued to intensify throughout the seventeenth and eighteenth centuries. Iroquoian peoples, like others in the Northeast, became increasingly involved in trapping beavers desired by European markets. In exchange for beaver pelts, natives received manufactured goods, especially metalware such as iron pots, knives, nails, and other tools and weapons. By the middle and late seventeenth century, they also obtained guns and ammunition.

The intensified trade economy solidified men's traditional roles. Whereas in previous eras men's responsibilities for hunting and trading had contributed supplementary products to basic resources produced by women, men's efforts in trapping and trading became increasingly critical to Iroquoian economies. In addition, as all native groups in the Northeast competed for access to resources in beaver and to trade goods, intertribal warfare expanded and casualties mounted. Furthermore, competition among the European powers, especially Holland, France, and Great Britain, led to each country's attempts to enlist native allies in their conflicts with one another, thus fomenting more armed hostilities. Military campaigns consequently became a further focus of Iroquoian men's activities. These responsibilities became increasingly important for the survival of local communities.

Although emphasis on warfare and trading economies enhanced men's prestige in Iroquoian societies, it did not undermine women's status as often occurs in many cultures. Two principal factors account for the maintenance of women's rights. First, Iroquois' participation in trade was made possible, in part, by women's labor. Because the supply of beavers in Iroquois territory was quickly decimated due to both a natural shortage and widespread overkill, the Iroquois had to trade for beaver pelts with other native groups who had a greater abundance. One of the products used in this exchange was the corn grown by Iroquois women. Women's labor was therefore a necessary ingredient in continuing the economic triangle: Iroquois corn was traded with northern native groups for beaver pelts, which were subsequently traded with Europeans for manufactured goods. To perpetuate this network, it was necessary for women to plant and harvest a larger surplus of corn. Economic interdependence of women and men that underlay the functioning of Iroquoian societies was thus not eroded by an emphasis on trade. In fact, increased trade may well have solidified recognition of the essential value contributed by both women and men.

Second, although warfare enhanced the social value of men's military skills, prestige accorded to warriors was not used to monopolize power in local villages. The absence of men's local control was due partly to the nature of Iroquois warfare and partly to the strength of women's status in their communities. Throughout most of the period of intense conflict—that is, the seventeenth and eighteenth centuries—men who engaged in warfare generally left their home communities on lengthy expeditions against a foreign group. They were often absent for months at a time, ranging as far west as the western Great Lakes, as far east as the maritime provinces of Canada, and as far south as Virginia and the Carolinas. Women who remained in villages maintained and perhaps even augmented their local authority. Although intertribal and international warfare did occasionally involve attacks on Iroquois settlements, this practice was not widespread until later in the period. Therefore, Iroquois men were not so much perceived as defenders of noncombatants as might have otherwise been the case.

In general, then, the first phase of European contact resulted in changes that enhanced productive contributions of both women and men without leading to exclusive emphasis on one or the other. The second period of societal transformation, however, did result in a shift in economic roles of the genders with a concomitant decline in women's status. This phase began with establishment of reservations (called "reserves" in Canada) in the late eighteenth century. Subsistence activities were reassigned as a result of a decline in hunting and trade and elimination of warfare. Canadian and American officials advocated a change in roles consistent with Anglo gender constructs. They urged the allocation of farming tasks to men and domestic activities to women. At first, both women and men resisted a change in their responsibilities. However, men were won over after it became clear that their traditional roles were forever eradicated by historical circumstances beyond their control. In addition, Canadian and American experts began to teach innovative farming techniques exclusively to men. New methods included use of plows and horses to replace traditional hoe technology employed by women.

As one might expect, women resisted the economic changes even more strenuously than men did because they recognized the danger of being displaced from labor that had supported their traditional status. However, in a fairly short period of time, Iroquois gender roles were essentially shifted. Such change was further solidified by the emergence at the turn of the nineteenth century of a revivalistic Iroquois religion, known by the name of its Seneca founder and prophet, Handsome Lake. In addition to offering religious solutions to community problems, Handsome Lake advocated a social program that had actually first been promulgated by Jesuit missionaries in the seventeenth century and was later championed by Quakers who had a great deal of influence on Handsome Lake (Bonvillain, 1986; Wallace, 1961, 1970). Among other cultural changes, Handsome Lake preached the ideal of nuclear family residence patterns and the authority of the husband/father as the head of household. The breakup of matrilineal extended family units eroded one of the bases of clan mothers' prestige and authority as well as eliminating a mechanism for solidarity among women. Isolation of women in separate nuclear families and their assignment to secondary domestic labor further undermined their status.

The final element that had previously contributed to Iroquois women's traditional prestige was their political participation in local and confederacy councils. Their roles in Iroquois politics were eroded during the late eighteenth and early nineteenth centuries. Canadian and American colonial agents generally refused to negotiate with women. They ignored women's opinions and advised Iroquois men to do likewise. Again, women resisted attempts to undermine their participation, but Iroquois men eventually followed the dictates of Anglo powers and assumed full responsibility for political affairs. Women were finally disenfranchised by elimination of clan chiefs appointed by clan mothers and their replacement with an elective system of leadership with exclusively male suffrage (Rothenberg, 1980). Dismantling the traditional political system thus combined with economic changes to transform gender roles and relations in conformity with Anglo values. Such transformation was a direct result of external pressure and the rewards offered by colonial powers to Iroquois men.

The Yanomamo of Brazil and Venezuela

In contrast to aboriginal Iroquoian culture, some horticultural societies in other areas of the world developed indigenous systems of gender that entailed male dominance. The Yanomamo (ya-na-MA-mo) of native South America exemplify such a group. They live in the Amazon region in borderlands of Brazil and Venezuela. Their total population numbers approximately ten thousand, although they reside in small villages in a dispersed settlement pattern throughout the region.

Yanomamo culture sanctions men's dominance over women in every feature of ideology and practice. Settlement patterns, social systems, subsistence activities, village leadership, and ceremonial practice are all dominated by men.

Residence patterns follow principles of patrilocality, based on affiliation among patrilineal kin. Villages consist of a few large dwellings that house several related families. Preference for village **exogamy** reflects and reinforces two features of inequality between men and women. First, because fathers arrange marriages for their daughters, village exogamy establishes **affinal bonds** between men in neighboring settlements. Men thus use their daughters to solidify alliances with other men. Second, the fact that wives move to their husbands' village effectively isolates women from their own kin, stranding them in unfamiliar communities and depriving them of any emotional support in the event of conflicts in their new households. Girls to be married have no right to object to marriages that their fathers contract for them. In fact, a reluctant bride may be beaten, not only by her husband but by her father or brothers as well.

Marital relationships additionally disadvantage women. Young girls, often as young as 8 or 9, are married to men in their 20s or 30s, resulting in substantial age differences between spouses that contribute to women's subordination because seniority itself confers authority.

Marriages serve to establish close, cooperative bonds, not between wife and husband but between two men as brothers-in-law. In fact, the brother-in-law relationship is "the most highly elaborated bond in Yanomamo society . . . [entailing] balanced and enduring reciprocity" (Shapiro, 1976, p. 92). Cooperation between brothers-in-law in hunting, raiding, ceremonial activities, and socializing is made possible by the exchange of women. In contrast, women do not establish lasting cooperative or supportive bonds with other women. Although the mother-daughter relationship is close, women always leave their mother's home when they marry and usually leave their natal community altogether because of preferences for village exogamy. Even in polygynous households, co-wives rarely engage in joint or cooperative work.

Polygyny is common and desired by all Yanomamo men. A man may contract multiple marriages through establishing alliances with several men who have daughters. Men of high social prestige are most likely to be able to arrange such unions for themselves because other men are likely to want to become their allies. Men also obtain wives by capture when raiding other villages.

Ceremonial activity highlights roles and relationships among men whether in communal or individual rites. Yanomamo villages participate in intercommunity ceremonial feasting that principally involve men as hosts and guests. Visiting men enter the host village dressed in warrior regalia and parade around the central plaza, recounting and boasting of their exploits. Visiting women, in contrast, "filter inconspicuously into the village, remaining in the peripheral area of the house" (Shapiro, 1976, p. 96). Later, men engage in ceremonial dialogues while women are relatively silent.

Individual ritual activity centers on shamanic curing, always the domain of men. With the use of drugs, they make contact with the spirit realm and gain powers. In contrast, women remain "ignorant" (Shapiro, 1976, p. 99).

Prestige in Yanomamo culture is principally based on success as a shaman and as a warrior. Warfare confers social value to men as a group and to the individual men who are most often victorious. Successful warriors also function as influential village leaders. Warfare is common in Yanomamo territory, although its frequency varies in different regions. It is characterized by raids against nearby villages with the aim of killing as many inhabitants as possible. Young women, however, are often captured and brought back to become wives. Yanomamo warfare is triggered largely by disputes over women and/or by men's desire to obtain wives from other communities (Chagnon, 1973). Because warfare pitting one Yanomamo settlement against others creates a dangerous situation for noncombatants, men's role in defending their home communities becomes a paramount necessity for survival. Men's success is rewarded both by their high social prestige and by the subordination of Yanomamo women.

Violence against women, in the form of both beatings and rape, is common. According to Chagnon's accounts, women may be subjected to beatings and sexual attacks. Women, whether married or unmarried, are vulnerable to assaults if they are in the forest unaccompanied by male kin. Danger of attacks obviously severely limits women's freedom to act as autonomous individuals.

Male dominance is also demonstrated by the frequent occurrence of female infanticide, which is practiced to such an extent that despite the high casualty rate of men in warfare, men greatly outnumber women. Female infanticide is connected to Yanomamo warfare because the scarcity of women creates an incentive for men's aggression against enemy villagers to acquire wives by capture.

Yanomamo subsistence activities reflect and enhance men's worthiness, whereas women's roles are simultaneously marginalized. The gender division of labor assigns productive work entirely to men. All necessary direct subsistence activities in farming, hunting, and fishing are performed by men. They clear and prepare fields; they plant crops, notably manioc, and they engage in hunting and fishing. Men thus contribute all resources consumed by their families. In marked contrast, women contribute no basic supplies. They perform domestic labor, including preparation of meals and child care. These tasks are considered secondary to those fulfilled by men.

In sum, every socially recognized avenue of achieving prestige in Yanomamo society is monopolized by men. They collect and produce resources, they defend their local communities and attack their enemies, and they function as village leaders. Systems of social organization and kinship help solidify men's authority by determining descent, household affiliation, and intervillage alliances.

In stark contrast, women have no access to socially valued achievements. They contribute no direct subsistence resources. They are victims of warfare rather than its victors. Residence patterns separate women from their kin groups, although in fact even their own relatives are unlikely to give them emotional or physical support. Women's subordination is especially marked by the frequent violence to which they are subjected.

The case of the Yanomamo raises two crucial questions regarding male dominance. One concerns the reasons accounting for development and entrenchment of men's power. The second concerns the reasons accounting for women's submission to domination by men. To begin with the latter issue, it is helpful to contrast women's roles and status in Yanomamo and Iroquoian societies. First, Yanomamo women can make no social claims on the basis of productive subsistence activities because they do not contribute, let alone control, necessary resources. In contrast, Iroquoian women collect and produce most of the foods consumed by their households, and they control distribution of resources in public contexts of civil and religious events in their villages. Their direct economic contributions are thus visibly demonstrated and socially recognized.

Second, whereas Iroquoian women are nurtured and supported by matrilineal kin groups and their solidarity is ensured by matrilocal residence patterns, Yanomamo women are separated from their homes and placed in what is often a hostile environment. A wife's isolation is especially marked for women taken as war captives, but it also is a feature of typical intervillage marriages.

Third, Yanomamo women have no possibility of gaining influence in their villages. Leadership is based solely on military prowess, a path of achievement blocked to women. The fact that Yanomamo warfare is characterized by attacks on nearby villages renders women vulnerable to danger but leaves them without any ability to defend themselves. Because men monopolize all weapons, they are the sole protectors of settlements. In contrast, the character of most of Iroquoian warfare meant that men left their home communities to engage in war against distant peoples. Women were rarely vulnerable to direct danger and therefore not dependent on men's protection for their survival.

Finally, any demonstration of resistance by a Yanomamo woman to the treatment she received was met with violence against her. Beatings by a father, brothers, or husband were common. Sexual assaults by men in her village or by strangers in the forest were frequent. Such a fate was unthinkable in Iroquoian society, where women's rights to their independence and the protection of their persons from attacks of any kind were socially recognized.

Whereas Iroquoian women's equality with men was validated in every societal domain, Yanomamo women's subservience is reflected in every aspect of life. Yanomamo women have no power to change their situation because any means of control has been effectively taken from them. Their powerlessness and dependence are created in part through processes of socialization in which ideological control is always first and foremost exercised. But women's subordination is also maintained by the knowledge that they have no alternatives. Because they have no means of even defending themselves physically, they must know that resistance is futile.

Returning to the first question concerning development and maintenance of male dominance in Yanomamo culture, several theories have been suggested. According to Marvin Harris (1974), male dominance among the Yanomamo is generated by warfare endemic in their territory. Men are socialized to be violent, to endure pain, and to inflict pain on others. Men's willingness to risk their lives in warfare is supported by social rewards given to them. Most notable among these rewards is their ability to subordinate women. The social system renders women incapable of resisting men's control. Polygyny, wife beating, and sexual assaults are visible public demonstrations of men's power and women's subservience.

Of course, an explanation of male dominance based on endemic warfare raises the need to explain such warfare. Harris contends that it is based on scarcity of resources and resulting population pressure. Because one of the goals of Yanomamo warfare is destruction of an entire enemy village, Harris claims that warfare serves as a means of population control. In addition, by eliminating competitors for resources, land is freed and allowed to lay fallow for some time, so it renews its nutrient base. Fallow periods are necessary in the Amazonian region where soil is of relatively poor quality and is quickly depleted.

Harris's interpretation is based on Yanomamo data provided by Napoleon Chagnon (1968, 1973). According to Chagnon, Yanomamo villagers frequently move to new locations because of the high incidence of warfare. That is, as raiding in an area intensifies, people abandon their villages and relocate to sites not currently in use. In this way, warfare can be viewed as a mechanism that disperses populations and forces them to utilize other zones for their farming and hunting.

Needs to disperse populations in areas of scarce resources have also been discussed by Janet Siskind (1973) as a factor explaining Amazonian peoples' practices concerning gender. According to Siskind, Amazonian cultures engage in several behaviors that artificially create a "scarcity of women" to limit populations and to generate conditions conducive to forcing people to relocate. Practices that lead to a scarcity of women include polygyny, female infanticide, and limitations on men's sexual access to women through strict sexual mores imposed particularly on women's activity.

Data from the Yanomamo exemplify effects of decreasing the number of available women as potential wives and thus creating jealousy and antagonism among men, which in turn results in fights within a community and raids against neighbors. Intravillage disputes often lead to fissioning of a settlement, dividing large settlements into smaller ones. Intervillage disputes lead to warfare that eventually results in relocations of people to safer peripheral areas. Although the underlying adaptive problem is a paucity of high-quality nutritious resources, women are culturally manipulated to facilitate dispersals of concentrated groups.

There is some corroboration for theories correlating male dominance and warfare by comparisons with other Amazonian peoples among whom warfare is not so prevalent. The situation for the Yanomamo in Brazil/Venezuela borderlands may be especially dire not only because of natural resource problems but also because of increased encroachments by whites in the area. According to William Smole's (1976) research with Yanomamo groups in other regions, warfare is more frequent in areas close to recent encroachments than in those more distant. And although women in the latter groups do not have status equal to that of men, they are not as totally subordinated as women in Yanomamo communities reported by Chagnon (1968) and analyzed by Harris (1974). Smole's study provides evidence of the impact on gender relations of pressures emanating directly and indirectly from outside contacts and modern national governments. As lands have been restricted, as resources have been eliminated, and as population pressure has increased, internal dynamics of gender antagonism that seem to be characteristic of the Amazonian region (Murphy and Murphy, 1974) have been intensified. Societal tensions have led men to become more hostile toward each other as reflected in increased raiding and intravillage fights. And men have displaced their collective anger onto an easily identifiable defenseless group within their communities—women.

Even the Yanomamo studied by Chagnon do not display totally homogeneous practices. Evidently there are some differences in gender relations in Yanomamo villages located in the center of a raiding area and those on the periphery of intense warfare. For example, Chagnon (1973) notes in passing that attitudes toward a wife's adultery differ in the two types of communities. In central villages, "trysts inevitably lead to fighting and often to killing. At the periphery, the affairs are tolerated if not institutionalized" (p. 135).

In sum, although Yanomamo society is clearly dominated by men, external factors need to be considered in addition to indigenous cultural developments. According to Shelly Kellman (1982), the problem with analyses by Chagnon (and Harris) is their "failure to consider historical and immediate events such as migration forced by the intrusions of development, contact with whites, [and] disease epidemics" (p. 23). Furthermore, Kellman refers to accounts by Father Saffirio, a Brazilian missionary working among the Yanomamo, who depicts much more peaceful communities than those described by Chagnon. Not only is intervillage raiding in this area relatively uncommon, but violence within a village is not so frequent. Moreover, consistent with Chagnon's statements concerning attitudes toward adultery in peripheral Yanomamo villages, a wife's extramarital affairs are not punished unless they become too frequent.

The Jivaro of Peru

A brief comparative look at data concerning Amazonian peoples in Peru sheds additional light on dynamics of gender relations in the Amazonian region. For example, among the Jivaro (HE-va-ro), a group with a total population of approximately twenty thousand dispersed in numerous small villages, male dominance is relatively weak. A number of instructive similarities and differences obtain between Jivaro and Yanomamo culture. Perhaps the most fundamental contrast between these societies lies in their economies. Whereas Yanomamo subsistence is based entirely on men's productive labor, Jivaro women contribute substantially to their households. They are responsible for planting, tending, and harvesting crops, notably manioc, sweet potatoes, and squash. These products supply most of the Jivaro's subsistence needs, although they are supplemented by fish and animal meat provided by men (Meggers, 1971).

In addition to planting and tending crops, Jivaro women control and perform garden rituals that must be enacted to ensure a good crop. Women are believed to have a "special relationship with plants" (Meggers, 1971, p. 60). According to Karsten (1935):

> Only a woman can act upon the female spirit of the manioc plant so as to make it produce an abundant crop; cultivated by a man it would yield but a meagre harvest. Only under a woman's care will the swine and the fowls increase and thrive, and the hunting-dogs become able to trace the game. (quoted in Meggers, 1971, p. 63)

Jivaro culture thus endows women with a critical role linking subsistence to the supernatural realm. Not only are women significantly responsible for ensuring success in their own productive activities, but also their ritual knowledge is necessary for men's success in hunting.

In other cultural practices, Jivaro and Yanomamo societies evidence several similarities. As among the Yanomamo, residence patterns and kinship systems favor men. Patrilineal descent determines kin groupings and also leads to preferences for patrilocality. But in contrast to the Yanomamo, although Jivaro women move to their husbands' villages and households, they are not vulnerable to frequent physical abuse. It is not so much that their relatives protect them but rather that social norms do not sanction the almost unrestrained violence to which Yanomamo women are subjected.

Similar to the Yanomamo pattern, intense warfare exists in the Jivaro region. It is characterized by attacks of one Jivaro village against another with the goal of annihilating an entire enemy village, destroying houses and crops as well (Meggers, 1971). Women and children are often spared and taken back to local settlements as captives. Warriors' abilities are socially rewarded, allowing them the means of achieving prestige and village leadership.

Polygyny is prevalent among the Jivaro. But in contrast to the Yanomamo, who practice polygyny despite scarcity of women, Jivaro polygyny results from the fact that constant warfare leads to high casualties among men, creating a population imbalance favoring women. Meggers (1971) reports that for the twenty thousand Jivaro as a whole, "females outnumber males by more than two to one" (p. 56). Therefore, polygyny among the Jivaro can be interpreted as an adaptive strategy to guarantee that all women marry and reproduce, thus ensuring continuity of the community.

Comparative data from the Jivaro and Yanomamo suggest it may be differences in productive roles that protect women's rights among the Jivaro and undermine Yanomamo women's status. Jivaro women's contributions are essential for survival and form a basis for protection of their rights. It may indeed be that Yanomamo culture prohibits women from engaging in productive work to justify their subordination. Constellations of productive contributions and gender relations are results of dynamic processes that generate, reproduce, and reinforce social rights and valuations. They demonstrate that societal activities and cultural values cohere to form unified constructs merging behavior and ideology.

The Igbo of Nigeria

Economic factors are critical to the development of gender constructs in societies throughout the world. Further evidence of this connection is provided by several horticultural tribal societies in West Africa, including the Igbo (I-bo) of Nigeria. An important feature of economies of these groups is their reliance on market trade conducted primarily by women. Women's control over local trade is key to their ability to establish a high degree of independence and autonomy in the context of a culture that otherwise is dominated by men. Women sell farm produce and handicrafts in town and regional markets to others who buy goods for their own households or who buy for resale to local villagers. Some women are able to make sizable profits in these exchanges. Through their control over market activities and the money they receive, tradeswomen establish independence in their households.

Data concerning the Afikpo Igbo, one of many local groups within the Igbo tribal configuration in Nigeria, provide insights into relationships between trading activities and social status. The Afikpo reside in more than twenty villages in eastern Nigeria. Although the Igbo speak a common language and recognize ethnic similarities, each village is autonomous. There are no overarching integrative structures uniting the more than five million Igbo people as a whole. Like other Igbo, Afikpo subsistence is based on horticulture. Tasks are strongly demarcated according to gender. Men plant yams, considered to be the staple crop. Rice, which is a product recently introduced, is the only plant grown by both men and women. Women plant and harvest all other crops, including manioc, cocoyams, maize, beans, and okra. Women also weed their husbands' yam gardens. Even when work has a collective focus, tasks are demarcated according to gender. For example, men harvest yams, but women and children carry the yams to the household yam barn (Ottenberg, 1965; Ottenberg and Ottenberg, 1962).

Other subsistence and household activities are likewise allocated according to gender. Men obtain fish from nearby rivers; women fish in ponds and streams. Men make bamboo frames for Afikpo houses, and women collect and carry mud for house walls; men put mud on the frames, and women smooth it when dry. Gender differentiation is extended to craft production: women are potters, and men make mats (Ottenberg, 1965).

In addition to their direct productive activities, women are responsible for processing crops once harvested, preparing meals, carrying loads, and caring for children. According to Ottenberg and Ottenberg (1962), "Women tend to take a larger part in economic production than the men, and they appear to work harder." As a result, "men have more leisure than the women" (p. 120).

Afikpo social organization favors men by preferences for patrilocal residence and patrilineal affiliation. Although the Afikpo have a kinship system of "double descent," tracing descent both through one's father and mother, father's lineage is considered more important.

Access to resources is complicated by both patrilineal and matrilineal claims. Most land is owned communally by matrilineages, but it is controlled by men, allotted to households by councils of elder men within a matrilineage. Unmarried men have rights to land under the jurisdiction of their own matrilineage; married men have rights to land controlled by their wife's matrilineage. Although women have access to their matrilineage's land, use rights are obtained indirectly through their husbands rather than directly on their own accord. Patrilineal groups also control some Afikpo land and are able to lay direct claims through men in the kin group (Ottenberg, 1965). Therefore, although patterns of access to land follow principles of double descent and inheritance, in all cases, men as members of either patrilineages or matrilineages are in control of allocation of land. Land is allotted to them as recognized heads of households.

Patrilineal affiliation further influences households through preferences for patrilocal residence. Male members of patrilineages thus are able to establish solidarity. Matrilineal groups, in contrast, are dispersed rather than unified.

Afikpo social norms require women to be deferential toward men, especially their husbands and elders. Ethics bestowing authority on one's seniors affect married couples because a husband is usually older than his wife. In polygynous households, a first wife generally has authority over subsequent wives, in part because she, too, tends to be the older. However, her position is never equal to that of her husband.

Political control is organized in villages by a system of age grades, a pattern common throughout much of Africa. Men are grouped into three age grades: elders, middles, and juniors. The middle group has the most responsibility for overseeing village affairs and for settling disputes. A council of elders functions as an advisory body to the middle group. Juniors act as messengers for other age grades. They also collect fines imposed by middle or elder councils, and they function as police in village markets. Within household compounds, elders of the resident patrilineage act as authorities. They allocate land and negotiate in family disputes.

Although Afikpo women are also organized into age grades, they belong to these groups in villages into which they marry rather than in their natal communities. Women's age grades provide mechanisms for women's solidarity, but they have no political functions. They have some impact on economic activities because they often organize women into cooperative work groups for planting and weeding tasks.

In contrast to the Afikpo, women and men in western Igbo communities are separately organized into political interest groups. In such a "dual-sex system" (Okonjo, 1976), each gender controls its own sphere of activity. Women collectively make decisions, settle disputes, and impose penalties involving other women; men do likewise for the men's domain. Each gender is officially represented by a titled leader. The leader of women, *omu*, is spoken of as the "mother of the community." Although the men's leader, *obi*, is said to be the head of the entire community, his authority is typically wielded in matters involving men.

When an incumbent *omu* was asked by Kamene Okonjo to describe her duties, she replied:

> The "obi" is the head of the men, and I am the head of the women. I and my cabinet represent the women in any important town gathering and deliberations. If decisions arrived at are such that the womenfolk are to be told about them, I get a woman to sound the gong to assemble the women. On less important occasions, my cabinet members pass the word around among the women by word of mouth.
>
> If there is drought, we curse whoever caused it. If there is sickness and people are dying, we curse whoever brought it. If there is sickness in the next town, I do something to insure that sickness does not enter this town. There are medicines we make at the entrance to the town. These are just a few of my duties. I am the mother of the people, and I have to insure in any way I can that they enjoy continued good health and happiness. (p. 50)

In addition to Igbo women's household and local productive tasks, they are principally involved in trade. Most Igbo women engage in trade, as do the women of a majority of disparate cultures throughout West Africa. Men also trade, but their participation is traditionally less extensive than that of women. Among the Afikpo and other Igbo communities, both local and regional markets function to redistribute goods. Most women are in some way involved in buying and selling local produce. In fact, according to I. U. Ukwu (1969), "Selling of local produce is considered as part of production" (p. 173). Trade therefore is an integral part of overall productive subsistence processes in which women are engaged. Women's roles in markets are extensions of their roles as primary producers. Moreover, Ukwu states, "With the differentiation of economic functions within the Igbo household, individual members retain to a large extent the personal control and rights of disposal of their produce" (p. 177). Women's marketing expertise encompasses men's products as well because women usually sell agricultural products grown by their husbands in addition to those in their own domain.

Tradeswomen tend to specialize in certain products, either raw or processed. The latter category includes steamed rice, roasted nuts, a fermented cassava drink (*gari*), and other cooked foods. Some women sell crafts, especially pottery. Specialization in goods is based partly on regional diversification and on personal skill. Igbo territory as a whole is ecologically complex, containing many distinctive ecosystems producing different kinds of crops. One function of trade, therefore, is to distribute a variety of produce to communities throughout the area. Tradeswomen, then, provide an important regional function in amassing and redistributing resources. Nutritional balance for the Igbo as a whole is achieved through their activities.

Most Igbo women are not full-time traders but rather engage in marketing as an extension of their roles in agricultural production. They supply their families with a variety of foods and obtain crafts and utensils made by others. However, some women do engage in more complex trading activities. Some function as intermediaries, buying from local producers and reselling produce in local and regional marketplaces. Others buy in large quantity from markets and then resell to villagers who do not go to market (Ukwu, 1969). Through these various efforts, women function as catalysts for wide redistributive networks.

The significance of tradeswomen's achievement in West Africa is underscored by the fact that ideologies of gender in these societies do not convey images of equality between women and men. Male dominance is transmitted through several cultural practices, including polygyny, wife beating, and the expected submissive demeanor of women interacting with men. But women who engage in trade are able to free themselves from stereotypical behaviors. Because their market business contributes significant support to their households, their husbands are loath to interfere with their activities or to make too many demands on their labor. Successful women have the income and prestige to manage on their own. They are therefore more likely than most to leave an abusive or domineering husband. If divorced or widowed, successful tradeswomen do not feel compelled to remarry because they know they can support themselves and their children.

Unlike Iroquoian culture, which thoroughly supports gender equality in ideological and material forms, and unlike Yanomamo culture, which explicitly maintains male dominance, Igbo culture conveys mixed messages. Male dominance is verbalized and enacted through the contrasting demeanors of men and women and through some restrictions on women's participation, but individual women are able to assert their independence through their critical control over economic exchange. Whereas Yanomamo women are not permitted to make any socially valued contributions to production or control any sphere of public life, West African women are vital producers, economic negotiators, and controllers of distribution and redistribution. They are able to translate their achievements in public socialized labor into a high degree of social autonomy. They do not dominate their husbands, but neither do they submit to domination.

Trading activities of West African women are thus interrelated with the economies and social systems of their societies. B. W. Hodder's (1969) comments on the Yoruba, an indigenous Nigerian kingdom, applies as well to the Igbo and other West African tribal peoples:

> Many social patterns of women may be correlated with, affected by, or even have arisen out of women's participation in trade. Many social relationships, in fact, are facilitated, perpetuated and even caused by the marketing complex. (p. 51)

Newly independent African countries, like the Igbo of Nigeria, have established compulsory education for both boys and girls.

Interrelationships between women's trading activities and their social status become further clarified through examination of significant changes in West African trading patterns that have occurred in this century as a result of the penetration of European economies into rural communities. At the beginning of the twentieth century, most Igbo markets were small in scale and were the sites of barter exchanges of locally grown produce and local crafts. For example, Afikpo women rarely traveled long distances to larger regional markets, in part because their needs were filled locally and in part because endemic warfare in the area made travel hazardous (Ottenberg and Ottenberg, 1962).

After British rule in Nigeria was extended through conquest of the entire Igbo region in 1902, economic transformations were effected in terms of both goods exchanged and the social and economic character of traders and trading. The diversification of products increased as new crops were introduced into Igbo economies. According to Ottenberg and Ottenberg (1962), new products "increased the volume of women's trade and did much to free them of their former economic dependence on men" (p. 129). Markets grew in size as more sellers and buyers frequented them. Growth was facilitated by improvements in roads and access to means of transportation. An end to internal warfare also contributed to people's willingness to travel long distances to collect supplies and to visit larger regional markets. Burgeoning market activity of Afikpo women contributed to their ability to function independently from their husbands' control. Introduction of new crops grown by women enabled them to obtain both food for support of themselves and their families and products to sell on the market. According to

Ottenberg (1959), an Afikpo tradeswoman who has her own source of supply "can say, 'What is a man? I have my own money!'" (p. 214).

Although these changes were significant and clearly boosted the vitality of marketing, most Afikpo women remained part-time traders. In contrast, by the middle of the twentieth century, some men had begun to engage in full-time trading. Sale of local agricultural products was still dominated by women, but men entered expanding fields of imported and manufactured goods, including clothing, utensils, and bicycles (Ottenberg and Ottenberg, 1962; Ukwu, 1969). Trade in these items is both more prestigious and potentially more profitable than selling local produce. It requires a large capital investment, well beyond the funds of most Igbo women.

Additional features of trade have benefited men while excluding women. First, people wishing to trade in manufactured articles have to deal with suppliers in urban centers. Most of these suppliers are associated with European companies that have a cultural bias against dealing with women (Mintz, 1971). Second, local traders of manufactured goods have to travel long distances to centers of supply. Such travel is restricted for women, in part by customary norms rendering women less mobile than men, and in part by women's household and productive activities that militate against their prolonged absence from home. In addition, as individuals and through local councils of elders, Afikpo men have exerted pressure on women to discourage them from engaging in long-distance trade (Ottenberg, 1959).

Men are able to amass larger capital funds than women because of their traditional control over land. Patterns of land use have been transformed as a result of colonial economic penetration in West Africa. Land has been increasingly removed from the sphere of small-scale family production and transferred to plantations growing produce for national and international markets. Such items as coffee and cocoa are now grown for export rather than for household or local consumption. In this process, control over land has been privatized. Land is no longer allocated by clans and lineages in which women had some contributing voice. Instead, it is owned individually, primarily by men. Many men have turned their land over to commercial farming, growing crops intended for national or export markets. They obtain cash income from the crops produced. Some men do not farm their own land but hire laborers or rent the land to others. Such men may invest their capital in acquiring manufactured goods that they sell in markets.

Markets in Africa have continued to grow in size and complexity, but their overall share in modern economic production and exchange has declined considerably (Mintz, 1971). The predominant share has shifted from the domain of women to that of men.

[In sum, the] traditional predominance of female traders in much of Nigeria is being threatened by the expansion of men's commercial activities. When this development is added to the virtual exclusion of women from export commodity activity, . . . expanded market and commercial opportunities in some spheres of West African trade are probably redounding more to the benefit of the male trader than to that of his spouse. (p. 264)

Igbo women have in the past reacted to threats to their autonomy by organizing collective resistance. An important episode in Nigerian colonial history was the 1929 "women's war" sparked by British authorities' imposition of taxation throughout the countryside. By that time, the British had imposed a system of colonial rule through selecting Igbo men to serve as "warrant chiefs" as intermediaries between the people and British authorities (Van Allen, 1976). Although warrant chiefs were nominally in charge of local courts, they acted at the behest of colonial officials. In 1926, the British began to tax men, but when they attempted to extend taxes to women in 1929, Igbo women in southern Nigeria rose up in protest. The women's war commenced when an Igbo warrant chief, under direction by a British district officer, entered the compound of an influential Igbo woman to count her sheep and goats for purposes of assessing her taxable worth. She and the chief came to blows, a scene witnessed by many other women. The women in the village called a communal meeting and decided to send word to others in the region that trouble was brewing. Women came from neighboring villages, entered the chief's compound, damaged his property, and demanded that the district officer arrest him (Leith-Ross, 1965). By making a formal protest, the women were exercising their traditional rights to demand redress for wrongs committed against them.

Word of events spread to tradeswomen in Aba, a major regional market center. Ten thousand women came to Aba and attacked European stores, banks, and the local prison. Two days of protest ensued, including traditional methods of "making war" such as dancing, singing insults, and publicly airing grievances (Van Allen, 1976). Elsewhere in Igbo territory, crowds of women dressed in war regalia burned European stores and mobbed police stations. The troops attacked the women, resulting in approximately fifty deaths and another fifty injuries.

The women's war ended shortly thereafter. Soldiers carried out punitive measures, burning or demolishing compounds and confiscating food supplies and other property as fines for damages (Van Allen, 1976). But during a Commission of Inquiry investigating the incidents, Igbo women articulated their objections, not solely to taxation but also to the imposition of a colonial system that contributed to undermining their autonomy. One woman said that they were fighting to preserve "the spirit of womanhood." Another remarked, "We are not so happy as we were before. . . . Our grievance is that the land is changed—we are all dying" (Leith-Ross, 1965, pp. 34, 38). Women asked British authorities to appoint some of their number to represent their interests on Native Courts and as district officers, a request "regarded by the British as irrational and ridiculous" (Van Allen, 1976, p. 74). Although some changes were instituted, women's traditional political roles were undermined, and their participation was marginalized.

Shifts in economic participation of women and men in West Africa resulting from colonial control and from the ensuing involvement of local producers in the world economy highlight the importance that trade has for women's status in these societies. As more land is turned over to production of export crops, locally grown produce that women previously bought and sold in markets is no longer available. Craftwork has also declined because of the substitution of traditional handmade cloth and pottery by manufactured clothing and utensils. To the extent that dealing in these latter items requires capital investment, women's participation in trade has generally been eclipsed by increases in men's involvement. With a decline in local market activity, women have become increasingly dependent on their husbands. As a result, women's autonomy has been restricted.

Where women continue to trade, their participation has become marginalized. They remain limited to small-scale, part-time marketing requiring little investment and returning relatively low profits. In modern sectors, most women traders deal individually with local buyers and sellers. Even in urban centers, they tend to be restricted to casual, informal economic spheres. They tend not to be hired as employees in trading establishments, partly because of continued high rates of illiteracy among women and continued cultural discrimination against women (Boserup, 1970).

COMPARING PASTORAL AND HORTICULTURAL SOCIETIES

Data concerning the various societies we have considered indicate several factors that seem to affect development and maintenance of either egalitarian gender relations or male dominance. Ability to exert control over resources is a prominent determinant of people's rights not only in economic domains but in social and political life as well. The specific economic mode on which a society bases its subsistence does not seem to be as significant as the factor of control over distribution of produce and goods. In all of the tribal societies that can be generally characterized as incorporating and enacting egalitarian gender constructs, women exert their rights to make decisions concerning economic activities. These rights are most prominent among the Iroquois, encompassing women's roles in household production and extending their roles as resource distributors into public domains. Navajo women also maintain rights to own resources (namely, sheep) independently and to make decisions concerning their use. Finally, although Igbo culture is characterized by male control in social and political spheres and contains overtly expressed ethics of male superiority, Igbo tradeswomen control market exchanges and benefit both economically and socially from their expertise in this sphere of life.

In contrast, male-dominated societies do not allow women to function autonomously in subsistence or value-producing activities. Among Plains tribes of the nineteenth century, women's productive labor was controlled by their fathers and husbands. Yanomamo women are completely excluded from direct productive work. Such exclusion is then used to justify their social subordination. Among the Nuer, women's work contributes to subsistence because they are assigned the job of milking cows, but their role is overshadowed by men's ownership of cattle and by an ideological link that the Nuer believe exists exclusively between men and cattle.

Examination of historical processes gives further support for the contention that gender constructs are rooted in economic modes. When relations of production have been transformed in a way that limits women's participation, their social and political rights have been restricted, and the social value accorded to women has diminished.

A second societal factor that seems to significantly affect women's and men's rights is postmarital residence rules. Matrilocal societies provide women with continued emotional support from their kin. Iroquoian and Navajo households based on matrilineal affiliation protect women's interests by establishing women's solidarity. In contrast, patrilocal residence patterns detach women from their kin groups and eliminate a potential source of support in the event of conflicts between spouses. Pastoral tribes of the North American Plains and horticulturalists in the South American Amazon all exemplify patrilocal societies that restrict women's physical and social activities. Male dominance is further exerted among these groups by the acceptability of violence against women. In Nuer society, although patrilocality is preferred, matrilocal residence is quite common. Decisions concerning postmarital residence depend on resources available to kin groups of husband or wife and on the numbers of people already living with each set of relatives. In such a flexible social environment, male dominance among the Nuer is possibly weaker than it was among Plains peoples and is certainly weaker than that among Amazonian peoples.

A third factor influencing gender constructs is the degree and type of warfare common in a region. Success in warfare usually confers social prestige on men. However, men's ability to translate their military achievements into control over women in their communities is in part related to the frequency of warfare and to characteristics of warfare. If warfare is absent or infrequent, men are obviously not able to exploit whatever recognition they might receive from engaging in a limited role.

Where warfare is generally directed against distant enemies and therefore requires men's absence from home for extended periods of time, warriors are less able to dominate the households that they have left behind. In addition, this type of external warfare often poses only a minimal threat to people who remain at home—namely, women, children, and elderly men. Iroquois culture exemplifies limits to male control deriving from external warfare.

Warfare directed against nearby settlements, however, creates conditions under which warriors can indeed translate their military dominance into social and especially gender dominance. Men can use their presence in home communities as a continual reminder of their warrior roles by enactment of rituals or other public displays in preparation for and upon return from raids. Furthermore, endemic warfare within a region places noncombatants in mortal danger and therefore assigns men roles as defenders and protectors. Warriors among the Plains and Yanomamo tribes clearly took advantage of their military roles to exert dominance in their settlements and households. Indeed, subordination of women may serve as a reward to compensate men for risks they take in warfare.

In sum, various societal factors make interdependent contributions to development of gender constructs. These constructs derive from social conditions and behaviors but are then justified and entrenched through ideological beliefs. Ideology reinforces and legitimates the prevailing social order. Through socialization processes, the social order is rendered invisible to those who live in it. But it is nonetheless powerful, encouraging both those who benefit and those who suffer to accept their proper roles.

Summary

Farming and pastoral societies exhibit numerous complexities in economies, social systems, and political integration. Some are based solely on a pastoral economy, some are horticulturalists, and others have mixed economies. However, the culture's mode of production seems to be less important in influencing gender constructs than other features of economic and social organization.

Control over resources and the rights to distribute produce and goods are critical in establishing an individual's autonomy and status. Among societies where gender equality is manifested, both women and men enjoy rights to resources, control over distribution of goods, and control over personal and household property. Iroquoian women were the primary producers and distributors of food for their households. They were publicly recognized as owners of farmland. Among the Navajo, both women and men have equal control over productive property (namely, sheep).

In male-dominated societies, men have monopoly control over resources. Yanomamo men were the sole producers of food and other goods. Women controlled no resources and made virtually no contributions to household economies except as processors of food and providers of services. Among the Nuer and the Plains cultures, men owned the animals that symbolized the wealth of their society.

Descent systems differ in the societies discussed. Some are based on matrilineal descent, some on patrilineal kinship, and others on principles of bilateral affiliation. However, the system of descent itself does not seem to be important in determining the quality of gender relations. Rather, postmarital residence rules seem to aid or impede women's autonomy. In matrilocal cultures, women can rely on support and protection from their kin, whereas in patrilocal households, women may be vulnerable to various kinds of restrictions and abuses.

As the economies and social systems of indigenous societies were transformed after European contact, women lost their roles as producers and distributors of resources and goods. Iroquoian women's household and community roles were restricted and marginalized, Plains women became secondary processors of furs and hides for a trade network controlled by men, and Igbo women lost their important status as traders in local and regional markets. In all cases, specific economic changes undermined women's status and resulted in restrictions on their independence.

REFERENCES

BEAUCHAMP, WILLIAM. 1900. "Iroquois women." *Journal of American Folklore,* 8 (49): 81–91.

BENDER, BARBARA. 1978. "Gatherer-hunter to farmer: A social perspective." *World Archaeology,* 10: 361–392.

BINFORD, LEWIS. 1971. "Post-Pleistocene adaptations." In *Prehistoric Agriculture* (ed. S. Struever). Garden City, NY: Natural History Press.

BONVILLAIN, NANCY. 1980. "Iroquoian women." In *Studies on Iroquoian Culture* (ed. Nancy Bonvillain). Man in the Northeast, Occasional Publications in Northeastern Anthropology no. 6, pp. 47–58.

———. 1986. "The Iroquois and the Jesuits: Strategies of influence and resistance." *American Indian Culture & Research Journal,* 10: 29–42.

BOSERUP, ESTER. 1970. *Women's Role in Economic Development.* New York: St. Martin's.

BROWN, JUDITH. 1975. "Economic organization and the position of women among the Iroquois." *Ethnohistory* 17 (1970). Reprinted in *Toward an Anthropology of Women* (ed. Rayna R. Reiter). New York: Monthly Review Press, pp. 235–251.

CARR, LUCIEN. 1883. "On the social and political position of women among the Huron-Iroquois tribes." In *Sixteenth Annual Report of the Peabody Museum of American Archeology and Ethnology,* Cambridge, MA: Peabody Museum, pp. 207–232.

CHAGNON, NAPOLEON. 1968. *Yanomamo: The Fierce People.* New York: Holt, Rinehart & Winston.

———. 1973. "The culture-ecology of shifting (pioneering) cultivation among the Yanomamo Indians." In *Peoples and Cultures of Native South America* (ed. D. Gross). New York: Doubleday Natural History Press, pp. 126–142.

CHARLEVOIX, PIERRE DE. 1761. *Journal of a Voyage to North America.* London: Dodsley. 2 vols. (Original work published 1721)

DIAMOND, JARED. 1995. "The worst mistake in the history of the human race." In *Peoples of the Past and Present* (ed. J.-L. Chodkiewicz). New York: Harcourt Brace, pp. 114–117.

EHRENBERG, MARGARET. 1989. *Women in Prehistory.* Norman: University of Oklahoma Press.

ENGELS, FRIEDERICH. 1972. *The Origin of the Family, Private Property and the State.* New York: International. (Original work published 1884)

EVANS-PRITCHARD, E. E. 1940. *The Nuer.* Oxford: Oxford University Press.

———. 1945. *Some Aspects of Marriage and Family among the Nuer.* Livingstone, Northern Rhodesia: Rhodes-Livingstone Institute.

———. 1951. *Kinship and Marriage among the Nuer.* Oxford: Clardendon.

EWERS, J. 1955. *The Horse in Blackfoot Indian Culture.* Bureau of American Ethnology, Bulletin 159. Washington, D.C.: Smithsonian Institution.

FLANNERY, KENT. 1973. "The origins of agriculture." *Annual Review of Anthropology,* No. 2. 274.

GOUGH, KATHLEEN. 1971. "Nuer kinship: A re-examination." In *The Translation of Culture* (ed. T. Beidelman). London: Tavistock, pp. 79–122.

HAMAMSY, LAILA. 1979. "The role of women in a changing Navajo society." *American Anthropologist,* 59 (1959): 101–111. Reprinted in *Women and Society* (ed. S. Tiffany). Boston: Eden Press Women's Publications, pp. 75–91.

HARRIS, MARVIN. 1974. *Cows, Pigs, Wars and Witches.* New York: Vintage.

HEWITT, J. N. B. 1933. "Status of women in Iroquois polity before 1784." In *Smithsonian Institution Annual Report for 1932,* Washington, D.C.: Smithsonian Institute, pp. 475–488.

HODDER, B. W. 1969. "Markets in Yorubaland." In *Markets in West Africa* (ed. B. W. Hodder and U. I. Ukwu). Ibadan, Nigeria: Ibadan University Press.

HOEBEL, E. A. 1960. *The Cheyenne.* New York: Holt, Rinehart & Winston.

HUNGRY WOLF, BEVERLY. 1980. *The Ways of My Grandmothers.* New York: Morrow.

JABLOW, JOSEPH. 1950. *The Cheyenne in Plains Indian Trade Relations 1795–1840.* American Ethnological Society, Monograph 19. Seattle: University of Washington Press.

KARSTEN, RAPHAEL. 1935. *The Headhunters of Western Amazonas.* Finland: Helsingors.

KELLMAN, SHELLY. 1982. "The Yanomamis: Their battle for survival." *Journal of International Affairs,* 36: 15–42.

KLUCKHOHN, CLYDE, AND DOROTHEA LEIGHTON. 1962. *The Navaho.* New York: Doubleday.

LAFITAU, JOSEPH. 1974. *Customs of the American Indians.* Toronto: Champlain Society. (Original work published 1724)

LEITH-ROSS, SYLVIA. 1965. *African Women.* New York: Praeger.

LEWIS, OSCAR. 1942. *The Effects of White Contact upon Blackfoot Culture.* American Ethnological Society, Monograph 6. Seattle: University of Washington Press.

LINDERMAN, FRANK. 1972. *Pretty-Shield: Medicine Woman of the Crows.* Lincoln: University of Nebraska Press.

LOWIE, ROBERT. 1954. *Indians of the Plains.* New York: McGraw-Hill.

MEGGERS, BETTY. 1971. *Amazonia: Man and Culture in a Counterfeit Paradise.* New York: Free Press.

MINTZ, SIDNEY. 1971. "Men, women, and trade." *Comparative Studies in Society and History,* 13: 247–269.

MISHKIN, BERNARD. 1940. *Rank and Warfare among the Plains Indians.* American Ethnological Society, Monograph 3. Seattle: University of Washington Press.

MORGAN, LEWIS. 1877. *Ancient Society.* New York: Holt.

MURPHY, YOLANDA, AND ROBERT MURPHY. 1974. *Women of the Forest.* New York: Columbia University Press.

OKEYO, ACHOLA PALA. 1980. "Daughters of the lakes and rivers: Colonization and the land rights of Luo women." In *Women and Colonization* (ed. M. Etienne and E. Leacock). New York: Praeger, pp. 186–213.

OKONJO, KAMENE. 1976. "The dual-sex political system in operation: Igbo women and community politics in midwestern Nigeria." In *Women in Africa* (ed. N. Hafkin and E. Bays). Stanford, CA: Stanford University Press, pp. 45–58.

OTTENBERG, PHOEBE. 1959. "The changing economic position of women among the Afikpo Ibo." In *Continuity and Change in African Cultures* (ed. William Bascom and Melville Herskovits). Chicago: University of Chicago Press, pp. 205–233.

———. 1965. "The Afikpo Ibo of Eastern Nigeria." In *Peoples of Africa* (ed. James L Gibbs). New York: Holt. Rinehart & Winston, pp. 3–39.

OTTENBERG, SIMON, AND PHOEBE OTTENBERG. 1962. "Afikpo markets 1900–1960." In *Markets in Africa* (ed. P. Bohannan and G. Dalton). Evanston, IL: Northwestern University Press, pp. 117–169.

ROTHENBERG, DIANE. 1980. "The Mothers of the Nation: Seneca resistance to Quaker intervention." In *Women and Colonization* (ed. M. Etienne and E. Leacock). New York: Praeger, pp. 63–87.

SAGARD, GABRIEL. 1939. *Long Journey to the Country of the Huron* (ed. G. Wrong). Toronto: Champlain Society. (Original work published 1632)

SHAPIRO, JUDITH. 1976. "Sexual hierarchy among the Yanomamo." In *Sex and Class in Latin America* (ed. J. Nash and H. Safa). New York: Praeger, pp. 86–101.

SISKIND, JANET. 1973. "Tropical forest hunters and the economy of sex." In *Peoples and Cultures of Native South America* (ed. D. Gross). New York: Doubleday Natural History Press, pp. 226–240.

SMITH, BRUCE. 1987 "The independent domestication of the indigenous seed-bearing plants in eastern North America." In *Emergent Horticultural Economies of the Eastern Woodlands* (ed. W. Keegan). Carbondale: Center for Archaeological Investigations, Southern Illinois University, Occasional Paper No. 7, pp. 3–47.

SMOLE, WILLIAM. 1976. *The Yanomamo Indians.* Austin: University of Texas Press.

THWAITES, REUBEN (ed.). 1906. *Jesuit Relations and Allied Documents 1610–1791 [JR].* Cleveland: Burroughs. 73 vols.

UKWU, I. U. 1969. "Markets in Iboland." In *Markets in West Africa* (ed. B. W. Hodder and I. U. Ukwu). Ibadan, Nigeria: Ibadan University Press, pp. 113–250.

VAN ALLEN, JUDITH. 1976. "'Aba Riots' or Igbo 'Women's War'? Ideology, stratification, and the invisibility of women." In *Women in Africa: Studies in Social and Economic Change* (ed. N. Hafkin and E. Bay). Stanford, CA: Stanford University Press.

WALLACE, A. F. C. 1961. "Cultural composition of the Handsome Lake Religion." In *Symposium on Cherokee and Iroquois Culture* (ed. W. Fenton and J. Gulick). Washington, D.C.: Bureau of American Ethnology Bulletin 180, pp. 143–151.

———. 1970. *Death and Rebirth of the Seneca Nation.* New York: Knopf.

WATSON, PATTY JO, and MARY KENNEDY. 1991. "The development of horticulture in the Eastern Woodlands of North America: Women's role." In *Engendering Archaeology: Women and Prehistory* (ed. M. Conkey and J. Gero). Cambridge: Basil Blackwell, pp. 255–272.

WEISS, LAWRENCE. 1984. *The Development of Capitalism in the Navajo Nation.* Minneapolis: MEP Publications, University of Minnesota.

WHITE, RICHARD. 1983. *The Roots of Dependency: Subsistence, Environment, and Social Change among the Choctaws, Pawnees, and Navajos.* Lincoln: University of Nebraska Press.

WITHERSPOON, GARY. 1975. *Navajo Kinship and Marriage.* Chicago: University of Chicago Press.

WRIGHT, RITA. 1991. "Women's labor and pottery production in prehistory." In *Engendering Archaeology: Women and Prehistory* (ed. M. Conkey and J. Gero). Cambridge: Basil Blackwell, pp. 194–223.

CHAPTER 4

Stratified Societies

In societies characterized by systems of social stratification, relations among individuals and kinship groups are founded not on egalitarian principles but rather on hierarchical ranking of people. The degree of segmentation and the strength of hierarchy vary cross-culturally. In some cultures, **rank** is of less consequence for social, economic, and political functioning than in others. In some chiefdoms, egalitarian ethics continue to organize relationships among people; in others, inequality and differentiation dominate societal interactions. Effects of stratification on gender constructs also vary. In some, gender relations are relatively egalitarian. Principles of men's and women's autonomy and worth may be socially recognized and ideologically supported. However, stratification in many chiefdoms may be based on the exercise of economic and political control by individual men competing with each other and/or by men as a group acting to restrict women's rights.

In this chapter, we examine data concerning representative stratified societies in three areas of the world: the Canadian Pacific coast, Africa, and Polynesia. We focus on interrelationships among social stratification, economic inequality, and political inequality and on the development of gender hierarchies. Historical transformations resulting from foreign contact and colonization are also considered as they affect gender relations.

THE HAIDA AND TLINGIT OF THE CANADIAN PACIFIC COAST

Native peoples inhabiting the Canadian Pacific coastal region developed cultures that were unusual in several respects. Although their economies were based on foraging, they lived in large stable villages and had complex systems of social ranking founded on individual and class differences. Pacific coast societies were, indeed, the sole examples worldwide of chiefdoms with a subsistence centered on foraging. As we discussed in Chapter 2, foraging societies tend to live in small, dispersed, temporary settlements. Social and political relations among foragers tend to be egalitarian and loosely structured.

Cultures of Pacific coast peoples, then, contrast sharply with the characteristic foraging mode. The uniqueness of these peoples is due in part to environmental conditions that differ dramatically from those experienced by most foraging groups documented in the ethnographic record. Unlike the scarcity of resources endured by many foragers, the Pacific Northwest provides an abundant variety of foods in different seasons. Moderate temperatures and frequent rainfall support an array of plants, fruits, and nuts that are readily gathered. The Pacific Ocean and numerous rivers, inlets, and lakes teem with fish and aquatic mammals. Dense forests are inhabited by many species of small and large animals. People living in this region are able to collect enough food not only for their daily survival but also for accumulation of large surpluses used in trade and in ceremonial displays and feasts.

The Tlingit (TLING-git) of Alaska and the Haida (HAI-da) of the Queen Charlotte Islands off the coast of British Columbia exemplify many cultural elements common to Pacific coast peoples. Their economies and sociopolitical organizations illustrate regional characteristics. Economic activities were allocated according to gender. Subsistence labor was intense during summer months when salmon, other species of fish, aquatic mammals such as otters and seals, and land animals such as beaver, deer, and moose were most plentiful. Men were primarily engaged in fishing and hunting these varied resources. Women were responsible for gathering the abundant wild plants, seaweed, fruits, and nuts. Their work also included the vital task of preserving and storing fish and meat caught during the summer. Fruits and some plants were also dried and stored. Large surpluses amassed in a short period of time were kept for use throughout the year. People were then freed of most subsistence activities and spent a good deal of time in social, ceremonial, and political activities. In autumn, Tlingit and Haida men set off on trading expeditions, exchanging their surpluses for those of other peoples supplied with their own distinct resources. Utilitarian and luxury goods such as wooden bowls, woven reed blankets, and decorated ornaments were also bartered. During winter months, ceremonial activities were prominent, including rituals of community renewal and initiation into ceremonial societies. Springtime was a period for preparation of fishing and hunting equipment in anticipation of the cycle of summer subsistence work.

Tlingit and Haida society was organized through matrilineal clans that determined descent, restricted marriage possibilities through rules of clan exogamy, and influenced patterns of residence. Clans were corporate groups, owning large plank houses in which their members lived and controlling access to resource areas. Clans also owned social property in the form of hereditary titles and chieftainships. Finally, they possessed ceremonial goods such as ritual paraphernalia and sacred myths and songs.

Within each clan, lineages were allotted economic resources and material and social property. Each lineage habitually used certain areas of beachfront and forest for fishing and hunting. Unity of lineages was demonstrated in settlement and housing patterns. Households were based on matrilineal affiliation, with a preference for **avunculocal residence**. Houses were ideally inhabited by a man, his own nuclear family, and his sisters' sons and their families. Boys sometimes went to live with one of their mother's brothers at about the age of puberty, although they might not make the move until after marriage. Avunculocal residence was consistent with the need to consolidate matrilineages in a social system emphasizing the prerogative of men to represent their kin groups. Households were headed by senior men. Lineages and **clans** were led by chiefs—that is, men who bore hereditary titles owned by their kin group.

The most important, highest-ranking man in a house was designated as the house chief. Similarly, the highest-ranking house chief in a clan was referred to as the clan chief, and the highest-ranking clan chief in a town was the town chief. Although these chiefs had no actual political power and could not control the actions of others, their position bestowed social prestige on the incumbent and necessitated public ratification in the form of ceremonial feasts.

When a man assumed a new title or chieftainship, he sponsored a public communal feast, called a *potlatch*. The chief invited people from rival clans to a potlatch at which he and his lineage mates displayed their wealth and distributed gifts of food and utilitarian and ceremonial objects to the assembled guests. Prestige accrued to a potlatch giver who was able to amass and distribute more wealth than had been given at previous feasts. In this way, potlatches were competitive and served both to raise the status of a host and to demean the position of guests, who subsequently attempted to outdo their former hosts at a later date.

Chiefs were wealthy and sought to increase their fortune and prestige through hard work and manipulation of kinship obligations to persuade their relatives to contribute goods to potlatches that the chiefs sponsored. In return, chiefs were generous, helpful, and conscientious in fulfilling responsibilities to their kin. As the prestige of a chief increased, so did the social status of his relatives. Links between the status of a chief and that of his kin offered a strong incentive for the latter's cooperation in a chief's potlatching.

Through feasting and redistributive giveaways, potlatching facilitated the intersection of native social and economic systems. Amassing, saving, and distributing wealth were critical social and economic goals. The status of hosts was validated, and the productive resources of a community were shared.

The social order of Tlingit and Haida societies was ranked, based on a combination of kinship, membership in social strata, and individual prestige. In addition to membership in lineages and clans, Tlingit and Haida people were identified according to three social groupings, generally referred to in English as "nobles," "commoners," and "slaves." The nobility consisted of chiefs, their matrilineal kin, and their own sons and daughters. Nobles were said to own houses and to be holders of the most prestigious hereditary titles. Nobles and their families were well respected and had "respect for themselves" (Blackman, 1982, p. 24).

Commoners were not respected and, among the Haida at least, were out-numbered by the nobles. They owned fewer possessions than the nobles. Commoners were said to be lazy and careless about their speech and demeanor. The slave class consisted of war captives or people purchased as slaves from other Pacific coast or inland groups. Their descendants were also in this class. Slaves were owned by nobles who thus benefited from their labor. Although chieftainships were held primarily by men, women sometimes became chiefs, principally if their lineages had no capable man to assume the position. But even in the absence of women's roles as chiefs, women's labor was crucial to the potlatching system. As already noted, women were responsible for preserving fish and other foods that could later be consumed or distributed to guests at potlatches. Women, then, not only were involved in household production but also had publicly recognized roles as distributors of resources in their communities. In addition, women were said to be responsible for protecting the household supplies that were given at potlatches. According to Laura Klein (1980):

> If a man had a good fishing season but was left with little material wealth at its end with which to potlatch or trade, it was his wife who was to blame. It is in a man's nature, it is said, to be friendly and to share good fortune with friends while it is a woman's responsibility to keep this tendency in check. (p. 93)

In addition to potlatches given to validate chiefs, feasts were sponsored by members of chiefly or commoner families for many different purposes. Some accompanied rites of passage, including rituals performed after a birth, naming of an infant, a girl's first menstruation, marriage, and death. These feasts marked social transitions and celebrated the unity of a family by publicly acknowledging important personal occasions.

Both men and women benefited from potlatches in numerous ways. They received gifts as guests and could function as hosts. Many types of potlatches were given by either gender. For example, women and men assumed new names and titles through public feasts. Among the Haida, both men and women sponsored potlatches to mark rites of passage, to avenge a wrong committed by someone else, or to redress a slight committed by the host. Some types of potlatches, though, tended to be associated exclusively with each gender. Funerary feasts and potlatches marking the building of a new house were hosted by men; potlatches celebrating a girl's puberty were hosted by women, typically a girl's father's sister (Blackman, 1982).

Gender equality in the potlatching system was demonstrated by the fact that sons and daughters were equally recognized through feasts given by their parents. A son's or daughter's birth, naming, puberty, marriage, and other accomplishments were publicly celebrated. The Haida expressed preferences for the birth of daughters, recognizing women's responsibility for procreation and continuity of matrilineages, but boys were also desired because they aided their maternal uncles in amassing wealth and eventually succeeded to uncles' titles and positions.

Maternal uncles had decisive roles in their nephews' and nieces' lives. They were involved in arranging marriages for these kin. Among the Haida, for example, marriage proposals were made by a boy's maternal uncle, who led a delegation of male matrilineal kin to the home of a girl's maternal uncle. Parents, especially mothers, of the prospective couple could offer advice, but the final decision was made by the uncle. Maternal uncles also bequeathed property to their nephews and were instrumental in selecting an heir to their own titles.

Even though Tlingit and Haida cultural constructs validated the equality of women and men, women were socialized to be somewhat deferential toward their husbands. Wives were expected to "show respect" to their husbands and to acquiesce to them in daily activities. George Murdock (1934) noted, however, that husbands did not assert their prerogatives in public and would be "ashamed" to do so. Men did not abuse their wives or deprive them of their essential autonomy.

Women owned property and had recognized rights to dispose of it as they chose. A woman's property remained her own after marriage and did not merge with that of her husband. The principle of individual control of goods and houses worked against women, though, in the event of divorce or the death of husbands. Divorce was fairly common and could be initiated by either spouse. Because men owned the houses in which they and their families lived, a divorced wife returned to her father's or brother's residence. A widow was expected to marry a man of her husband's lineage, preferably a younger brother or nephew. These men were often many years junior to the widow. Her seniority gave her a great deal of influence over her young husband, but she had little, if any, choice in selecting her spouse (Blackman, 1982). If a widow did not remarry quickly, she was obliged to leave her deceased husband's house. Although widowers also tended to remarry, often marrying a sister of their deceased wife, they had more latitude in choosing a spouse and, in any case, had no fears of being forced to leave their homes.

Pacific coast cultures conveyed complex messages about women's and men's status and authority. In some domains, separation of tasks and rights was clearly demarcated. Subsistence activities were allocated according to gender; rights to inheritance of property were differentiated so that women inherited goods from their mothers, whereas men inherited property and titles from their mother's brothers; interpersonal demeanor was at least ideally gender linked. However, egalitarian valuation of women and men was a prevailing principle and led to the essential independence and autonomy of both.

Equal, although different, participation of men and women in the potlatch system was a crucial reflection of societal attitudes. Although men generally succeeded to chiefly titles, women's roles in potlatching were recognized. Women had responsibility for accumulating gifts to be distributed and in apportioning those gifts to guests. According to observers of the Tlingit in the late nineteenth century, "since very ancient times the women have been the keepers of the family treasures, they are generally in a position to dictate terms" (Knapp and Childe, 1896; quoted in Klein, 1980, p. 94).

Rights of Tlingit women to "dictate terms" extended from household and community distribution to market exchanges. Trading along the Pacific coast and inland territory was a traditional endeavor of Northwest peoples. Although most traders were men, women frequently participated in expeditions. According to Klein (1980), a woman often accompanied men to "assure that the male traders got a good return for their goods. She, in other words, set the prices" (p. 94).

Women's participation in trade continued after contact with European merchants. Pacific coast peoples became engaged in the Euro-American fur trade beginning in the eighteenth century. They were contacted by Russian, Spanish, British, and American traders who sought skins of otter, marten, seal, and fox. As elsewhere in North America, native peoples obtained manufactured goods in exchange for animal furs. A large variety of goods was procured, but the majority of items were iron tools and guns that contributed most to men's activities and thus favored men's roles. Household supplies such as flour, cloth, and kettles were also obtained (Blackman, 1982).

Many European traders complained about the hard bargains driven by native women and native men's insistence on complying with their wives' terms. As Klein (1980) comments:

> There are a number of stories [from the nineteenth century] that tell of deals vetoed by wives and of men who refused to go to a certain trading post because the trader's native wife would not allow them to cheat him. The manipulation and saving of wealth was in the hands of women; this is considered their duty and responsibility. (p. 93)

Numerous accounts by European traders contain complaints against the influence of native women and the acquiescence of native men. For example, Wood (1882) recounted:

> The Alaskan [Tlingit] women are childish and pleasant, yet quick-witted and capable of heartless vindictiveness. Their authority in all matters is unquestioned. No bargain is made, no expedition set on foot, without first consulting the women. Their veto is never disregarded. I bought a silver-fox skin from Tsatate, but his wife made him return the articles of trade and recover the skin, in the same way I was perpetually being annoyed at having to undo bargains because "his wife said *clekh,*" that is, "no." I hired a fellow to take me about thirty miles in his canoe, when my own crew was tired. He agreed, I paid him the tobacco, and we were about to start when his wife came to the beach and stopped him. He quietly unloaded the canoe and handed me back the tobacco. (quoted in Klein, 1980, p. 97)

Although Wood may have exaggerated the "unquestioned" authority of Tlingit women, his accounts accurately indicate the importance attributed to women's opinions and their contributions to family decisions. Independence and social prestige of women were not limited to the Tlingit. Europeans who traded with the Haida noted, with annoyance, the same patterns. For example, Joseph Ingraham, writing in the 1971, commented:

> Here in direct opposition to most other parts of the world, the women maintain a precedency to the men in every point insomuch as a man dares not trade without the concurrence of his wife. Nay, I have often been witness to men being abused by their wives for parting with skins before their approbation was obtained. (quoted in Blackman, 1982, p. 35)

Other observers occasionally described physical beatings meted out by women to their husbands who traded without consent, one noting, "[T]here is no mercy to be expected without the intercession of some kind female" (quoted in Blackman, 1982, p. 35). Although some traders' comments were probably exaggerated, they demonstrate two noteworthy points. One is the fact of women's autonomy in their own activities and their influence over those of their husbands. The second is Europeans' propensity to be amazed—and annoyed—at the independence of native women.

Economic and political changes wrought by contact between Pacific coast peoples and European, American, and Canadian merchants and officials have had varied effects on traditional gender relations. In some ways, social transformations have supported underlying principles of gender equality, but in other respects, women's status was negatively affected. Among the latter consequences, an early impact of European trade on women's lives was the high incidence of prostitution. According to numerous accounts throughout the nineteenth century, women sometimes prostituted themselves voluntarily; in other cases, their sexual services were exploited by male relatives. Not only was women's personal degradation involved in this business, but venereal disease evidently spread rapidly and caused many illnesses and deaths. Population decline among Pacific peoples resulted directly from deaths from syphillis and also from frequent cases of infertility among survivors (Blackman, 1982).

Swift decreases in population, additionally caused by widespread disastrous epidemics of smallpox in the late nineteenth century, led to a marked emphasis on women's procreative roles to ensure community survival. This responsibility can be viewed as both positive and negative. It clearly recognized women's vital contribution to their lineages, but it also increased physical and social burdens for mothers.

Another societal impact resulting from drastic population declines was the creation of imbalances between the number of chiefly titles and the availability of qualified men to assume them. As a consequence, noble women were frequently selected to be chiefs. Any gain in women's status from their positions as chiefs and the ensuing prestige obtained through potlatching was soon undermined by laws enacted by the Canadian government that established a system of elected leaders to replace hereditary chiefs. The government also implemented policies that ended in dividing lands traditionally held communally by lineages into individual allotments assigned to men as heads of households. These changes decreased women's authority and social prestige.

Canadian authorities, prompted by Anglican missionaries, attempted to eradicate potlatching, which they viewed as a wasteful pagan ceremony. Pacific coast peoples continued to potlatch, although traditional public displays were transformed into private household feasts. The emphasis on potlatching as a household activity reestablished important roles for women. Not only did women hold prominent positions as hosts or wives of hosts, but the objects used as potlatch gifts shifted from those associated with men to those associated with women. Among the Haida, for example, instead of spoons and feast bowls traditionally carved and owned by men, potlatch distributions generally involved china, silverware, and tablecloths considered to be women's property.

Division of clan and lineage land by Canadian authorities and assignment of land to individuals affected household composition and the position of women. Land ownership usually was awarded to men, thus undermining women's prestige as the persons through whom inheritance ensued. Nuclear family households further isolated wives from their matrilineal kin. The new system was accompanied by increased recognition of the authority of husbands and fathers.

Innovations in Pacific coast economies also had varied impacts on gender roles. As already discussed, men's and women's labor and decision-making rights continued in the context of Euro-American trade in the nineteenth century. By the early twentieth century, commercial fishing replaced the fur trade as a major source of income for indigenous peoples in the region. Because fishing had always been a prestigious male occupation, men readily shifted from providing fish for domestic and ceremonial consumption to working for commercial fisheries. Women's traditional roles as processors and preservers of fish were similarly transferred to industry as women were widely employed in numerous canneries in British Columbia. Although both men's and women's traditional work has been transferred to the modern economy, men's labor is given greater social prestige and compensated with higher salaries. Women therefore are likely to at least partially depend on their husbands' incomes. Subsequent changes in the fishing industry altered women's opportunities. Due to declines in profits from small-scale local operations, many canneries were closed. Ensuing unemployment has disproportionately affected women workers, whereas men are still engaged as fishers, boatsmen, and dockworkers. Many women have shifted to employment in service and retail sectors. These jobs are generally paid at low rates. However, their availability has encouraged women to continue their educations to acquire literacy and other skills necessary for public jobs (Klein, 1980).

Many insights into Pacific coast cultures, and both the change and continuity of traditional gender roles, can be gleaned from two published autobiographies of native people, one recounting the life of a Haida woman, Florence Davidson (Blackman, 1982), and the other of a Kwakiutl man, James Sewid (Spradley, 1972). Kwakiutl culture is similar in its general content to that of the Haida and Tlingit with the exception that Kwakiutl kinship is organized around patrilineal rather than matrilineal clans. Because Kwakiutl men inherit titles and property from their fathers, fathers and sons form the basic kinship and coresidence groups. In many significant respects, Davidson's and Sewid's lives display similar themes. Both people are concerned with having "respect for oneself." Respect also should be shown to others. By fulfilling kinship and community obligations, all people, both men and women, gain respect and prestige in their society.

Davidson and Sewid are high-status people who would be referred to in the traditional social system as "nobles." Sewid is the holder of chiefly titles, inherited through his own lineage and clan as well as from relatives of his wife. Davidson, the daughter of a well-known Haida carver, is a member of a chiefly family and the wife of a titled man. Respect, therefore, accrues to them in part because of their social status. However, high rank entails many responsibilities. As in the past, these responsibilities include interpersonal behaviors and community actions. As individuals, people of high status must be considerate of others, show moderation and self-control, and carry themselves with a dignified demeanor. In addition, they should help others in their communities who are less fortunate. Davidson's circle of concern tends to be more limited than that of Sewid. Her activities revolve around church-sponsored events and neighborhood "doings." In contrast, Sewid is an elected leader and has served as chief of his village and as a Kwakiutl representative to native organizations in British Columbia and elsewhere in Canada.

Although the difference in Davidson's and Sewid's spheres of activity is partly attributable to their personalities, their gender is probably an additional factor. Indeed, the difference in their personalities is likely attributable to their socialization into gender. As discussed earlier, Haida women were taught to be deferential toward their husbands. The fact that this traditional ideal is still valued is demonstrated by Davidson's experience: "Before I got married my mother used to tell me to have respect for my husband. Don't let him wash dishes or his own clothes. She told me not to wash my husband's clothes with mine, to keep his separate" (Blackman, 1982, p. 94). The latter restriction followed from Haida notions of gender separation and ritualized avoidances. Men's activities, especially their economic success, could be harmfully affected by contact with a woman's menstrual blood.

Women's behavior was often expected to be circumspect. Women were socialized to take care not to offend others and not to be domineering or boastful. As a woman fulfilled the valued roles of wife and mother, she gained respect and was able to widen her circle of activities and influence. Elder women, particularly those from high-status families and those with many children, can take on positions of prestige and leadership. Davidson, for example, is a deacon active in the local Anglican church and a giver of elaborate feasts and potlatches.

Men, too, are not expected to take prominent roles in their communities until they are more experienced and older, although the age at which they begin to exercise their influence is younger than for women. Men of high rank are socialized at an early age to prepare themselves for later positions of responsibility and prominence. For instance, Sewid was given much attention as a child because he was the eldest son of a highly titled man who died shortly before the younger Sewid's birth. All of the father's names and positions thus passed to his son (Spradley, 1972). Sewid describes the attitudes and actions of his family in terms of "respect" given to him because of his social position and inheritance:

> Mary Bell [Sewid's maternal grandmother] had a lot of respect for me. She thought the world of me just like my other grandmother, old Lucy [Sewid's paternal grandmother]. Mary used to speak very highly of me and she did everything I wanted her to do as a young boy. If I asked her to do anything for me she would do it. It was the Indian custom to always put the oldest child first in everything they did and then the rest would follow. Since I was born to a well-to-do and very highly respected family and was the oldest son they treated me with respect. The Indian custom was all respect, and they were going to try to respect me in the same way that they would have respected my father if he had still been alive. (p. 26)

It is important to note that Sewid's words are not boastful of his own qualities but rather that they recount the prestige accorded to him as an incumbent of a respected social position. As Sewid recalled:

> They [Sewid's relatives] were all teaching me how to be a leader of my people when I grew up. Cause this was the aim of my parents. They wanted to see me uphold my name, because this would be the beginning of our name which had been down, lost these past years when my grandfather died and my father died, and there was a gap between them. And that's all they used to tell me when I was a little boy, "Never forget that name." (p. 44)

The strength of kin ties and obligations are strikingly demonstrated in both Davidson's and Sewid's lives in the periods preceding their marriages. Both entered arranged marriages against their own personal wishes. In Sewid's case, he was a teenager, not quite 14 years old, when he overheard his mother and grandparents discussing plans to propose a marriage to the parents of a 15-year-old girl. Although Sewid expressed his objections in private to his mother on the grounds that he was too young, his feelings were ignored. Even his grandmother, with whom he felt emotionally close, discounted his resistance, claiming that it was her happiest wish to see him married and a father before she died. Sewid then acquiesced:

> Well, that is what made me kind of give in. I didn't want to get married but of course I had no business to my own personal opinion. I had no business to try and argue or anything like that because I knew that the older people knew what was right for me. I never did like to argue with anybody that was older than me but I always liked to respect what they said to me. (p. 67)

That Sewid's wife-to-be, Flora Alfred, was a member of a high-status family and would bring with her the access to prestigious titles were undoubtedly recognized as benefits to the marriage. As an additional incentive, given the competitive context of Kwakiutl culture, "There were quite a few people who wanted to marry Flora Alfred. A lot of these families heard about me getting the best of them and they tried everything to stop it" (p. 67). Once the marriage was set, Sewid adjusted to it well and recalled that his wedding, occurring in December, was "the best Christmas present I had in my life" (pp. 70–71).

Although in retrospect Davidson also recalled happy years of married life, her feelings in opposition to her marriage continued beyond the ceremony itself. A proposal was brought to Davidson's parents by lineage relatives of her husband-to-be. Her parents made no comment but referred the delegation to her maternal uncle, in keeping with traditional rights of a maternal uncle to decide on marriages for his sister's children. When Davidson was informed by her mother, she was advised "not to say anything about the proposal because they were high-class people" (Blackman, 1982, p. 95). Davidson, who was 14 years old at the time, objected because she felt she was too young and wanted to continue her schooling. Her mother countered with sentiments similar to those expressed by Sewid's relatives:

> Don't say anything. Your uncle thinks it's best for you to marry him. He's a noble. He's going to respect you all your life and if you don't want to marry him you're going to feel bad all your life. He belongs to clever people; you're not going to be hard up for anything. We need a young man's help, too. You must remember that. We belong to chiefs too and you're not supposed to talk any old way. You have to respect yourself more than what you worry about. (p. 96)

Although Davidson continued to resent her forthcoming marriage, she decided "not to say anything much as I disliked it." But her internal resistance came to the fore during the ceremony: She refused to utter the marital pledges. Davidson recalled:

> I was stubborn. I guess I thought I wouldn't be really married if I didn't answer when they asked me. I felt bad the whole time. . . . I felt real bad because I was a married woman. Everybody but me was real happy. I don't remember any more about the wedding, it was too awful. (p. 99)

Despite this inauspicious beginning, Davidson grew to be pleased with her marriage. Her life with her husband, Robert Davidson, clearly exemplified the respect Haida couples ideally show toward each other and the complementary interdependence and autonomy that each experiences.

The Kpelle of Liberia

In contrast to Pacific coast societies, male dominance may be an expressed ideological construct in some stratified societies. However, even in many such cultures, women and men may lead autonomous lives, each gender receiving positive social recognition. West African cultures offer examples of the combination of men's dominance and women's autonomy. For instance, the Kpelle (KPE-lay) of Liberia exemplify some characteristic West African cultural practices. Among the Kpelle, gender constructs support the "belief in the formal superiority of men over women" (Gibbs, 1965, p. 230). But examination of the roles and rights of women and men reveals that women make significant recognized contributions to their families and have both economic and social independence despite public control exercised by men.

Kpelle economy is based on farming, providing both food for subsistence and surplus sold for cash income. Rice is the most important crop, although a wide variety of other foods are grown, including manioc, yams, okra, bananas, citrus fruits, and peanuts. Some phases of farming are joint activities of men and women and others are gender linked. Men cut down trees in fields in preparation for plantin, and then women and men clear the fields of undergrowth. Men and women engage in farming, although the crops produced are distinct: men are responsible for producing rice; supplies of other foods are in women's domain and are obtained by their labor.

A couple farms on land allotted to men as heads of households within patrilineages. Land controlled by patrilineages is awarded to men as the last link in a chain of hierarchical jurisdictions. All Kpelle land is said to be owned by paramount chiefs, each of whom controls his own territory. Within the jurisdiction of each paramount chief, lands are divided into towns under the stewardship of town chiefs. In turn, towns are divided into sections administered by section elders. Finally, elders divide their sections into acreage for each patrilineage resident within them. Grants of land entail **usufruct rights** under the control of heads of households. A man, then, gains use rights as a member of a patrilineage. Women work on land allocated to their husbands.

Although men are the holders of land use rights, women have a great deal of control over the produce of the land. They make decisions about which crops to grow and in what amount. According to Gibbs (1965):

> One of [a woman's] significant roles is regulating the flow of rice from the granary. Keeping the key, she guards the reserve of seed rice and also determines how much rice is to be used for subsistence and how much her husband may sell. (p. 208)

In addition, women determine the planting of other crops on acreage allotted to them by their husbands. They "have complete control over the income from these individual plots" (p. 201).

Women obtain income from the sale of surplus produce. Unlike numerous peoples in West Africa, the Kpelle do not participate in large regional markets, but many women sell a portion of their crops to people in their villages or to travelers who stop by to purchase food from displays in front of a woman's house. Some women sell only raw produce; others sell prepared foods and crafts, especially pottery and net bags. Income derived from market sales is controlled by the woman who earns it.

Kpelle households consist of nuclear families residing in proximity to kin based on principles of patrilineal descent and affiliation. That is, nuclear dwellings headed by men are located near those of their fathers and/or brothers. Members of a polygynous family all live in the same house, although each wife has her own room that she shares with her children. A man's economic responsibilities include his obligation to supply his wife (or wives) and children with rice and to fulfill other material needs such as provision of clothing and household goods. Material items are purchased by cash obtained from sale of rice and other products as well as from occasional wage labor on nearby plantations. In addition to monetary expenses incurred to supply their households, men are currently required by the Liberian government to pay hut taxes in cash.

Marriage patterns among the Kpelle provide several options entailing differences in the strength of bonds between couples and the rights that a man exercises over children born of the union. The ideal form of marriage involves transfer of bridewealth from a husband's patrilineage to that of his wife. This is the standard normative type of union. It permits a husband and his lineage to claim children produced by the marriage. A second form involves performance of bride service rather than payment of bridewealth. In this type of marriage, a couple resides with the wife's family for a fixed period of time agreed upon by the parties concerned. During this period, the husband performs labor for his **affines**. Children born to the couple during the years of service belong to the wife's lineage rather than to the husband's.

A third marital option is "male concubinage." It entails a union between a poor man and one of the wives of a chief or wealthy man. Such a marriage provides benefits for two kinds of men. First, a poor man who would otherwise have few marital prospects can marry and ally himself with a wealthy person. Second, a wealthy man who is either already a chief or aspires to become one can gain clients in a dependent relationship. The client's dependence is translated into political support for the patron. Because the client and the patron's wife farm land controlled by the patron, the latter obtains products of their labor that he can sell for cash income or can distribute to others in displays of generosity. Finally, because the woman remains the legal wife of the patron, children born to the client couple belong to the patron's lineage rather than to that of their biological father.

Kpelle marriages, then, are basically differentiated in terms of the legal status of women and the ensuing rights that men and their lineages may claim over a woman's children. If a woman is a full legal wife—that is, in a standard marriage with payment of bridewealth—her children belong to her husband's patrilineage. If a woman's legal status is in transition—that is, during the period of bride service—her children belong to her patrilineage and cannot be claimed by her husband. If a woman is the legal wife of a patron even though she lives with another man, her children belong to the patron.

Determination of social rights to children is critical in cases of divorce as well as in forms of marriage. Rates of divorce among the Kpelle are "moderately high" according to Gibbs (1965). Divorces are granted by formal courts under the jurisdiction of district chiefs. Proceedings involve public hearings to determine the party at fault. Women usually initiate divorce, in part because fixing of blame is most often placed on the initiator, and men are reluctant to be publicly criticized. Even though women are characteristically blamed for failure of their marriages, their request to be divorced is usually granted. A man who wishes a divorce may mistreat his wife so she will seek a formal divorce in court. In this manipulative manner, he obtains his objective but is not publicly faulted.

In several respects, divorce benefits both wife and husband in an unhappy marriage. A wife who seeks a divorce is given her freedom and thus is personally satisfied. A husband, whether or not he wants to be divorced, retains two prerogatives: he receives the return of bridewealth that he had initially transferred to his wife's kin, and he retains rights as father to his children. Such rights significantly include the privilege of receiving bridewealth for his daughters when they marry.

Although women and their children are clearly manipulated in Kpelle marriages and divorces, women have socially recognized rights to fair treatment. According to Gibbs, relations between spouses are properly marked with "reserve and respect." One symbolic expression of spousal relationships is the linguistic usage of "respect forms" couples employ in addressing each other.

Despite ideological constructs supporting male dominance, Kpelle women exercise their autonomy stemming from critical roles in household economies. Moreover, their productive roles are not confined to the domestic sphere. Women sell crops they plant and crafts they create. And they control the dispersal of income derived from their labor. Women's contributions are acknowledged by their husbands' lack of interference in their pursuits. If a woman experiences abuse or extreme personal domination from her husband, she has the option of seeking a divorce. As Gibbs (1965) notes:

> The crucial role women play in farming and in regulating the household economy means that they are a source of wealth and much sought after. Knowing this, they are quick to leave a husband who displeases them, for they are always welcome elsewhere. (p. 214)

One place where a woman is always welcome is in the polygynous household of a wealthy man who aspires to become a chief. Chiefs are selected by councils of elders from among members of the Kpelle upper class, called "upright persons." Men in this class are influential and respected. They must also be generous and helpful to people in need. Through their generosity, wealthy men gain political support and use this support in their bids to be chosen as chiefs. Such men often attract dependent clients through agreeing to unions between their wives and poor men. Wealthy families enjoy some slight benefits in standards of living relative to those of common people, but differences are minimal. The major advantage to wealth is the social prestige and influence associated with it. Such social rewards are derived from the successful manipulation of wealth and the successful manipulation of the dependent people it attracts.

Two additional classes comprise the majority of Kpelle society. The middle class consists of ordinary people who have use rights to land in territory allotted to their patrilineages. The lowest class consists of poor people who for various reasons have little or no land and therefore must work for others either in paid service or through patron-client relations.

In sum, Kpelle society, and numerous similar cultures in West Africa, contain mixed messages about gender. An ideology of male superiority is reflected in political authority of men, in men's control of land, and in men's manipulation of women's sexuality through marriages and the children produced. However, despite social and political dominance exercised by men, women retain their autonomy and a degree of social rights. A woman's ability to free herself from an abusive husband is a significant reflection of her independence. Women's rights even in the context of male dominance can clearly be traced to their decisive influence in economic production. Their control is exercised both in household subsistence and in market exchanges.

Comparison of Kpelle and Pacific Northwest societies reveals some behavioral similarities despite differences in ideological constructs. Among Pacific coast peoples, ideologies of gender equality are overtly expressed and supported. In contrast, Kpelle beliefs emphasize male superiority. But the social rights of women and men among the Kpelle and the Haida and Tlingit are similar in certain respects. Women's autonomy in all these groups is reflected in their ability to control household production and to determine the terms of economic exchange. Indeed, women's status and influence are both reflected in and derived from their economic roles.

THE MPONDO OF THE TRANSKEI

Interrelationships between economic activities and women's status can be highlighted by data from another stratified African society where women's economic roles are limited relative to men's and their social rights are correspondingly restricted. The Mpondo (PON-do) chiefdom, located in the Transkei region of South Africa, illustrates patterns of marked social stratification and male dominance. Economic and political factors intersect and combine to endow chiefs with power over commoners and to give men rights to dominate women.

Mpondo land is said to be owned by paramount and district chiefs. Chiefs in turn allocate use rights to portions of land to other men who are heads of lineages and households. Through control of land, chiefs are able to control access to resources in the form of acreage for farming and for grazing cattle. By granting access to land, chiefs create dependent clients who in return support the chiefs' political aspirations (Sacks, 1979).

Wealth in Mpondo society is measured by individual ownership of cattle. Cattle, owned exclusively by men, literally and figuratively embody a man's wealth. Most men own some cattle, although, of course, wealthy men and chiefs possess a great number of animals. Cattle are important not only as the source of subsistence products such as milk and meat but also as tokens in economic, social, and political exchanges. For example, cattle are given in bridewealth transactions by men in a husband's lineage to those in a wife's kin group. Cattle are thus economic symbols of bonds created through social relationships. Cattle are also received by men as payment for services rendered. In addition, cattle function in Mpondo ritual life when they are distributed at public feasts and on ceremonial occasions marking rites of passage such as marriage and funerals. Finally, chiefs distribute cattle from their herds to men who give them loyalty and political support (Sacks, 1975). Recipients benefit from the gift of cattle; chiefly donors benefit from both the loyalty offered and the social prestige rendered to generous benefactors.

Men thus receive cattle from each other in the context of many different types of interactions. They also obtain cattle by raiding neighboring peoples. These raids are carried out by groups of men organized by chiefs who enlist participants with promises of cattle confiscated in the raids.

Whereas Mpondo men are distributors and recipients of cattle, women have no direct roles in this vital system of exchange. They do not own cattle, cannot obtain them through raiding, and do not direct their distribution. In fact, women are themselves exchanged for cattle in transfers of bridewealth.

Women's roles are restricted to direct subsistence production. They produce crops grown on land under their husbands' control. Women's labor therefore benefits the patrilineage into which they marry. But their labor is for household consumption only. A significant contrast between women's and men's productivity, therefore, is that while women work to produce goods for use, men work to produce and distribute goods (namely, cattle) that have value both for use and for exchange. Men are involved in wide social and political networks cemented by acquisition and redistribution of private property in cattle. Denying women access to these networks renders them secondary in economic production and inconsequential in political maneuvering.

Mpondo men's social dominance is enacted in several practices concerning women's demeanor and behavior. Wives are expected to be deferential toward their husbands. Many ritualized restrictions affect their actions. For example, a woman must not walk too close to an elder man in her husband's lineage. When outdoors, she must walk behind, rather than in front, of the huts in the village. And she cannot drink milk from her husband's cows during the first year of marriage. Because milk is an important component of Mpondo diets, a woman's father gives her a heifer to take to her marital residence so she will have milk to drink (Sacks, 1979). Although restrictions are gradually eased with the passage of years of marriage, and especially with the birth of children, they visibly reflect and reinforce a wife's isolation in her husband's community. These various **taboos** are aimed specifically at women as wives marrying into patrilocal households. Unmarried women who live as daughters and sisters resident in their natal homes are not so restricted.

Ideological constructs supporting male prerogatives are expressed in Mpondo culture by a double standard in regard to sexual activity. Premarital sexual behavior on the part of girls is severely criticized and punished, whereas boys' behavior is considered normal and acceptable. Similarly, adultery is more sternly condemned when committed by wives than by husbands.

Attitudes toward divorce are ambiguous. Either a husband or a wife may initiate divorce. Marital conflicts are often motivated by adultery, although such acts are not considered legitimate grounds for divorce. That is, a husband who divorces his wife because of her affair cannot claim a return of bridewealth from her kin. If a divorce is considered legitimate—that is, for dereliction of a wife's duty—the woman's kin must return bridewealth to her husband. Even if a wife initiates a divorce, bridewealth is returned by her family if she is deemed to be at fault.

A husband's dominance over his wife is extended to encompass her interactions with his kin. A woman defers to her husband's relatives. This principle is shown not only through her circumspect behavior toward her husband's male kin but also through the social superiority of a man's sister over his wife. Sisters who reside in their natal family compound can demand labor from their brother's wife and can even demand that she obtain goods from her own kin. Women sometimes refer to their husband's sister as "female-husband," linguistically reflecting the social prerogatives of the latter.

Among the Mpondo, social attitudes toward women are complicated by differentiation between wives and sisters. According to Karen Sacks (1979), "Mpondo [lineages] subordinate women as wives and make them group members as sisters" (p. 192). However, distinctions between wives and sisters are obliterated among women in the chiefly class. Restrictions are imposed on elite women regardless of their relationship to men in their residential households. These restrictions tend to limit more seriously the behavior of women in the chiefly class as compared to their effect on the lives of nonchiefly women.

THE TONGA OF THE SOUTH PACIFIC

Contrast in behavior of members of different strata or classes is a fairly characteristic feature of stratified societies. In such societies, gender segmentation often develops or intensifies among members of higher strata. As societies historically are transformed into more complex, hierarchical polities, gender inequality is a common consequence of overall social change. That is, as class segmentation intensifies, gender roles often become more rigid. As elite men increase their political power, they restrict activities of women within their class. Women and men of nonelite groups are subordinated as well, although the character of their subordination varies.

To examine the dynamics of gender and social stratification, we turn to data concerning periods of social and political transformation in the Tongan Islands, a group of Polynesian islands in the South Pacific. Data from Tonga demonstrate how differentiated gender roles and relations in a chiefdom society can become increasingly hierarchical as a chiefdom is transformed into a kingdom. In this process, women's rights are undermined, and the social value traditionally bestowed on them is demeaned.

Traditional Tongan society was based on a system of ranking in which no two individuals were of equal rank. Three abstract principles were used to determine an individual's status relative to others: seniority, an older person outranking a younger; gender, a man outranking a woman; and sisterhood, a sister outranking her brother (Gailey, 1987). Application of principles of status obviously could lead to inconsistent ranking. Such ambiguity left open actual determination of rank to possibilities of maneuvering on the basis of contrasting criteria and personal claims.

The Tongan system of stratification divided the populace into two primary social strata distinguishing chiefs (*eiki*) and nonchiefs (*tu'a*). These two groups contrasted fundamentally in their relationship to land and in their roles in subsistence. Tongan land was controlled by paramount chiefs who then allocated portions to lower or district chiefs. Chiefs were perceived as guardians but not exclusive owners of Tongan land. Each chief alloted use rights to land under his jurisdiction to heads of lineages, usually men, who were resident in the chief's district. In return for use of land, families owed a part of their produce to the chiefs.

Tongan chiefs were incumbents of prestigious titles held by high-ranking lineages. Succession to a title was awarded on the basis of several criteria including geneological closeness to the predecessor. Preference for patrilineal **primogeniture** was strong but not exclusive. That is, although a chief's eldest son was a likely successor, other men could make rival claims based on additional criteria, including geneological connections through the previous chief's sister as well as personal wealth, ability, and charisma. The importance of descent through a sister was especially apparent if the prior chief had no surviving children. Because sisters were of higher status than brothers, a chief's sisters' sons outranked his brothers' sons and therefore were strategically positioned to succeed. But claims through sisterhood could be made even in opposition to a chief's own sons, particularly if a sister were senior to the deceased chief.

Chiefly people did not usually engage in subsistence activities but instead obtained food and goods from the productive work of others. As we amplify later, chiefly people depended on goods supplied by commoner men and by both chiefly and nonchiefly women. Through collection of products of other people's labor, chiefs "generate a politically utilizable surplus" (Sahlins, 1970, p. 211). Surplus resources supported the chiefs and their families and were also used to sustain dependent functionaries, attendants, and warriors who thus owed their well-being to the chief's largesse. In return, they were loyal followers.

Tongan economy entailed a strict division of labor based on gender. Two kinds of goods were therefore produced: women's products, called *koloa*, or "valuables, wealth"; and men's products, called *ngaue*, or "work" (Gailey, 1987, pp. 97, 101). The word *koloa* was extended to refer to anything produced by a woman, including a newborn baby. Because they were made by women, k*oloa* items were considered more valuable than *ngaue*. Although the value of *koloa* reflected the social worth of women, both *koloa* and *ngaue* were necessary and fulfilled daily needs of household members.

Differentiation of roles and responsibilities according to gender encompassed subsistence activities and the production of crafts. Tongan subsistence was based on horticulture and fishing. Nonchiefly men carried out farming tasks, producing crops such as yams, coconuts, and a variety of vegetables. They supplied their families with fish and turtles obtained in the open seas. Nonchiefly women collected shellfish in shallow waters and reefs and also fished in lagoons. They extracted oil from coconuts and blended it with flowers to be used as a salve to protect the skin.

In addition to subsistence activities, men were responsible for cooking, an occupation that carried low prestige in Tongan society. Other household tasks were not linked to gender but were performed by both women and men. These included child care and building of houses. Production of crafts, utensils, and weapons was assigned according to gender and rank. Nonchiefly men made canoes and weapons. Nonchiefly women made mats, bark cloth (called *tapa*), bedding, and net bags. Although chiefly people usually did not engage in horticulture or fishing, they did produce certain crafts. Men made rope and decorations on weapons; women made bark cloth and wove bark mats. Indeed, craft production in Tonga was extensive, an example of the economic diversity and specialization found in most complex Polynesian societies (Sahlins, 1970).

Koloa, or women's wealth, was employed as the medium of exchange in social, economic, political, and ritual contexts. In other words, women's work provided the means for publicly demonstrating underlying societal relationships and obligations. *Koloa* thus gave visible evidence of women's roles in integrating the multifaceted networks of Tongan society.

Distribution of *koloa* was ritualized in ceremonies of ascension to chiefly titles. To validate his or her rank, a new chief presented women's valuables to relatives and supporters (Gailey, 1987). *Koloa* products included bark cloth and mats made by chiefly and nonchiefly women. The value of a particular item was determined by several factors, principally the status of the maker (*koloa* made by a high-ranking woman was more valuable than that produced by a woman of lower rank), the status of the person who ordered its production (*koloa* commanded by a chief or his sister was high in value), the time involved in producing the item, and the age or history of the product (an older item, especially one that had been made or owned by someone of high rank, was more valuable than a new item).

In addition to its use in validating chiefs' rank, *koloa* was given as barter for other items, payment for services rendered, or gifts on special occasions including rites of passage. People could exchange *koloa*, both parties giving and receiving valuables, but *ngaue*, or men's products, could not be given in return for *koloa* because they were inherently of less value than *koloa*.

Nonchiefly people produced goods both for their own households and for the benefit of chiefs. Chiefs' prerogatives included their right to obtain products and services from commoners. They commanded collective labor by men who farmed the chiefs' fields and by women who produced mats, plain and decorated bark cloth, and other valuables. Although (as in all chiefdoms) most rights and obligations in Tongan society emanated from kinship relations, the right of chiefly people to obtain subsistence support from commoner households signaled their dominance over nonkin. Tongan society, then, conformed to Sahlins's (1970) summary of dynamics in Polynesian chiefdoms:

> The success of [chiefdoms] is the control that can be developed over household economies. For the household is not merely the principal productive unit, it is often quite capable of autonomous direction of its own production, and it is oriented towards production for its own, not societal consumption. The potential of Polynesian chieftainship is precisely the pressure it could exert on household output, its capacity both to generate a surplus and to deploy it out of the household towards a broader division of labor, cooperative construction, and massive ceremonial and military action. (pp. 214–215)

The Tongan social system included two groups intermediary between chiefs and commoners. These groups functioned as "buffers between the lower-ranking nonchiefly people and the chiefs" (Gailey, 1987, p. 87). They generally did not engage in subsistence work but rather were supported by the fund of goods given by commoners to chiefs. One such group was known as *matapules,* a word literally derived from words meaning "a cutting edge" (*mata*) and "authority" (*pule*). *Matapules,* then, were metaphorically the "face or surface of authority." They were said to have been originally foreign immigrants from other Polynesian societies, probably Fiji and Samoa. They functioned in Tonga as artisans, warriors, administrators, and attendants to chiefs. The *matapule* grouping was internally ranked depending on the particular job performed. For example, chiefs' attendants were of higher rank than artisans. Attendants and administrators performed important roles for chiefs as overseers of cooperative work commanded of commoners by chiefs. They also called together assemblies of commoners to advise them of chiefs' directives.

A second intermediary group of chiefs' attendants was called *mu'as.* These people were offspring and descendants of intermarriages between chiefs and *matapules.* They were often engaged in watching over young members of chiefs' families to ensure that the youths conformed to norms of public etiquette and morality. The caretaking roles of *mu'as* were significant because the likelihood of a particular man succeeding to a chiefly title was in part based on his behavior and public reputation. Although high rank clearly brought substantial benefits, it also incurred obligations to act in a suitable manner.

The various strata tended to be **endogamous**. Although lower-ranking people certainly preferred to marry someone of higher rank, those of high rank looked upon such unions as disadvantageous to their own status.

Marital alliances were used by chiefly people to validate and consolidate high rank. At the highest levels, among paramount chiefs, marriage between a brother and sister was the most direct form of exclusion of counterclaims. Another strategy employed by the most powerful chiefs to consolidate their dominance and exclude rivals was arranging marriages of their high-ranking sisters to foreigners. By such marriages, Tongan chiefs simultaneously forged alliances with leaders of other chiefdoms and eliminated competition from sisters' sons, who instead became chiefs in their mothers' marital communities.

The authority of sisters was not limited to chiefly strata, although among chiefs it played critical roles in political maneuvering. Among all groups, one's father's sister held high social status within the family and wielded authority over her brother and his children. Rights of a sister, called *fahu* rights, included the ability to command labor and products from her brother and his wife and children, to arrange or veto marriages of her brother's children, and to adopt her brother's children. A sister who was angered by her brother or his family could place a curse on them that was thought to result in their sterility. If a sister was senior to her brother, status and *fahu* rights were even more enhanced.

Fahu rights extended from a woman to her children in relation to their mother's brother and his descendants. That is, people could make claims for labor and products of their maternal uncles and cousins.

Tension between principles of patrilineality incorporated in Tongan lineages and the prerogatives of sisters and their descendants prevented institutionalization of strict patrilineal inheritance. Although men held public positions with administrative power, women wielded great authority. Women's prerogatives were derived from their place in kinship networks, but because kinship was not separated from politics, women as sisters and as fathers' sisters had influence over public life.

In Tongan society, women and men had different responsibilities, but both were accorded prestige in specific domains, and each had autonomy and independence. These principles were demonstrated, for example, in attitudes toward sexuality, marriage, and divorce.

Premarital sexual activity was common for both girls and boys. Only among the chiefly strata were restrictions placed on girls' behavior. High-ranking daughters were watched closely to assure their chastity, but among the majority of Tongans, most people engaged in sexual relations prior to marriage. In fact, it was customary for a woman to give a plaited mat (*koloa* wealth) as a gift to the first man with whom she had intercourse.

Tongan marriages were monogamous for nonchiefly people, but chiefly men often had several wives. The highest-ranking men additionally had concubines. Concubines were not legal wives but lived in the chief's household and were usually attendants to the chief's legal wives. Secondary wives were typically younger than the first or primary wife. They were often close relatives of the first wife, preferably younger sisters or daughters of the first wife's brother. In either case, a primary wife had authority over the others. A younger sister would, by the principle of seniority, defer to her elder. A woman's brother's daughter would also be deferential, both because of the first wife's seniority and because the first wife was the younger woman's father's sister and therefore wielded the authority inherent in the *fahu* relationship.

In Tongan marriages, husbands and wives were expected to show respect toward each other. A wife's behavior was customarily deferential toward her husband, but if a wife outranked her husband, he often deferred to her.

Attitudes toward extramarital sexual activity were somewhat ambiguous. Ideally, both husband and wife should be faithful, but Tongans recognized that this ideal was not always fulfilled. If adultery became public knowledge, divorce often ensued. As might be expected in a society where rank influenced many disparate domains of life, strictures against adultery were stronger among chiefly people, especially regarding men who had affairs with a chief's wife. Such a man was in grave danger of being killed, either on orders of the chief or by one of his own relatives who took the action to forestall the chief's revenge against the entire kin group.

Although marriage was ideally a lifelong commitment, in fact a majority of Tongan marriages ended in divorce. According to William Mariner, a British observer of Tongan culture in the early nineteenth century, approximately two-thirds of Tongan couples were divorced (Mariner, 1827; cited in Gailey, 1987, p. 131). Many people evidently remarried several times during their lives. Divorces were initiated only by husbands, but no social stigma was borne by either party. Divorced people of either gender were expected to remarry, but many did not. Because women were not economically dependent on their husbands, they had no survival need to remarry. A divorced woman could always receive material support from her brothers and their wives and children through her *fahu* claims to their labor.

Widows who were still in their childbearing years were expected to remarry, but the choice was theirs. They too could be sustained by their brothers and families and therefore were not compelled by economic constraints to remarry. Widows' independence was curtailed only among people of the highest strata. A widow of a primary paramount chief might commit suicide or be killed at his funeral.

Violence against women in the form of beatings and rape was extremely rare. A wife might be beaten by her husband as punishment for adultery, but otherwise such behavior was considered reprehensible. In fact, a man who chronically or severely beat his wife might be killed by her relatives. Rape was socially condemned and punished. According to Gailey (1987), rapes, although rarely committed, were most often perpetrated by young chiefly men against unmarried nonchiefly women.

Documentary evidence provided by British traders, missionaries, and other observers of Tongan society in the nineteenth century indicates that violence in any form was relatively rare. All people could expect to be treated with respect. Despite an overt principle of ranking that endowed men with higher status than women, men's behavior toward women was not domineering or disrespectful.

Mariner (1827) noted, for example, that men usually "show [women] attention and kind regard" (quoted in Gailey, 1987, p. 123). Furthermore, he stated, "At meals, strangers and foreigners are always shown a preference, and females are helped before men of the same rank, because they are the weaker sex, and require attention" (p. 134). Similarly, William Anderson, a doctor on the ship of Capt. James Cook, commented in 1777:

> The province allotted to the men is. . . far more laborious and extensive than that of the women. . . . [W]e find them [women] eased of laborious employments but treated with that respect to which they are often more justly entitled than their lordly masters, and have even a great sway in the management of affairs. (Beaglehole, 1969; quoted in Gailey, 1987, p. 123)

In sum, at the time of contact with Europeans, Tongan women and men had important, although differentiated, social rights. They exercised their rights in different domains and by claims to different kinds of relationships. Men had authority as husbands, and women wielded authority as sisters and fathers' sisters. However, tensions existed in relationships between women and men, especially among chiefly people who aspired to sustain or elevate their rank. Both men and women were assertive as they maneuvered to better their own status and that of their children and to increase their social and political power.

As in all chiefdoms, power and prestige were not divorced from the kinship groups in which they originated. And in the domain of kinship, women and men had dual roles: men as husbands and brothers, women as wives and sisters. The dual roles gave each woman or man authority in one type of relationship while rendering the person subordinate in another.

Tongan society, however, did not remain static. Indeed, seeds of political and social transformation were inherent in the Tongan chiefdom as individual chiefs vied with each other for power and control. But contact with Europeans beginning in the seventeenth century accelerated processes of change and channeled subsequent cultural shifts in particular directions. Among the consequences was a reworking of gender constructs so as to increase men's authority while women's social, economic, and political claims were undermined.

Tongans first encountered European traders and explorers in the seventeenth century. Sporadic contact continued throughout the eighteenth century, but in the early 1800s, trade and whaling in the South Pacific became more frequent and sustained. As elsewhere throughout the world, Tongans were willing participants in commercial dealings with Europeans. Through trade, they obtained metal goods such as axes, nails, and knives. They also procured beads and cotton and wool cloth. Tongan men and women eagerly traded for these utilitarian items. In exchange, they brought native resources such as fish, coconuts, yams, bark cloth, and other crafts. Women, especially unmarried nonchiefly women, offered sexual services in exchange for manufactured goods from traders and sailors.

Women's participation in trade was common. High-ranking women chiefs were among those dealing directly with traders. For instance, a British missionary, James Wilson (1799/1968), noted:

> [A] woman of rank paid us a visit; she was attended by many chiefs, and a vast number of females. . . . After her came four stout fellows carrying a bundle of cloth. . . . [T]his was presented to the captain, who gave her in return such things as fully satisfied her. (p. 108; quoted in Gailey, 1987, p. 148)

Chiefs were keenly interested in trade with the British. They especially wanted to obtain firearms. Acquisition of a substantial number of weapons intensified Tongan disputes over succession to chiefly titles, disputes that sometimes led to warfare between men making rival claims to inheritance. By the middle of the nineteenth century, motives of warfare widened to include quests for land under jurisdiction of rival chiefs (Gailey, 1987). As a result of efforts by a number of high-ranking chiefs to enlarge their domains and increase their power, rivals each attempted to establish control over all of Tonga. Such competing attempts led to a critical fundamental transformation of the Tongan polity from a chiefdom into a kingdom under the leadership of one paramount ruler. This far-reaching change commenced in the early 1800s and was finally institutionalized in 1845 by the assumption to the title of king by a paramount chief named Taufa'ahau, known also as George I.

Expansion of trade throughout the nineteenth century had a crucial impact on the traditional division of labor and especially on the value of *koloa*, or women's wealth. At first, coconut oil, processed by women, was an important trade item. It was employed by Europeans to light lamps and manufacture soap. As a result of its use as a trade commodity, women's production of coconut oil intensified (Gailey, 1980). Concomitantly, women's importance in commerce enhanced their status. Trading coconut oil, a *koloa* product, for European valuables was consistent with Tongan principles of exchange. However, after the middle of the nineteenth century, the world market for coconut oil declined. Instead, Europeans sought dried coconut, called *copra*. But because collection and processing of coconuts was *ngaue*, or men's work, the shift to trade in copra began a realignment of traditional Tongan beliefs about the inherent value of women's and men's products.

As copra production intensified throughout the rest of the nineteenth century, men spent more time in this endeavor and less time in fulfilling other subsistence and domestic tasks. As a result, women were compelled to engage in work such as farming and cooking that carried low status. Women also occasionally helped in copra production (men's work) to amass a greater supply destined for trade. Although women's participation increased their households' income, it further altered the traditional division of labor.

Women's work and their production of *koloa* were also affected by the importation of European manufactured cotton and wool cloth. Two interrelated factors led to undermining women's roles. First, cotton and wool replaced traditional bark cloth, one of the most highly valued *koloa* items. Second, because cotton cloth was purchased with cash, men's access to money from copra production changed Tongan concepts of value. Had cotton been obtainable on the basis of an exchange for a woman's product, the traditional system of values could have remained intact. Instead, men's labor was used to procure a valuable trade item. Women's wealth was thus undermined in a dual process of material replacement and ideological reconstruction.

Codification of laws and enactment of a Tongan constitution in the mid-nineteenth century solidified the state's power and men's authority over women. Many Tongan laws and government policies were instigated under the influence of Wesleyan Methodist missionaries from Great Britain who began their mission activities in Tonga in the 1820s. Tongan chiefs quickly sought to ally themselves with the Wesleyans because they viewed the missionaries as powerful and wealthy. Chiefs realized the missionaries were potential sources of firearms that could then be used in their own plans to enlarge their jurisdictions and control (Gailey, 1987).

As advisers to the king and his associates, the Wesleyans came to play a critical role in shifting traditional gender relations. Such shifts were direct and indirect results of a wide range of societal changes.

Wesleyans fostered several significant changes in Tongan principles of inheritance, assignment of productive tasks, and authority patterns within kin groups. In all, their goal was to transform Tongan social, economic, and political life so as to conform to standards considered "civilized" and "moral" by European society. First, use rights to land were granted individually to men as heads of their households. After the establishment of the Tongan kingdom in 1845, Tongan land was nominally owned by the king, but it was allocated for use to men. Inheritance of land rights passed patrilineally from father to son. Competing claims through father's sisters were legally negated.

Second, domestic economic tasks were shifted by assigning the responsibility of cooking to women. Men were drawn out of household work into producing copra and bananas for export and/or into wage-earning occupations. Women's work roles were restricted, thus rendering them increasingly dependent on their husbands for support. The value of *koloa* was undermined, both by replacement of bark cloth by cotton and by laws that forbade making or wearing *tapa*. Although this law was in effect only from 1875 until 1880, when it was repealed under enormous public pressure, it demonstrates the lengths to which the government under Wesleyan guidance was prepared to go to lessen women's productive contributions and consequently undermine their status.

Women's authority was further harmed by legal bans against the exercise of *fahu* rights. A woman can no longer lay claims to her brothers and their families. This shift resulted in dependence of a woman on her husband because other means of support were eliminated. As a result of multiple factors, then, women's status within their households declined, and the quality of their relationships with family members shifted. According to Gailey (1980):

> These processes [have] resulted in restriction of Tongan women's authority as sisters, and the redefinition of their role as wives in such a way as to transform what was simple deference behavior toward husbands into structural and economic dependency. (p. 318)

A third societal change affected inheritance of chiefly titles. A woman can no longer inherit titles from her father unless she is the firstborn child with no brothers. Even in this case, if her father had a brother, the brother's claim takes precedence. The daughter, however, can inherit after her uncle's death.

Finally, Wesleyans attempted to alter Tongan attitudes and behaviors concerning sexuality and marriage. By legal statutes, women who engaged in premarital or extramarital sexual activities were punished by fines, imprisonment, or forced labor on royal plantations (Gailey, 1987).

Historical transformations, stemming both from motives of traditional Tongan chiefs and from external pressures from British colonial authorities, resulted in benefits for men of the chiefly strata. Although women of this group colluded in the process of state formation to increase their wealth and the power of their close kin, they lost rights relative to chiefly men. Nonchiefly people of both genders experienced a decline in their economic and political autonomy. However, among people in this stratum, too, women's roles and prestige were disproportionately decreased.

Tongan culture exhibited shifts in traditional gender constructs as the chiefdom was transformed into a state. Such shifts are not unmotivated but are in fact fundamental to the emergence of state society. Chapter 5 pursues and elaborates the examination of interconnections between gender hierarchy and the functioning of states.

SUMMARY

Gender constructs in stratified societies are linked to participation in household economies and in community affairs. Among the Haida and Tlingit, men and women both had productive economic roles. Men fished and hunted, and women gathered plant and marine resources. Women had important decision-making rights in economic distribution within households and in intergroup trade. They participated with men in planning and hosting family and ceremonial potlatches that validated and increased the status of their kin groups. Women's equality and autonomy was therefore manifested in critical spheres of social life.

Among the Kpelle, ideological and religious precepts stress men's superiority, but women maintain some autonomy and rights to decision making as a result of their productive farming roles and their control over the produce of their labor.

In Mpondo society, men's dominance over women is solidified by their ownership over the valued resource of cattle. They own, distribute, and exchange wealth in cattle in a wide variety of contexts, including economic production, ceremonial display and distribution, and political power maneuvers. Because women are excluded from ownership of cattle, they cannot attain prestigious and influential roles in their society.

In the Tongan chiefdom, women asserted numerous rights to familial and public status. They produced valued goods (that is, "women's wealth"), influenced decisions regarding ascendancy to chieftainships, and exerted authority, or *fahu* rights, in relation to their brothers and their brothers' children. Men also had varied rights and statuses. They contributed subsistence resources, functioned as chiefs of their lineages, and had authority in their families as husbands and fathers.

After European contact, the economic, social, and political participation of women declined among the Pacific coastal cultures and the Tongan people. Haida and Tlingit women's roles in trade were marginalized and ignored by European merchants. Among the Tonga, women's wealth was obliterated by the importation and substitution of European products. Women's role in household economies declined with a focus on production for export, and their critical status as sister and father's sister was undermined and finally outlawed.

REFERENCES

BEAGLEHOLE, JOHN (ED.). 1969. *The Journals of Captain James Cook.* 3 vols. Cambridge: Cambridge University Press.

BLACKMAN, MARGARET. 1982. *During My Time: Florence Edenshaw Davidson, a Haida Woman.* Seattle: University of Washington Press.

GAILEY, CHRISTINE. 1980. "Putting down sisters and wives: Tongan women and colonization." In *Women and Colonization* (ed. Mona Etienne and Eleanor Leacock). New York: Praeger, pp. 294–322.

———. 1987. *Kinship to Kingship: Gender Hierarchy and State Formation in the Tongan Islands.* Austin: University of Texas Press.

GIBBS, JAMES. 1965. "The Kpelle of Liberia." In *Peoples of Africa* (ed. James L. Gibbs). New York: Holt, Rinehart & Winston, pp. 197–240.

INGRAHAM, JOSEPH. 1971. *Joseph Ingraham's Journal of the Brigantine Hope on a Voyage to the North West Coast of North America 1790–1792* (ed. Mark D. Kaplanoff). Barre, MA: Imprint Society.

KLEIN, LAURA. 1980. "Contending with colonization: Tlingit men and women in change." In *Women and Colonization* (ed. Mona Etienne and Eleanor Leacock). New York: Praeger, pp. 88–108.

KNAPP, FRANCES, AND RHETA CHILDE. 1896. *The Thlinkets of Southeastern Alaska.* Chicago: Stone & Kimball.

MARINER, WILLIAM. 1827. *An Account of the Natives of the Tongan Islands* (ed. John Martin). 2 vols. Edinburgh: Constable.

MURDOCK, GEORGE. 1934. "The Haidas of British Columbia." In *Our Primitive Contemporaries* (ed. George Murdock). New York: McGraw-Hill.

SACKS, KAREN. 1975. "Engels revisited: Women, the organization of production, and private property." In *Toward an Anthropology of Women* (ed. Rayna R. Reiter). New York: Monthly Review Press, pp. 211–234.

————. 1979. *Sisters and Wives*. Westport, CT: Greenwood.

SAHLINS, MARSHALL. 1970. "Poor man, rich man, big-man, chief: Political types in Melanesia and Polynesia." *Comparative Studies in Society and History*, 5: 285–303 (1963) Reprinted in *Cultures of the Pacific* (ed. Thomas Harding and Ben Wallace). New York: Free Press, pp. 203–215.

SPRADLEY, JAMES (ED.). 1972. *Guests Never Leave Hungry: The Autobiography of James Sewid, a Kwakiutl Indian*. Montreal: McGill-Queen's University Press.

WILSON, JAMES. 1968. *A Missionary Voyage to the Southern Pacific Ocean 1796–1798*. New York: Praeger. (Original work published 1799)

WOOD, C. E. S. 1882. "Among the Thlinkits in Alaska." *Century Magazine*, 24: 323–339.

CHAPTER 5

Agricultural States

S tate societies are characterized by many forms of stratification. They typically consist of several classes or **castes** that are differentiated in terms of access to economic resources, social prestige, and political power. Classes are fundamentally different from stratified rankings that are found in chiefdoms. In class societies, inequalities obtain in people's access to resources and means of production. An elite class maintains control over production and wields its control in various types of social and economic relations. Elites may directly own resources and permit access to others only on the condition of receiving a portion of produce or goods or their equivalent in rent or money. They may compel common people to render services as subsistence laborers, craftspeople, or domestic workers. Because class-based systems obviously entail some degree of exploitation of nonelites, they necessarily develop mechanisms to minimize or eliminate resistance. These mechanisms take many forms, including legal restrictions backed up by fines and punishments, threats and/or use of military action against resisters, and a myriad of indirect but powerful means of ideological control that convince people the system itself is legitimate, just, and/or inevitable.

Of course, degrees of inequality existing between classes and modes of control exerted by elites vary in different states and at different historical epochs in each society. Similarly, rights of nonelites may be recognized or curtailed to varying degrees.

In addition to economic and political distinctions, state societies often develop or intensify gender hierarchies as another means of segmenting the populace. Roles and responsibilities are generally demarcated according to gender and are rigidly construed. The power of the state is wielded primarily, if not exclusively, by men, and women's autonomy is curtailed. Ideological constructs supporting men's dominance permeate state cultures in many domains of life, including the valuation of work performed by women and men, the legal rights to which they are entitled, and the quality of their social interactions as experienced in familial and public settings.

In this chapter, we analyze gender constructs in several agricultural state societies. We begin with data concerning the Inca of Peru, examining the development of the Incan empire in the Andes and its later destruction by Spanish colonizers. We then turn to data from India and China, focusing on dynamics of gender in traditional Indian and Chinese culture as well as the extent of change in gender relations in recent decades.

THE INCA OF PERU

The Incan empire developed over many centuries, growing out of Andean cultures centered around Cuzco, Peru. The Incas themselves were members of two dominant lineages that gradually increased their wealth and power over other kin groups, eventually transforming Andean cultures into a hierarchical state society. The state did not remain limited to its area of origin but rather expanded in the fifteenth century to encompass an estimated six million people living in what is now Peru and Ecuador (Rowe, 1950). The empire was enlarged by incorporating indigenous cultures and transforming them in the process.

As in all state societies, the Incan state developed through differentiation of its population into stratified classes and the appropriation of wealth and power by an elite group. Although elites in the Incan state clearly reaped enormous material and social benefits from their advantages, some rights of commoners, founded in preexisting kin-based Andean cultures, were legitimated and sustained.

Pre-Incan Andean cultures contained egalitarian principles related to land ownership and access to resources. These ethics coexisted with a burgeoning system of stratification allowing certain people to enhance their social prestige and wield political authority over others.

Andean land was under the control of localized kinship groups called *ayllus*. An *ayllu* consisted of people living within a particular territory. It was a corporate entity and exercised control over allocation of land to households resident within it. Because the available land was located in a relatively fixed area, *ayllu* leaders periodically reassigned allotments to adjust to changes in household composition. Land was apportioned to male heads of households on the basis of family size. Each married man received one measure (*tupu*) of land for himself and his wife. For each of his sons, he received an additional *tupu*; for each daughter, one-half *tupu*. When a son married, he was allotted the portion of land originally given to his father on his behalf. Although in most cases daughters relinquished their share of land upon marriage, some reports indicate that married women sometimes retained usufruct rights to land in their natal *ayllus* (Silverblatt, 1978, 1980).

Ayllus were endogamous communities. Postmarital residence was preferably patrilocal, but actual choice in any instance was made after consideration of the size and composition of husband's and wife's family and the resources available to each household.

Communal rights to resources within an *ayllu* were recognized and enacted through redistribution of foods and goods to community members. Any family or individual in need received aid from others. This system of redistribution was based on egalitarian ethics and "effectively checked individual accumulation of wealth and power" (Silverblatt, 1980, p. 152).

Despite the fact that all people had rights to resources and sustenance, some individuals were of higher social status than others. These people, known as *curacas*, had political influence in their communities and constituted a governing body of some sort, although the ways in which they exercised their power are currently unknown. Although there were both men and women *curacas*, it is uncertain whether the women had solely economic privileges or whether they also had roles in decision making and leadership of their communities (Silverblatt, 1987). In pre-Incan cultures located along the northern coast of Peru, women *curacas* held positions of community leadership; elsewhere in the region, their roles are not well documented (Silverblatt, 1978).

Curacas had social and economic privileges similar to chiefly people in chiefdom societies. They had rights to obtain products from the labor of others. In return for goods received from common people, *curacas* were obligated to be helpful and generous to those in need. Therefore, although their status endowed them with material, social, and political advantages, they had responsibilities toward the populace over whom they exerted authority.

As Incan society developed, it continued features of Andean egalitarian reciprocity while it also intensified preexisting trends toward stratification and increased the privileges and power of elites. Incas appropriated some portion of land held by *ayllus*. Land in the empire was allocated to three separate spheres: the "land of the Incas" supported the Inca elite, state bureaucrats, and military; the "land of the Sun" supported members of the official state religion; and the remaining land supported local communities with no interference in traditional usufruct patterns. Ordinary peasants were compelled to farm the lands devoted to the Incas and the state religion and to deliver the produce obtained. These resources were tribute used to sustain members of the Incan upper class as well as numerous administrators, artisans, and religious specialists whose activities supported elite power. Because most government functionaries and craft specialists were men, the tribute system benefited men more than women.

In addition to demands on agricultural work, common people were obligated to perform other kinds of labor, known as *mita* service. Men were enlisted to construct and maintain public works projects such as palaces, temples, forts, irrigation systems, and roads. Some men were conscripted into army units under Incan command. Others were trained from childhood to serve as runners in an elaborate postal system, carrying messages throughout the empire (Rowe, 1950). Women were compelled to spin and weave cotton and wool cloth for Incan garments or for trade to other areas.

Burdens of giving tribute in labor or goods to the Incan elite were assigned not to individuals but rather to households. Each household was treated as the unit that had collective responsibility to fulfill its obligations. Work was assigned within a household depending on availability and capacities of individuals. The fact that only married people were obliged to perform *mita* service recognized the economic interdependence of men and women. That is, if at any given time a husband was performing his service, his wife was able to assume the husband's usual responsibilities or at least recruit someone to fulfill them. Similarly, a husband could provide or arrange for labor to carry out his wife's tasks when she was engaged in weaving cloth for the Incas.

Although Incan society was highly stratified and power rested exclusively with the upper class, pre-Incan egalitarian ethics somewhat tempered elites' behavior. Chiefly generosity was shown to followers to consolidate elite power and retain support from the vast network of officials and local leaders on whom Incan rulers depended. In addition, basic survival requirements of all people were met by maintenance of granaries and warehouses from which *curacas* could obtain supplies for members of their *ayllus* in times of famine or intense need. These goods were, of course, derived from surpluses originally expropriated by elites from the labor of commoners. However, the ability of needy people to obtain a portion of supplies indicates that there were limits to the degree of exploitation to which they could be subjected. The Incan system further indicates that ethics of reciprocity underlying social relationships and uniting people in kin-based societies were kept alive among the populace even as the Incas intensified their political control.

Generosity on the part of elites, though, was not altruistic. According to John Rowe (1950):

> [Incan] paternalistic concern for the material well-being of its subjects was admitted by the rulers themselves to be nothing but enlightened self-interest, for they realized that a healthy, happy people work better and produce more than one suffering from want and injustice. (p. 273)

The Incan state was headed by a supreme ruler who maintained his power through a complex network of agents, bureaucrats, armies, and priests. These various people transmitted demands of elites to local communities and ensured that they were fulfilled. Administrative power was exclusively a male domain. Most of the emperor's closest advisers and aides were chosen from among the men in his lineage. Succession to the position of emperor was not rigid, but a current ruler usually selected and trained one of his sons to assume the post.

The ruler's wife, known as *coya* or "queen," was his own sister. Marriage between a brother and sister at the highest level of state functioned to consolidate power and minimize struggles over succession. Marriages between siblings were absolutely forbidden to all except the emperor and *coya*.

The *coya* had substantial public influence in her own right. She participated in Incan public life in both economic and administrative capacities. She owned land and could dispose of its produce. The *coya* was obligated by principles of reciprocity to redistribute some of the surplus delivered to her. She often held huge public feasts as demonstrations of her generosity. As an example of their contributions to Incan society, *coyas* had special lands that they used for experimentation with new strains and varieties of crops (Silverblatt, 1978). Finally, a *coya* might occasionally wield political power, governing from Cusco in the absence of her husband.

The rights of other elite women in the Incan state are currently unknown (Silverblatt, 1980). However, upper-class women contributed productive and symbolic labor as weavers of special cloth used to make clothing for ritual occasions.

Although the exact nature of gender relations among the Incan nobility is uncertain, one indication of Incan male dominance was the practice of polygyny among elites. In contrast to norms of monogamous marriages among commoners, elite men usually had several wives. The emperor, in fact, had many wives in addition to the *coya*, who was always his first and primary wife. Subsequent wives were often daughters of important local and foreign leaders. They thus were the tokens of political and military alliances on which Incan rule depended.

Among the common class, gender constructs were based on Andean ideological beliefs that emphasized the interdependence of all natural forces and of all people. Balance and reciprocity between women and men were consistent with the desired equilibrium thought to underlie and unite the universe. The necessity of balance was expressed in the division of labor within households, assigning complementary tasks to husbands and wives. Women's work included weaving, farming, herding, food preparation, and child care. Men's work centered on farming and herding. A great variety of crops was grown, principally maize, potatoes, beans, tomatoes, and cotton. Domesticated animals, including llamas, ducks, guinea pigs, and dogs, were herded and tended by both women and men. Many tasks were performed cooperatively by a married couple. For instance, husbands prepared fields by use of foot plows while wives accompanied them, breaking up clods of earth with hoes (Rowe, 1950; Silverblatt, 1987).

Balance and autonomy of the genders was expressed in the Andean kinship system, based on a principle of **parallel descent** (Silverblatt, 1987). Descent and inheritance followed gender-linked lines so that men considered themselves descended from their fathers, whereas women descended from their mothers. Inheritance of property and of usufruct rights to land in *ayllus* typically followed these parallel lines as well. Parallel descent and inheritance created strong gender identity and solidarity.

In conjunction with principles of parallel descent, the sibling pair of brother and sister was of primary importance in kinship unity. Therefore, inheritance could flow through men from a mother's brother to sister's son and through women from a father's sister to brother's daughter. Within sibling groups, authority was based on birth order regardless of gender. Rights to autonomy for Andean women and men were demonstrated in marriage practices. Although parents tended to arrange marriages of their daughters and sons, approval by the couple was necessary. Wedding rituals included a balanced mutual exchange of gifts between families of both spouses.

In the Incan state, attitudes and behaviors concerning sexuality, marriage, and divorce differed between elite and peasant classes. Among the latter, trial marriages were common, indicating that prenuptial sexual activity was considered normal and acceptable. Among elites, however, girls' chastity was expected and deviations were punished.

Similar differentiation in possibilities of divorce distinguished elite and common people. Peasant couples could divorce if they chose. Such action carried no stigma. In contrast, marriages between elites were legally sanctioned by Incan authorities and hence could not be dissolved. However, because only the first marriage of an elite man was ritually marked, it was only this union that could not be terminated. Husbands could easily divorce secondary wives (Rowe, 1950).

Widows of elite men were barred from remarriage except to a brother of their deceased husband. In some cases, sons inherited secondary wives from their fathers so long as the women had not yet borne any children.

Although concepts of balance and interdependence between the genders remained as an ideal in rural communities, Incan economic and political control eventually led to development of competing ideological constructs. Attitudes of elite men toward women clearly reflected men's privilege and dominance. According to Silverblatt (1987), because Incan rule spread through military conquest, the prestige of men as warriors increased, resulting in the warrior emerging as the principal image of manhood. An ideology of conquest, then, distorted the traditional balance believed to obtain between men and women. As men were identified with war, women became perceived as inferior. In a symbolic manifestation of these constructs, groups defeated by the Incas were referred to as "conquered females" (Silverblatt, 1978).

A significant consequence of male domination in Incan society was elite men's control over women's sexuality, reflected in requirements for girls' premarital chastity and women's marital fidelity. In addition, Incan officials confiscated young virgin girls (called *acllas*) from rural villages to serve the emperor or other elites. These girls were often daughters of high-status people in local communities. They were sent to centers for training in each province. There they were taught to spin and weave and were instructed in various ritual specialties. After their training, some *acllas* were compelled to become wives or concubines of elite men. Others were given by the emperor to influential men to obtain and/or retain their loyalty. Still others were chosen to serve as virgin priestesses in religious cults dedicated to Incan deities.

When non-Incan Andean peoples were defeated and absorbed by the Incan state, they were compelled to donate young girls to become *acllas*. Appropriation of these girls thus became symbolic of a people's subordination (Silverblatt, 1978).

Formation of the Incan state affected relations between women and men in ways similar to the pattern we discussed for Tonga in chapter 4. Differences in roles that existed in prestate cultures were turned into hierarchical relationships as privileges of class extended throughout the society. For the Incas, according to Irene Silverblatt (1987):

> As class relations supplanted kinship, gender became a trope embracing relations of power and articulating them. Class formation, transforming cultural distinctions into reflections of its own exploitative image, took gender distinctions and made hierarchical differences. (p. 212)

Some evidence of the deterioration of women's status in the Incan period comes from archaeological excavations and the examination of living spaces and skeletal remains. Christine Hastorf's (1991) study of the Sausa, a group indigenous to the Andes for several thousand years, revealed data that can be interpreted as reflecting changes in women's roles and status. For instance, examining an archaeological site spanning the years A.D. 200 to 1532 uncovered a significant increase in food production, especially maize, during the period from 1460 to 1532, corresponding to the time of deepening Incan control and incorporation into the expanding Inca empire (p. 140).

Study of structures and soil samples in an early Sausa village uncovered large concentrations and varieties of foods, leading to the conclusion that the structures were within women's domains of living and working. Because samples of maize, a sacred and ritual food, were found in patio areas of structures, Hastorf suggests that its preparation and consumption was likely a group activity (p. 143). However, the lack of remains of other foods in the patios suggests that these were not sites of casual or routine eating. Instead, patios seem to have been used for special preparation and consumption of maize, possibly in the form of *chicha* or beer, a drink considered sacred and consumed on ritual occasions.

In the later periods of Sausa habitation, the amount of maize found at the sites increased considerably, coinciding with greater demands from the Inca ruling elites on local populations for resources given as tribute. Interestingly, the maize remains were found at more restricted areas within structures rather than distributed throughout them. This change may reflect greater restrictions on women's activities at the same time as there were greater demands on their labor (p. 148). Presumably women's labor was put to the service of facilitating the social and political activities of men.

Skeletal remains from the Sausa sites support the contention that women's status declined during the Inca period. Until about A.D. 1460, the people's diet emphasized several varieties of tubers with a relatively small amount of maize. Studies of sexed skeletons indicate that women and men consumed roughly the same types of foods. After 1460, however, differences between the genders became significant, particularly in the increase in consumption of maize by men, probably in the form of *chicha* (Hastorf, 1991, p. 150). Consumption of *chicha* took place then (as now) in the context of rituals, political activities, and communal, state-organized work tasks. Men seem also to have been eating more meat than women were eating.

What these data together indicate is growing involvement of men in community and regional activities and obligations, symbolized by the consumption of *chicha*. And although it was women's labor that produced *chicha*, they were restricted in its consumption and in participation in the activities that called for its use.

Although the rise of the Incan state and the expansion of its empire extracted burdens from women and men and curtailed some of women's activities more than men's, there were also contradictory tendencies and signs of resistance. For example, parallel descent as an organizing principle of kinship and of inheritance kept gender identities intact, continuing the strength of women's rights to land and wealth. Elite women maintained their membership in political and religious organizations and their access to political and religious authority through descent from other women (Silverblatt, 1991, p. 147). And the Incan queen remained a central state figure both as the wife of the king and in her own right, owning land, controlling labor, and wielding state power.

Ideologies and symbolisms of gender did relegate women to subordinate status in some contexts. For instance, as the Inca empire expanded, defeated peoples were referred to as "female," and young women from defeated groups were demanded as tribute to become "wives of the Inca" or "wives of the Sun" (p. 151). The former were married to Inca elites while the latter were dedicated to the service of Imperial gods. However, although some defeated peoples and their young women accepted these roles, others resisted, refusing to send their daughters into service. And some women consigned to a life of religious obligation refused to obey the rules of chastity incumbent upon them. Finally, because the women taken from vanquished groups were the symbols of the group's defeat, women who resisted Incan control came to symbolize ethnic identity and sovereignty.

Despite the burdens placed on rural communities, remnants of traditional egalitarian principles remained even in the context of superimposed control by Incan elites. However, indigenous beliefs and practices were thoroughly weakened by the cultural and military onslaught of Spanish invaders who arrived in Incan territory in 1532. Spanish conquerors not only overthrew the Incan state apparatus and looted its riches but also sought to transform all aspects of social, economic, and political life in the empire. Their interference in the lives of rural peasants was more intense than had been the experience under Incan control.

After destroying Incan rulers and their military forces, Spanish authorities moved to co-opt members of elite classes to forestall resistance to Spanish domination. Incan elites were granted privileges to land and resources that they had not been able to assume in traditional times. For example, they received individual grants to land in the countryside over which they had complete control and thus received personal income. Because this land was confiscated from the peasantry, the land base of rural people was eroded. To sustain themselves, they were forced to work on farms owned by elites or to seek employment, at extremely low wages, in mines or manufactories under Spanish or elite native ownership.

Both men and women among elite classes benefited from economic advantages allowed them by Spanish colonizers. They participated in trade with the Europeans and enriched themselves in the process. However, patriarchal attitudes inherent in Spanish culture affected women's lives. Under prior Incan rule, women had been able to own property and retain control over it after marriage. But Spanish laws turned married women into legal minors, denying them the right to own land independently of their husbands. Women needed male guardians to act for them in legal transactions (Silverblatt, 1980). Not surprisingly, husbands and male guardians often ignored a woman's wishes and disposed of her property to benefit themselves.

Women and girls were denied equal treatment in all public domains. Girls were not permitted to attend schools that were operated exclusively for elite boys. And despite women's traditional responsibility to spin and weave cloth, they were not allowed entrance to craft guilds or to paid employment in urban craftshops. They were, however, hired at low wages to perform domestic service for Spanish and native elites and clerics.

Demands on nonelites for tribute in goods and labor greatly increased after Spanish domination. Men were forced to work on farms or in mines, and women were compelled to weave cloth. In some cases, men fled their local communities to evade conscription into forced labor, but this practice left their wives with greater burdens in sustaining their families. At the same time, demands on women's labor in the form of producing cloth or performing domestic service for elites, Spanish landlords, and priests increased, further curtailing their ability to maintain daily subsistence activities in their households. Even when both husband and wife were present at home, tribute and tax requirements led to their impoverishment.

Spanish officials established control over rural communities by co-opting indigenous *curacas*. This group, traditionally endowed with high social status and some political authority, colluded with Spaniards in return for exemption from labor service or tribute in goods or taxes. They then served the colonial government by collecting taxes and ensuring that peasants fulfilled their work obligations. However, in keeping with Spanish patriarchal attitudes, women *curacas* were denied any power in local polities.

Sexual exploitation of women was a further reflection of Spanish values and a further curtailment of women's autonomy. Rape and forced prostitution became common abuses to which rural and urban women were subjected. These outrages were committed by Spanish colonizers and priests. Indeed, according to Felipe Guaman Poma de Ayala (1956), an indigenous chronicler of postconquest Peru, clergy were the worst offenders:

> The priests want money, money and more money [so they force women] to serve them as spinners, weavers, cooks, breadmakers. . . . Women had honor . . . during the epoch of the Incas in spite of the fact that they were idolatrous, but now the clergy and parish priests are the ones who first violate them and lead them to sin. (quoted in Silverblatt, 1980, p. 169)

In addition to abuses by Spaniards, some native women were sold to the Spanish by male relatives who thus evaded tribute or labor service (Silverblatt, 1980). The only women who fared well under colonial rule were those among the elite classes who became legal wives of Spaniards. Because few Spanish women emigrated from Europe, especially during the first thirty years after conquest, Spanish men sought indigenous wives.

A final mode of attack against native women surfaced in witch-hunts organized by Catholic priests. Women who were leaders or participants of native religious cults dedicated to female deities were systematically accused and executed as witches. Women healers were similarly persecuted.

In sum, Andean cultures experienced several waves of transformation as they were first incorporated into the expanding Incan empire and then engulfed by Spanish conquest. In the period of Incan state formation, social stratification incipient in Andean society increased. It was reflected in differential social prestige and in rights of elites to expropriate a portion of goods and labor from commoners. However, local lifeways were not totally disrupted, allowing indigenous egalitarian values to survive to some extent. Gender constructs expressing equality of women and men and their necessary interdependence remained operative in rural communities. Among elites, however, women's autonomy was restricted as social stratification and state control intensified.

Spanish domination obliterated Andean and Incan people's independence, extracted heavy burdens in the form of labor and produce, and decreased people's legal rights. Although most indigenous men and women were impoverished as a result, Spanish patriarchal practice exacted specific tolls on women as their previous rights to property and inheritance were negated, their participation in local polities was barred, their position as ritualists was attacked, and their bodies were sexually exploited.

INDIA

In turning next to data concerning two highly stratified and complex agricultural states—India and China—we see that ideological constructs supporting male dominance were intensified during historical periods of consolidation of state power. They remained strong well into the modern era and in fact continue today to varying degrees. Differences currently obtain among various groups within these nations with respect to adherence to traditional gender constructs. Many differences are correlated with class, education, religious beliefs, and urban/rural dichotomies.

Despite the unique circumstances of each society, traditional gender relations and attitudes toward women and men in India and China were quite similar. Likewise, the modern governments of these two nations have taken steps legally to support gender equality. In both cases, such steps have had uneven successes.

India is a nation of enormous ethnic, linguistic, and religious diversity. In addition to cultural differences, the populace is further segmented on the basis of rural/urban living, class and/or caste membership, education, and occupation. All of these distinctions have a bearing on gender relations experienced by individuals because norms in different groups vary.

Despite the diversity existing in India, certain behavioral and ideological patterns obtain throughout most of the nation. These patterns derive from an intensely patriarchal culture that dominated Indian society for thousands of years and continues with great strength even as modern reform movements have achieved some measure of success.

Most people in India reside in rural villages, have little or no formal education or contact with the national government, and hence generally live according to age-old traditions. In these villages, patriarchal social systems predominate. For most, patrilineal descent and patrilateral affiliation are the basis of household and community organization. Large extended families, often called *joint families*, reside together. These residence groups consist of a couple, their sons and sons' families, and their unmarried daughters. Women move to their husbands' homes upon marriage. Men are the recognized heads of households and wield authority over their wives and children. Marriages among India's Hindu people are monogamous, whereas polygyny is possible for Muslims and is practiced by wealthy men.

Among rural villagers, economic tasks are allocated according to gender. Men are primarily responsible for supplying their families with food, either produced through their own labor on their farmland or purchased with money received for paid employment. Farmers employ a variety of intensive techniques, including fertilizers, irrigation, and use of plows drawn by bullocks. Surpluses for sale in local markets are desirable as they provide income to enhance a household's standard of living (Jacobson, 1974).

Women's work consists mainly of food preparation, child care, and other domestic tasks. Women in many areas of India also participate in food production, especially in regions where rice is cultivated. There they engage in weeding and harvesting the crops. In other areas, women aid in harvesting grains such as wheat and millet and a variety of vegetables and fruits.

In areas where women engage in agricultural work, their status appears to be higher than among groups in which women do little or no direct productive labor. The Indian pattern of linkage between economic productivity and women's status is thus consistent with patterns found elsewhere in band, tribal, and chiefdom societies.

Male dominance and the resulting subordination of women have been accepted in Indian culture throughout its history, spanning millennia. In the earliest documented historical era of Indian society, the Vedic period (4000 to 300 B.C.), patriarchal constructs and practices were already instituted. Men dominated their households and communities, excluding most women from arenas of productivity and value.

However, women in Vedic society were not totally subordinated. Mothers had some authority in their families, and daughters were well treated by their parents. Although sons were preferred, girls were given the same opportunities as boys for education and religious training. In fact, many chroniclers of India's Vedic history were women. And some elite women were trained in military and administrative skills (Narain, 1967).

Vedic attitudes toward sexuality, divorce, and widowhood were relatively flexible, certainly as compared to practices of later periods. Although a girl's premarital chastity was the ideal, girls who had sexual experience before marriage were not shunned. Similarly, divorce was a possible escape from an unhappy marriage. It was usually initiated by husbands, but wives, too, could seek a divorce. Finally, widows were encouraged to remarry, often to a brother of their deceased husband.

Despite their ability to exercise some social freedoms, women were not legally independent of male control. As daughters, they were legal wards of their fathers; as wives, they were legally dependent on their husbands. A woman was not permitted to inherit property unless she was the only child.

Patriarchal practices and values inherent in Vedic society intensified in the post-Vedic period. The systematic codification of Hindu laws undertaken in early post-Vedic centuries was especially responsible for giving official sanction to strengthened patriarchal rights and decreases in women's status. The laws or code of Manu (ca. second century B.C.) were the most influential set of pronouncements on gender roles and values. According to Manu, a woman's highest duty (dharma) was to serve her husband:

> By a young girl, by a young woman, or even by an aged one, nothing must be done independently, even in her own house.
>
> In childhood a female must be subject to her father, in youth to her husband, when her lord is dead, to her sons; a woman must never be independent.
>
> By violating her duty towards her husband, a wife is disgraced in this world; [after death] she enters the womb of a jackal, and is tormented by diseases [the punishment] of her sin. (quoted from Buhler, 1964, in Wadley, 1988, p. 30)

Much of the ideological justification for the subordination of women was founded on Hindu beliefs in the inability of women to control their own passions. Women were perceived as inherently both dangerous and nurturing. Left to their own inclinations, they are unpredictable and therefore at least potentially threatening. Under male control, though, they become safe and benevolent. According to Manu:

> Through their passion for men, through their mutable temper, through their natural heartlessness, [women] become disloyal towards their husbands. . . . Knowing their disposition, which the Lord of creatures laid in them at the creation, to be such, [every] man should most strenuously exert himself to guard them. (p. 31)

On the basis of such attitudes, numerous practices oppressive to women became institutionalized throughout India in post-Vedic society and lasted well into the modern era. These included requirements of female chastity, child marriage, wife beating, disfigurement of widows, and *sati*, or the immolation of widows on their husbands' funeral pyre.

Further restrictions on women's activity were imposed when India came under Muslim rule in the twelfth century. At that time, the Islamic custom of *purdah*—that is, seclusion of women—began as a practice in some areas of India, particularly in the north, and by the fifteenth century, it was well established. Purdah entails the restriction of women to their homes. In addition, women must wear veils to cover their heads and faces when in the presence of men. The extent of coverage and contexts in which it is necessary vary among different groups, ranging from veiling of wives in the presence of elder male affinal relatives to complete coverage by all women in the presence of any man (Jacobson, 1974). Although the practice of purdah in India began with Muslims, it spread to some Hindus because it was reinterpreted as consistent with ancient Hindu precepts concerning the need to control women. Restrictions on women's activities and the extent of veiling tend to be greater among Muslims than among Hindus.

In any case, however, purdah is both a material and symbolic manifestation of women's dangerous potential and the need to control their activities. Women are perceived as threatening and defiling to men. In a sense, purdah is an extreme version of restrictions common to all Indian ethnic groups that affect women during menstruation. Contact with a menstruating woman is considered extremely polluting for other people. The woman therefore must refrain from touching others or preparing food or even entering a kitchen during the five days of ritual impurity beginning with the onset of each menstrual period. Although women may look upon these practices as granting them monthly respite from laborious household burdens, the social and personal messages encapsulated and transmitted have negative meaning concerning the danger to men that women inherently pose.

Preference for sons, already discernable in Vedic society, intensified in later centuries. It was shown in numerous behaviors and ideological constructs. Sons were considered necessary not only to support their parents in this life but to conduct proper funeral rituals that guaranteed eternal happiness for a parent's soul. The birth of a daughter was considered an unfortunate event because a girl could not perform any economic or ritual benefit for her parents. Indeed, daughters were liabilities because at their marriage, parents were required to give dowries to a husband's family.

As a consequence of marked preference for sons, female infanticide was often practiced. Although currently illegal, female infanticide still occurs in India. It is achieved through direct action of killing infants and by "maternal neglect" of daughters. In a modern study of the practice among the Kallars, a rural caste grouping in the state of Tamilnadu, S. Krishnaswamy (1988) cites records of a district hospital suggesting that of approximately 600 girls born each year to Kallar mothers, 450 are killed. The incidence of female infanticide is undoubtedly even higher because many Kallar women give birth at home rather than in hospitals, and the fate of their daughters is totally unknown. Another statistical indication of the rate of female infanticide is the fact that 70 percent of Kallar children under the age of 10 are boys.

In addition to statistical evidence, Krishnaswamy refers to midwives' accounts of witnessing killings of daughters, often accomplished by feeding the baby with poisonous substances from plants. In one case, a father killed his newborn daughter by stepping on her throat. Krishnaswamy reports a common Kallar belief that "if you kill a daughter, your next child will be a son" (p. 189), thus giving an added incentive to the practice. Regardless of current legal prohibitions against female infanticide, Kallar parents are evidently quite willing to discuss their behavior. As one woman told Krishnaswamy:

> Since I do not want the first child to be a female baby I wanted it to be killed. But my husband feels that we should wait for the second child. If that also happens to be a female baby we will definitely kill the second one. (p. 188)

Finally, that female infanticide among Kallars is far from disappearing is supported by statistics indicating a decline in the female-to-male sex ratio from 1971 to 1981. Krishnaswamy accounts for the continuation—indeed, possible rise—of female infanticide as a consequence of increasing pressure for dowries demanded by prospective in-laws of daughters and the resulting economic costs of raising girls.

A report released in 1998 indicates continuation of female infanticide in rural South India, especially, but not only, in Kallar communities (Jeeva et al., 1998). An intensive study of 120 respondents revealed that a majority of the families admitted to having killed one of their daughters shortly after her birth. Of the 57 Kallar women surveyed, 48 said that female infanticide had occurred in their families. About one third (12) of the 39 members of the Dalit castes interviewed also reported the practice. In both groups, the husband, with or without aid from his mother, committed most of the killings. Only four Kallar women and two Dalit women admitted to having perpetrated the acts themselves. Although dowry demands may be a factor in perpetuating female infanticide, more than half of the women interviewed denied being themselves the targets of dowry harassment. Analyses that interpret female infanticide in the context of violence against women are supported by the fact that nearly all of the women interviewed said they had been repeatedly beaten by their husbands, often when the men had been drinking alcoholic beverages heavily.

A further review of data collected indicated that in the study period, about 10% of girls were victims of infanticide (George et al., 1998). Moreover, 72% of all of the deaths of female infants resulted from infanticide whereas all of the deaths of male infants resulted from natural causes. Additional data from hospitals confirm similar trends. For example, of approximately 600 female births among the Kallar in one regional hospital, about 570 girls "vanish" and of these, hospital authorities estimate that about 80% (more than 450) are infanticide victims.

Jeeva et al. (1998) suggest that female infanticide is associated with the decline in women's status that has resulted from economic changes since the "Green Revolution" promulgated by international development agencies in India and other Asian countries since the 1960s. Intensive agricultural development has favored men's employment in technologically advanced farm work while women farmworkers have lost their jobs and therefore their income contributions to their families. As their productive roles have become more limited, their status has declined. The gender power imbalance, always a feature of patriarchal societies, has been intensified. In this context, some men have prospered and with their prosperity, the ability to give large dowries when their daughters marry has become a prestigious status symbol. Although wealthy people can afford such luxuries, poor people often imitate the style in an attempt to raise their own perceived status even though they can ill afford to do so. The dowry system therefore renders daughters a financial liability and provides an incentive for families to rid themselves of a financial burden.

Additional research and data from the southern Indian state of Tamil Nadu tell the same story. There, government statistics indicate that in the year 2006, there were a reported 2568 cases of female infanticide (Sridhar, 2006). However, although infanticide is illegal, only 16 cases were pursued by the authorities.

Negative attitudes toward girls are also demonstrated by patterns common in many areas of India of neglect of daughters through insufficient feeding and inattention to their illnesses. Unwanted girls eventually weaken and die, ostensibly from natural causes. Patterns of "maternal neglect" are, in Ashis Nandy's (1988) words, "a weird expression of woman's hostility toward womanhood and also, symbolically, toward her own self" (p. 71). They are, moreover, a reflection and instantiation of the strength of socialization that successfully teaches women their own unworthiness.

Neglect of daughters' illnesses has been found to be widespread in northern India, where patriarchal family and social systems are especially entrenched. Surveys conducted by staff of the Ludhiana Christian Medical College in the state of Punjab document numerous cases, including the following:

> In one village, I found a girl [who had] an advanced case of tuberculosis. I asked the mother why she hadn't done something sooner because now, at this stage, the treatment would be very expensive. The mother replied, "Then let her die. I have another daughter." The two daughters sat nearby listening, one with tears streaming down her face. (quoted in Miller, 1993, p. 423)

Similar instances of neglect, in effect "passive infanticide," have been documented throughout the region. In one study of a district in the Punjab, India's wealthiest state, 85 percent of all children who died between the ages of 7 to 36 months were female. Although all socioeconomic classes discriminated against daughters, disparities in mortality rates were strongest among the higher, privileged classes. Economic motives therefore cannot be attributed as causative. In fact, where economic pressures on families are greatest, relative female mortality rates are lower, presumably because girls' labor is needed most in poor families.

According to research sponsored by the World Bank in 1999, India's female children continue to suffer from neglect compared to the treatment received by boys (Claeson, Bos, and Pathmanathan, 1999). Girls are more likely to be seriously ill and to die between the ages of one month and five years than are boys. Indeed, at every age between birth and five years, mortality rates for girls are higher than for boys (ibid.: 20). These differences are due principally to two causes. First, girls have higher rates of malnutrition because boys are given preference for food both in terms of quantity and quality. Second, when girls fall ill, they are less likely than boys to be taken to doctors or other health care specialists for medical treatment. As a consequence of these patterns, Indian girls are 30 to 50% more likely to die by age five than are boys.

Although rates of neglect of girls vary somewhat among different segments of the Indian population, evidence of girls' disadvantages in food and health care is widespread throughout the country. It occurs in both urban and rural communities, among Hindus and Muslims, and by parents in all classes. In fact, the presence of economic resources and access to good health care facilities does not necessarily benefit daughters. Excess resources may be diverted to sons while daughters languish in need of proper nutrition and medical treatment.

Evidence further suggests that some Indian families take advantage of modern medical technology not to aid their daughters' survival but rather to cut it short. One study of hospital records from a large city in western India concluded that women often use amniocentesis to determine the sex of their fetus so they can abort daughters. In a one-year period, all of the 250 fetuses that were determined to be male were kept to term; 430 of the 450 female fetuses were aborted.

The destruction of daughters, whether before or after birth, has significant harmful effects on mothers as well. In addition to the self-negating symbolic meaning it must transmit, demeaning and devaluing the woman herself, a mother's health is affected by what Miller (1993) calls "over-reproduction," forcing "women to bear many children in the attempt to produce several sons" (p. 432).

In the 1980s and 1990s, new technologies were developed that could aid in the determination of the sex of a fetus. Ultrasound techniques were relatively cheap and became easily available throughout much of India. As a result, rates of abortion of female fetuses have risen. In response to trends that some government officials fear will widen the sex imbalance between males and females, in 1994 the Indian parliament enacted the Prenatal Diagnostic Techniques (Regulation and Prevention of Misuse) Act that made it illegal to use sonograms or other prenatal testing for the sole purpose of determining the sex of the fetus. However, authorities rarely pursue cases against either technicians or doctors who administer the procedures or parents who request them. Health clinics and roving trucks provide services even in remote rural communities. Their relatively cheap price and convenience make them accessible for many families. Advertisements proclaiming "Pay 500 rupees [US $14] now rather than 5 lakhs [US $14,000] later" appeal to parents who want to avoid costly dowries for their daughters (Rajan, 2006).

Abortion of female fetuses has negative consequences for women. Not only is it psychologically damaging by reinforcing negative attitudes about females but it also leads to multiple pregnancies and repeated abortions. Women who risk their health and potentially their lives may also have difficulty conceiving and bringing a baby to term.

No one knows the exact numbers of aborted female fetuses but a study published in the prestigious British medical journal The Lancet estimates that about 500,000 female fetuses are aborted annually in India (Jha et al., 2006). Over the last 20 years, therefore, the researchers conclude that as many as 10 million baby girls were never born. To support their claims, the report cites data from a Special Fertility and Mortality Survey of more than one million households. The study documents the sex ratio of first-, second- and third-order births. For example, there were 871 firstborn females for every 1000 males. These figures suggest a deviation from the expected near parity of sex ratios in the absence of intervention. When the firstborn was a girl, the sex ratio of the second child was 759 females per 1000 males. And when the first and second child were girls, the sex ratio for the third child was 719 females per thousand males. In contrast, when the first child was a boy, the sex ratios for second and third births were about equal.

These recent figures supplement data on sex ratios throughout India over the last several decades, indicating increasing disadvantage for females. For example, the number of girls per 1000 boys in the age group from birth to 6 years was 962 in the year 1981 but had fallen to 945 in 1991 with a further decline to 927 by 2001. Furthermore, the sex ratios of children living in urban areas is even more imbalanced than for those living in rural communities. That is, in 2001, there were 906 girls per 1000 boys in cities while in rural areas the comparable figure was 934 per 1000. Disparities in numbers of girls and boys begins at birth and then increases at each age for the next five years, reflecting higher mortality rates for girls. These facts provide additional evidence of neglect of girls through unequal access to nutrition and health care.

Families with greater resources and better educations were more likely to avoid having second and third order girls. That is, mothers who were educated at least through grade 10 were less likely than illiterate women to give births to girls. The data reflect sex ratios averaging 683 per 1000 males for more educated mothers and sex rations averagin 829 per 1000 males for illiterate mothers.

Taken altogether, Jha et al. (2006) conclude that sex determination of fetuses followed by selective abortion if the fetus was to be a girl accounts for the imbalance in sex ratios. Comparing the Indian data with worldwide sex ratios suggest a natural ratio of about 952 980 girls per 1000 boys. Therefore some 13.6–13.8 million girls should have been born in India in 1997 but instead, only 13.1 million girls were born, leaving a deficit of about one half or three quarters million female births in one year alone.

In response to a continuing decline in the number of female births, some activists and government authorities promote a program called the White Cradle Baby Scheme (Sridhar, 2004). The government sets up cradles in public places so that parents who have unwanted daughters can leave the babies for adoption without any penalty to themselves. While this plan may save some girls' lives, some activists believe that it transmits the wrong message, encouraging people to give up their daughters and thus undermining rather than advancing concepts of women's worth.

Another manifestation of male dominance in Indian culture is the practice of child marriage. In early periods of Vedic society, girls were expected to marry in their middle or late teens, but administrative and religious writings dating from 400 B.C. began to advise that girls be married soon after puberty. Child marriage thus became the norm by approximately A.D. 100 and continues even today in many Indian communities despite laws prohibiting it.

Child marriage is one method of controlling females and has two important consequences. First, the chastity of a young girl, usually married before or shortly after the onset of menses, is virtually assured. A girl's chastity is an absolute requirement for a respectable marriage, although boys' premarital sexual activity is permitted. Second, a wife who relocates at such a young age to her husband's household generally accepts her subordination because it is based not only on gender but also on age. She is thus easily dominated by her husband and especially by his elder relatives, perhaps most particularly by his mother. Indeed, as many researchers of Indian culture have noted, wives often experience their most intense oppression at the hands of their mothers-in-law rather than of their husbands (Chitnis, 1988).

Wives' domination by their mothers-in-law is due, in part, to the quality of relationships between spouses. Newlywed couples rarely are acquainted prior to their marriages. Unions are arranged by parents or other relatives without any need to gain consent of either prospective bride or groom. Once married, couples actually have little interaction in a husband's joint household. The husband is himself a young man and lives under his father's authority. As a subordinate in his father's household, he takes great care not to signal a shift away from his first allegiance to his parents. Because wives are perceived as potentially destabilizing to established familial order, married sons refrain from showing too much affection or even concern for their wives. Couples rarely interact publicly and do not engage in extended conversation when other family members are present. A wife thus spends most of her time in the company of other women in the household. These women, unmarried daughters and in-marrying wives, are all under the supervision of the elder woman. A new daughter-in-law is typically met with some degree of hostility by her husband's mother and sisters. As a result, authoritative statuses are immediately established and reinforced.

A woman's position, both in the general context of Indian culture and in the specific experience of individuals, is strengthened only when she becomes a mother. Motherhood defines a woman's social and personal identity. "Each infant borne and nurtured by her safely into childhood, especially if the child is a son, is both a certification and a redemption" (Kakar, 1988, p. 44). Pregnancy changes a woman's status from an obedient servant of little consequence to a future mother at the center of household attention. Her mother-in-law, previously stern and domineering, becomes solicitous and concerned. In addition, a pregnant woman's household burdens are lightened, and other family members cater to her needs.

Given the marked improvement in the treatment a woman receives when she is pregnant and after she becomes a mother, women desire to produce many children. Sons, of course, are strongly preferred, but daughters at least prove that a woman is not barren, a condition that renders a woman totally valueless.

Marriage and even motherhood are not unmixed blessings for Indian women, however. Physical abuse of women was, and is, common, perpetrated both by husbands and their relatives. Such violence is justified on the basis of ancient beliefs, codified by Manu, of the need to control women to render them safe and benevolent. In the context of patrilocal residence, ideally coupled with norms of village exogamy, wives have little recourse. Their own natal families live in other villages and may not have knowledge of the abuse to which they may be subjected. In any case, parents generally do not give emotional support to a daughter who attempts to leave an abusive marital situation. In fact, they often urge her to return to her husband and even deliver her back to her in-laws.

Wife beating continues as a serious problem in modern Indian society. Statistics on its incidence are lacking, but some researchers estimate that well over 50 percent of married women experience some form of physical abuse (Flavia, 1988). A contemporary survey of women who sought aid from shelters for battered wives indicated that people of all ages, classes, educational, and occupational groups were equally likely to be affected. The lack of parental support for victims is graphically recounted by one interviewee (quoted in Flavia, 1988):

> I was desperate, but I could not return to my mother's house because I had two younger sisters and my mother felt that if I came back it would be difficult to get them married. So I stayed on. Once I was so desperate I poured kerosene over myself, but my husband entered the room and stopped me before I could light the match. I was expecting my first child. When I went to my mother's house for delivery I stayed for three years. But finally my mother grew frantic because my younger sisters were not getting proposals. So she took me, my daughter, 10 tolas of gold and Rs. 2000 [Indian currency] and left me in my husband's home. Today I have three children and I live as a prisoner in my own home. (pp. 157–158)

In 1983, the Indian government enacted laws making domestic violence a criminal offense but perpetrators are rarely pursued legally. Still, official statistics suggest that rates of violence against wives have not declined in the early 21st-century. Estimates remain that more than 50% of married women are victims of some form of physical and/or sexual violence committed by their husbands. Attitudes that condone such violence are widespread. For example, researchers from the International Center for Research on Women who interviewed men in the state of Punjab discovered that about 80% of the men think that a husband has the right to physically punish a wife who is "disrespectful" while 60% think that a man is justified in beating his wife if she "does not follow instructions" (Zutshi, 2004). Research conducted in the northern Indian state of Uttar Pradesh similarly documents high levels of both physical and sexual violence against wives (Koenig et al., 2006). This study questioned husbands about their behavior. About 25% of the total 4520 male respondents admitted to having used some form of physical violence against their wives in the 12 months prior to the survey while 30% admitted to having physically forced their wives to have sexual intercourse. Significantly as well, about a third of the men reported that when they had been children they had witnessed their own fathers beating their mothers.

In past centuries, the fate of widows in India was certainly unenviable. Under conditions of intensifying male dominance in post-Vedic society, widows lost all respectability and sympathy. They were customarily disfigured and shunned. They were denied the right to remarry regardless of their age. Thus, many young women, even girls, were forced to live alone or at the mercy of unsympathetic consanguineal or affinal relatives. The practice of *sati*—that is, immolation of widows—became common among some high-status castes. Widows were coerced into throwing themselves on the flames of their husband's funeral pyre. *Sati* continued well into the modern era. It is currently illegal but is occasionally reported even today.

During the many centuries following the decrees of Manu and other Hindu lawgivers, practices that restricted and oppressed women gained wide acceptance and became integral parts of Indian culture. Patriarchal attitudes and behaviors reflective of male dominance did not begin to abate until the nineteenth century. At that time, a number of prominent Indian men advocated changes in law to eliminate some of the most severe practices. Among the first goals was the abolition of *sati*. Other practices, such as child marriage, disfigurement of widows, and denial of widows' rights to remarry, also came under attack during periods of agitation for reform beginning in the first half of the nineteenth century. Significantly, these reform movements were initiated by elite men who had been exposed to Western education under British colonial rule in India that commenced in the eighteenth century. Women did not become active on their own behalf until late in the nineteenth century (Chitnis, 1988).

In addition to goals of eliminating oppressive practices, reformers championed the cause of education and opportunity for girls as well as boys. Finally, they advocated granting women rights to own and inherit property independently of men.

Many reform activists became disillusioned with the failure of British colonial administrators to respond favorably to their demands for changes in law. This timidity was occasioned by British unwillingness to take on social and cultural issues that might arouse Indian resistance to their rule. However, some legal prohibitions were enacted during this period to ameliorate women's situation. These included outlawing *sati* (1829), permitting widows to remarry (1856), raising the age at which girls could be married to 12 years (1860), providing for divorce and for a woman's right to inheritance (1872), and allowing married women to own property (1874) (Narain, 1967).

As movements for national liberation and Indian independence from Great Britain gained force, new leaders emerged who also advocated equality for women. Among these was Mahatma Gandhi, who developed his philosophy of nonviolence and "moral power" based, in part, on the "pure and gentle, but firm and tenacious strength which, he emphasized, women continuously display in life" (Chitnis, 1988, p. 87). Gandhi also believed that success of the struggle for India's independence required the full participation of all its citizens and thus urged women to join actively in public life.

Since Indian independence in 1947, the central government has taken steps legally to ban many practices oppressive to women, including child marriage, *sati*, and dowry. It has also enacted laws to support equal rights for women in property ownership, inheritance, and educational and employment opportunities. But enormous problems remain in terms of people's knowledge of these laws and rights and in terms of enforcement. Because most Indians live in rural areas and are illiterate, they are unlikely to be aware of legislation prohibiting such traditional practices as child marriage and dowry. Literacy rates in India are extremely low, and even more so for females. Only 24.8 percent of Indian women are literate, a rate that is approximately half the percentage of 46.9 percent for men. But even when aware of existing legislation, many people are unwilling to claim their rights because of intense social pressure to conform to local norms and continue traditional behavior.

There are numerous reports of continuation—indeed, acceleration—of outlawed practices. For instance, attention has been given in the Indian press and governing circles concerning the rise of dowry demands despite the fact that dowry is currently illegal. Dowry was traditionally a gift in the form of goods or money given by a wife's parents to the family of a prospective husband. Although outlawed by the Dowry Prohibition Act (1961, amended in 1984 and 1986), dowry has now become a demand on the part of a husband's family (Ghadially and Kumar, 1988). Such demands specify amounts of cash or goods necessary to contract a marriage. Young men of high status, good educations, and favorable employment prospects command large sums. In many cases, dowry demands are currently made after a marriage is contracted and even after a wedding has occurred.

Public controversy has been stirred in India over dowry because of the increasing incidence of deaths of young wives whose families have not satisfied the dowry demands of their in-laws. Rehana Ghadially and Pramod

Kumar (1988) report a study indicating that of a registered 179 "unnatural deaths" of young married women in Delhi in 1981–1982, 12 to 16 percent were dowry related. In two-thirds of these cases, young women committed suicide; the remaining one-third were murdered by their affines (in-laws). The families involved were of all social classes, educational levels, and occupations. Ghadially and Kumar also report a study in the Indian state of Maharashtra concluding that dowry deaths rose from 120 in 1984 to 211 in 1985, an increase of 64 percent. Government statistics indicate the seriousness and frequency of the problem of violence against wives motivated by dowry conflicts. According to figures from 2001, nearly 7000 women were killed by their husbands and in-laws over dowry payments deemed inadequate. And many thousands more are seriously injured (BBC News, 2003).

Retaliation against wives whose families have failed to meet dowry demands takes many forms, ranging from verbal abuse to physical violence. Women frequently suffer kicks, burns, and beatings. Most of the women studied who died as a result of their treatment died of burns; hanging, poisoning, and strangulation also occurred.

A disturbing finding in studies of dowry abuse and death is the fact that the wife's parents are sometimes aware of the violence perpetrated against their daughter but do nothing to give her emotional or legal support. In fact, the abused daughter is told to endure her situation rather than stir social controversy that would negatively affect her family's reputation.

Dowry and the related mistreatment and deaths of women were the impetus to the birth of the feminist movement in India. Beginning in 1979, women's groups staged public protests to bring the issue of dowry harassment out in the open. As a result, many families of abused and murdered daughters came forward to give testimony and ask for redress. The Indian government responded in 1980 with passage of laws against dowry-related crimes, mandating police investigation of the death of any woman who had been married less than five years at the time of her death. Legislation passed in 1983 strengthened the first law, making "cruelty to a wife a cognizable, nonbailable offense" and stipulating that "cruelty" included both mental and physical harassment (Kumar, 1995, p. 68). Cases reported as suicides (frequently involving death by dousing and burning) could be investigated as "abetment to suicide," shifting the burden of proof to the woman's husband and his family. In addition, amendments required autopsies of women who died within seven years of marriage.

The burgeoning movement for women's rights in India also tackled the issue of rape, focusing first on "custodial rape" that is, rape perpetrated by police and by landlords or employers. Although the government again responded with favorable legislation, spelling out the meaning of custodial rape and mandating ten-year prison terms for those convicted, in 1988 the Indian Supreme Court, in a precedent-setting decision, reduced the sentence of a convicted rapist because of the conduct of the victim—an unmarried woman with a lover (Kumar, 1995, p. 72).

While the women's rights movement has gained considerable public support, opposition has been voiced especially on the part of religious fundamentalists of both the Hindu and Moslem faiths. Islamic leaders objected to the Indian parliament's attempt to extend statutes protecting a woman's ability to seek divorce and to obtain economic support from her ex-husband, claiming that such legislation violates Islamic personal law. In addition, some traditional and nationalist Hindus have sought to extol the practice of *sati* as an honorable act on the part of a widow. This issue took center stage in 1987 after a young widow was immolated on her husband's funeral pyre, although there was considerable uncertainty about whether she was a willing or unwilling sacrifice (Kumar, 1995, pp. 80–81). Public sentiment was marshaled both in outrage against the event and in support of the practice, the former pointing out the abrogation of women's rights and the latter claiming rights to Hindu identity.

Another area of controversy in India concerns the use of amniocentesis to determine the sex of a child prenatally. Such tests are freely provided under Indian health care, as are a myriad of contraceptive and abortion services. Discovery through amniocentesis of a female fetus often results in a mother's decision to abort. This practice demonstrates the strength of preference for sons and has resulted in continuation of an unbalanced sex ratio in India, currently standing at 933 females to 1,000 males (Chitnis, 1988).

Practices demonstrative of male dominance tend to be most intense in rural communities, but townspeople and city dwellers are not free of traditional gender constructs that limit women's activity and undermine their social worth. Class membership, education, and occupation also intersect in complex ways in the manifestation of traditional norms. Generally, urban middle and upper class people with advanced educations are less constrained by attitudes supportive of male dominance than are people living in rural areas and having little or no exposure to modern education. However, even college-educated professional people frequently agree that women's first responsibility is to fulfill their roles as wives and mothers and only secondarily to pursue their careers (Sharma, 1986). These attitudes often contradict actual economic contributions. For instance, in a study of urban households in the city of Shimla, North India, Ursula Sharma (1986) found that despite overt values emphasizing women's responsibilities to their domestic roles, those women who worked in the paid labor force contributed a substantial portion of the family's income. Furthermore, although wives' earnings tend to be less than husbands', the disparity is caused by the fact that women are generally paid lower wages than men even for the same work rather than by differences in time spent in paid employment.

In addition to unequal pay, other kinds of discrimination against working women adversely affect their ability to gain adequate incomes. For instance, Johanna Lessinger's (1986) study of tradeswomen in the large southern India city of Madras discovered numerous difficulties encountered disproportionately by women engaged in market activities. Many unskilled, uneducated women make their livelihood selling fresh fruit, vegetables, and flowers in open retail markets. But in contrast to societies in Africa, the Caribbean, and Latin America, Indian market women are far outnumbered by men. Those women who do sell goods in Madras are in retail sales only; none are in the more profitable wholesale sector. Women tend to be concentrated in less desirable marketplaces and to sell highly perishable items that garner relatively low profits. Significant also is their exclusion from the more lucrative field of sales to hospitals, schools, and factories (Lessinger, 1986).

Lessinger accounts for many of Madras's tradeswomen's problems by reference to patriarchal attitudes toward women's participation in paid employment and activity outside the home. Although women in her study entered the workforce because of dire economic necessity and thus fulfill their duties to maintain their families, they are often met with hostility because they contradict traditional norms of women's seclusion. Women's difficulties in establishing themselves as wholesalers or as sellers to hospitals and other public facilities stem, in part, from harassment they receive when interacting with strangers, creditors, or administrators. Such harassment is often verbal and/or sexual, manifested as insults and threats of sexual violence.

As a counterclaim to criticism that they are immoral because they violate principles of women's seclusion, Lessinger (1986) reports that tradeswomen "invoke another set of cultural ideals, that of self-sacrificing motherhood. . . . Their departure from the norm of retiring female modesty is always recast as a variant of female domestic responsibility" (pp. 587–588).

Women thus attempt to resolve an ideological dilemma occasioned by material conditions of their poverty. However successful they may be in justifying their behavior, their need to do so demonstrates the strength of patriarchal attitudes still dominating Indian society. Efforts of the Indian government, both nationally and regionally, and efforts made through education and health care services to protect women from oppressive practices and to grant women equal rights and opportunities have been only partially successful. But for the vast majority of India's people, living in rural areas and largely unaffected by public policies, traditional values and behaviors persist unabated.

It is certainly true that most Indian men do not benefit materially from their patriarchal culture. Most Indian people, men and women, live in poverty, obtain little or no formal education, receive inadequate health services, and are subordinated in a rigid hierarchical system of caste and class. However, women's experience is made more oppressive because of ideological constructs that undermine not only their material rights but also their very sense of social and personal worthiness.

China

Gender constructs and behaviors that developed in India are not entirely unique. In fact, many complex hierarchical state societies employ gender differences as a means of subordinating one-half of the populace and rewarding the other half. As a result, both women who are subordinated and men who are rewarded can be controlled. Potential resistance to state power can be muted by convincing women of their powerlessness and convincing men that the system offers them benefits. Although such systems become established to further economic and political goals of elites, they are explained and justified through ideological constructs. Even when material conditions change, ideological beliefs and attitudes may continue with great strength. We have seen that Indian customs that discriminate against women are still practiced despite decades of governmental and educational efforts to eliminate them. In turning now to another predominantly agricultural state, China, we will see that similar patriarchal attitudes and behaviors hold a tenacious grip over many Chinese citizens, regardless of official policies to foster equality of women and men.

Traditional Chinese culture, like that of India, was intensely patriarchal. Patriarchal gender relations and the ideological constructs supporting and justifying them were developed through several millennia of Chinese history. They were interconnected with an extremely hierarchical social and political order growing out of a history of internal warfare among feuding warlords who continually attempted to expand their control over larger territories and to deepen their rule over the populace. Centralized imperial dynasties took hold in the eighth century, succeeding one another after wars among rivals. To stabilize and expand political and military power, ruling classes adopted and promulgated philosophies that expounded the legitimacy of state control. The thought of Confucius (551–479 B.C.) and his disciples was especially influential. A cornerstone of this philosophy was the notion of "filial piety," which ordained obedience toward one's social superiors. All Chinese owed obedience to the emperor, sons must obey their fathers, and women must be subordinate to men.

Although documents chronicling early periods of state development in China indicate the low status of women and in fact enshrine and justify women's inferiority, some evidence from the archaeological record may point to the high status of particular women and perhaps of women as a group. Excavations at Niuheliang, a site in northeastern China dating from about 3500 to 3000 B.C., reveal a ceremonial center of great size and importance (Nelson, 1991, p. 302). The site contains a large ceremonial building, life-size female statues, and several burials of high-status individuals. The temple is constructed of several rooms containing clay statues of women, some decorated with paints and jewels. Although there is no confirmation in written documents about the statues, a likely hypothesis is that because the building was used as a ceremonial center, the statues probably represented female deities. And although the presence of female deities does not necessarily correlate with high social status for women, it does suggest an intriguing possibility that during earlier periods of Chinese state formation, women may have had high social status and religious authority.

Some corroborating evidence of the status of women exists in an excavation of the "richest grave that has ever been found [in China] with all the burial goods intact" (p. 304). This is the resting place of Fu Hao. Some records indicate that she was a consort of a king while others state that she was a "leader of armies" (p. 304). In any case, she was a woman of great wealth and high social standing.

Male dominance was manifested in numerous social, economic, political, and religious spheres. The social domain was organized through lineages and clans based on patrilineal descent. Households consisted of members of patri-lineages, dominated by the eldest male. His wife, unmarried children, and married sons and their wives and children were all under his absolute authority. The rule of a head of household was often quite cruel, with a resulting high level of intrafamilial violence. Wives and children were frequent victims of beatings meted out by husbands/fathers. Because postmarital residence was patrilocal, wives could rarely depend on their own relatives for support in times of conflict with their affines (Wolf, 1974). A wife experienced extreme subordination within her husband's household, especially when she was young and had not yet borne sons to carry on her husband's lineage. Compounding the problem of low status for wives based on their gender, the fact that wives were customarily much younger than their husbands added to their social inferiority. Because seniority was a critical dimension of hierarchical order in Chinese society and family life, a wife's youthful age contributed to her subordination.

As in India, women were dominated by men in various kinship relations. Girls were ruled by their fathers, wives by their husbands, and widows by their brothers and sons. In addition, wives were controlled by their mothers-in-law, who acted as "surrogates for male authority" (Diamond, 1975, p. 376). Mothers-in-law could be quite cruel to their sons' wives, abusing them verbally and physically. Wives had few, if any, allies in their husbands' households. Husbands offered their wives little emotional or strategic support if conflicts arose between a wife and her affines. In keeping with notions of filial piety, a man's allegiance was first and foremost to his parents. His wife was decidedly secondary and could not depend on him for social solidarity.

As a consequence of the isolation and hardships many women were forced to endure, the suicide rate among young wives was higher than for any other age and gender categories (O'Kelly and Carney, 1986). Only after they reached middle or old age and had adult sons did women receive any deferential treatment. Because sons were the sole possible allies for a woman, mothers attempted to control their sons through establishment of strong emotional bonds (Wolf, 1974). Given the sternly authoritarian relationship between fathers and sons, sons gravitated to the emotional warmth showered on them by their mothers.

Patriarchal attitudes were reflected in a marked preference for sons. Sons were necessary for the social, material, and spiritual well-being of their parents. Through sons, patrilineages maintained their continuity. Of course, it was not sons themselves who provided progeny; rather, the sons possessed the ability to marry and thus recruit women to produce offspring, particularly male offspring, for their lineages. Given these circumstances, marriages of eldest sons were especially significant events in a family's life. Enormous

Chinese farmers plant rice
using traditional methods.

expense was therefore often incurred in paying bridewealth for the wife of an eldest son and in celebrating the marriage with an elaborate and expensive wedding.

The economic division of labor contributed further justification for preference for sons. According to gender-assigned tasks, men were primarily responsible for agricultural production. They prepared fields and planted and harvested crops. Women's work was usually confined to domestic household tasks, including food preparation, household maintenance, and child care. When additional labor was required for farmwork at harvest time, women, especially among poor families, helped in the fields. Families who were more prosperous generally hired men and women as agricultural workers. Patriarchal relations embedded in Chinese culture were demonstrated in paid employment because the wages of women workers were given to their fathers or husbands rather than to the worker herself (Diamond, 1975).

Women living in prosperous households were restricted to domestic labor and in fact were ideally restricted to the physical confines of the home.

Indeed, the Chinese word for "wife," *neiran,* literally means "inside person" (Croll, 1982). Women's social subordination was justified, in part, by their economic dependence on men (Wong, 1974). Preference for sons was rationalized on the basis of their economic productivity and their contributions to their parents' sustenance. Sons' material assistance continued as parents grew older and came to depend totally on their sons' labor.

Finally, sons fulfilled crucial religious functions for their parents. In accordance with Chinese beliefs, sons performed necessary rituals at parents' funerals. Ceremonies dedicated to deceased parents, especially to fathers, were conducted daily, and parents' death days were marked annually.

Given the productive and socially valued roles allotted to men and the fact that these roles were systematically barred to women, sons were markedly preferred over daughters. This preference was repeatedly enacted in Chinese life and was also enshrined in Chinese philosophy. The Chinese scholar Mencius, a disciple of Confucius, stated, "There are three unfilial acts; the greatest of these is the failure to produce sons" (quoted in Wong, 1974, p. 230). Similarly, the ancient *Book of Odes,* compiled three thousand years ago, states, "When a son is born, he is laid down on couches, and is given a piece of jade to play with. When a daughter is born, she is laid on the floor, and is given a piece of tile to play with" (p. 131).

Daughters frequently received even worse treatment than just prescribed. Female infanticide was quite common, resulting in a distorted sex ratio. As an alternative to infanticide, daughters were sometimes sold into slavery or prostitution by poor families who thus not only gained immediate financial rewards but also freed themselves of the need to present a dowry at their daughter's marriage.

Marriages were arranged by fathers of the prospective couple without any need to consult either bride or groom. Girls generally were married in their late teens but were often betrothed as children. Many marriages were arranged at the time of a girl's birth. These betrothals functioned to solidify alliances between men, using their children as tokens.

Girls' chastity before marriage was absolutely essential. Indeed, because children in a household were segregated by gender at an early age, many girls had little knowledge of sexuality. Their initiation into sexual relations after their weddings often was brutal. Husbands, of course, were not constrained by premarital restrictions. In fact, men frequented brothels to gain sexual experience before marriage (Wong, 1974).

Several interrelated practices in traditional China contributed to a scarcity of marriageable women. Widespread female infanticide was the most obvious cause, but, in addition, many young girls were sold by their fathers into concubinage to wealthy men. Others were sold into houses of prostitution, and once defiled in this way, they were considered unfit for marriage. The shortage of women resulted in many men's inability to marry. These men were socially humiliated because not only were they without the sexual and domestic services of a wife, but they were also unable to produce legitimate sons. Patriarchal control over women thus intersected with hierarchical relations based on wealth, to the detriment of women and poor men.

Traditional customs related to divorce further discriminated against women. Divorce could be initiated only by husbands. Proceedings against a wife could be occasioned by several conditions, among them her disobedience to her husband or his parents or her failure to produce a son. Divorce carried no stigma for a husband, but a divorced woman was shamed.

Ideally, widows were not supposed to remarry. Despite the norm, widows were sometimes sought after by poor men who were unable to find other suitable women willing to marry them. Because widows had few alternatives, they often agreed to such unions to escape the social stigma and economic hardships of widowhood.

Throughout her life, then, a woman was subordinated and controlled, primarily by the men in her household or by the mother and elder sisters of her husband. Restrictions were placed on her behavior, barring her from social contacts outside the family, denying her the value of contributing productive labor to family subsistence, and excluding her from many significant ritual contexts. It is important to stress that the denigration of women was the result of first blocking their participation in society. Economic and religious roles performed by Chinese men could just as well have been performed by women. But by denying women rights to function as independent and valued members of society, Chinese society made women's consequent dependence into a justification for their unworthiness.

A symbolic and meaningful mark of the social distinctiveness of men and the social nonbeing of women was (and still is) shown by different naming patterns for males and females. In a study of naming practices in Hong Kong and Taiwan, Rubie Watson (1993) found that although both girls and boys are given personal names that may be motivated by literary sources or an event occurring near the time of the child's birth or a wish for the child's future, boys' names have positive or prestige implications, whereas girls' names more often have negative meanings. For example, an eldest boy might be called "Eldest Luck," but a second or third girl might be named "Too Many" or "Little Mistake." In addition to differences in the names themselves, acquisition of subsequent names distinguishes males and females. Throughout a man's life, he acquires new names that indicate social standing in his household and community and confer prestige to their holder, such as a school name given by a teacher, a marriage name selected when a man marries, a "courtesy" name that marks economic or social success, and a posthumous name given to honor a man's life. Women, in sharp contrast, have only their personal name. In fact, even this name is dropped from usage when a woman marries; but rather than acquiring a new marriage name as men do, a woman becomes known thereafter by kin terms in reference to her husband and children—that is, as "X's wife" or "X's mother." In old age, a woman is simply called "old woman" by everyone except her closest relatives. Finally, a woman's nonbeing is forever memorialized on her tombstone where, instead of personal, courtesy, and posthumous names engraved for men, a woman's existence is subsumed under her father's surname, and she is listed eternally as "Family of X."

Restrictions on girls and women in traditional Chinese society were symbolized and physically manifested by the practice of foot binding. The feet of young girls at the age of 4 or 5 were bound with tight cloths so their toes curled under their feet. As the children grew to adulthood, their feet became progressively more deformed, and normal walking became impossible. As a result, adult women took tiny, faltering steps on feet sometimes 3 inches long. This brutal deformity was inflicted on women beginning in imperial circles in the tenth century. Foot binding quickly spread among other elites, and by the twelfth century, it was widely used throughout all social classes. Only among very poor people where women's agricultural labor provided a necessary financial contribution to family survival did daughters escape the torture of having their feet bound.

Traditional patriarchal customs did not begin to change until the early twentieth century. By that time, imperial Chinese dynasties had been overthrown through military defeats by the British in the Opium War of 1839–1842 and by the Japanese in 1895. Chinese elites were exposed to Western values through contact with Western traders and administrators as well as through Western education. Although nineteenth-century European and American cultures were also patriarchal, the forms they took were certainly milder. As a result of contacts and pressures exerted by European authorities, some traditional Chinese practices came under attack. For instance, foot binding was outlawed in 1902, although the ban was widely ignored until the 1950s when the new communist government undertook a vigorous campaign to eliminate the practice.

In the early twentieth century, nationalist movements sprang up in China, principally in urban areas, to free the nation from foreign control. These movements combined their political goals with a strong social agenda aimed at dismantling Confucian ideologies that subordinated the majority of Chinese people to benefit the privileged elite. Among the many activists and reformers of the period were numerous women, mainly from families of prosperous merchants or landed gentry. They were well educated and assumed leadership positions within the nationalist movements (Gilmartin, 1989).

The Chinese republic was established in 1911, led by Sun Yat-sen. In the early 1920s, the two major parties, the National Party (Guomindang) and the Chinese Communist Party, became allies, but they severed their solidarity in 1927. In the ensuing years, members of the Guomindang launched campaigns against the communists, most of whom fled to the countryside and began to organize among the peasantry. The Guomindang was especially brutal in its attacks against women activists, raping, torturing, and murdering more than a thousand (Stacey, 1979).

Those women who survived continued their work among peasants and organized women's committees throughout China. Such committees sought and aired complaints made by rural women who were encouraged to "speak bitterness" about their lives publicly. Once this process began, it gained popularity. Many women spoke of the hardships of their marriages and the brutal treatment they received from husbands and affines. However, despite the Communist Party's initial sympathy for the cause of women's rights, many leaders tempered their attack against patriarchal practices common in rural communities. They feared arousing men's hostility and thus weakening their base of support. They focused their attention on campaigns for land reform that were obviously popular among the peasantry. Party officials continued to value and encourage women's participation both before and after the establishment of the communist state in 1949, but they reneged on their earlier commitment to women's equality (Gilmartin, 1989). Also, although the party remained strenuous in attacking Confucian ideals that bound poor peasants to their social superiors, it abandoned the vigorous fight against patriarchal practices within the family that subordinated women to men's control.

The Chinese government did enact several laws that attempted to transform social and familial relationships between women and men. For instance, the Marriage Law of 1950 declared that the "New-Democratic marriage system is based on the free choice of partners, on monogamy, on equal rights for both sexes, and on the protection of the lawful interests of women and children" (quoted in Wong, 1974, p. 242). The law further declared the legal age of marriage for women to be 18 years and for men, 20 years. The Chinese government currently encourages even later marriages to limit population growth, advocating that women marry between the ages of 23 and 27 and men between 25 and 29.

Additional laws have banned child marriage, bridewealth, and dowry. These laws are often ignored, however, particularly in the countryside where patriarchal attitudes remain strong and government intervention is weak. Although divorce is legal, social barriers to a wife's seeking an end to her marriage are still difficult to overcome. Pressure to remain in an unhappy marriage is also exerted by male political cadres in rural communities who oppose women's full emancipation. As one peasant woman remarked, "To get a divorce, there are three obstacles to overcome: the obstacle of the husband, the obstacle of the mother-in-law, and the obstacle of the cadres. The obstacle of the cadres is the hardest to overcome" (Stacey, 1979, p. 314).

Male dominance is still evidenced in modern Chinese society in several domains. Although the notion of equality between women and men within families has become superficially accepted among educated urban people, women continue to bear the responsibility of fulfilling domestic tasks even though they are full-time workers in outside paid employment. Their "double day" includes housework and child care.

Among rural people, who make up the vast majority of Chinese citizens, patriarchal attitudes are prevalent in the kinds of work assigned to women and men and in the rewards given for work. When communal farms were established through land reform programs in the mid-1950s, all men and women were expected to contribute productive agricultural labor. The government clearly understood that economic development in China depended on the full participation of all residents. Encouragement for women's work was generally successful. In the one year between 1957 and 1958, when the government launched its strongest effort, rural women's rate of employment jumped from 60 percent to 90 percent (Croll, 1982). However, assignment of jobs on the communes is often linked to gender. For instance, a study by Elizabeth Croll (1982) of Jiang village indicates that women's tasks consisted principally of such work as tending pigs and poultry, collecting manure, breeding silkworms, and hoeing fields. All of these jobs are consistent with women's traditional domestic tasks rather than reflective of innovative departures from traditional norms.

Women's participation in rural work tends to be greater in those areas where agricultural production is intense, as in regions producing cotton, tea, and rice. Women also participate fully in direct production where other kinds of occupations, such as rural industries or construction work, are available for men. Women therefore function as a reserve labor force ready to be absorbed into agricultural work when needed. But their opportunities to perform other jobs in rural communities is limited by men's monopoly. For example, Croll's study of Jiang village reveals the allocation of work for women and men shown in Table 5.1. As these statistics demonstrate, even though nearly the same number of women and men are employed, all women except one work in agricultural production, whereas two-thirds of the men work in farming and one-third have other occupations.

Women currently constitutes 45% of the total employed workforce in China (SD Dimensions, 2006). And they constitute about 60 or 70% of the agricultural labor force as men in rural communities have increasingly migrated to urban areas seeking employment with higher salaries and prestige (United Nations Development Programme, 2002). Although women's employment has grown, women are the most likely to be laid off in times of economic downturn. They make up 61% of the unemployed. In addition, women's wages are generally lower than those received by men. In urban areas, the gender gap in wages declined from 82.6% in 1988 to 80% in 1999 (Liu, Zhang, and Kung, 2004). And in rural areas, women earn consistently less than men, although the difference depends on the region (Rozelle, 2002). Overall, women earn about 83.9% of men's earnings (Shu and Bian,

TABLE 5.1   Allocation of Work

Type of Work	Men	Women	Total
Agricultural production team	27	38	65
Occupations outside team	13	1	14
Total	40	39	79

SOURCE: Elizabeth Croll, "The sexual division of labor in rural China." In *Women and Development: The Sexual Division of Labor in Rural Societies* (New York: Praeger, 1982), p. 230.

2003). Still, women's contributions to their household's income have grown steadily. In 1950, shortly after the Communist revolution in China, women contributed about 20% of family income. In 2004, women's share of family income grew to 40% (Marquand, 2004).

Another significant factor discriminating against rural women workers is the system of assigning "work points" for daily labor. Work points are given for one's work and are used to measure one's contribution to the commune. Ten work points are considered equal to one full day's labor. Croll's investigation shows that whereas men are usually allotted ten points for their day's work, women tend to be given fewer points, even when they perform the same work as men. Nationwide surveys indicate that women receive, on average, two points fewer per day than men (Stacey, 1979).

Although the system of land reform and collective ownership of resources has aided all rural people, men retain control over land use and production. Traditional patterns of leadership continue to endow men with greater authority than women both within kinship groups and communes (Diamond, 1975). In fact, collectivization of farms has increased men's dominance because it has strengthened small patrilineal units.

The Chinese government continues to rely on the one child policy in order to reduce population growth. The policy pertains to urban couples, mandating that they have only one child, unless either or both of the parents belong to an ethnic minority or unless they are themselves only children. In rural areas, couples may have a second child. Although this policy has led to a decrease in the population growth rate, a favorable outcome, it has also unwittingly encouraged the use of prenatal sex determination testing, particularly ultrasound technology with a consequence that female fetuses may be aborted. In 2000, the overall Chinese sex ratio was about 117 males to 100 females (U.S. Department of State, 2006). These data reflect an increasing imbalance in the last 20 years when the sex ratio was 108.4 males to 100 females (Arnold and Liu, 1986). Even more striking, for second births, the ratio in 2000 was about 152 males to 100 females (U.S. Department of State, 2006). Infant mortality rates are also higher for females than for males. For example, figures for 2006 indicate that the male infant death rate was 20.6 deaths per 1000 live births while for females the figures were 25.94 deaths per 1000 live births (CIA, 2006). Since generally worldwide, male infants have higher mortality rates than females, these figures suggest parental intervention, whether in the form of outright infanticide or in the form of nutritional and health care neglect.

Surveys of mothers' attitudes about the number and sex of their children reveal continuation of preference for sons. Older women are especially likely to prefer sons to daughters but the pattern is attested among younger women as well. For example, survey and focus group research in three Chinese provinces reported 54–58% of women who had one son but no daughter said that they were satisfied with their reproductive situation while only 31–50% of women who had one daughter and no sons reported being satisfied. A majority, 73–99%, of respondents who had two children said they were satisfied with their situation regardless of the sex of their children (Hardee, Xie, and Gu, 2004).

The Chinese sex ratio imbalance is one of the most extreme in the world. It rests on an ideology of male dominance and preference for sons that remains strong in both rural and urban China despite laws against infanticide and against the use of prenatal testing to determine the sex of the fetus and the consequent abortion of females. One of the practical outcomes of the sex ration imbalance is that an estimated 40 million men are currently unable to find spouses (Jha, 2006).

A final factor contributing to the sex ratio imbalance is that the rate of suicide of Chinese women is the highest in the world, five times the world average (Zuckerman, 2000). Chinese women account for 21% of all women worldwide but 57% of global female suicides. And suicide accounts for 4.5% of female deaths in China in contrast to the worldwide figure of 1.6% of female deaths. Finally, rural women commit suicide at a rate three times higher than urban women. According to Zuckerman (2000:10), suicide among women is a response to complex life situations, including " . . . the unbearable stress women feel for belonging to be 'wrong' gender" in addition to heavy workloads, domestic violence and unhappy marriages.

Also reflective of preference for sons is the rate at which couples renounce their pledge to have one child. Of those couples with daughters, 12.5 percent reneged; half that proportion—that is, 6.7 percent—of couples with sons did so. Similarly, when a woman became pregnant with a second child, differential choices to abort the fetus were made depending on the sex of her first child. If the first was a girl, 18.6 percent of mothers decided to abort, whereas if the first child was a boy, 26.4 percent aborted.

As a result of continued preference for sons and strategies used by parents to favor sons, an unbalanced sex ratio among children remains in China. Arnold and Liu (1986) cite the figure of 108.4 males to 100 females.

In sum, then, although the Chinese government has undertaken strenuous efforts to raise women's status, guarantee them equal rights in marriage and work, and eradicate the most brutal features of patriarchal control, these efforts have had only partial success. Traditional beliefs maintain their force even though many material conditions of life have been radically transformed. One of the age-old justifications for male dominance was men's productive contributions to their families and elder parents, but this rationalization is swept away by women's full participation in agricultural work and by government programs providing financial support and health care to elders. It is therefore on the ideological plane that patriarchal attitudes remain. This fact demonstrates the critical role played by ideological constructs in continuing practices that have no material necessity. However, despite the maintenance of some degree of male dominance in Chinese society, it must be remembered that tremendous advances have been made in less than fifty years in eradicating some of the most brutal forms of patriarchal control. These advances have come about because of two interrelated efforts: first, a transformation of material conditions and relations of

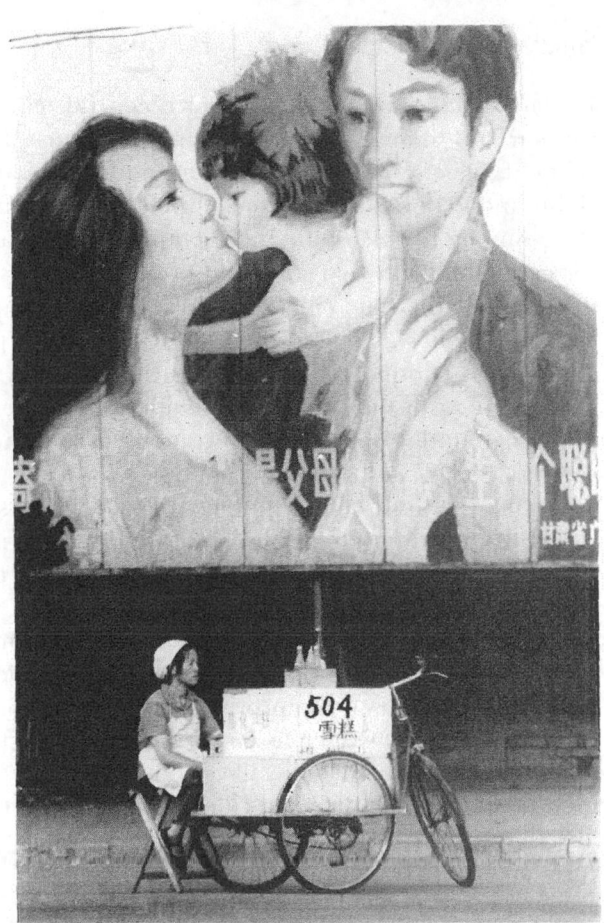

Large billboards throughout China remind people of the one-child-per-family policy.

production, and, second, a concerted attack on traditional social and religious beliefs. These dual strategies are interdependent and equally critical to achieve lasting fundamental change in gender constructs.

Economic changes in China toward a market economy have led to cuts in governmental expenditures for health care. Medical costs are covered by private insurance but only 60% of China's urban dwellers have some form of health insurance and a much smaller 10% of rural residents are covered for health costs (Forney, 2003). In response to an impending crisis for rural people, the Chinese government intends to establish a cooperative program of medical coverage for rural areas but it will not go into effect until at least 2010.

Elderly people in China are particularly hard-hit by the loss of free medical care. They generally have low incomes and little savings. In addition, the success of the "one-child" program leaves many elderly people with few children to help support them. And as the first cohort of people are born under the "one-child" program, they will be burdened by the care of elderly parents and grandparents without siblings to share the responsibilities (Kaneda, 2006).

SUMMARY

In state societies, as political power is centralized under the control of men, women lose their autonomy and independence. Ideological constructs and religious beliefs are used to reinforce and legitimate restrictions on women's rights and to devalue and demean their very personhood.

Among people of the Incan empire, the social and ideological supports for gender equality that existed in prestate cultures were maintained to some degree after the state emerged. However, these supports were attenuated as state authorities increased their control over the populace. After the Incan empire was conquered by the Spanish, women's status declined and their rights were vastly diminished. Although both women and men lost their independence under Spanish rule, women carried multiple burdens based on their race, class, and gender.

In India and China, intense patriarchal systems restricted women's rights in their households and communities, trivialized women's contributions to production, and denied women access to political participation. Religious and philosophical ideologies negated women's worthiness and devalued all of their potential roles except that of motherhood.

The modern governments of present-day India and China have taken numerous steps toward improving women's status in their nations. In India, traditional practices such as female infanticide, child marriage, dowry, and widow burning are currently illegal. In China, the government has outlawed infanticide, foot binding, and child marriage. However, in both nations, some illegal practices still exist among some sectors of the population, especially in rural areas, where government control is minimal and patriarchal traditions are deeply entrenched.

REFERENCES

ARNOLD, FRED, AND LIU ZHAOXIANG. 1986. "Sex preference, fertility, and family planning in China." *Population and Development Review*, 12: 221–246.

BBC NEWS. 2003. www.news.bbc.co.uk, 2003/07/16.

BUHLER, GEORG. 1964. "The laws of Manu." In *Sacred Books of the East*, vol. 25 (ed. Max Muller). Delhi: Motilal Banarsidas.

CENTRAL INTELLIGENCE AGENCY. 2006. "The World Factbook, China." www.cia.gov/publications/ factbook.

CHITNIS, SUMA. 1988. "Feminism: Indian ethos and Indian convictions." In *Women in Indian Society* (ed. Rehana Ghadially). Newbury Park, CA: Sage, pp. 81–95.

CLAESON, MARIAM, EDUARD BOS, AND INDRA PATHMANATHAN. 1999. Reducing Child Mortality in India: keeping up the pace. Washington D.C.: The International Bank for Reconstruction and Development: The World Bank.

CROLL, ELIZABETH. 1982. "The sexual division of labor in rural China." In *Women and Development: The Sexual Division of Labor in Rural Societies* (ed. Lourdes Beneria). New York: Praeger, pp. 223–247

DIAMOND, NORMA. 1975. "Collectivization, kinship and the status of women in rural China." In *Toward an Anthropology of Women* (ed. Rayna R. Reiter). New York: Monthly Review Press, pp. 372–395.

FLAVIA, AGNES. 1988. "Violence in the family: Wife beating." In *Women in Indian Society* (ed. Rehana Ghadially). Newbury Park, CA: Sage, pp. 151–166.

FORNEY, MATTHEW. 2003, May 12. "China's failing health system." *Time*, Asia.

GEORGE, SABU, ABEL RAJARATNAM, AND B. D. MILLER. 1998. "Female Infanticide in Rural South India." Search Bulletin, July–September 1998, 12 (3), pp. 18–26. SNDT Churchgate.

GHADIALLY, REHANA, AND PRAMOD KUMAR. 1988. "Bride-burning: The psycho-social dynamics of dowry deaths." In Women in Indian Society (ed. Rehana Ghadially). Newbury Park, CA: Sage, pp. 167–177.

GILMARTIN, CHRISTINA. 1989. "Gender, politics, and patriarchy in China: The experiences of early women communists, 1920–1927." In Promissory Notes (ed. S. Kruk et al.). New York: Monthly Review Press, pp. 82–105.

GUAMAN POMA DE AYALA, FELIPE. 1956. Nueva cronica y buen gobierno (trans. L. B. Galvez). Lima. 3 vols.

HARDEE, KAREN, ZHENMNG XIE, AND BAOCHANG GU. 2004. "Family planning and women's lives in rural China." International Family Planning Perspectives, 30 (2): 68–76.

HASTORF, CHRISTINE. 1991. "Gender, space, and food in prehistory." In Engendering Archaeology: Women and Prehistory (ed. Margaret Conkey and Joan Gero). Cambridge: Basil Blackwell, pp. 132–159.

JACOBSON, DORANNE. 1974. "The women of North and Central India: Goddesses and wives." In Many Sisters: Women in Cross-Cultural Perspective (ed. Carolyn Matthiasson). New York: Free Press, pp. 99–176.

JEEVA, M., GANDHIMATHI, AND PHAVALAM. 1998. "Female Infanticide: philosophy, prospective and concern of SIRD. Search Bulletin, July–September 1998, 13 (3), pp. 9–17. Location:SNDT Churchgate.

JHA, PRABHAT et al. 2006. "Low male to female sex ratio of children born in India: national survey of 1.1 million." The Lancet, 367: 211–218.

KAKAR, SUDHIR. 1988. "Feminine identity in India." In Women in Indian Society (ed. Rehana Ghadially). Newbury Park, CA: Sage, pp. 46–68.

KANEDA, TOSHIKO. 2006. "China's concern over population aging and health." Population Reference Bureau. www.prb.org.

KOENIG, M. et al. 2006. "Individual and contextual determinants of domestic violence in North India." American Journal of Public Health. 96 (1): 132–138.

KRISHNASWAMY, S. 1988. "Female infanticide in contemporary India: A case-study of Kallars of Tamilnadu." In Women in Indian Society (ed. Rehana Ghadially). Belmont Park, CA: Sage, pp. 186–195.

KUMAR, RADHA. 1995. "From chipko to sati: The contemporary Indian women's movement." In The Challenge of Local Feminisms: Women's Movements in Global Perspective (ed. Amrita Basu). Boulder, CO: Westview.

LESSINGER, JOHANNA. 1986. "Work and modesty: The dilemma of women market traders in South India." Feminist Studies, 12: 581–600.

LIU, PAK-WAI, JUNSEN ZHANG, AND CHING YI KUNG. 2004. "What has happened to the gender wage differential in urban China during 1988–1999?"

MARQUAND, ROBERT. 2004, December 17. "Women in China finally making a great leap forward." The Christian Science Monitor.

MILLER, BARBARA. 1993. "Female infanticide and child neglect in rural North India." In Gender in Cross-Cultural Perspective (ed. Caroline Brettell and Carolyn Sargent). Upper Saddle River, NJ: Prentice Hall, pp. 423–435.

NANDY, ASHIS. 1988. "Woman versus womanliness in India: An essay in social and political psychology." In Women in Indian Society (ed. Rehana Ghadially). Newbury Park, CA: Sage, pp. 69–80.

NARAIN, VATSALA. 1967. "India." In Women in the Modern World (ed. Raphael Patai). New York: Free Press, pp. 21–41.

NELSON, SARAH. 1991. "The 'Goddess Temple' and the status of women at Niuheliang, China." In Engendering Archaeology: Women and Prehistory (ed. Margaret Conkey and Joan Gero). Cambridge: Basil Blackwell, pp. 302–308.

O'KELLY, CHARLOTTE, AND LARRY CARNEY. 1986. Women and Men in Society, 2nd ed. Belmont, CA: Wadsworth.

RAJAN, V. G. JULIE. 2006. "Will India's Ban on Prenatal Sex Determination Slow Abortion of Girls?" Hindu Women's Universe. www.hinduwomen.org.

ROWE, JOHN. 1950. "The Inca culture at the time of the Spanish conquest." In Handbook of South American Indians (ed. Julian Steward). Washington, D.C.: Smithsonian Bureau of American Ethnology, Bulletin 143, vol. 2, pp. 183–330.

ROZELLE, SCOTT. 2002. "Gender wage gaps in post-reform rural China." The World Bank, Development Research Group.

SD (Sustainable Development) Dimensions. 2006. "Asia's women in agriculture, environment and rural production: China." www.fao.org/sd.

Sharma, Ursula. 1986. *Women's Work, Class and the Urban Household: A Study of Shimla, North India.* London: Tavistock.

Shu, Xiaoling, and Yanjie Bian. 2003. "Market transition and gender gap in earnings in urban China." *Social Forces*, 81(4): 1107–1145.

Silverblatt, Irene. 1978. "Andean women in the Inca Empire." *Feminist Studies*, 4: 37–61.

———. 1980. "Andean women under Spanish rule." In *Women and Colonization* (ed. Mona Etienne and Eleanor Leacock). New York: Praeger, pp. 149–185.

———. 1987. *Moon, Sun, and Witches: Gender Ideologies and Class in Inca and Colonial Peru.* Princeton, NJ: Princeton University Press.

———. 1991. "Interpreting women in states: New feminist ethnohistories." In *Gender at the Crossroads of Knowledge: Feminist Anthropology in the Postmodern Era* (ed. Micaela di Leonardo). Berkeley: University of California Press, 140–174.

Sridhar, Lalitha. 2004. "Treating infanticide as homicide is inhuman." InfoChange News & Features.

Stacey, Judith. 1979. "When patriarchy kowtows: The significance of the Chinese family revolution for feminist theory." In *Capitalist Patriarchy and the Case for Socialist Feminism* (ed. Zillah Eisenstein). New York: Monthly Review Press, pp. 299–348.

United Nations Development Programme China. 2002. "Gender equality in China." www.unchina.org.

U.S. Department of State. 2006. www.state.gov/2006.

Wadley, Susan. 1988. "Women and the Hindu tradition." In *Women in Indian Society* (ed. Rehana Ghadially). Newbury Park, CA: Sage, pp. 23–43.

Watson, Rubie. 1993. "The named and the nameless: Gender and person in Chinese society." In *Gender in Cross-Cultural Perspective* (ed. Caroline Brettell and Carolyin Sargent). Upper Saddle River, NJ: Prentice Hall, pp. 120–132.

Wolf, Marjorie. 1974. "Chinese women: Old skills in a new context." In *Woman, Culture and Society* (ed. Michelle Rosaldo and Louise Lamphere). Stanford, CA: Stanford University Press, pp. 157–172.

Wong, Aline. 1974. "Women in China: Past and present." In *Many Sisters: Women in Cross-Cultural Perspective* (ed. Carolyn Matthiasson). New York: Free Press.

Zuckerman, Elaine. 2000. "China, country gender review." *World Bank*. East Asia and Pacific Region and the Gender Methods. Thematic Group. Poverty Reduction and Economic Management Network.

Zutshi, Minna. 2004. "Veiled Agony: Domestic violence: Women deny it, men trivialise it." Jalandhar, Online Edition. www.tribuneindia.com.

CHAPTER 6

Industrial Economy: The United States

In Europe and the United States of the late eighteenth century, innovations in productive modes began a process that transformed agricultural societies into industrial nations. In this chapter, we trace the historical development of industrialization in the United States and its interrelationships with constructs of gender. Industrialization and its use of people's labor had significant impacts on gender relations obtaining in preexisting social and economic forms. Inequalities between women and men were in some ways widened and in other ways narrowed by new economic relations. As we shall see, industrialization developed through the use of women's labor and then marginalized women as it became fully established as the dominant productive mode in the United States.

Coexisting with the growth of industrialization were other types of economic forms. Small-scale independent farmers continued to carry out agricultural production, slaves worked on large plantations, hired laborers in towns and cities engaged in various craft or service occupations, and numerous Native American communities attempted to pursue their traditional foraging or horticultural practices. Many different types of productive modes thus contributed to the overall American economy. Each type conditioned its own array of productive roles, and each was characterized by different kinds of relations between women and men. We focus here on those roles and relations developed and maintained in the industrial sector because this sector was a radical departure from historically prior economic modes and has come to dominate most national economies and, indeed, the world economy.

EARLY INDUSTRIAL DEVELOPMENT

Industrial production began in the United States in the late eighteenth and early nineteenth centuries. It was founded in and grew out of capitalist economic relations separating people into a class that owned and controlled means of production and one that did not. Industrialization had begun in Great Britain in the eighteenth century as an outgrowth of cottage piecework in the making of textiles and clothing. Initially, women were paid by merchants to produce cloth and garments in their homes. This mode of production was relatively inefficient given the social context in which it was carried out. That is, women's responsibilities to maintain their households and care for their children often interrupted their work weaving and sewing. Eventually, cottage piecework was shifted to manufactories owned and supplied by capitalists who hired workers and directed their labor physically separated from homes and household duties.

In some cases, whole families were hired to work in the factories. Husbands/fathers maintained their authority over the working group consisting of themselves, their wives, and their children. The system of family-based production that preexisted in farming households continued intact. But married women had difficulties fulfilling their domestic and child care responsibilities when they left their homes to work in factories. They therefore dropped out of the labor force.

Married women's return home solidified a dichotomy between paid employment in the public sector and domestic labor in private households. No longer were families cooperative economic units; rather, differentiation of spheres of activity and labor specialization became the norm.

With the advent of the industrial revolution, large factories transformed both the landscape and the lives of people in previously rural areas.

VIEW OF THE ARCHITECTURAL IRON WORKS

12TH & 14TH STS EAST RIVER, NEW YORK.

By 1820, technological innovations transformed manufacturing processes by incorporating complex machinery and new sources of energy. These innovations enabled workers to create more product in the same amount of time. In the end, hand manufacturing was replaced by machine industrial production. Use of complex and powerful machinery resulted in a further shift in labor patterns. The employment of children became inefficient because they could not operate heavy or complicated equipment. In addition, public disclosure of children's illnesses and injuries caused by long working hours and unsafe conditions led to demands for legal protections against the abuse of children. Consequently, as children were barred from many manufacturing jobs, men and young women remained the primary factory employees.

In the United States, industrial production began around the turn of the nineteenth century. But it did not organize all aspects of economic life at that time. Many independent farmers continued to obtain their subsistence primarily from the crops they grew and the animals they tended. Farming households fulfilled most of their material needs directly, although some commodities had to be purchased. Money to buy goods was gained through the sale of surplus crops, animal products, or crafts made in the home. Although work performed by household members was differentiated by gender and age, farm families pooled their labor to fulfill collective needs. Men's primary responsibilities included the bulk of farmwork and house construction. Women performed domestic labor, entailing preparation of food, manufacture of clothing, household maintenance, and child care. They also aided in farmwork when additional labor was needed.

Farming households were organized through patriarchal authority patterns. Men as husbands/fathers were the recognized heads of households and dominated wives and children. Women's status, although subordinate, was not totally devoid of influence or prestige. Wives and husbands contributed interdependent labor to their families and were recognized as equally necessary to household functioning. But women's social worth was secondary to men's, and women were denied legal rights to own property or to participate equally in political and religious domains.

During the early nineteenth century, the independence and self-sufficiency of farming families was gradually eroded by growing needs to purchase commodities. At the same time, transformations of production in manufacturing resulted in owners' need to hire workers for the burgeoning industrial sector. These two processes coalesced in the development of industrial production.

One of the first industries to develop in the United States was that of textiles. Manufacture of textiles was concentrated in Massachusetts mill towns, most notably Lowell and Waltham. Young women constituted the bulk of mill operators. They were drawn from farm families, the daughters of independent farmers. Many poor families needed extra income to buy the growing number of commodities, such as shoes, household utensils, and tools, that were usually purchased rather than produced by family members. Unmarried

Young women provided a source of cheap labor for the textile mills of Lowell, Massachusetts

daughters were available for outside employment because their direct productive contributions to their families was not as critical as that of sons. In the farming economy, daughters generally aided in farmwork and housework, but sons were central to agricultural production because they, along with their fathers, contributed the major share of labor.

Conditions of employment in the textile mills were in many ways consistent with social norms of propriety and decency recognized as legitimate for young women from respectable families. The women lived in dormitories provided by employers, took communal meals, and were accompanied by chaperones when they went shopping in town on their day off (Dublin, 1977).

Mill life was compatible with the social context of the times in that patriarchal relations obtaining within households were reproduced in the mills. Men were owners and supervisors, controlling the organization of production; young women labored as necessary but subordinate workers. In a sense, women's participation at the workplace was similar to their participation at home under their fathers' authority.

Although living and working conditions were acceptable, considering the standards of the era, most young women who worked in the mills did so out of dire economic necessity. Many began their employment after the death of a parent, crop failure, or the threat of a loss of farms (Matthaei, 1982). The women generally sent most of their wages back to their parents and were thus critical to their families' survival.

In a short period of time, conditions of work and living in the mills changed dramatically. Because of competition from European imports, textile manufacturers began to reduce costs of their operations in Massachusetts.

They lowered the wages paid for work, ceased providing living quarters for workers, and demanded longer hours of work or in other ways sped up production. Under these circumstances, workers' dissatisfaction increased, leading to protests and strikes in the 1830s and 1840s organized by young women in the mills. Workers' unity was extremely high, a consequence of their communal living and working conditions and of their social homogeneity (Dublin, 1977). In 1845, mill operatives founded the Lowell Female Labor Reform Association to press for workers' rights and also for women's social rights. In one statement reflective of women's militancy, a mill operative wrote to her state legislator:

> Bad as is the condition of so many women, it would be much worse if they had nothing but your boasted protection to rely upon, but they have at least learnt the lesson which a bitter experience teaches, that not to those who style themselves their "natural protectors" are they to look for the needful help, but to the strong and resolute of their own sex. (Letter from *Voice of Industry*, March 6, 1846; quoted in Amott and Matthaei, 1991, p. 101)

In response to work stoppages, many women were fired. They had become expendable because of a new source of laborers—namely, the growing number of poor immigrant women and men who flocked to the United States in hopes of escaping poverty in Europe. Because immigrants' living and working conditions were even worse in their native lands than in the mills, they eagerly took the jobs abandoned in protest by Americans. By 1852, half of the workers in textile mills were immigrant women and children (Bose, 1987).

American mill workers' commitment to their jobs was tempered by the social context from which they came and by future expectations that they shared. They were young, unmarried women who anticipated marriage and motherhood. On average, millworkers were employed for four and a half years, most leaving to marry (Matthaei, 1982). They hoped subsequently to take up the domestic roles typical of, or at least idealized by, American family life. According to this ideal, husbands supported their families while married women remained at home and fulfilled domestic duties.

Marginalization of Women in Industry

Among poor families, the American ideal could not be maintained. Both men and women had to seek incomes to sustain their households. Many married women remained at home and earned money through such sources as factory outwork, sale of foods or crafts produced at home, and providing room and board for lodgers (Bose, 1987).

In addition to home-based incomes, many women obtained money through paid employment. By the end of the nineteenth century, manufacturing and industrial development had expanded considerably. By 1900, rates of women's labor force participation had reached nearly 20 percent; that is, approximately five million women were employed (Fox and Hesse-Biber, 1984). They labored in a wide range of occupations: 40 percent worked in domestic and personal service jobs (for example, cleaning, laundering, cooking); 25 percent in textile and garment manufacturing; 18 percent in farming; 10 percent in trade and transportation as saleswomen, secretaries, and accountants; and 9 percent in professional jobs, primarily teaching.

Although rates of employment of married women remained low, large numbers of single, widowed, and divorced women were wage earners. Approximately half of the women in these latter categories who were younger than 45 were employed, as indicated in Table 6.1.

Despite their labor participation, women remained marginalized in the industrial sector by intersecting links between gender segregation in employment and unequal remuneration for work performed by women and men. Segregation between the genders entailed the assignment of different types of work to men or women. Some occupations were considered appropriate for women and others for men. For example, industrial jobs requiring the operation of large machinery were undertaken by men, whereas women were employed in so-called light industries such as those producing soap, hats, and cigars (Hartmann, 1979). Even where both men and women worked in the same industry, they were differentiated according to specialization. In the manufacture of boots and shoes, for instance, men were employed as cutters and finishers, and women were stitchers and sewers (Matthaei, 1982).

In addition to occupational segregation, hierarchical patterns within a workplace differentiated women and men. Workplaces that employed women

TABLE 6.1   Percentage of Women in the Labor Force, by Marital Status and Age, 1890

Age	Marital Status				
	Unknown	Single	Married	Divorced	Widowed
15–24	29.0	37.3	6.4	53.5	50.0
25–34	17.2	55.0	4.8	55.0	56.0
35–44	13.2	48.1	4.5	50.1	54.2
45–54	12.9	41.0	3.9	37.0	44.5
55–64	12.0	32.3	3.0	24.5	32.9
65	8.3	17.7	2.3	11.0	18.1
All ages	18.9	40.5	4.6	29.3	49.0
Unknown	30.8	44.0	14.2	39.2	58.2

Labor force participation rate computed from the number of women in the labor force divided by the number of women in the population.

SOURCE: Julie Matthaei, *An Economic History of Women in America*, p. 130. Copyright © 1982 by Julie A. Matthaei. Reprinted by permission of Schocken Books, published by Pantheon Books, a division of Random House, Inc.

were characterized by a typical patriarchal authority structure in which men served as supervisors and overseers, whereas women were subordinate workers.

Distinctions of work and responsibilities between men and women were generally not necessitated by physical abilities. They were instead arbitrary and artificial reflections of gender stereotypes that insisted on differentiation of women and men. But the process did not merely attribute distinctions between the genders; it assigned men more valued roles than women and rewarded both accordingly.

A further feature of economic relations contributing to women's marginalization and secondary status was the fact that women generally received lower wages than men did, even when both performed the same jobs. This differential in pay—or "gender gap," as it is now called—was (and is) often masked by the concomitant segregation of work and workplaces. That is, if men and women labor at different trades or occupy different positions at work, disparities in their pay can be rationalized as consistent with their particular tasks and duties. But the gender gap in wages is in reality a reflection and reinforcement of patriarchal relations widespread in society. Men's social dominance can then be justified by the fact that they earn more money than women do.

In addition to gender, distinctions of social class affected the public and domestic roles people performed. As industrialization and wage work expanded, the lifestyles of women in middle- and upper-class families contrasted sharply with that of working-class women (Bose, 1987). Among prosperous families, women were relegated to purely domestic roles. Indeed, a man's ability to support a wife and children was a signal of his economic success. In contrast to prosperous women, poor women were engaged in earning incomes, either through paid employment or through home-based strategies for gaining money.

The Cult of Domesticity

In the middle of the nineteenth century, a cultural construct currently referred to as the *cult of domesticity* developed as an ideological justification for separation of the genders and for the relegation of women to the domestic sphere. Its popularity grew throughout the nineteenth century, and it remains in one form or another as a dominating construct in American society. According to the cultural ideal, vastly separate roles and domains are ordained for women and men. Men are assigned responsibility for providing material support for their families; women are suited to perform domestic tasks.

The cult of domesticity was consistent with ideological beliefs about men's and women's innate interests and capacities. Men were perceived as competitive and aggressive. They vied with each other for material rewards, the measure of their success. In contrast, women were seen as innately nurturing and passive. They willingly—indeed, happily—strove to provide comfort and calm to other family members. The separation of spheres of activity was seen as a God-given mandate, expressed, for example, in the following words of George Burnap in 1841:

> The question has been raised, and often discussed, whether the original intellectual endowments of woman are as great or rather the same as those of man. It is a question, however, which never can be settled and which is unimportant to decide one way or another. . . . But whatever may be the original equality of the sexes in intellect and capacity, it is evident that it was intended by God that they should move in different spheres, and of course that their powers should be developed in different directions. They are created not to be alike but to be different. . . . This radical and universal difference points out distinctly a different sphere of action and duty. (quoted in Matthaei, 1982, pp. 116–117)

The cult of domesticity provided explanations for men's place at work and women's place at home. It justified capitalist and industrial relations in that it offered a rationalization for competition in the workplace as stemming innately from men's nature. Competition among men was also legitimated by the popularization of Darwinian notions of evolution and competition among species. Analogous to biological processes, economic and social competition was seen as natural and indeed inescapable. Charles Darwin wrote little about gender, but the few words he penned concerning human instincts were consistent with cultural notions of psychic and moral distinctions between women and men. For instance, Darwin believed that women were "naturally more tender and less selfish than men" (Sayers, 1987, p. 72).

Women had no "natural" place in the competitive work environment. Instead, their job was to create a "haven in a heartless world" (Kessler-Harris, 1982) for their husbands returning from a tiring day competing with other men for economic success. Notions of the home as a respite from the world were popularized by public leaders and writers. For instance, according to Harriet Beecher Stowe, writing in *House and Home Papers* (1865):

> The very idea of home is of a retreat where we shall be free to act out personal and individual tastes as we cannot do before the wide world. . . . Our favorite haunts are to be here or there . . . and our whole arrangement the expression, so far as our means can compass it, of our own personal ideas of what is pleasant and desirable in life. This element of liberty is the chief charm of home. "Here I can do as I please," is the thought with which the tempest-tossed earth pilgrim blesses himself or herself, turning inward from the crowded ways of the world. (quoted in Matthaei, 1982, p. 109)

Although Stowe claimed that both men and women had "liberty" at home, one wonders, given the social domination of men over women, how much freedom of action was in reality possible for women.

The cult of domesticity assigned mothers primary responsibility for a child's upbringing. Devotion to training children to be well-adjusted members of their culture was seen not only as a feature of women's natural inclination but also as their duty to society. In *The Claims of the Country on American Females*, published in 1842, Margaret Coxe wrote:

> To American mothers . . . is then committed, in a special manner, the solemn responsibility of watching over the hearts and minds of our youthful citizens who are soon to take their places on the public arena, and to give form and individuality to our national character. (quoted in Matthaei, 1982, p. 113)

Women who were compelled by economic necessity to join the labor force were continually reminded that by working outside the home they were neglecting their proper duties to nurture their husbands and children. Husbands of working women were similarly made to feel derelict in their duty. Because the ideal man was one who supported his wife and children, a man whose wife worked was not fulfilling his proper role and was therefore less than a real man. Such husbands sometimes turned their frustration against family members, taking the form of violence against wives and children.

Labor leaders also used constructs of the cult of domesticity to advocate restricting women's involvement in wage work. Such efforts were occasioned by competition between employed women and men that intensified by the beginning of the twentieth century. For instance, according to Samuel Gompers, president of the American Federation of Labor, writing in 1906:

> We know to our regret that too often are wives, sisters and children brought into the factories and workshops only to reduce the wages and displace the labor of men—the heads of families.
>
> I contend that the wife or mother, attending to the duties of the home, makes the greatest contribution to the support of the family. . . . [T]he wife will, apart from performing her natural household duties, perform that work which is most pleasurable to her, contributing to the beautifying of her home and surrounds. . . . There is no necessity for the wife contributing to the support of the family by working—that is, by wage labor. . . . The wife as a wage-earner is a disadvantage economically considered and socially is unnecessary. (quoted in Berch, 1982, p. 41)

Although such statements offered women a role having some positive value, they supported cultural ideals of women as "natural" homemakers, finding "pleasure" in "beautifying" their homes. And, of course, they justified excluding women from paid employment.

A potential departure from the precepts of the cult of domesticity was set in motion in the middle of the nineteenth century when a few colleges and universities began to offer higher education for women. In 1832, Oberlin College in Ohio, previously for men only, opened its doors to women students. Soon other colleges in the Midwest also permitted women to enroll. The first college for women, Wheaton College, was founded in 1834, followed by Mount Holyoke in 1837 (Sapiro, 1986). After the Civil War, prestigious colleges such as Vassar, Wellesley, and Smith were established

(Fox, 1989). However, most institutions offering advanced education for women did so within the ideological and social constructs of women's accepted roles. Women were schooled in domestic science, child rearing, and the arts and humanities. They were encouraged to be chaste and mindful of their familial duties.

Even though the education provided for women tended to support most of the prevailing cultural stereotypes, ideological attacks were mounted against women who dared to envision anything other than a domestic life for themselves. Science and religion combined to give justifications for restricting women to the home. Religious leaders spoke of the God-given roles of women and men ordained in the Scriptures. Scientific experts wrote of innate biological differences between the genders that suited them each for their societal roles.

In addition, medical doctors voiced their own set of warnings, specifically admonishing women against striving for advanced educations and professional careers. According to medical experts, a woman's biological energy was limited and should not be channeled into more than one pursuit. Doctors claimed that because women's natural and proper goal is motherhood, and because schooling and working dissipate some of a woman's vital energy, she can cause irreparable harm to her ability to procreate if she tires herself through education and a career. Doctors of the late nineteenth and early twentieth centuries advised that a woman's reproductive organs tend to atrophy and are rendered nonfunctioning if she taxes her mind or body. The words of Dr. P. Moebius, a German scientist, set the tone for American physicians:

> If we wish woman to fulfill the task of motherhood fully she cannot possess a masculine brain. If the feminine abilities were developed to the same degree as those of the male, her maternal organs would suffer and we should have before us a repulsive and useless hybrid. (*Concerning the Physiological and Intellectual Weakness of Woman*; quoted in Ehrenreich and English, 1978b, p. 131)

This warning was taken to heart by numerous experts and expounded with great fervor. For example, to those women interested in obtaining college educations, Dr. R. R. Coleman advised:

> Women beware. You are on the brink of destruction: You have hitherto been engaged in crushing your waists; now you are attempting to cultivate your mind: You have been merely dancing all night in the foul air of the ballroom; now you are beginning to spend your mornings in study. You have been incessantly stimulating your emotions with concerts and operas, with French plays, and French novels; now you are exerting your understanding to learn Greek, and solve propositions in Euclid. Beware!! Science pronounces that the woman who studies is lost. (quoted in Ehrenreich and English, 1978a, p. 128)

Such ideas were widely promulgated and accepted as rationalizations for restricting women's activities. Not only were objective proofs entirely lacking, but the experts blindly overlooked the fact that many poor women worked a tiring double day as paid employees and unpaid housewives and in addition produced children.

Indeed, the popularity of medical opinion concerning procreation was influenced by population dynamics in the United States. In the middle and late nineteenth century, birthrates among middle- and upper-class women began to drop considerably, whereas fertility among poor white women, African American women, and immigrants remained relatively high. As a result of the disparity among classes and races, many public leaders cautioned prosperous white women about the dangers of "race suicide" (Gordon, 1982). Using the advice and warnings of medical experts as an argument, they urged white women to produce more children.

Public policies concerning contraception and abortion changed during the period of fears of race suicide. Prior to the mid-1800s, abortion had been legal in the early months of pregnancy—that is, before "quickening" or fetal movement was evident. It had been a common procedure; in fact, numbers of abortions rose in the 1840s, particularly among married women who already had children. But campaigns organized by physicians soon succeeded in convincing most states to outlaw abortion. In 1860, the Catholic Church also condemned the procedure, although it, too, had previously accepted it.

Occupations for Women

Despite strong pressures to keep women in the home, some women obtained advanced and specialized educations. Many of these women subsequently felt restricted by traditional domestic roles. They endeavored instead to pursue professional careers. Educated young women often gravitated to professions that were compatible with the accepted stereotype of women's nature, including such fields as nursing, teaching, and social work. Women could translate their potential as nurturers into tending the sick, educating children, and improving the lives of the poor and helpless.

Professional women gained some prestige, especially if they performed work consistent with social edicts concerning women's morality and dedication to social service. For many women, careers became an acceptable and even respectable alternative to marriage and motherhood (Matthaei, 1982).

Increasing numbers of women from all social classes entered the workforce. Technological changes played a role in opening up new types of employment for women. For example, the invention of the typewriter in 1873 was especially significant in transforming office work from a domain for men to one for women (Fox and Hesse-Biber, 1984). Prior to that time, men were the primary office workers. In 1870, of a total of 76,639 office workers, only 1,869, or 2.5 percent, were women (Davies, 1979). Men were typically employed as clerks and accountants in small firms where hard work and dedication were rewarded with raises and promotions. Employees had personal relationships with their employers and developed loyalty to the firm. As businesses grew in size and complexity by the turn of the twentieth century, occupations within companies were increasingly differentiated in terms of responsibilities and authority. Many low-level jobs became dead ends. The invention of the typewriter allowed specialization in only one skill to define one's work and place in the organization. Men were generally disinterested in this work because it was repetitive and monotonous and particularly because it led to no career advance. Women were then recruited to fill the growing number of secretarial positions as men moved up the administrative hierarchy.

The feminization of clerical work was eventually supported by ideological constructs that linked secretarial duties to those of wives. For instance, in a series of articles on women in business published in *Fortune* magazine in August 1935, secretaries were equated with wives:

> Women occupy the office because the male employer wants them there. It is doubtless true that women take to the work nicely. Their conscious or subconscious intention some day to marry, and their conscious or subconscious willingness to be directed by men, render them amenable and obedient and relieve them of the ambition which makes it difficult for men to put their devotion into secretarial work. ("Women in Business II," p. 55, quoted in Davies, 1979)

Similarly, men of that era, who no longer commanded the same authority in the home as their fathers and grandfathers had, relished the authority afforded them in their role as employers:

> [A male employer]... resented the loss of his position [in the household]. He regretted the old docility, the old obedience, the old devotion to his personal interests. And finding himself unable to re-create [it] in his home he set about re-creating it in his office. What he wanted in the office was something like the vanished wife of his father's generation—someone to balance his checkbook, buy his railroad tickets, listen to his side of the story, give him a courageous look when things were blackest. ("Women in Business II," p. 55; quoted in Davies, 1979, pp. 257–258)

Secretarial work was considered a respectable job for an educated woman. Requirements for literacy and specialized training contributed to its appeal (Matthaei, 1982). In addition, educated women often turned to office work as a career alternative because they were barred from entry into many other professions. Finally, the fact that secretaries were paid higher wages than factory workers gave women from working-class families an incentive to continue their educations and gain the necessary skills.

Scientific Housework

Birthrates continued to fall through the early twentieth century. This trend occurred for all social classes and races but was most marked among white middle- and upper-class women. Because many women had few children, a potential existed for boredom and dissatisfaction with domestic roles. In response, a new ideological construct was advanced to justify the accepted order separating the genders. According to precepts of the "scientific management of housework," women were encouraged to improve standards of cleanliness, orderliness, and efficiency in their homes. A woman was expected to spend a great deal of time cleaning and tidying her home, planning and preparing meals, purchasing consumer goods, or supervising a staff of servants and cooks in every detail of home maintenance. Women were told to take pride in their management of the household just as men took pride in their accomplishments in the workplace. For example, according to Ida Tarbell (1913), a leading exponent of scientific housework:

> Housekeeping is a many-sided business calling for training in theory and practice for scientific management. It needs as varied qualities as any business known to human beings, and yet as things are now girls and women are getting only the most superficial and artificial training in it. It needs to be formulated and professionalized and every girl should be taught at least its principles: at the same time she should be taught its relation to all economic and social problems and in particular to the problems of the cost of living. (quoted in Matthaei, 1982, p. 158)

Principles of scientific housework not only gave an aura of professionalism to domestic labor but also cohered with necessities of capitalist expansion. Because one of a housewife's important tasks was managing her budget and supplying her family with commodities, she played an important role in the proliferation of consumer goods produced by growth in the industrial sector. Links between housewives and consumerism were made explicit, for example, by another scientific manager, Bertha Richardson. In *The Woman Who Spends: A Study of Her Economic Function* (1904), Richardson compared women's prior and present economic roles:

> In the relationship of women to the getting and spending of money, the world has seen a most interesting change. Years ago, when our nation was a nation of country folk, women did little of the spending, but helped much in the production of wealth. . . . Production of most of the needs of life centered around the home. Women very naturally came into close touch with this production. . . . The country has moved to town. Women can now buy all the necessities they at one time had to manufacture. Today women are not spinning and weaving; they are buying dress goods and linen. They are not producing; they have thrown off the yoke of economic production. They only spend.
>
> On account of the change in the economic conditions of production, women have gained a whole new field of economic activity, that of consumption. Their problem is not, What shall be produced to satisfy my needs? but, How shall I spend to satisfy my needs? (quoted in Matthaei, 1982, pp. 164–165)

A second ideological rationalization for women's domestic duties was the emphasis on proper child rearing. Mothers' responsibilities for their children's health and success became paramount. The advice of medical experts concerning harm to reproductive processes by thinking or working women was used as an argument in support of this construct. That is, to guarantee bearing a healthy baby, a mother should refrain from dissipating her mental or physical energy in educational or occupational pursuits. Children's health therefore was directly correlated with a mother's activities. Sickly children were a signal of and punishment for her lack of sole commitment to motherhood.

But a mother's responsibilities did not end with the birth of a healthy child. Thereafter, she was urged to create a home environment conducive to a child's physical, intellectual, and moral development. Attention had to be paid to every detail of children's growth; care had to be given to make them happy so that they would become successful as competitive men or dutiful women.

Changing Attitudes toward Child Care

By the late nineteenth century, children were becoming the focus of their mother's attention and indeed were playing a central role in the life of the family, at least among the urban middle classes. The cult of domesticity and the movement for scientific housework lay the foundation of much of the shift in familial focus toward creating a physical and emotional environment that would nurture the child. The house had to be maintained and cleaned to safeguard the child's health, and the mother had to devote her emotional and physical energy in attending to the child's needs as defined by a growing cadre of experts.

Such an interpretation of child and home life was a radical change from earlier centuries in the United States and Europe. For example, in the European Middle Ages, children were thought to be "demonic, animalistic, ill-formed and fragile" with a marked propensity for evil (Hays, 1996, p. 22). Wrapping children in swaddling clothes curbed their aggressive impulses and also kept them out of the way of their parents, who were busy working in the fields or house. In addition, misbehaving children were given opium to calm them or were whipped to punish them. Children were taught their place in a hierarchical household system that mirrored the relationship between subject and king. Using biblical symbolism, Sharon Hays (1996) notes, "In this scenario, fathers were the shepherds, mothers were the sheepdogs, and children were the sheep, lowly and stupid yet valuable when they were ready for market" (p. 23).

Later, during the seventeenth and eighteenth centuries, attitudes among the European bourgeoisie began to change with the influence from philosophers and moralists of the Enlightenment. Children were then thought to be innocent and malleable, open to guidance in a loving household. The importance of home life and schooling was stressed. These attitudes did not reach the United States, however, until the nineteenth century. By mid- and late century, the values of domesticity held sway, emphasizing the role of the wife/mother in creating an atmosphere of purity, calm, and piety. A child's conscience, reasoning ability, manners, and morals were to be developed through "affectionate persuasion" (Hays, 1996, p. 31). Emphasis on the maternal role coincided with economic changes that left urban, middle-class women with little opportunity for employment outside the home and therefore gave them meaningful work to do inside. Thus began what Hays calls the "cultural contradictions of motherhood": "The world was increasingly thought to be dominated by impersonal relations and the competitive pursuit of self-interested material gain, yet within it the tiny enclave of the family was to operate according to an opposing logic" (p. 34).

By the end of the nineteenth century, even greater responsibilities were placed on mothers not only to mold their children's moral character but also to be attuned to their emotional, behavioral, and cognitive development. By the mid-twentieth century, children were firmly established as the center of the middle-class family. In contrast to earlier times, when children were trained to become proper adults, "the child (whose needs are interpreted by experts) is now to train the parent" (Hays, 1996, p. 45). Child care, having become "expert-guided" and "child-centered," also became "more emotionally absorbing, labor intensive, and financially expensive" (p. 46). But as more was (and is) demanded of mothers and as mothers become central to the child's development, mothers are poised to take both the praise and the blame for the results.

Although the constellation of behaviors and values involved in "intensive mothering" is normative in the United States, there is not uniform opinion about what children's needs are or how best to satisfy them. Hays's research carried out in the 1980s with mothers of different socioeconomic classes reveals some views on the subject. Whereas middle-class mothers were more apt to negotiate or reason with their children and to give them options to choose from, working-class mothers were more likely to set rules for expected behavior and to seek obedience and compliance. These differing approaches can be contextualized in the lives and realities faced by the two groups. As one working-class mother noted, "Discipline, that's very important to me. Because if children can't respect their own mother and father, they're certainly not going to respect a boss, or an employer, or the law. And that's important" (Hays, 1996, p. 94).

Finally, American attitudes and practices should also be understood as representative of only a small percentage of the world's people. A study of 186 contemporary cultures found that individual mothers were the principal caretakers of children in only 20 percent of the sample. Child care in the majority 80 percent was shared among women or among women and older children (Hays, 1996, p. 20).

WOMEN AND WORK THROUGH THE MIDDLE OF THE TWENTIETH CENTURY

Increased demands on a woman's time in housekeeping and her devotion to home and family members kept her confined to domestic life. However, only women from prosperous families could fulfill the idealized roles made popular through the cult of domesticity, the movement for the scientific management of housework, and all other various elaborations. Working-class women were compelled by economic necessity to gain incomes in paid employment. As inflation increased, as men's wages failed to keep pace with rising prices, and as costs of maintaining households and rearing children mounted, middle-class women also were increasingly drawn out of their homes into the workforce.

As more women entered paid employment, competition between men and women intensified. Although employers often were biased against women because of patriarchal prejudices, they sometimes preferred hiring women because women were generally less demanding and more docile than men. Owners and managers of factories reported preferring women workers principally because they were "better adapted, cheaper, more reliable and more easily controlled" than men (Matthaei, 1982, p. 213). Women were willing to work for lower wages and sought fewer job benefits or guarantees. Women's timidity stemmed from their socialization as subordinates. In addition, many women expected to work only temporarily, ending their employment when they married or became mothers. If already married, they accepted the dominant societal view that women's work was secondary and supplemental. For these various reasons, then, women workers were less concerned with conditions of employment than were men.

Whereas women's social and personal identities were focused on their present or anticipated familial roles, men's identities centered on their public work roles. As more women entered the workforce, men felt economically and personally threatened. The segregation of jobs according to gender helped buffer the competition between men and women, but women began to make small inroads into men's domains. In response to this trend, men organized and joined labor unions to protect their interests. Although ostensibly dedicated to bettering conditions for all workers, most unions in the nineteenth and early twentieth centuries discriminated against women, barring them from membership or relegating them and their interests to auxiliary status (Berch, 1982).

Labor unions thus functioned to solidify men's dominance in the workplace. When men were faced with competition from women, who often were willing to work for lower wages, unions had two possible responses. They could have advocated equality of pay for women and men to remove the financial incentive for employers to hire women rather than men. Instead, they advocated restrictions on women's employment as a strategy for maintaining men's advantages. Therefore, as Heidi Hartmann (1979) concludes, rather than choosing to engage in a fight against capitalist control, labor unions sided with patriarchal privilege as they fought against women's opportunities.

In another response to competition from women workers, labor leaders and public figures advocated enactment of "protective legislation" ostensibly protecting women workers from harmful conditions on the job. Beginning in the late nineteenth century, hours for women workers were lessened, night work in some occupations was forbidden, and exposure to dangerous chemicals, materials, or machinery was banned. Although these restrictions appear beneficial, they carry a hidden agenda rendering women less attractive employees and therefore hurting their chances of being hired.

The transparency of this approach is made clear with the realization that, until recently, protective legislation did not apply to those fields where women were ghettoized. For instance, secretaries who were routinely exposed to dangerous chemicals and nurses who performed backbreaking duties in their care of patients had no specific legal safeguards against injury on the job (Hubbard, 1983). Even in the current context, protection of the health of women workers focuses on problems related to biological reproduction. In some cases, pregnant women are restricted from certain types of work, including work in technical and chemical industries; in other cases, all women of childbearing age are barred. Such limitations on women's employment are not actually designed to safeguard women but rather are directed toward "fetal protection" (Rose, 1988). They thus continue the definition of women as mothers.

Focus on women's reproductive potential surfaced when women objected to "protective" limitations. When women argued for their right to participate as free workers on their own behalf, courts sided with patriarchal interests restricting women. In the language of the U.S. Supreme Court, deciding against the plaintiff in *Muller v. Oregon* (1908) and upholding Oregon's laws limiting women's working hours, society's interest in women's roles as potential mothers outweighed a woman's individual rights:

> A long time on her feet at work, repeating this from day to day, tends to injurious effects upon the body, and as healthy mothers are essential to vigorous offspring, the physical well-being of woman becomes an object of public interest and care in order to preserve the strength and vigor of the race. . . . [H]er physical structure and proper discharge of her maternal functions—having in view not merely her own health, but the well-being of the race—justify legislation to protect her from the greed of man. The limitations which this statute places on her contractual powers, upon her right to agree with her employer as to the time she shall labor, are not imposed solely for her benefit, but also largely for the benefit of all. (quoted in Berch, 1982, pp. 46–47)

Despite the social and legal barriers to women's employment, participation rates for women continued to rise in the twentieth century. The period during World War I (1914 to 1917) witnessed a shift in women's employment as women replaced men who had joined the army (Fox and Hesse-Biber, 1984). Women were able to obtain jobs that had previously been barred to them, including managerial positions and jobs in heavy industry. Patterns of employment among women changed as well. As white women were increasingly hired as office workers, teachers, saleswomen, and telephone operators, African American women moved into domestic and service occupations.

After the war ended, many women, recruited through slogans of patriotism to the war effort as well as economic necessity, were pressured to leave the public sector and return to home life. Although some women did so, many others remained in the workforce. Their motivations were partly economic and partly personal. Economic needs of families continued to grow as inflation rose and real wages fell. The expansion of varieties of consumer goods provided another incentive for women to increase their families' income and consequently raise their standard of living. Also, many mothers worked to support children through college so that a child's future occupational choices would be enhanced.

In addition to financial reasons, women continued to work because of social and personal benefits they received. Rather than isolation in small households, they experienced social comraderie and stimulation from contact with other workers (Ferree, 1987). Even in dull jobs, women found personal fulfillment through their interactions with others.

The years of the Great Depression, beginning in 1929, witnessed another cycle of shifts in men's and women's employment. Industrial and construction jobs were hardest hit, throwing millions of men out of work. Although women lost jobs too, occupations in the service sector dominated by women because of gender segregation did not suffer as much (Bose, 1987). But attitudes toward working women, especially if married, turned more hostile. Wives of unemployed men were, among others, vocal in their attacks against married working women. Some states passed laws barring employment of married women.

The Depression was shortly followed by World War II, a period of change yet again. Millions of men entered the army, leaving millions of jobs unfilled. As during World War I, women heeded the call to do their patriotic share by joining the workforce. They were employed in jobs that until then had few women, including heavy industry, craft specializations, and administrative or managerial positions. Job opportunities for all women improved during the war. African American women obtained work in industry that had previously been closed to their participation (Bose, 1987). Not only was there a large increase in the numbers of married working women, but women with young children also entered public labor.

Despite rises in rates of employment and widening of the range of occupations available to women, women were still faced with gender segregation in workplace hierarchies and the gender gap in wages. Even though women often took wartime jobs previously held by men and performed the same work, they were generally paid less than men (Fox and Hesse-Biber, 1984).

After the war, men returned to reclaim their jobs, pushing women out of work or at least out of the positions they had taken. Many women, though, remained in the workforce, motivated by the dual factors of economic necessity and personal interest.

WOMEN, MEN, AND WORK INTO THE TWENTY-FIRST CENTURY

Throughout the twentieth century, rates of women's labor participation rose steadily. Each spurt of increase in both the nineteenth and twentieth centuries had been fed by workers from different social categories. At first, young, unmarried women made up the bulk of workers. Then immigrant women,

TABLE 6.2 Percentage of Women in the Workforce

	1950	1960	1970	1980	1985
Married women					
No children under 18	30.3	34.7	42.2	46.0	48.2
Children aged 6–17	28.3	39.0	49.2	61.7	67.8
Children under age 6	11.9	18.6	30.3	45.1	53.4
Never married	50.5	44.1	53.0	61.5	65.2
Widowed, divorced, separated	37.8	40.0	39.1	44.0	42.8
All women	33.9	37.7	43.3	51.5	54.5

SOURCE: Adapted from *The American Woman 1988–89: A Status Report*, edited by Sara E. Rix, p. 127. By permission of W. W. Norton & Company, Inc. Copyright © 1988 by the Women's Research and Education Institute.

single and married, added to the workforce. Married, native-born women constituted the next contingent, entering and staying in paid employment in large numbers in the 1940s. During the 1940s, 1950s, and 1960s, most married working women were older women whose children had grown up. But since then, working mothers with young children have taken jobs in addition to their domestic responsibilities. Table 6.2 presents data for women's labor force participation from 1950 through 1985. It indicates trends since 1950 in employment of women in different marital categories (Blank, 1988).

By 2004, the total labor force participation rate for women was 59.5 percent compared to 73.5 percent for men. Rates varied for different age cohorts, with the highest levels for women between the ages of 25 and 55. Less than half of women (44.8 percent) aged 16 to 19 were in the labor force. The level of participation rose dramatically to 70.8 percent for women aged 20 to 24 and 74.1 percent for the next cohort aged 25 to 34. Women aged 35 to 44 had a slightly higher labor force participation rate of 76.0 percent, and the next group aged 45 to 54 had the highest rate at 76.8 percent. Labor force levels then dropped considerably to somewhat over half (49.6 percent) for women aged 55 to 64. Those older than 65 had the lowest rate, only 10.6 percent (U.S. Department of Commerce, 2005, Table 570).

A majority of women with children at all ages were in the labor force in 2003 regardless of their marital status. Table 6.3 displays comparative statistics.

TABLE 6.3 Labor Force Participation Rates for Women with Children, 2003 (percentages)

Marital Status	With Children Aged 6–17	With Children under 6
Single	77.6	70.2
Married with husband present	77.0	59.8
Widowed, divorced, or separated	84.8	74.3

SOURCE: U.S. Department of Commerce, *The United States 2004–2005. National Databook*, Table 579.

Even a majority of married women, with husband present, who have a child age 1 year or younger are in the workforce. In 2003, 54.6 percent of white married mothers with infants and 63.6 percent of African American married mothers with infants were working outside the home (U.S. Department of Commerce, 2005, Table 580) .

Despite the growth in numbers of women who are in paid employment, discrimination in wages and lack of access to all kinds of jobs still hinder women's equality as workers. The gender gap in pay continues to be a constant source of inequity for women. Women are paid, on average, less than men in all occupations and for all age cohorts. When salaries are compared for women and men with comparable educations and comparable numbers of years of experience, the gender gap remains. Note the relevant data from the 1980s through the early twenty-first century presented in the accompanying series of tables. Table 6.4, illustrating earnings by workers' age and sex for 2002, indicates that only among the youngest workers (aged 15 to 24) do women earn annual salaries about $2,000 less than men, the smallest gap. This fact does not presage a future trend but rather reflects the low wages of young, inexperienced men. The gender discrepancy for whites was greater than for African Americans or Hispanics (see Table 6.5).

TABLE 6.4   Median Yearly Earnings of Full-Time
Workers, by Sex and Age, 2002 (in dollars)

Age	Women	Men
Total	16,812	29,238
15–24	7,582	9,642
25–34	21,649	30,677
35–44	22,322	37,892
45–54	25,165	40,969
55–64	19,165	36,277
65 and over	11,406	19,436

SOURCE: U.S. Department of Commerce, *Databook 2005*, Table 677.

TABLE 6.5   Yearly Earnings by Sex and Race, 2002 (in dollars)

	Women	Men
White	16,652	30,240
Black	16,282	21,466
Hispanic	12,583	20,189

SOURCE: U.S. Department of Commerce, 2005, Table 678.

TABLE 6.6   Median Family Income by Family Type, 1995

Married couple, wife in the paid labor force: $55,823
Married couple, wife not in the paid labor force: $32,375
Male head, no spouse present: $30,358
Female head, no spouse present: $19,691

SOURCE: U.S. Department of Commerce, 2005, Table XXX.

Income statistics for 1995 analyzed by family type reveal the important contribution of married women to their households but also reveal that "female-headed" households fare the worst (see Table 6.6).

Families with children generally have lower median incomes than those without children, but the relative standings by family type are maintained, as shown in Table 6.7 (Costello, Miles, and Stone, 1998, p. 329).

Poverty rates for women are consistently higher than for men. Data reported for 2002 indicate that 13.3 percent of females and 10.9 percent of males lived in poverty (U.S. Department of Commerce, 2005, Table 686).

When disaggregated by race, data reveal that Native American, African American, and Hispanic women are the most disadvantaged (see Table 6.8).

When analyzed by family type, female-headed families are most likely to be living in poverty. The data are presented in Table 6.9.

Data concerning the "working poor" (people in the workforce whose earnings are below poverty level) also indicate gender and racial disparities, as displayed in Table 6.10.

Women's difficulties in the workplace are additionally reflected in data concerning work schedules and multiple jobs. In 2001, 30.0 percent of employed

TABLE 6.7   Median Income of Family with Children, 1995

Married couple: $49,969
Male head, no spouse present: $26,990
Female head, no spouse present: $16,325

SOURCE: U.S. Department of Commerce, 2005, Table 686.

TABLE 6.8   Poverty Rates by Sex and Race, 2002 (percentages)

	Females in Poverty	Males in Poverty
White	10.1	8.1
African American	26.7	22.8
Hispanic (of any race)	24.2	21.1
Native American	27.2	24.0

SOURCE: U.S. Department of Commerce, 2005, Table 682.

TABLE 6.9   Poverty Rates by Family Type and Race, 2002

	Percentage in Poverty			
	All Races	White	Black	Hispanic
All family types	9.6	7.8	21.5	19.7
Married couple	5.3	5.0	7.9	15.0
Female head (no spouse present)	26.5	22.6	35.8	35.3
Male head (no spouse present)	12.1	9.9	20.9	17.0

SOURCE: U.S. Department of Commerce, 2005, Table 690.

men worked in jobs with flexible schedules while 27.4 percent of women had similar advantages. This pattern may appear to be surprising given the assumption that there are greater demands on women's time at home. Women also are more likely than men to have more than one job. In 2003, 5.1 percent of male workers held more than one job, whereas 5.6 percent of female workers held multiple jobs (U.S. Census Bureau, 2005, Tables 589, 590). Women may be compelled to work multiple jobs because their average earnings are lower than men's wages. Furthermore, marital status has a different effect on multiple job-holding for women and men. That is, married men are more likely than single or divorced men to work at multiple jobs, whereas single or divorced women are more likely than married women to be multiple job-holders.

Tables 6.11 and 6.12, displaying figures for earnings by workers' education and experience, indicate that women do not gain relative to men by pursuing their educations or by amassing years of experience. In fact, as educational attainment increases and as job tenure increases, the dollar difference in earnings of women and men widens. Note that for college graduates and workers with professional degrees, the gender discrepancies are especially remarkable: Men's earnings are more than 50 percent higher than those of women.

Table 6.13 compares women's and men's salaries for selected occupational categories. As demonstrated, the gender gap in pay is larger among occupations requiring more education, skill, and training than among jobs that are relatively

TABLE 6.10   Percentage of Full-Time Workers Described as "Working Poor," by Sex and Race, 2003

	Men	Women
White	4.4	4.9
Black	7.2	12.5
Hispanic	10.9	10.9
Asian	4.5	5.1

SOURCE: U.S. Department of Labor Statistics, 2005, Table 27.

TABLE 6.11   Median Annual Earnings of Year-Round
Full-Time Workers by Sex and
Educational Attainment, 2002 (in dollars)

Educational Attainment	Women	Men
Fewer than 9 years	8,965	15,132
1–3 years of high school	10,613	19,802
High school graduate	15,972	27,526
1–3 years of college	20,002	35,032
College graduate	30,788	50,600
Professional degree	44,748	88,216
All education levels	18,965	32,471

SOURCE: U.S. Department of Commerce, *Statistical Abstract 2004–2005*, Table 677.

unskilled. Therefore, women's efforts to improve their status by obtaining education and training are eclipsed by men's relative advances.

Finally, statistics on salaries that are disaggregated according to race demonstrate that gender is the most critical factor in wage differentials (see Table 6.14). Although African American and Hispanic men receive, on average, lower salaries than white men, all groups of men earn substantially more than either white, African American, or Hispanic women. Suffering from both gender and racial discrimination, African American and Hispanic women earn the least.

TABLE 6.12   Mean Hourly Earnings of Full-Time Workers
by Tenure on Current Job, 1984 (in dollars)

Years of Work Experience by Tenure on Current Job	Hourly Earnings		
	Women	Men	Ratio of Women's Earnings to Men's
Experience < 5 years	5.88	7.19	.82
On job < 2 years	5.72	7.07	.81
On job 2 years	6.07	7.33	.83
Experience 5–9 years	6.95	8.35	.83
On job < 2 years	6.36	7.74	.82
On job 5 years	7.45	8.89	.84
Experience 10–19 years	8.07	10.95	.74
On job < 2 years	6.56	9.50	.69
On job 10 years	8.53	12.01	.71
Experience 20 years	8.15	12.41	.66
On job < 2 years	6.12	10.20	.60
On job 10 years	9.10	13.02	.70

SOURCE: U.S. Census Bureau, *Current Population Reports, 1987*, Table F; cited in Rix, 1988, p. 390.

TABLE 6.13　Median Weekly Earnings of Full-Time Workers, by Sex
and Occupation, 1996 (in dollars)

Occupational Category	Women	Men	Women's Wage as Percentage of Men's
Managerial and professional	616	852	72.3
Technical, sales, and administrative support	394	567	69.5
Service occupations	273	357	76.5
Precision production, craft, and repair	373	560	66.6
Operators, fabricators, and laborers	307	422	72.7
Farming, forestry, and fishing	255	300	85.0

SOURCE: U.S. Bureau of Labor Statistics, *Employment and Earnings, January 1997*, Table 39; cited in
Costello et al., 1998, p. 309.

In addition to inequities in pay, women continue to face occupational segregation in terms of both types of jobs for which they are hired and workplace
hierarchies. Table 6.15 presents percentages of women and men in occupational
categories, and Table 6.16 gives percentages of women in selected occupations.

Although women's median earnings in all occupations fall below those
of their male colleagues, ratios recorded for 2004 vary depending on the field.
The data are presented in Table 6.17.

Data on administrative stratification within "women's" occupations reveal
that positions of authority are dominated by men. For example, Table 6.18
contains figures for percentages of men within selected occupations and their
distribution in occupational hierarchies (Fox and Hess-Biber, 1984, p. 134).

TABLE 6.14　Median Annual Earnings of Full-Time Workers,
by Sex and Race, 2001 (in dollars)

Race and Sex	Earnings
White:	
Women	16,652
Men	30,240
African American:	
Women	16,282
Men	21,466
Hispanic:	
Women	12,583
Men	20,189

SOURCE: U.S. Department of Commerce, *Statistical Abstracts 2005*, Table 678.

TABLE 6.15 **Employed Women and Men, by Occupation, 2004 (percentages)**

Occupation	Women	Men
Managerial	13.2	15.7
Professional specialty	24.5	16.7
Service occupations	19.9	13.2
Sales occupations	12.2	10.9
Administrative support, clerical	22.8	6.3
Construction and extraction	0.3	11.1
Transportation	1.9	9.7
Operators, laborers	7.6	20.2
Farming, forestry, fishing	0.3	1.1

SOURCE: U.S. Bureau of Labor Statistics, 2005, Table 19.

TABLE 6.16 **Women as Percentage of Workers in Selected Occupations, 1996**

Occupations	Women as Percentage of Total Employed
Airplane pilots and navigators	1.4
Architects	16.7
Auto mechanics	1.2
Carpenters	1.3
Clergy	12.3
Computer programmers	30.8
Dental assistants	99.1
Dentists	13.7
Economists	54.4
Editors, reporters	55.7
Financial managers	54.0
Firefighters	1.8
Lawyers, judges	29.0
Librarians	82.7
Managers, medicine and health	75.3
Mechanical engineers	6.9
Physicians	26.4
Registered nurses	93.3
Social workers	68.5
Teachers, college and university	43.5
Teachers, elementary school	83.3
Telephone installers, repairers	13.9
Welders	5.0

SOURCE: U.S. Bureau of Labor Statistics, *Employment and Earnings, January 1997*, Table 11; cited in Costello et al., 1998, p. 287.

TABLE 6.17   Median Usual Weekly Earnings of Full-Time Wage and Salary Workers, by Industry and Sex, 2004 annual averages

Industry	Women's earnings as percent age of men's
All employees aged 16 years and over	80.4
Agriculture and related industries	90.0
Construction	94.9
Manufacturing	71.1
Wholesale and retail trade	73.3
Transportation and utilities	81.8
Information	74.1
Finance and insurance	58.4
Real estate and rental and leasing	91.0
Professional and technical services	64.6
Management, administrative, and waste services	91.7
Educational services	81.1
Health care and social assistance	73.9
Arts, entertainment, and recreation	82.5
Accommodation and food services	86.4
Public administration	76.4

As is shown, men hold a disproportionate number of positions of authority even within occupations in which women are crowded. Patriarchal relations of dominance and subordination are thus reproduced in the workplace. Benefits to men include the prestige and personal autonomy associated with authority as well as high salaries relative to nonadministrative workers.

All of these various sources of statistics amply demonstrate that women who work outside the home continue to suffer from discrimination and devaluation. Gender segregation, exclusion from administrative positions in workplaces, and

TABLE 6.18   Intraoccupational Stratification

	Occupation				
	Nursing	Elementary Teaching	Secondary Teaching	Academic Library	Social Work
Percentage of men:					
In occupation	1.1	16	50	37	37
In administration in occupation	45.7	80	94	70	66

SOURCE: Fox and Hess-Biber, 1984, p. 134.

inequities in pay all contribute to women's continued marginalization in the industrial economy.

Housework

Women who remain at home and fulfill the traditional patriarchal ideal of domestic roles also suffer. They are demeaned by the trivialization of their labor in social reproduction. Just as the worth of women's paid labor is systematically undervalued, the worth of labor contributed by wives and mothers is devalued. Trivialization of women's domestic work is reflected, for example, in the phrase "just a housewife" that women themselves often use as a self-definition. But the work of social reproduction performed by such women is vital to society and to the economic system. Social reproduction entails the care and sustenance of people so that they are able to contribute productively to society. Necessary tasks include obtaining and preparing food, maintaining the physical premises of the home, purchasing clothing and other material goods, tending to family members when they are ill, and planning and supervising children's education. Wives and mothers perform these and other duties in their daily activities. Women, therefore, "perform a great deal of socially necessary work but do not receive payment for it" (Ciancanelli and Berch, 1987, p. 247). Although non-employed wives are perceived as dependent on their husbands, husbands are in actuality also dependent on their wives. Just as men contribute their wages to support of families, women contribute their unpaid labor to family survival.

Devaluation of women's household work results, in part, from the social context in which it is performed. According to Penelope Ciancanelli and Bettina Berch (1987), housewives do the work of social reproduction "in the guise of familial responsibility" (p. 249). That is, housewives purchase food and clothing, prepare meals, clean the house, wash the clothes, and attend to other needs of family members. Their roles contrast with the role of paid employees who have contractual relationships with their employers. Whereas hired workers have socially and legally recognized obligations to perform labor for their employers, wives and mothers are perceived to be fulfilling their domestic responsibilities through voluntary choice.

Housework is also devalued, in part, because it is unpaid (Eisenstein, 1979). Given capitalist values implicit in economic and social relations, social worth is measured by money obtained through one's labor. Therefore, work that is accorded no monetary valuation is consequently given no social accounting. The fact that the gross national product (GNP) includes paid household labor performed by a hired worker but not unpaid daily labor performed by a woman in her own home is an indication of the link between productivity and paid employment. Because housewives are not paid, they are not considered productive.

In addition to benefits in the quality of family life derived from women's housework, if families were to hire an outsider to accomplish the work of social reproduction, the cost in wages would become a drain on household members' income. Because wages generally must be adequate to cover workers' subsistence costs, salaries for all workers would have to be raised to cover expenses for domestic service. The fact that women perform domestic duties without compensation allows wages to remain relatively low. Women's unpaid work, then, helps perpetuate the existing economic system and helps stabilize the relationship between employers' costs and profits. According to Eli Zaretsky (1973):

> The wage labor system is sustained by the socially necessary but private labor of housewives and mothers. [Their work] constitutes a perpetual cycle of labor necessary to maintain life in this society. In this sense, the family is an integral part of the economic system under capitalism. (p. 79)

Research documenting housewives' time reveals that only since the 1980s have the hours of work spent in the home begun to decline despite the increase in supposedly labor-saving technology. Studies conducted in 1912, 1929, 1943, 1953, 1967, and 1973 all found that women averaged from 52 to 56 hours per week in caring for their homes and family members (Schor, 1992, p. 86). Several theories help explain the stability of these figures. Although time spent in some tasks, such as food preparation, has declined, other tasks, particularly shopping, child care, and cleaning, have increased because standards of cleanliness, attention to child rearing, and consumerism have risen. At the same time, commercial alternatives or socialization of housework (i.e. hiring homecare workers) have been eliminated because of both economic and ideological disincentives. In addition, housework, and particularly shopping and cleaning, were encouraged because they supported a capitalist system needing outlets for an ever-growing array of consumer products. Note, too, that beginning in the late nineteenth century, a wife dedicated solely to the care of her home and family became a symbol of middle- and upper-class privilege. With the decline of family farms and businesses as well as social and economic barriers to women working outside the home, housewives spent more time attending to the needs of family members. Once a "market wage . . . was eliminated as an alternative (and lucrative) use of a housewife's time," the value of her time became "artificially deflated" (Schor, 1992, p. 94). Furthermore, since housewives are supported by the same share of their husbands' wages no matter how little or much work they do, it costs their husbands no additional rate to expect more services.

However, because more married women now seek employment outside the home for both personal and economic reasons, the number of hours spent in housework has correspondingly begun to decline. Time spent in housework for employed women is even lower—about two-thirds of the amount of nonemployed wives and mothers (Schor, 1992, p. 103). Men are also beginning to do a share of work in the home, especially child care, when their wives are employed. Still, although a majority of both women and men report that they think men should share in housework, women continue to do the bulk of the tasks. Judith Schor's survey found that 24 percent of wives in her sample did all the work in the home, whereas an additional 42 percent said that they did most of the work (p. 104).

Recent research indicates an overall decline in the number of hours spent on housework, attributable to several factors. First, women who work outside the home, a majority of American women, have less time to spend on housework. Second, people are having fewer children, making less demands on domestic tasks. And, standards of household cleanliness have either declined somewhat or families are willing to tolerate less cleanliness (Bianchi et al., 2000). Gender, marital status, and parenthood affect the amount of household labor a person performs. Although husbands now spend more time performing household tasks than previously, wives are the major domestic workers. Women's time in housework averages about two or three times the number of hours spent by men (Coltrane 2000). Married women spend more time in housework than unmarried women but married men spend less time in housework than unmarried men (Bianchi et al., 2000:197). Among married couples, domestic tasks are gender-linked. Women performed most of the tasks such as cooking, cleaning, and doing laundry while men's housework centers on shopping in stores and doing housework repairs.

Patriarchal Society and Capitalist Economy

Patriarchal social relations and capitalist economies thus are interconnected. Of course, patriarchal systems predated the origin of capitalism and exist in cultures without capitalist economies, but as capitalist economies developed, they incorporated and utilized preexisting patriarchal relations. They continue to do so. The marginalization of women serves the interests of both capitalist economies and patriarchal social systems. Capitalism benefits by women's availability to enter the workforce at relatively low wages and under unstable conditions. Women are willing to work for less than men because of their socialization in a male-dominated culture that systematically undermines their self-worth. They are taught to view themselves primarily in terms of familial relationships, especially as wives and mothers, rather than as workers. In addition, women are socialized to be docile and obedient to authority. These personality traits are fostered within families and are subsequently manipulated by employers in their control over women workers.

Capitalist economies also benefit from men's adherence to patriarchal values. Because men are socialized to accept the idealized version of American family life, they expect to support a wife and children. To do so, they must obtain and retain a job. Men therefore become bound to their work and often endure difficult conditions out of fear of losing their jobs and falling short of society's and their own expectations. Although women's secondary status presumably raises men's self-esteem, it also results in women's dependence on men and men's dependence on their jobs. Capitalist relations, then, subordinate men to their employers just as patriarchal constructs subordinate women to men.

But as a group, men receive benefits from capitalist systems. Relative to women, men are given social and economic rewards in higher wages, more prestigious jobs, and greater authority in the workplace. At home, men continue to benefit from traditional relationships, treated with deference by their wives and children. Indeed, restrictions on women's entry and participation in paid employment and their marginalization in the public sector contribute to solidifying men's control at home because when women's productive roles are limited, they remain dependent on their husbands.

Recent Ideological Attacks on Gender Equality

Since the nineteenth century, each period of increase in women's participation in the labor force has called forth an ideological attack by supporters of patriarchal values. The cult of domesticity warnings against harm to women's reproductive capacities and concepts in the scientific management of housework were among the earliest constructs offered to justify excluding women from paid employment. Following World War II, a new twist was added to the argument. Intense interest in personal psychology, spurred by the popularization of Freudian theories, led to the development of several interrelated concepts. Men and women were no longer viewed as differentiated solely on the basis of physical characteristics and social interests but were thought to be distinct in their inner psyches. Men were inherently aggressive, assertive, driven to competition and domination, whereas women were passive and docile and, in fact, wanted to be dominated. Psychic differences were innate and therefore immutable. Indeed, attempts to behave in ways that contradicted one's psychic nature were not merely futile but produced warped, destructive personalities. Although many of these attitudes were already enshrined in social and religious teachings of earlier periods, a new breed of experts—namely, psychologists—added their voices to the chorus.

Interest in psyches was not limited to those of adults. Children's psychic development also became of special concern. One's earliest years of life were seen as critical to emotional growth and adjustment, and mothers' responsibility for their children's mental health became paramount. A child's failure in school, delinquency, or inability to establish good relationships with others were blamed on his or her mother. A mother's job, then, consisted of selfless devotion to the interests of her children. Mothers who, by poverty or through divorce or widowhood, were compelled to work outside the home received some sympathetic understanding, but middle- and upper-class women who sought professional careers were targeted as selfish and destructive.

Despite the popularity of such notions, the 1960s and 1970s witnessed a resurgence of social and legal pressures for women's rights and equality in the workplace and in society. The women's movement gained force along with other movements for social, economic, and political change current at the time. Among the issues of concern were discrimination against women in hiring and promotions, sexual harassment on the job, disparities in pay for women and men, gender segregation, and the burdens of working women's "double day." In addition, activists focused on the discrimination inherent in patriarchal social attitudes that restricted, trivialized, and demeaned women. Finally, issues related to reproductive rights became central to providing meaningful lifestyle choices for families.

As in earlier times of social change, supporters of patriarchal values turned to another series of experts who advocated maintaining traditional roles and relationships. Leaders and adherents of various religious organizations voiced their beliefs about the sanctioned roles of men as authorities and heads of families and of women as subordinate and nurturing followers.

Religious beliefs combined with social constructs of the idealized American family. Women who asserted their rights to social, economic, and legal equality were seen as attacking the structure of American society. However, in reality, the ideal of the American family consisting of a working husband and nonemployed wife has been elusive for most Americans. A majority of actual households are composed of people in quite different circumstances. In fact, couples who both work, unemployed husbands, separated or divorced people, widows or widowers, single parents, or unmarried people living alone constitute a larger percentage of households than does the idealized family. Government statistics indicate that in 1989, 79.2 percent of American households consisted of a married couple. Of these, more than half of the wives were in the paid labor force. Therefore, only 33.5 percent of all American households conform to the idealized cultural construct of a husband and nonemployed wife. Table 6.19 presents data of forms of family composition, indicating a trend toward decreasing percentages of married-couple families and of households with nonemployed wives.

Despite the hard evidence, proponents of various religious or moral teachings continue to enshrine the traditional image. Science, too, currently plays its part in rationalizing traditional gender roles. For instance, concepts proffered by sociobiologists claim that distinctions in social behavior of women and men are derived from innate genetic differences. Sociobiologists begin with the erroneous assertion that certain activities or character traits are universally associated with women and others with men and then deduce

TABLE 6.19   **Family Composition as Percentage of Total, 1970–1989**

Family Type	1970	1980	1989
Married-couple families	86.7	81.7	79.2
Wife in paid labor force	——	41.0	45.7
Wife not in paid labor force	——	40.7	33.5
Male head of household, no spouse present	2.4	3.2	4.4
Female head of household, no spouse present	10.9	15.1	16.5

SOURCE: Calculations from U.S. Bureau of the Census; cited in Ries and Stone, 1992, p. 253.

that these features must be genetically programmed. For example, note the conclusion stated by Edward Wilson (1975):

> In hunter-gatherer societies, men hunt and women stay at home. This strong bias persists in most agricultural and industrial societies, and, on that ground alone, appears to have a genetic origin. . . . My own guess is that the genetic bias is intense enough to cause a substantial division of labor even in the most free and most egalitarian of future societies. . . . Even with identical education and equal access to all professions, men are likely to continue to play a disproportionate role in political life, business and science. (quoted in Lewontin, 1983, p. 247)

Wilson's opinion is premised on a superficial understanding of human cultures, ignoring cultural diversity and the complexity of human history. Contradicting the stance of sociobiologists, data presented by many anthropologists (some of which are discussed in previous chapters) demonstrate that men are not the only people who hunt and women do not always stay at home. Wilson and other sociobiologists assume universality when it does not exist and then posit a genetic basis as explanatory.

Because sociobiologists claim a biological basis for human behavior, they admit no possibility of sociocultural explanation or variation. They can therefore conclude, as did Stephen Goldberg (1973):

> Human biology precludes the possibility of a human social system whose authority structure is not dominated by males, and in which male aggression is not manifested in dominance and attainment of position, of status and power. (p. 78)

According to Goldberg, this state is not only a biological and social reality but an emotional one as well. He claims that in all cultures, "the *feeling* of both men and women [is] that the male's will dominates the female's" (p. 31; emphasis in original). "The ethnographic studies of every society that has ever been observed explicitly state that these feelings were present; there is literally no variation at all" (p. 67).

Characteristics of human cognitive processes are also gender linked, according to sociobiological theories. Goldberg (1973) states categorically:

> The stereotype that sees the male as more logical than the female is unquestionably correct in observation, and probably correct in its assumption that the qualities observed conform to *innate sexual limitations analogous* to those relevant to physical strength. (p. 204)

Therefore, "society's socializing girls from careers in mathematics may well be an acknowledgment of hormonal reality" (p. 204). Goldberg's opinion seems to be a curious echo of nineteenth-century warnings for women to stay away from Euclid. Arbitrary analogies and conclusions found in the sociobiological literature and supported by no data would be merely ludicrous were they not taken as authoritative by many in the United States to justify patriarchal attitudes and practices.

Lawrence Summers, then president of Harvard University, stirred controversy in 2005 when he stated publicly that women might lack " . . . an intrinsic aptitude for math and science" (Finder and Zernike 2006). Although his comments were greeted with dismay by the majority of academics at Harvard and elsewhere and Summers was forced to resign his position the following year, his remarks indicate the continuance of prejudicial attitudes about girls and women.

Sociobiologists also assert that women's roles in child care and other domestic tasks are outcomes of biological adaptations related to reproduction. According to their theories, because pregnancy lasts nine months, mothers have an innate physical and psychic "investment" in a child that is far more intense than that of fathers, whose role in procreation consumes less time and energy. Moreover, because a woman can have fewer children in her lifetime than a man potentially can, she is more concerned with her offspring's survival and development (Hubbard, 1983). Despite the mathematical logic employed, this theory, too, ignores the role of culture and socialization. It dismisses the importance of learned behaviors and of learned expectations and attitudes. As Ruth Hubbard (1983) concludes:

> Human living necessarily involves an interplay between biological and social forces. We have no way of knowing what people's "real" biology is, because the concept has no meaning. There is no such thing as human biology in the pure. In other words, what we think of as . . . biology is a political construct, not a scientific one. (p. 6)

Some scientists have contended that men's aggressiveness and women's docility are based on innate hormonal differences. However, critics point out that hormonal levels are not immutable but rather are sensitive to psychological, physical, and social factors (Lowe, 1983). For instance, levels of testosterone, a male hormone supposedly responsible for aggressiveness, are altered under various conditions, including changes in social environment, exercise, psychological states, and physical stress.

In addition to biodeterministic theories championed by sociobiologists, a number of anthropologists have popularized various notions that help support traditional gender constructs. Erroneous views that male dominance is universal, men behave aggressively in all societies, and women are everywhere socially devalued lend further "scientific" credence to the acceptability—indeed, inescapable destiny—of patriarchal relations. But these anthropologists ignore data derived from their own field indicating the importance of social and cultural learning, and the importance of culture, in shaping people's behavior and attitudes. They ignore cross-cultural evidence of differences in the roles allotted to men and women and the values associated with each. Finally, they ignore the importance of understanding cultural and historical conditions in which various social formations and relationships develop and are maintained. Ignorance of history and trivialization of human cultural diversity and human potential are succinctly asserted in, for example, the following statement by anthropologists Lionel Tiger and Robin Fox (1978):

> Nothing worth noting has happened in our evolutionary history since we left off hunting and took to the fields and the towns—nothing except perhaps a little selection for immunity to epidemics, and probably not even that. "Man the hunter" is not an episode in our distant past: we are still man the hunter, incarcerated, domesticated, polluted, crowded and bemused. (quoted in Smith, 1983, pp. 93–94)

All of the religious, moral, and scientific theories currently popular have an underlying social and political message in support of traditional gender constructs. Each field adds its own slant to the theme legitimating patriarchal relations. Although critics continually point out the fallacies and inconsistencies in evidence and arguments propounded, as each theory is debunked, new propositions are offered that transmit the same basic message. As women have entered the workforce to stay, as both women and men have questioned patriarchal expectations and constructs, adherents of the traditional order develop and support theories that explain and assert the logic, legitimacy, and inevitability of men's dominance and women's subordination.

In the next four chapters, we examine more closely the import of practices and attitudes that convey symbolic messages in addition to their overtly behavioral content. Domains of health, religion, and language exemplify interrelationships between actions and symbols as they reflect and reinforce prevailing gender constructs.

SUMMARY

Industrial production developed in the United States by utilizing women's labor in the manufacture of textiles. Women's working and living conditions in the New England mills were acceptable for the times. However, as competition from European products increased and as poor immigrants entered the country, mill owners sought to maintain and increase their profits by lowering wages, lengthening workdays, and allowing working conditions to deteriorate.

Competition among sectors in the growing industrial workforce, including American and immigrant women and men, gradually resulted in the marginalization of women's participation, the relative decline in their wages, and restrictions on their ability to secure and maintain employment. As labor became socialized out of the household, women were relegated to work within the domestic sphere—and in the domestic sphere, women's unpaid labor in providing services and processing or acquiring goods has been trivialized. In practice, however, the tendency to relegate women exclusively to housework was never complete throughout the society. Class and race were critical factors in determining a woman's role in her family and in paid employment.

Nonetheless, powerful ideological constructs developed to legitimate restrictions on women's participation in the workplace and in public life. Notions conveyed through a series of forms, including the cult of domesticity, scientific management of housework, psychoanalysis, and sociobiology, have all contributed to limiting women's roles and undermining their personal and social equality.

Trends throughout the twentieth century have resulted in the increased participation of women in paid employment. Rates of employment for all groups of women have risen. Single women and women without children in the household continue to be the largest sector. But mothers with young children have increasingly taken jobs outside the home. Currently, a majority of such mothers are in the workforce.

Despite gains in employment, women face discrimination in the workplace. The gender gap in pay continues, as does occupational segregation. Patriarchal attitudes can still be found in familial and public life.

REFERENCES

AMOTT, TERESA, AND JULIE MATTHAEI. 1991. *Race, Gender and Work: A Multicultural Economic History of Women in the United States.* Boston: South End Press.

BERCH, BETTINA. 1982. *The Endless Day: The Political Economy of Women and Work.* New York: Harcourt Brace Jovanovich.

BIANCHI, SUZANNE, et al. 2000. "Is anyone doing the housework? Trends in the gender division of household labor." *Social Forces*, 79 (1): 191–228.

BLANK, REBECCA. 1988. "Women's paid work, household income, and household well-being." In *The American Woman 1988–1989: A Status Report* (ed. Sara Rix). New York: Norton, pp. 123–161.

BOSE, CHRISTINE. 1987. "Dual spheres." In *Analyzing Gender* (ed. Beth Hess and Myra Marx Ferree). Newbury Park, CA: Sage, pp. 267–285.

DURNAP, GEORGE. 1841. *The Sphere and Duties of Woman and Other Subjects.* Baltimore, MD: Murphy.

CIANCANELLI, PENELOPE, AND BETTINA BERCH. 1987. "Gender and the GNP." In *Analyzing Gender* (ed. Beth Hess and Myra Marx Ferree). Newbury Park, CA: Sage, pp. 244–266.

COLTRANE, SCOTT. 2000. "Research on household labor: Modeling and measuring the social indebtedness of routine family work." *Journal of Marriage and the Family,* 62 (4): 1208–1233.

COSTELLO, CYNTHIA, SHARI MILES, AND ANNE STONE. 1998. *The American Woman 1999–2000: A Century of Change—What's Next?* New York: Norton.

COXE, MARGARET. 1842. *The Claims of the Country on American Females.* Columbus, OH: Whiting.

DAVIES, MARGERY. 1979. "Women's place is at the typewriter: The feminization of the clerical work force." In *Capitalist Patriarchy and the Case for Socialist Feminism* (ed. Zillah Eisenstein). New York: Monthly Review Press, pp. 248–266.

DUBLIN, THOMAS. 1977. "Women, work, and protest in the early Lowell mills: 'The oppressing hand of avarice would enslave us.' " In *Class, Sex, and the Woman Worker* (ed. Milton Cantor and Bruce Laurie). Westport, CT: Greenwood, pp. 43–63.

EHRENREICH, BARBARA, AND DEIRDRE ENGLISH. 1978a. *For Her Own Good: 150 Years of the Experts' Advice to Women.* New York: Anchor.

————. 1978b. "The 'sick' women of the upper classes." In *The Cultural Crisis of Modern Medicine* (ed. John Ehrenreich). New York: Monthly Review Press, pp. 123–143.

EISENSTEIN, ZILLAH. 1979. "Developing a theory of capitalist patriarchy and socialist feminism." In *Capitalist Patriarchy and the Case for Socialist Feminism* (ed. Zillah Eisenstein). New York: Monthly Review Press, pp. 5–40.

FERREE, MYRA. 1987. "She works hard for a living: Gender and class on the job." In *Analyzing Gender* (ed. Beth Hess and Myra Marx Ferree). Newbury Park, CA: Sage, pp. 322–347.

FINDER, ALAN, AND KATE ZERNIKE. 2006, February 21. "Embattled President of Harvard to Step Down at End of Semester." *The New York Times.*

FOX, MARY. 1989. "Women and higher education: Gender differences in the status of students and scholars." In *Women: A Feminist Perspective*, 4th ed. (ed. Jo Freeman). Mountain View, CA: Mayfield, pp. 217–235.

FOX, MARY, AND SHARLENE HESSE-BIBER. 1984. *Women at Work.* Mountain View, CA: Mayfield.

GOLDBERG, STEPHEN. 1973. *The Inevitability of Patriarchy.* New York: Morrow.

GOMPERS, SAMUEL. 1906. *Labor and the Employer.* Salem, NY: Ayer.

GORDON, LINDA. 1982. "Why nineteenth-century feminists did not support 'birth control' and twentieth-century feminists do: Feminism, reproduction and the family." In *Rethinking the Family* (ed. Barrie Thorne and Marilyn Yalom). New York: Longman, pp. 40–53.

HARTMANN, HEIDI. 1979. "Capitalism, patriarchy, and job segregation by sex." In *Capitalist Patriarchy and the Case for Socialist Feminism* (ed. Zillah Eisenstein). New York: Monthly Review Press, pp. 206–247.

HAYS, SHARON. 1996. *The Cultural Contradictions of Motherhood.* New Haven, CT: Yale University Press.

HUBBARD, RUTH. 1983. "Social effects of some contemporary myths about women." In *Woman's Nature: Rationalizations of Inequality* (ed. Marian Lowe and Ruth Hubbard). New York: Pergamon, pp. 1–8.

KESSLER-HARRIS, A. 1982. *Out to Work: A History of Wage-Earning Women in the United States.* New York: Oxford University Press.

LEWONTIN, R. C. 1983. "Sociobiology: Another biological determinism." In *Women and Health: The Politics of Sex in Medicine* (ed. Elizabeth Fee). Farmingdale, NY: Baywood, pp. 243–259.

MATTHAEI, JULIE. 1982. *An Economic History of Women in America.* New York: Schocken.

RICHARDSON, BERTHA. 1904. *The Woman Who Spends: A Study of Her Economic Function.* Boston: Whitcomb & Barrows.

RIES, PAULA, AND ANNE STONE (eds.). 1992. *The American Woman 1992–1993: A Status Report.* New York: Norton.

RIX, SARA (ed.). 1988. *The American Woman 1988–1989: A Status Report.* New York: Norton.

ROSE, MICHAEL. 1988. "Reproductive hazards for high-tech workers." In *The American Woman 1988–1989: A Status Report* (ed. Sara Rix). New York: Norton, pp. 277–285.

SAPIRO, VIRGINIA. 1986. *Women in American Society.* Palo Alto, CA: Mayfield.

SAYERS, JANET. 1987. "Science, sexual difference, and feminism." In *Analyzing Gender* (ed. Beth Hess and Myra Marx Ferree). Newbury Park, CA: Sage, pp. 68–91.

SCHOR, JULIET. 1992. *The Overworked American: The Unexpected Decline of Leisure.* New York: HarperCollins, Basic Books.

SMITH, JOAN. 1983. "Feminist analysis of gender: A mystique." In *Woman's Nature: Rationalizations of Inequality* (ed. Marian Lowe and Ruth Hubbard). New York: Pergamon, pp. 89–109.

STOWE, HARRIET BEECHER. 1865. *House and Home Papers.* Boston: Tichnor & Fields.

TARBELL, IDA. 1913. "The cost of living and household management." *Annals of the Academy of Political and Social Science,* 48.

TIGER, LIONEL, AND ROBIN FOX. 1978. "The human biogram." In *The Sociobiology Debate* (ed. Arthur Caplan). New York: Harper & Row, pp. 57–63.

WILSON, EDWARD. 1975, October 12. "Human decency is animal." *New York Times Magazine.*

ZARETSKY, ELI. 1973. "Capitalism, the family, and personal life." *Socialist Revolution,* 13–14: 69–125.

CHAPTER 7

Global Economic Development

Agricultural and industrial development programs sponsored by national governments or international agencies have been promoted as a means of strengthening the economies, raising standards of living, and improving the health of impoverished rural communities in the so-called underdeveloped or developing world. Development theory has emphasized the importance of modernizing in technology, agricultural production for trade, and industrialization dependent on a mobile labor force. When measured by indices such as gross national product (GNP), median family or household income, and longer life expectancy within an entire nation, economic advances can be demonstrated, but researchers have questioned the impact of economic development on different sectors of the population. In many cases, development programs have primarily benefited men, whereas women often find that their economic, social, and political security has deteriorated. Planners and advocates who are sensitive to women's concerns should therefore be aware of the possible consequences of such programs rather than simply assume that they are gender-neutral and universally beneficial.

The differential effects of development on men and women were first systematically explored in Ester Boserup's (1970) *Women's Role in Economic Development*, which effectively argues that modernization has contributed to a decline in women's status. In a survey of farming systems in Africa and Asia, Boserup found that although women are the primary subsistence farmers in Africa where land is under collective control of lineages and farming technology is relatively simple, agricultural development projects have often resulted in alienating land from women's use, concentrating it instead in the hands of large landholders who are nearly always men. In contrast, men do most of the farmwork in Asia, where land is owned individually and production involves more complex technology. Development programs in Asia have harmed women too, however, because women's income from employment as farmworkers has declined as mechanization has increased. In addition, Boserup pointed to the invisibility of women's economic contributions in household subsistence and maintenance work, in home craft industries, and in the informal labor sectors of urban centers.

Boserup's criticism of development theory has in turn come under criticism by researchers who note that she ignores a central aspect of women's work and a contributing factor in their subordination—namely, the gender division of labor in the household and its interrelationship with patterns and symbols of women's subordination. Women's role in biological and social reproduction (that is, household maintenance and services, child care, and care of sick and elderly members) is pivotal to understanding the ways in which women are limited in their ability to seek work outside the home as well as to understanding ways in which their work of social reproduction is marginalized. According to this critique:

> Domestic work performs a crucial role for the functioning of the economic system. It is linked with markets both by way of what it purchases and by what it provides—the commodity labor power that is exchanged for a wage. In the average household, this work is done by women and is unpaid. Women's unique responsibility for this work, and their resulting weakness in the labor market and dependency on the male wage, both underlie and are products of asymmetric gender relations. (Beneria and Sen, 1986, p. 151)

Furthermore:

> The maintenance of the asymmetric of division of labor and women's ongoing responsibility for the production of life and for subsistence production forms the base upon which production of surplus value and mainly male productive labor can be built. Female (subsistence) productivity still constitutes the base of male (surplus producing) productivity. . . . Because of the preservation of the basic structure of the asymmetric division of labor between the sexes, these changes do not lead to greater equality between women and men but, rather, to a polarization between them. The social definition of women as housewives plays a vital role in this polarization. (Meis, 1982, pp. 5–6)

Therefore, because of the interrelationship of social reproduction and economic production, attempts to address women's participation in nonhousehold productive labor will not be adequate without also addressing women's social reproductive burdens and the limitations on their public participation because of economic, social, and ideological restrictions.

To understand how projects aimed at "modernization" could in fact worsen women's lives, it is necessary to situate the programs in the context of women's rights, responsibilities, and opportunities in their traditional societies and then examine how development has transformed the conditions under which women live. In many countries of the developing world, women contribute substantially to their households as primary subsistence farmers, producing crops for their families. Agricultural development programs undermine women's productive roles and hence lead to deterioration of their social position in several ways. First, most programs are aimed at converting land from subsistence use to production of crops for national and international trade. To make commercial endeavors profitable, large accumulations of land are necessary. Through access rights in traditional land-controlling and lineage systems, men are able effectively to take land away from their wives. As a result, women eventually lose their important economic and social roles as subsistence food producers. In addition, national and international organizations lending money for land purchases primarily deal with men, partly because of indigenous patterns of landholding and partly because of (perhaps unconscious) biases that favor men while not recognizing women as potential controllers of land and business. As the male monopoly on agriculture for export increases, women become correspondingly less visibly productive and more dependent on their husbands.

Patterns of labor and household responsibilities further contribute to a deterioration of women's lives. As men's activities become concentrated on growing crops for export, either as landowners or as hired farmworkers, more of the family's subsistence tasks and burdens shift to their wives. Women continue, where possible, to grow crops for household use but can no longer depend on their husbands for help with farmwork, especially with preparing the fields for planting, formerly a man's task. In addition, household maintenance work such as cleaning, gathering wood for fuel, and hauling water are performed solely by the women of the family. Rural-to-urban migration of landless men in search of jobs also results in increased responsibilities for wives left at home with full burdens of household maintenance.

Finally, women agricultural laborers, principally performing unskilled work, lose income and productive roles as development projects encourage the increased mechanization of technology and labor, primarily performed by men. As unskilled women workers lose jobs and access to incomes, their economic dependence and social marginalization deepen.

Development programs aimed at industrial growth have also had ambiguous effects on women's lives. Projects that concentrate capital and job creation in heavy manufacturing requiring high levels of training and skills have predominantly sought male employees. Men have benefited disproportionately because of agency and employer bias and because job training and education programs in many countries are often aimed at boys and men and have not equally recruited or enrolled girls and women.

In many countries, particularly in Africa and Latin America, the growth of industrialization has led to a decline in household craft production. This trend has affected women's contributions and consequently their economic independence because women were heavily involved in making goods for household use as well as textiles, pottery, basketry, and other valued items that could be traded locally or regionally. As their participation in craft production declines, women lose a significant source of income.

In contrast to skilled, technologically complex jobs employing men, many companies have recruited women for low-skilled work in textile manufacturing and electronics assembly plants, especially in Asia, the Caribbean, and Latin America. Echoing the patterns of earlier industrialization in nineteenth-century Great Britain and the United States, multinationals seek young, unmarried women as their employees for low-skilled, monotonous work (Fuentes and Ehrenreich, 1983). Job creation in this sector has had ambiguous benefits for the workers. Studies demonstrate that the women themselves have ambivalent attitudes toward their work and working conditions. However, even though when compared to wages for similar industries in the United States and Western Europe, earnings in developing countries are exceedingly low, by national standards they are often relatively high. The ability to earn money gives the women a sense of independence and self-respect. Workers who live in cities or export zones far from their families enjoy their freedom from parental control. But despite some positive rewards, the industrial context in which the women find themselves often replicates the relations of dominance and subordination found in traditional households. Employers and supervisors establish patriarchal relations with the young subordinate women, severely restricting their autonomy on the job (Ong, 1987). In addition, most available jobs offer no possibility of advancement or improvement, they are often temporary, and they pay low wages. Workers have no union representation, few if any health benefits, and no job security.

Socialist nations' record of economic development is also ambiguous. Socialist governments such as those in Eastern Europe, China, Cuba, and Africa have promoted women's full and equal economic participation both as a means of economic advance for the nation as a whole and in particular as a means for improving the social status of women. These policies have been formulated on the basis of writings by Karl Marx and Friedrich Engels (especially Engels's (1884/1972) *The Origin of the Family, Private Property, and the State*), which discuss the causes of women's subordination worldwide. According to Engels, women's low status in society stems from their isolation in household, production and the societal barriers to women's participation in public economic, social, and political life. To break with past restrictions, socialist governments encouraged women to work for wages outside the household and thus loosen traditional patriarchal relations that devalued and marginalized women.

When viewed solely from the perspective of employment, socialist nations have a markedly positive record. Women in socialist societies contribute as much or nearly as much as do men to productive labor outside the household. Their active participation is (or was) coupled with legislation guaranteeing equal opportunity and equal education for all people and protecting women's rights in social spheres such as marriage, divorce, and reproductive control.

However, despite these significant advances, women in socialist nations have faced many of the same kinds of discrimination as their sisters in capitalist societies. Women's work in the public sector is not compensated at the same rates as men's work. The occupations in which women are heavily represented tend to have lower social prestige than fields dominated by men. Working women are the primary homemakers and caregivers in their households because husbands are still reluctant to accept their share of family maintenance responsibilities. And women have not attained positions of political power comparable to men or proportionate to their numbers. Furthermore, since 1990 and the fall of socialist governments in Eastern Europe, women's economic and social gains have proved to be precarious. Women's unemployment rates far exceed those of men. Legal protections and guarantees of reproductive control have been dismantled in some countries. In the remaining socialist countries, traditional patriarchal attitudes have persisted despite official attempts to eradicate them.

Because women's status in developing nations, as in all nations of the world, derives from multiple causes, hope for improvement must be found in contesting their marginalization in public economy and subordination within their households. As Lourdes Beneria (1982b) suggests:

> The solution to women's oppression rests both on their full participation in non-home production under conditions of equality between the sexes, and the transformation of household relations and gender asymmetries so that relations of dominance and subordination between the sexes are eliminated. At the policy level this approach implies that any effort to eliminate discrimination by sex in the productive sphere cannot ignore other issues related to reproduction—such as the burden of the "double day" that women face when they work outside the household, a burden still common in most countries. (pp. xiii–xiv)

Women's marginalization in public economy is reflected in their overrepresentation in low-paying occupations and their simultaneous underrepresentation in jobs garnering high prestige and high salaries. In addition, women routinely earn less than men for performing similar tasks with similar requirements of education and skill. In the home, women's lack of equality can take many forms. In most countries, as Beneria notes, women workers face the double burden of working for wages in the public sector and performing unpaid work as caretakers in the home. Furthermore, because of social and religious ideologies, women may be restricted to the home and thus barred from public employment and community involvement.

Women's actual contribution in world economy is often distorted and rendered invisible because of the inadequacy of research and statistics on labor force participation in the public sphere and because women's economic contributions in the home are ignored. In national and international economic studies, productive work or "active labor" is generally interpreted as participation in income-earning activities. Because much of women's work is in subsistence agriculture, home craft production, or the "informal" labor sector in urban environments, their economic contributions are often seriously underestimated. For example, following a still-used definition promulgated in 1938 by the International Labor Organization, "housework done by members of a family in their own homes is not included in the description of the gainfully occupied" (Beneria, 1982a, p. 122). Women's economic contributions are generally overlooked in calculations of GNP statistics. In addition, census classifications of workers according to their "main occupation" tend to underestimate or distort women's economic contributions because they are classified as home workers without detailing their specific contributions not only to subsistence but also to extra-household income such as making foods or crafts for sale. Because many women are omitted from categories of "active work," women's needs in economic development and the effect of development projects on their lives are either ignored entirely or thought to be inconsequential.

Women's participation in areas of public production are limited in many countries because of their relative lack of skills and training. These disadvantages stem from routine discrimination against girls in public education and job training programs. In most developing nations, literacy rates for girls are far below those for boys. Girls do not enter primary or secondary schools at rates equal to boys, usually because patriarchal family ideologies dismiss education for girls as useless or dangerous. If families must pay for their children's education, they are more reluctant to bear the expense for daughters than for sons. Families rationalize these biases on the basis of assumptions that daughters will marry soon after graduation and will not be income-earning workers or that daughters are needed at home to help care for younger siblings or perform household maintenance tasks. As a result of these ideological and practical restrictions, boys obtain better educations and learn skills related to income-earning activities in the public sector. These skills range from basic literacy to the ability to handle complex machinery or technologies.

Development programs in agriculture and industry often ignore the root causes of women's lack of technological knowledge and in fact may contribute to the increasing gap between men's and women's skills and training. For example, agricultural development projects create or exacerbate distinctions between subsistence food production and cash crops for trade and export and then recruit men for training in technological skills needed for intensive production, whereas women remain concentrated in subsistence work utilizing simple technology (Chaney and Schmink, 1976, pp. 164–165). Industrial development projects entail similar processes. Men are trained for and recruited into more highly skilled manufacturing jobs, whereas women cluster in low-skilled occupations. As a result, women's work receives less financial reward and consequently less social value.

An important issue in economic improvement is, of course, the development and dissemination of technologies. Women are often marginalized by a combination of factors. When teaching advanced, mechanized technology in programs aimed at modernizing both farming and industry, development planners typically bypass women. And even when women might have access to sophisticated technologies, because of their lack of education relative to men, they may not be able to learn the necessary skills as quickly and efficiently as men. But national governments and international agencies have a role to play in the ways that they promote economic policies at the local level. Although there is sometimes a bias against women's involvement, women's labor is certainly tapped by multinational corporations seeking workers to produce garments and electronics parts in many Third World countries.

Subsequent sections of this chapter will discuss studies of development programs and their effect on women's lives in Latin America, Africa, India, Asia, the Pacific, and socialist societies. The chapter will end with a presentation of demographic, educational, economic, and political data compiled by the United Nations Division for the Advancement of Women.

LATIN AMERICA

Latin American development has generally led to the growth of large agribusiness conglomerates that control huge expanses of land worked by a labor force whose members have lost access to their own land. As agribusiness corporations expand, peasants are forced to sell their land because they are unable to compete with large firms that can afford the capital investment for advanced technology and are therefore able to produce more crops at a cheaper price. Women are affected by this type of agricultural expansion in several ways. Some may be hired as farmworkers under conditions of temporary employment and low wages. Their labor is exploited without long-term benefits or security for themselves or their families.

A common response to agricultural development, however, is that women from peasant communities whose families own little or no land may migrate to urban centers to seek jobs. According to Elizabeth Jelin's (1986) analysis of population trends in seven cities in seven Latin American countries, the majority of female migrants are young, unmarried women, the daughters of poor peasant families. Because their labor at home is superfluous, women move to the cities both in the hope of obtaining income-producing employment and to relieve their families of the burdens of supporting them. Older women with children constitute a second group of migrants. They generally do not find jobs outside their households but instead continue as the primary caretakers of social reproduction, preparing foods, purchasing goods, and performing other hosehold maintenance tasks.

Each class of women tends to adjust to life in the city in different ways. Many young women initially find employment in domestic service, later leaving to obtain other kinds of jobs or to marry and become housewives. Older women with children may earn income, not by seeking outside employment but rather by working in their homes, either producing goods or performing services for sale. For example, they may sew or mend clothing, take in washing and ironing, or care for children from other families. These are tasks that housewives perform for their own household and are consistent with their schedules and skills. Jelin (1986) notes, "Since the tasks are practically the same ones performed at home for her family and may be performed on a part-time or irregular basis, they are added to the woman's responsibilities, without having to break the household routines or change the family organization" (p. 135).

Women's participation in agriculture and industry in Brazil exemplifies many of the general trends in Latin America. Women's role in agriculture depends on the level of technology employed. The introduction of complex technology and mechanization tends to reduce the numbers of workers overall and especially the number of female workers, who are disfavored because of their relative lack of skills but also because men tend to monopolize the few jobs that remain. Glaura Vasques de Miranda (1977) documents that in Brazil between 1940 and 1970, there were both a net and a proportional decline in the number of women employed in agriculture and a parallel rise in the number of men: 47 percent of all working women were in the agricultural sector in 1940, but by 1970 that number had dropped to 20 percent (p. 264). Vasques de Miranda also found that women's agricultural employment varies with overall development. In those areas where agriculture is more highly developed, fewer women work in the farm sector, whereas in less intensively developed regions, more women work in agriculture (p. 266). In the industrial sector of Brazil, female workers are concentrated in low-skilled, temporary, low-paying occupations both because of their lack of education and training and because of social prejudices.

Class, however, is a significant determinant of women's participation in the labor force. Rates of employment increase significantly with education. That is, among illiterate women, only 6.4 percent of married and 19.7 percent of single women were in the active workforce, whereas 65.8 percent of married women and 77.2 percent of single women with university educations were in paid employment (Vasques de Miranda, 1977, p. 270). Women of low socioeconomic status have labor participation rates about 8 percentage points lower than those of other social classes despite the fact that they might be motivated to work to supplement their husbands' low incomes. Women with more education and higher socioeconomic status tend to concentrate in fields such as education, clerical work, and service occupations in which literacy and skill are necessary.

Class and marital status were found to be significant factors affecting women workers in Mexico City as well (Arizpe, 1977). In conformity with prevalent cultural attitudes, most middle-class Mexican women did not work outside the home, although a small percentage of those with university educations had professional careers. In addition, a small but significant number of middle-class women were owners of restaurants or shops selling foods, clothing, and books. Their business income was often a significant supplement to their husbands' wages and helped to support their families in the style to which they aspired. In contrast, women of lower classes were often involved in temporary, informal sector activities such as work as domestic servants or as street peddlers and petty merchants (pp. 32–33). Prostitution was another source of income for women of all social groups, although the majority of prostitutes came from the lower classes.

Because of the scarcity of jobs in agriculture and industry, women who live in the cities of Latin America often find themselves in the informal labor sector. Although classical theories of development predict a transformation from an agricultural to an industrial economy and either ignore the informal labor sector or consider such work to be temporary, according to Lourdes Arizpe (1977), "[d]ata show that the displaced labor from agriculture enters the informal labor sector, most often in the cities which provide a large market for such jobs, and remains there" (p. 26). Industrial development does not provide sufficient employment for all job seekers and therefore creates a marginal population that "survives by low income, intermittent wage or self-employment. In other words, workers are pushed into the informal labor sector and into the services as a result of insufficient demand in the manufacturing sector, and they are destined never to leave them" (p. 27). However, many women fill occupations in the informal labor sector not solely because industrial jobs are lacking but because of such cultural factors as the sex typing of jobs, the need for women to have flexible work schedules to accommodate their household and family responsibilities, and cultural attitudes about the value and/or appropriateness of women working outside the home.

In the 1960s, the Mexican government embarked on a policy of industrial development in conjunction with multinational corporations principally based in the United States that it hoped would attract investment, create jobs, and alleviate some of its soaring rates of unemployment and poverty. The Border Industrialization Program (BIP), inaugurated in 1965, was also a response to the closing of legal opportunities for Mexican migrant farmworkers who had been able to enter the United States for seasonal work under the Mexican Labor Program (also known as the *bracero* program), a bilateral agreement regulating migrant labor that was in effect from 1942 until 1964. When the *bracero* program was discontinued, unemployment in the border region of Mexico jumped to between 40 and 50 percent (Fernandez-Kelly, 1983, p. 209). According to procedures outlined by the BIP, foreign companies established what has come to be known as the *maquiladora* system. *Maquiladoras* operate plants in border towns that function as subsidiaries of the multinationals even though they are on Mexican soil. The plants receive electronics parts or precut garment pieces made in the United States or in overseas factories that are then assembled into a finished product and can reenter the United States under a special agreement at low tariff rates. The companies evade high tariffs by first exporting parts and then importing marketable products from their subsidiaries. They also benefit from agreements with Mexico that enable them to lease or acquire land at low prices and to pay little or no local taxes. Finally, and critically, they have access to a constant supply of workers willing to work for low wages with few, if any, job benefits.

By the 1990s, well over five hundred companies were operating through the BIP, employing more than half a million people. The overwhelming majority (about 85 percent) of *maquiladora* workers are young women who have enough education to be literate but who have not advanced in schooling enough to have higher aspirations. Some one-third of the workers are single parents and heads of households (Fernandez-Kelly, 1997, p. 526). Women are favored as employees because of their willingness to do repetitive or monotonous work, accept low wages, and follow orders. Men, in contrast, are not actively recruited because, said an electronics plant manager, "The man in Mexico is still the man. This kind of job is not doing much for his macho image. It's just a little quirk of a different culture. They'd rather run a factory" (Fuentes and Ehrenreich, 1983, p. 30).

The establishment of the plants has affected internal migration patterns in Mexico. Because of widespread poverty throughout the country, young women by the tens of thousands have left their interior villages and arrive at the border zones eager to take any kind of employment that will pay them a steady wage. As a result, gender roles within families are often reversed. In contrast to customary expectations that men work to support their families, wives and daughters now provide the major household income. But rather than being fully appreciated for their efforts, negative stereotypes about female workers are widespread. They are said to be sexually promiscuous and are blamed for breaking apart the traditional Mexican family.

Although in the past, families preferred investing in the education of their sons, now daughters are encouraged to continue at school so that they will be literate and qualify for factory jobs that pay relatively high wages. However, despite the contribution that women make to their families, marital friction often ensues because of husbands' continued desire to control their wives' behavior and options (Warren and Bourque, 1991, p. 300).

AFRICA

Commercialization of agriculture and expansion of industrialization in Africa have followed trends similar to those found in Latin America. Shifts from subsistence farming to cash cropping have deprived women of access to land and of productive roles in household subsistence. For example, in many traditional farming communities in sub-Saharan Africa, women were often the primary producers of subsistence and local trade goods. Women controlled the land that they farmed and the crops that they obtained. Land was typically allotted for household use by land-controlling lineages, following matrilineal or patrilineal affiliation depending on the prevailing descent principle. Postmarital residence was consistent with patrilocal preferences even when descent was reckoned matrilineally. But even though married women farmed land allotted to their husbands, they controlled the distribution and consumption of produce. Where farm surplus was traded outside the household, the woman who produced the crops also determined the use of the money received. Especially in West Africa, some women were able to attain a great deal of economic independence as local and regional traders (see Chapter 3 for a discussion of African tradeswomen). Because of their central role in economic production and distribution, West African women were able to demand the respect of their husbands and to protect their own autonomy despite living in societies where male dominance was evident in actual and symbolic features of culture. In such societies, women participated in community decision making on behalf of their individual and group interests.

Furthermore, women bear increased burdens in household maintenance because of their husband's concentration in agriculture or migration to towns and cities seeking industrial employment. Mass production of clothing and household goods also deprives women of customary opportunities to produce and sell crafts in local or regional markets. The decline in the markets of Western Africa undercuts women's trading activities, one of the most secure and status-enhancing productive roles traditionally available to them. Women's social prominence, based on their role as traders, has been radically reversed because no other cultural institutions support their autonomy in the context of religious and ideological values that otherwise promote male dominance. According to Leith Mullings (1976):

> Since women have virtually been excluded from the industrial labor force, few alternatives to marketing exist in the urbanizing and industrializing sectors. Women, then, find themselves in a commodity economy where their traditional productive role has been devalued and where they have limited access to the new means of production. (p. 249)

In addition to intensifying gender inequality, industrial development in Africa has either created or deepened differences in class based on ownership of land. Many men lost their access to means of production as they lost access to land traditionally controlled by lineages. As community-based societies were transformed, political power and decision making became less communally focused and more concentrated in the hands of a few individuals who eventually ignored customary economic and social responsibilities to lineage members. Although changes in social relations in traditional African villages have harmed everyone, women's status has declined disproportionately. Mullings (1976) characterizes the relations between men and women in traditional village communities as

> equal but asymmetrical in that men and women did not participate in the same roles [but] equality to access to the means of production limited the extent to which the asymmetry of roles produced relations of domination and subordination. . . . With the advent of private property and the emergence of classes, . . . relations between the sexes became both asymmetrical and unequal. It appears that the existence of asymmetry often provided the basis for the development of inequality under changed conditions. (1p. 263)

Mullings's assessment derives from a study of the Ga town of Labadi in southeastern Ghana. Ga women traditionally held positions of prominence and prestige because of their valued roles as cultivators of land and as traders of goods produced by themselves and their husbands. They also decided how to spend money earned from trading even when trading their husband's produce. Market women were under no obligation to share their earnings with their husbands, evidently often keeping all of the proceeds because they worried that their husbands would not spend the money on the household as they did (p. 252).

As industrialization expanded in Ghana, women's status declined because of both the decrease in trade and the scarcity of new jobs available. Women have not obtained commercial, industrial, or service sector jobs at the same rates as men. As commonly as elsewhere, women do not have access to education and job training for skills necessary for professional, managerial, clerical, and industrial jobs and therefore cannot be recruited to those positions.

In addition, industrialization and the growth of town life has led to an emphasis on nuclear family residency that tends to limit women's mobility and independence because of their responsibilities in household maintenance and child care (Mullings, 1976):

> Traditional kinship patterns were such that a woman and child were less dependent upon a particular man: responsibility for individuals was vested in the lineage. The residential system, based on compounds of matrilineal kin, meant that there were several women who could cook for a woman's husband and look after a woman's children if necessary. (pp. 253–254)

In contrast, women's mobility has now been curtailed because their presence is required at home.

Mullings also documents the decline in women's political visibility in Ga towns. Political roles were traditionally divided between male and female "captains" who represented their lineages. The town itself had two chiefs, a male and a female (called *mantse* and *manyei*, respectively), each responsible for making decisions for their constituency. Quoting a male town chief, Mullings (1976) reports that the *manyei* "had control over all the women in the town," making decisions concerned with everyday life and "the attitudes of the men toward the women" (p. 255). British colonial administrators helped strengthen the power of the male chief as he became a liaison between colonial officials and the populace, but they undermined the power of the female chief, whose authority they ignored. By the 1970s, the office of *manyei* was "moving toward oblivion" (p. 254). At that time, the male chief of Labadi reported that he had "set certain educational qualifications for the office [of female chief] that had not been met" (pp. 254–255).

Women of West Africa have become increasingly involved in rural-to-urban migration. In fact, rates of female migration in the last quarter of the twentieth century probably outpaced that of males, reversing an earlier pattern of predominantly male migration. Migrants are motivated by "actual and perceived opportunities for employment, education, and/or marriage in the cities" (Sudarkasa, 1986, pp. 178–179). Migration in West Africa has an older colonial history that

> redirected economic activity *away from* the precolonial production and trade centers in the interior *toward* the coastal administrative, production, and commercial centers established or promoted by the colonial regimes. By the imposition of taxes, the introduction of various goods and services that had to be purchased with European currencies, and the passage of compulsory labor laws, colonial governments virtually and literally forced people to move away from those areas which could not provide them with adequate cash incomes. (p. 179)

According to Samir Amin (1974), in the fifty years between 1920 and 1970, migrants and their children from the interior to coastal West Africa numbered at least 4.8 million people, a figure that accounted for 21 percent of the coastal population and 26 percent of the inland population. Throughout most of the century, male migrants sought jobs in the expanding commercial and administrative centers, while most female migrants were accompanying their husbands. Where women were able to earn money, they generally were self-employed in farming, trading, service sector occupations, and craft production. The majority were involved in trade, continuing a traditional pattern of female domination of local and regional trade. During the last quarter century, however, a significant portion of female migrants have been young, single women seeking jobs in commercial, clerical, or industrial occupations. When they fail to find such work (probably a likely outcome), they often turn to trading and other informal sector occupations (Sudarkasa, 1986, pp. 182–183). Indeed, women migrants have continued their traditional roles as traders and are prominent catalysts in the spread of technical innovations and the diffusion of knowledge and skills from urban to rural areas. Their roles as traders have made them

> responsible for most of the small scale distribution of the overseas manufactured goods imported into some parts of West Africa. They have also been instrumental in moving commodities from one West African country to another, thereby making foodstuffs, textiles, housewares, medicinals, etc. available to consumers who would not otherwise have access to them. In many instances, female commercial migrants have also helped to introduce new types of machinery, for example, pepper grinding machines and flour mills, and to promote new techniques for getting tasks accomplished. . . . In their persons, female migrants have been perceived as the embodiment of the material and cultural offerings of the city or the foreign land. (pp. 188–189)

INDIA

In a study of lace makers in the city of Narsapur in the state of Andhra Pradesh, India, Maria Meis (1982) has documented how commercialization and expansion of the industry have marginalized the women who are the primary producers. Lace making was initiated as a commercial enterprise by the wife of a Scottish missionary in the middle of the nineteenth century to provide women with an income-earning occupation. Lace table mats and doilies were sent to England and Scotland for sale among relatives and friends of the missionary workers. Profits were used to buy thread for lace production, and the rest was paid to the workers. The industry remained under the control of women until 1970, when two men took over the export of lace as a business venture. They established a "putting-out" system similar to earlier cottage industries in Europe. The work was divided into component processes, each woman specializing in producing one part of the pattern or decoration rather than creating the entire item as before. The separate pieces were collected by agents of the owners and were later joined together by finishers. By 1980, the business had blossomed, and about sixty additional firms were established to export lace, employing between 150,000 and 200,000 workers. Further expansion responded to growing demand for handicrafts in Europe and the United States. From an annual income of about one million rupees in 1970, the Narsapur lace industry jumped to eight million rupees by 1978. In fact, about 95 percent of foreign exchange earnings from all handicrafts exported by the state of Andhra Pradesh was generated by the lace industry of Narsapur.

The industry attracted investors because of its simple and inexpensive technology and the low wages paid to the workers. Investors were primarily from an agricultural caste (called *Kapu*) who had made large profits after the "green revolution" of the 1960s and 70s but who lacked markets for farm products and therefore turned to lace exporting (Meis, 1982, pp. 9–10). Most of the workers also belonged to the Kapu caste but were of the poorer classes.

As lace making became more profitable, men began to replace women in all capacities except as primary producers. Whereas previously women had been employed as agents to bring threads to the lace makers and collect pieces for assembly into the final product, men were increasingly hired as agents, supposedly because they were more mobile. The expansion of the lace industry and its integration into a world market system thus led not only to class differentiation within particular communities but also to the masculinization of all nonproduction jobs, especially of trade, and the total feminization of the production process. The dividing line between men and women is the integration of their products into the market. Men sell women's products and live on the profits from women's work (Meis, 1982, p. 10).

As the process of commercialization deepened, the economic exploitation of women producers increased. They work long hours for low wages while the profits from export trade are extracted by others. Women's marginalization is also reflected in an ideology, stated openly by men, that women workers are just "sitting in the house," not really devoting their time to work. The women also think of themselves as housewives even though they are significant earners in their families and even though they generally spend six to eight hours per day making lace, leaving them with little leisure time after their housework and other caretaking tasks:

> Although many of the women were the actual breadwinners of their families because the men had lost their land (due to indebtedness or because they were jobless), the men did not change their ideas; they said that the women of the community did only housework. (Meis, 1982, p. 11)

According to Meis, "What is so striking about this industry is the fact that the primary producers have become virtually invisible" (p. 14). Even though nearly 200,000 women worked as lace makers in the 1970s, they were not counted as workers in census statistics. Finally, as Meis notes:

> [W]omen are not simply left behind while men monopolize the new and profitable areas of the economy; they are deliberately "defined back" into the role of housewives. Only if the women remain outside the organized sector and are socially defined as housewives can the double exploitation of their labor go on. (p. 26)

The green revolution in South Asia and East Asia has had a profound impact on the economies of the countries concerned and on the patterns of labor necessitated by increased concentration on agricultural output. In India, the green revolution went hand in hand with land reform programs that were instituted after the nation's independence in 1947. Through the efforts of international agencies, primarily the Ford Foundation, high-yield varieties of grain seeds were made available, leading to a radical transformation of traditional agricultural practices. Because of the types of seeds used, farmers could no longer keep seeds from one year to the next but rather had to purchase new seed stocks annually, entailing additional expense. Chemical fertilizers and pesticides also had to be purchased, replacing animal manure as the principal fertilizer. Finally, irrigation projects involving complex machines and technology had to be financed and built. Because of the expenses involved, intensive production was necessary to ensure profits needed for further investment in technology. As a result of intensification, land quickly became depleted of nutrients.

At first, agricultural production required more laborers and increased work from each. Women's participation rose as small landholding households found it necessary to have additional help in the fields to pay the yearly expenses of seeds and fertilizers. However, human labor was eventually replaced by machinery for preparing fields, harvesting, and threshing grain crops. In addition, the increased mechanization of agriculture led to gender segregation of workers. Men were trained and hired to work with complex machinery and technology on a permanent basis, whereas women were concentrated in the casual labor force recruited for seasonal tasks (Sen, 1982, p. 47).

ASIA

Development programs, when aimed at expanding economic growth, may increase opportunities for women while at the same time increasing their overall burdens. For example, following its independence in 1965, the government of Singapore devised economic strategies for rapid industrialization by providing tax incentives to foreign capital investment. They also embarked on wide-ranging social programs such as universal education, public housing, and national family planning, along with regulations that severely restricted labor union organizing and political dissent (Wong, 1986, p. 208). Since then, social indicators generally show an improvement in women's lives. Labor force participation rates for women increased dramatically from only 21.6 percent in 1957 to 41.9 percent in 1979 (p. 209). By 1995, women's economic activity rate had risen to 51 percent, accounting for 39 percent of the adult labor force (UN Division for the Advancement of Women, 2005).

Most women workers are young and unmarried. In fact, because they expect to leave the workforce upon marriage and childbearing, they are marrying later in life, primarily to delay child rearing and prolong their years of employment. There has also been an increase in married women seeking employment outside the home because of rising costs and the desire of families to maintain or improve their standard of living.

Although women are represented in all sectors of employment, they are especially concentrated in light manufacturing such as textiles and electronics that have been drawn to Singapore and other Asian countries since the 1970s. These jobs generally require few technical skills but are monotonous and often temporary, and they compensate workers at low wages. Women are also concentrated in the informal sector because it may be an attractive alternative for mothers with children and household responsibilities.

While universal education is promoted by the Singapore government, gender differences persist in the types of schooling pursued. Women tend to enter academic and vocational programs but are underrepresented in technical schools. Because of their lack of technical training, even women with high school degrees are concentrated in low-paying light industrial work or in commercial and service occupations where they receive low pay for jobs with low status. As in the United States, women generally receive less pay than men for comparable jobs. Also as in the United States, educational acheivement only widens the income gap between men and women.

Social and cultural norms continue to retard women's equal participation in their nation and continue to overburden women's work. Housework and child care remain primarily the responsibility of wives and mothers. Aline Wong (1986) notes:

> In Singapore, and in other developing countries, it is clear that expanded opportunities have not necessarily altered the sexual division of labor. As long as sexual segregation characterizes the occupational world and women are bound by

domestic responsibilities, they will remain a peripheral workforce. Singapore's dependent economic development also tends to transform women into a type of reserve labor force. (pp. 222–223)

Studies of women factory workers in Taiwan indicate that actual experience may contradict the generally held notion that when women enter the labor force, their status in their communities and families rises because they are able to contribute to household support. The rapid growth of government-sponsored export processing zones in Taiwan that concentrate on labor-intensive light industries has led to dramatic increases in jobs for young women. Many girls from poor families leave school after completing primary education to enter the workforce. While young women who work outside the home report benefits from socializing with other young women, they remain bound by cultural values that subordinate women in both the workplace and the home (Kung, 1976).

Although the women may appreciate the independence they obtain from working away from home, they do not generally experience satisfaction on the job, principally because of their low wages. Lydia Kung's (1976) study of factory workers revealed that while most were dissatisfied with their jobs, women without high school educations realized that they would never be able to obtain employment in higher-status, better-paying jobs and so were resigned to their economic position. In contrast, women with high school educations or those who were employed while continuing their high school courses experienced frustration because they felt that they were capable of achieving higher status but were blocked from doing so because of economic realities and social restrictions. Because of the prestige of education in Taiwan, many factory workers who were high school graduates resented the fact that supervisors and coworkers with more seniority were often not as well educated as they were (p. 45). For example, one young woman reported being ashamed of the kind of work that she did even though other occupations do not pay much more than factory work: "But it sounds so much better to be working in an office, especially among people at home who have the notion that 'it does not seem right' if you have been through high school but work in a factory" (p. 45). Another commented, "This kind of factory work is a job where you 'cannot lift your head high.' It is a low status occupation and does not give a person any face" (p. 46). These concerns are especially strong in a society where one's public image is of critical social and psychological importance.

Young women workers also expressed ambivalence about their independence. Although they appreciated the opportunity to travel, work outside the home, and associate with other women, they were aware of their subordinate position in the workplace and of the cultural values that limited their ability to participate equally in their homes and receive social prestige and rewards. Feelings of excitement and independence tend to be stronger among workers at the beginning of their employment histories: "The factories that once represented a wider world, or at least one means of entry to the outside society, appear progressively more confining as one's stay lengthens" (Kung, 1976, p. 51). Women also eventually begin to feel that they are "wasting away" by remaining in factory work during their youthful years.

Although familial attitudes toward daughters have changed now that they are economic assets whose contributions to a family's income are appreciated, it is difficult for young women to assert their independence and be treated as equals in the household setting because of their gender and age. While daughters recognize the difficulty of their ambiguous status, they accept the social and cultural values that obligate sons and daughters to provide assistance for their parents.

Young women are socialized to accept subordinate status in their families, recognizing that their brothers will likely receive better educations and opportunities. Still, they see that their ability to earn wages and contribute to their households has improved their lives, gaining them independence and some measure of respect (Warren and Bourque, 1991, p. 294).

The Pacific

Economic development is not only characteristic of large, highly structured and centralized nations but is also a process affecting small, relatively isolated communities. For example, islands in Melanesia and Polynesia have increasingly become incorporated into national and international export networks. Margaret Rodman's (1993) study of the production of copra (dried coconut) as a cash crop on the Melanesian island of Vanuatu (formerly called New Hebrides) demonstrates the gradual but eventual patterns of globalization and yet also documents the ways in which rural villagers have been able to escape total domination from the world market by maintaining a diversified subsistence and cash economy.

People of Vanuatu became involved in the European trade for sandalwood in the first half of the nineteenth century and expanded their exposure to world economies by working on plantations in New Zealand and Australia in the second half of the century. The islanders thus became familiar with European manufactured goods and evidently desired to acquire them. British and French commercial interests competed in New Hebrides, eventually acquiring large landholdings in the islands. With neither European government able to oust the other, the two foreign powers established the Condominium of the New Hebrides in 1914 and set up joint administration of the islands.

By that time, coconuts had become Vanuatu's main crop, but most people retained customary patterns of communal land tenure, extended family households, and traditional descent and ceremonial systems (Rodman, 1993, p. 173). The islanders grew their own coconuts on small plantations established on the outer islands because much of the land on the large islands had already been turned into plantations under foreign commercial control.

At first, islanders sold raw coconut meat, but by 1930, they had begun to produce dried copra and thereafter earned more income. Because of the simple technology (splitting coconuts and drying the meat in the sun), islanders could produce copra on an occasional basis when they wanted money to purchase store goods without disturbing their subsistence activities and communal ceremonial life. Gradually, however, production expanded in the rural islands so that by 1982, small landowners were producing three-fourths of all copra exports from Vanuatu.

Expansion of copra production had an important consequence in solidifying status differences among the islanders. Because of their access to land through lineage systems, chiefs were able to amass more land and extract more income from trade in copra. However, traditional norms of reciprocity and the obligatory generosity of chiefs in material and ceremonial exchanges tempered the development of status differentiation and inequalities of wealth.

In the early 1980s, world prices for copra declined, and the local market collapsed. At that time, the Vanuatu government sponsored a fisheries development program to diversify sources of income and employment as well as to provide islanders with fish, utilizing a local resource that by the 1980s had been replaced by imported canned fish (Rodman, 1993, p. 178).

The shift from copra to fishing has had an impact on gender relations and contributions to household economies. Although most land under copra production was owned or controlled by men, both men and women worked cooperatively in the fields. The fisheries industries, however, tend to recruit men because fishing in deep water is an occupation traditionally reserved for men. By custom, in contrast, women fish within protective reefs. Still, women continue some traditional roles by marketing the fish locally.

The national government has attempted to recruit islanders to fishing on a more than occasional basis, but most rural villagers resist full incorporation into a national or global economy, preferring to rely on traditional subsistence production supplemented by income-producing activities when deemed necessary for the purchase of goods, clothing and equipment. As Margaret Rodman (1983) notes:

> Only by maintaining access to their means of production and reproduction—in other words, by maintaining a variety of potential sources of income, food, and social support—can rural islanders ensure continued self-reliance. Ironically, this strategy of individual self-reliance inhibits the achievement of national self-reliance and constrains capitalist development. (p. 181)

In fact, then, it is the Vanautu islanders' refusal to become fully incorporated into the global economy that has protected their traditional life and has allowed them to resist the social effects of development that are evident elsewhere in the world, especially increases in social stratification and gender inequality.

In some Pacific societies, where women have traditionally had a high degree of autonomy and economic independence stemming from their productive roles in horticulture despite societal ideologies that support male dominance, they have been able to counterbalance trends stemming from economic development and the world market economy that might otherwise marginalize their contributions. For example, in the highlands of Papua New Guinea, women have developed a system of savings and loans called *wok meri* ("women's work" in neo-Melanesian jargon). *Wok meri* networks consist of small groups of women who together save earnings obtained from selling vegetables and from employment on plantations or as domestic workers (Sexton, 1993, p. 117). Each *wok meri* group establishes exchange networks with similar units and may set up a banking system for making small loans to group members. *Wok meri* groups establish fictive mother-daughter relations with one another that replicate the reciprocal obligations and responsibilities between actual kin.

Both women and men note that *wok meri* began as a response to women's complaints that their husbands spent most of the money they received from their own work on leisure activities such as playing cards and drinking beer. To assure provision of their households, women pooled their resources while simultaneously keeping their savings and earnings away from their husbands' control.

Each *wok meri* group is led by one or two "big women," a title and position that replicates the customary role of the New Guinea "big man," who is both a lineage head and a prominent participant in community redistribution and exchange. *Wok meri* units model their meetings on traditional ceremonial exchanges and rituals, but reversing the ritual system in which women play supportive roles to male leaders, men function as "bookkeepers" and "chairmen" in *wok meri* groups. *Wok meri* units rely on young, educated men to keep accounts of monies collected and dispersed because most women have no formal education (Sexton, 1993, p. 120). The male "chairman" accompanies women when they leave the village to visit other *wok meri* groups and fulfills the customary role of speaker at meetings. However, the chairman is typically younger than the "big woman" who heads the *wok meri*, consistent with the norm that seniority is a critical feature of status and authority.

The amount of money collected and invested by *wok meri* groups was originally quite small, but by the 1980s, many groups had accumulated enough funds to establish themselves as intermediaries in the coffee export business, buying coffee from producers and selling it to processors and wholesalers. Some groups also bought land for coffee production and trucks that they leased for transporting coffee and fuel.

The *wok meri* movement began as a response to women's desire to control the money that they earned, contradicting traditional property rights that vested control of land and resources in men and patrilineage groups. Most resources, such as land, coffee, trees, and pigs, continue to be owned by men (Sexton, 1993, p. 126). Furthermore, since men own land, they own the coffee trees and therefore the coffee produced and the money received for its sale. As elsewhere in the developing world, when traditional economies shifted to a focus on cash crops, the ownership of land became increasingly individualized, and women lost their productive economic roles. However, as Lorraine Sexton (1993) notes, although

> changes in the economy had, on the whole, a detrimental effect on women's economic rights, the relative weakening of male authority brought about by pacification and missionization has allowed women to take steps to respond to the deterioration of their economic rights. (p. 125)

Wok meri, then, is a structured response by women to the perceived decline in their economic status relative to men. It is a form of collective resistance that enhances women's solidarity. *Wok meri* may also be a way for women to bypass traditional avenues of economic success—namely, land ownership. Women are able to amass and reinvest money that they earn from sales of goods and labor and collectively gain economic independence and social status.

In other areas of Papua New Guinea, women have suffered a loss of status and an increase in burdens because planning agencies do not address the potential harmful consequences to women when their traditional productive roles are lost in the context of a society influenced by ideologies of male dominance. To boost agricultural production, the government inaugurated programs in the 1970s for voluntary resettlement of people in districts where farming would be partially subsidized. Prospective settlers could apply for land in settlement communities provided that they agreed to produce targeted crops and sell exclusively to either the central government or multinational companies financing the ventures. Families applying for land are assigned "labor units" based on a scoring system that counts women as half a unit but men as full units. Because their labor is undervalued, women find it difficult to receive land without a husband or sons whose labor will be counted at a higher rate. For example, only 2 of the 150 settler blocks in the Gavien Rubber Settlement were assigned to women (Cox, 1987). Both female recipients were wives of influential men who worked for the government.

Although planning agencies assume a gender division of labor in which women produce food crops for household subsistence and men concentrate on cash crops, in reality women also produce cash crops. In fact, 80 percent of the women working in the region worked on cash crops in addition to their subsistence tasks (Cox, 1987, p. 36). However, by emphasizing the production of crops for export, the importance of subsistence farming is devalued, consequently lowering the status of and marginalizing women who are the main food producers. In addition, women's burdens increase because of their work for their families and for export.

Settlement regions are administered locally by government officials and a local management board made up of settler delegates, all of whom are men, thus effectively muting women's voices and interests. Women's lack of political participation and inability to manage business affairs are the results of their lack of formal education. Although literacy rates among the entire population are quite low, they are even lower for women; Cox (1987) noted that only about 10 percent of girls and women were even minimally literate (p. 39). Nearly all of the women (95 percent) were unaware of the status of household loan obligations to local development banks, having no knowledge of the amount of money borrowed or the repayment schedules.

In contrast to women's experiences in Papua New Guinea, women living on two Tahitian islands, Tubuai and Rurutu, demonstrate that they can maintain or even enhance their status in societies undergoing change when traditional cultural values supporting gender equality are not subverted. In the 1960s, the government of Tubuai initiated agricultural development projects oriented toward the growing of potatoes and green vegetables. These programs were largely successful, involving both men and women by granting financial support and technological training to all. By the early 1990s, approximately 43 percent of potato farmers were women (Lockwood, 1997, pp. 511–512). Women's involvement in farming represented a break with the traditional division of labor that had limited women to performing domestic tasks. But they were able to use their customary access to communal land and their new access to government programs to produce crops for export.

On the island of Rurutu, in contrast, economic expansion has focused on the sale of crafts such as woven mats, hats, and quilts, skills traditionally in women's domain. Craft production, in fact, is now the island's major income-generating occupation, allowing women's economic contributions to be seen as maximal to the welfare of their families. Men concentrate on selling crops from small garden plots, but their efforts are supplemental rather than central.

On both Tubuai and Rurutu, women's rights are protected by indigenous views that people control the products of their labor and the income received. Although residents of both islands have been exposed to Western value systems through government agencies, public education, and missionaries, "Tahitians never accepted notions of male superiority and female inferiority, continuing to see men and women in a largely egalitarian, interdependent way that afforded mutual respect for both" (Lockwood, 1997, p. 515).

SOCIALIST SOCIETIES

The record of socialist nations in establishing gender equality is decidedly ambiguous. Although socialist governments in Eastern Europe, the Soviet Union, China, Cuba, Africa, and the Middle East have officially advocated policies aimed at combating discrimination against women, they all suffer to varying degrees from failure to recognize the critical link between public production and social or household reproduction. They also have rarely confronted and have thus failed to eradicate patriarchal attitudes stemming from traditional ideologies. Influenced by the writings of Friedrich Engels, socialist thinkers and planners have espoused the theory that women's equality can be achieved by participation in public economic production. In addition, recapitulating Karl Marx and Engels, they recognize that a nation's progress toward equality and human rights can be measured by the status of women. However, in practice, the economic and social policies of the existing or formerly socialist countries have not led to full equality for women either in the public spheres of economic production and political participation or in the household spheres of structure of family life, patterns of work, and authority.

Most socialist nations have made great strides in a relatively short time in increasing women's participation rates in paid employment. However, serious discrepancies remain between the salaries received by men and women for comparable work. In addition, women are underrepresented in political office, especially in central governing and policymaking ministries and offices. Finally, working women carry the familiar burdens of the "double day."

In a study of agricultural development policies in four socialist societies (the Soviet Union, China, Cuba, and Tanzania), Elisabeth Croll (1986) reports that while both men and women are heavily recruited into paid agricultural work, women generally are concentrated in less skilled, nonspecialist, low-paying, and low-prestige jobs. In addition to these general trends, women face specific difficulties in each country. In China, women farmworkers are discriminated against by a policy of determining wage scales based on a point system that allocates more points and skilled jobs to men and assigns women to less skilled work, earning fewer points and therefore lower wages (Croll, 1986, p. 231). In Cuba and the Soviet Union, women are also concentrated in nonspecialized jobs, often recruited as temporary workers at peak seasons. Finally, in contrast to the other three nations where men were traditionally the producers of crops, Tanzanian women farm land assigned to them through either their own or their husband's lineage. Recognizing the customary centrality of women in food production, the Tanzanian government has implemented policies of expanding agricultural output by concentrating on independent farmers owning small plots of land because it believed that such a policy would protect women from the loss of status encountered in development schemes based on large accumulations of land. However, although Tanzanian women continue to be the primary producers of both subsistence and cash crops, control of land and farm products remains a male prerogative, and women therefore are essentially "laborers for [their] husbands" (Croll, 1986, p. 239). Only women who live independently or are the heads of households have benefited from Tanzanian policies because they are assigned land in their own names.

Tanzania remains a predominantly agricultural country. Most adults are employed in agricultural work or are domestic subsistence farmers: 84% of females and 74% of males work in the agricultural sector (Government of Tanzania, 2001). However, rates of unemployment and underemployment are higher for women than for men. For both men and women, the second most common occupation is listed as "domestic helpers, cleaners, laborers," although the rates vary by gender: 4.6% for women and 7.5% for men. And women are more likely than men to be economically inactive (56–44%). Finally, women's incomes average about two-thirds that of men. Some of women's disadvantages are interrelated with and compounded by the fact that about a third of all females never attended any schooling while about one-fifth of males are uneducated.

The Tanzanian government has established economic programs and legal institutions to ameliorate women's economic and social burdens (United Nations, 1996). However, lack of funds hampers their ability to fully implement these plans. In addition, cultural factors and traditional attitudes also impede progress for women.

In Mozambique, a country in western Africa that won its independence from Portugese colonial control in 1975, the economy is dominated by agricultural production. In 1980, shortly after independence, 83 percent of the workforce (defined as adults over 12 years of age) was engaged in agriculture; 93 percent of these workers were engaged in "family agriculture" (Kruks and Wisner, 1989, p. 161). Today, according to data compiled by the United Nations, 95.9 percent of the female labor force and 70.3 percent of the male labor force are engaged in farming. The Mozambiquan government has pursued a policy of increasing agricultural production by establishing rural cooperatives. Although the government recognizes the continuing centrality of women as principal family producers, development programs ignore their vital contributions and instead orient modernization strategies toward men. Government agencies render women economically invisible by defining only 42 percent of adult women as "economically active" despite their primary role in family subsistence production (Kruks and Wisner, 1989, p. 156). The main thrust of the government's policies concerning women is to attempt to promulgate nuclear family households and dismantle traditional polygynous marriages. However, as Sonia Kruks and Ben Wisner (1989) note:

> To attempt to end the polygamous household and to encourage women to enter public production without simultaneously attempting to define a new division of domestic labor within the family is to demand of rural women an even more extensive "double day" than they have now. (p. 160)

The establishment of cooperative production in rural areas provides a strategy for easing the individual burdens of women in the fields and at home, but these benefits have not been fully realized.

Social policies in socialist nations have had a mixed record as well. A brief review of some of the relevant issues will suffice here. Most socialist governments have enacted legislation protecting women's rights to control biological reproduction. These efforts are based not only on principles of women's rights but on perceived needs to limit population growth. In the Soviet Union, in contrast, the government had an ambivalent stance because of severe population losses experienced both during the revolutionary period and even more markedly during World War II, when some twenty million Soviet military and civilian residents died. Financial incentives were therefore offered to women who had children. Rewards and social pressures did not have much effect, however; most women limited the number of children they had because of inadequate child care facilities and the likely burdens of the double day of wage-earning mothers.

In China, official government policies aimed at establishing gender equality have not been successful. Particularly in the countryside (where the majority of Chinese people live), patriarchal attitudes remain entrenched. Many families have strong preferences for sons, manifested in part by their lack of participation in governmental one-child programs when their first child is a daughter. In the family, wives continue to be subordinate to their husbands and daughters to their parents (see Chapter 5 for a lengthy discussion of these issues).

In Tanzania, the government promotes the idea of reproductive control but gives it only mild support because traditional ideologies in both patrilineal and matrilineal societies reenforce beliefs that women's most important role is producing children for the continuity of the lineage (Kruks and Wisner, 1989, p. 242). Children are also valued because of their potential contributions to rural farm production. Although some women adhere to traditional notions, others have lobbied for recognition of their rights to control reproduction. As one woman said, "Tanzania women have shown their loyalty to their menfolk and the nation. It is now the nation's duty to provide them with the opportunity to have a say in the one question which concerns them most deeply" (quoted in Croll, 1986, p. 243).

Child care and housework remain primarily women's responsibilities despite official policies that enunciate the need for a more equal sharing of household maintenance work between wives and husbands. Of all countries (socialist and nonsocialist), the Cuban government has taken the most direct and emphatic positions concerning the social rights of women, but these efforts have met with limited success because of the strength of traditional ideologies. The 1974 Marriage and Family Code that is read to couples at their wedding ceremonies has done little to change the actual burdens of women despite its insistence that husbands take equal responsibilities for household maintenance and child care and despite widespread public recognition that husbands ought to share these tasks with their wives. In addition, restrictive attitudes toward women's sexuality have survived despite official promulgation of gender equality. Although the government provides free contraceptive and abortion services, many Cubans, particularly of the older generation and in rural communities, fear that such services, and even the discussion of sex, will lead to promiscuity (Croll, 1986, p. 237).

The Cuban government has continued to stress the importance of women's economic development and social rights. Despite economic problems for the country as a whole, the unemployment rate is relatively low, standing at 5.5 percent. And unlike in many other countries, both socialist and capitalist, women's rates of unemployment are not substantially different than those for men. Economic and political data indicate that women occupy a wide range of jobs including those requiring advanced skills and responsibilities. Nearly all people in Cuba are literate, both males and females. Women comprise about 62 percent of university students (Cuba Solidarity Campaign, 2004). Women account for 66.4 percent of all technicians, 87 percent of administrative workers, 53.9 percent of service workers, 33.5 percent of managers and 43.3 percent of state sector workers (Cuba Solidarity Campaign, 2004; Government of Cuba, 2000). Women are well represented in government and legal positions. They account for 35 percent of the members of Parliament, 16.1 percent of the governing State Council, 18 percent of government Ministers, and 22.7 percent of Vice-ministers. Sixty-one percent of attorneys are women, 49 percent of judges are women, and 47 percent of the judges of the Cuban Supreme Court are women (ibid.). Still, despite these real gains and the prominence of women in public life, cultural attitudes continue to burden women with disproportionate share of household responsibilities even when they are gainfully employed outside the home.

In the early years following the Cuban revolution of 1959, the government initiated a wide-ranging program of economic redistribution and strategies for economic growth by encouraging the participation of all Cuban men and women as wage earners in industry and agriculture to increase productivity. By the end of the 1970s, however, the difficulties faced by Cuba (primarily instigated by the deepening U.S. economic blockade) led to a change in economic and social policy. For example, the government was no longer able to subsidize universal free child care and health care. Once families had to pay for part of the expense of child care, some women, especially those who received low wages, left the workforce to stay home and take care of their children. Furthermore, although the Cuban constitution guarantees employment, the guarantee applies to heads of households, and because in practice males are usually defined as heads of households, it is men who effectively have guaranteed jobs, women have guaranteed access to employment only if they are heads of households (Nazzari, 1989, p. 120).

Another important piece of Cuban legislation mandates that pregnant women receive a fully paid leave of six weeks before childbirth and an additional twelve weeks following. Yet, although this legislation protects working mothers' income, it acts as an unstated excuse for preferring to hire men rather than women. In the early years following the Cuban Revolution, the effects of this law were not serious because companies did not have to show a profit, but since the late 1970s, when economic pressures forced the Cuban government to require that businesses and factories be profitable, the need to compensate women for eighteen weeks of maternity leave put pressure on companies to avoid hiring women.

Still, despite these drawbacks, participation rates of women in employment grew steadily until the late 1980s (Bengelsdorf, 1997, p. 231). Since then, however, the Cuban economy has experienced a sharp downturn since the collapse of the Soviet Union and the withdrawal of economic support as well as a contraction in markets for Cuban products in Eastern Europe. As a consequence, unemployment rates have risen, expensive social services such as child care and health care have been reduced, and many Cuban families face dire hardship. Although there has been a loss of employment across many sectors of the Cuban economy and the policies for job cuts have been officially gender-neutral, in effect women have been more vulnerable to job loss because of their lack of seniority. Since women tend to be the most recently hired, they are likely to be fired before their male colleagues. According to UN data for 1995, the economic activity rate for men was 77 percent, whereas for women it was only 47 percent. Women accounted for 38 percent of the adult labor force.

The fragility of the advances made by women in socialist countries in terms of economic participation, legal protections, and social equality is demonstrated by changes that have taken place in the former Soviet Union and Eastern Europe since the collapse of the socialist systems at the beginning of the 1990s. In the former Soviet Union, for instance, the "inefficiencies" of the economy have been addressed by instituting a market system that has, among other things, resulted in drastic reductions in employment. Although all sectors of the economy have experienced declines, women have suffered disproportionately. For example, in 1993, approximately 70 percent of people officially listed as unemployed were women (Waters and Posadskaya, 1995, p. 353). Because of continuing fears of population decline and falling birthrates (so low that Russia now experiences a population decline), pressure on women to become full-time mothers and housewives has increased considerably. The resurgence in defining women as childbearers and homemakers indicates that changes in social attitudes necessary to protect advances in women's status have not been realized.

In the Russian Federation, most adults are economically active and employed. However, gender discrepancies disadvantage women. According to Russian government statistics, women are more than twice as likely as men to be unemployed (Russian Federation, 2006). And although a majority of professional and technical workers are women (64%), women's earned income is 0.64 percent of men's income (Human Development Reports, 2005). A further indicator of the fragility of women's status in the former Soviet Union is the fact that women's political representation on the national level has plummeted. In the 1980s, women constituted approximately 33 percent of the deputies in the Supreme Soviet (the highest government body in the USSR) and approximately 50 percent or more in lower-level governmental organizations. After the elections of 1991, however, women accounted for only 5.6 percent of national deputies and were even less represented in regional and local governing bodies (Waters and Posadskaya, 1995, pp. 352–353). Similar dramatic declines in women's political representation and increases in unemployment rates have occurred throughout Eastern Europe.

UNITED NATIONS SOCIAL AND ECONOMIC DATA

In the developing world, as in developed nations, women's status is reflected in statistics on population, literacy rates, income, labor force participation, occupation, and representation in parliaments, decision-making bodies, and appointed ministerial positions. Reports published by the UN Division for the Advancement of Women and the Department of Economic and Social Affairs document patterns of discrimination that result in women's marginalization in the paid labor force, their relatively low average wages, and their underrepresentation in official governing bodies. The following sections present some of the relevant data.

In the majority of countries, population figures reveal more or less equal numbers of women and men, but in some regions, disturbing countertrends to the expected parity are evident. In all but three of the forty-six nations in the "developed" world (that is, Eastern and Western Europe, Australia, Canada, Japan, and the United States), the number of women is equal to or slightly greater than the number of men, but nowhere is the ratio of women to men below 95:100. In some countries in the developing world, however, men outnumber women by a considerable margin. Table 7.1 lists countries where the proportion of women to men is less than 95:100.

The figures in Table 7.1 should be understood in comparison to countries in the developed world where, because of roughly equal access to nutrition and health care, the number of adult women equals or more commonly exceeds that of men. Therefore, one can assume that where the proportion of women falls significantly below the adult male population, girls have suffered disproportionately from factors such as infanticide, neglect, poor nutrition, and inadequate health care. These factors probably contribute to the exceedingly low ratio of women to men in some countries of the Middle East and Asia, where extreme patriarchal social and religious ideologies create conditions and practices that harm girls' and women's chances of survival.

Girls and women in many developing nations also suffer because of their lack of education. Boys' greater access to education is reflected in statistics on enrollment in schools, especially at higher levels. Unequal opportunities for education result in much lower levels of literacy for women than for men. Even in the developed world, where nearly all of the adult population is literate, women are somewhat more likely to be illiterate than men except in Malta and the United States, where men's rates of illiteracy exceed those for women. Throughout the rest of the world, however, illiteracy rates are higher overall, and the gender discrepancy favoring men is much more marked. In Latin America and the Caribbean, illiteracy rates may be fairly low for the population as a whole (10 percent or less in Argentina, Cuba, Chile, Martinique, the Antilles, Trinidad and Tobago, and Uruguay), but in other countries they may near or surpass 50 percent (El Salvador: women, 56.1 percent, men, 44.5 percent; Haiti: women, 76 percent, men, 69.4 percent). Gender discrepancies in illiteracy widen even more in many Asian and Middle Eastern nations, where

TABLE 7.1   Ratio of Women to Men in Various Countries, 2005

AFRICA (55 COUNTRIES):

Number of countries with ratio between 95:100 and 100:100: 9

Countries with ratio of less than 95:100:

Libya	94

ASIA (49 COUNTRIES):

Number of countries with ratio between 95:100 and 100:100: 17

Countries with ratio of less than 95:100:

Bahrain	76
Brunei	93
Afghanistan	94
Jordan	92
East Timor	93
Kuwait	67
Oman	78
Pakistan	94
Qatar	48
Saudia Arabia	85
United Arab Emirates	47

OCEANIA (18 COUNTRIES):

Number of countries with ratio between 95:100 and 100:100: 4

Countries with ratio of less than 95:100:

Cook Islands 90	90
Polynesia	94
Northern Mariana Islands	91
Palau	89
Papua New Guinea	94
Samoa	92
Solomon Islands	94

LATIN AMERICA

Number of countries with ratio between 95:100 and 100:100: 11

SOURCE: *Demographic Year Book 2005, Population and Vital Statistics Report, Sex and Age Annual 1950–2050.*

women's rates exceed those of men by 20 or 30 percentage points. Countries where the discrepancies are greatest include Afghanistan, Bangladesh, China, India, Iraq, Iran, Jordan, Malaysia, Pakistan, Syria, Turkey, and Lebanon. Similar patterns are attested in Africa, where the widest discrepancies of 20 to 30 percentage points or more are found in Algeria, Burundi, Cameroon, Cape Verde, Congo, Ivory Coast, Egypt, Kenya, Liberia, Libya, Malawi, Mauritania, Morocco, Mozambique, Rwanda, Sudan, Togo, Tunisia, Uganda, Tanzania, and Zambia. In fact, the only African nations where men's and women's literacy is nearly comparable are Botswana, Namibia, Reunion, South Africa, and Swaziland (UN Department of Social and Economic Affairs).

In much of the developing world, girls' school enrollment has increased during the last several decades, but it still falls below that of boys. For example, a study of education in Papua New Guinea revealed that whereas about 70 percent of school-age boys were attending primary school, only 58 percent of girls were enrolled despite the government's target of full enrollment for all children (Yeoman, 1987, p. 108). Provincial figures vary considerably: in six provinces, less than 50 percent of girls attend school (p. 118). Several key factors contribute to the low enrollment of girls, but

> the most important factor affecting both enrollment and retention is the attitude of parents (particularly fathers) to the status and education of women. Where parents are keen to see their daughters educated, most other factors can be overcome. (p. 120)

Of parents interviewed, 89 percent thought it important for their sons to go to school, but only 56 percent considered it important for their daughters to be educated (p. 122). Although these data refer to a relatively small population, it is likely that similar attitudes are held elsewhere in the world and contribute to low rates of school attendance and literacy for girls and women.

In most of the world, women suffer socially and politically from their lack of visibility as active economic contributors in government statistics and perhaps in public conceptions. However, women's invisibility does not reflect their actual lack of economic participation but rather the recording biases that either ignore or underestimate their substantial contributions. Keeping this in mind, the following tables present 2005 figures compiled by the UN Department of Economic and Social Affairs. The data detail the "economically active population," which includes all persons, either employed or unemployed but seeking work, such as "employees, persons working on their own account, unpaid family workers, and members of the armed forces." In addition, "in the internationally recommended definition, production of primary products such as food stuffs for own consumption and certain other non-monetary activities are considered economic activity." However, the reporting of statistics varies from country to country because different standards are used to determine occupation and hours worked. Furthermore, women are often underrepresented because they "account for the major portion of persons engaged in those economic activities that are the most difficult to measure."

Women's share of the adult labor force is highest in developed regions, but even there, country-to-country variation is attested (see Table 7.2). Women constitute nearly half (that is, 48 or 49 percent of the adult labor force) in Belarus, Bulgaria, the Czech Republic, Estonia, Finland, Latvia, Lithuania, Moldova, the Russian Federation, Slovakia, Sweden, and the Ukraine. These countries comprise Scandinavia and the former Soviet Union and former Eastern Bloc countries. Women's share of the adult labor force is below 40 percent in Bosnia, Italy, and Malta. In the rest of the world, women's

TABLE 7.2   Women's Share of the Adult Labor Force, 2005

Region	48–50 percent	Less Than 40 percent	
Africa (55 countries):			
	Burundi	Algeria	Swaziland
	Ghana	Ivory Coast	Tunisia
	Malawi	Egypt	Morocco
	Zimbabwe	Liberia	
	Rwanda	Nigeria	
	Uganda	Sierra Leone	
	Tanzania (51%)	Mauritius	
Asia (49 countries):			
		Afghanistan	Oman, Malaysia
	Cambodia (52%)	Bangladesh	Pakistan
	Viet Nam	Hong Kong	Qatar, Phillippines
	Kazakhstan	Cypress	Saudi Arabia
	Mongolia	India	Syria
		Iran, Jordan	United Arab Emirates
		Iraq, Japan	Sri Lanka
		Lebanon, Kuwait	Yemen
Oceania (18 countries):			
		Fiji	
		Marshall Islands	
		Samoa	
		Micronesia	
		Tonga	
Latin America and the Caribbean (39 countries):			
	Grenada		Mexico
	U.S. Virgin Islands	Belize	Nicaragua
	Antilles	Chile	Panama
	Bahamas	Costa Rica	Paraguay
	Barbados	Dominican Republic	Peru
			Suriname
		Guatemala	Trinidad and Tobago
		Guyana	
		Honduras	

SOURCE: UN Secretariat, Department of Economic and Social Affairs.

labor force participation rates tend to be lower than in developed regions, although again with variation.

Data on employment and occupation indicate regional and national patterns in the distribution of the labor force according to sector. In UN tables, the following categories are disaggregated: agriculture (farming, hunting, forestry and fishing); industry (manufacturing, mining, utilities, and construction); and services (wholesale and retail trade, restaurants, hotels, transport, communication, financing, real estate and business services, community, social and personal services). In most of the developed world, the fewest people participate in the agricultural sector, but nevertheless male workers outnumber female workers. Women tend to be significantly concentrated in services and underrepresented in industry. The gender discrepancy may be quite marked; differences of 20 to 30 percent are the norm. Data from the United States are typical: 15.2 percent of working women are employed in industry, whereas 34.6 percent of men are so employed; in contrast, 83.5 percent of working women and 61.4 percent of working men are employed in services.

Sectoral employment in Africa and Asia contrasts significantly from patterns in the developed world. The majority of African and Asian women in the labor force are heavily concentrated in agriculture and are correspondingly underrepresented in industry and services. In many countries, in fact, nearly all working women are employed in agriculture, and although men may also be heavily represented in that sector, the percentage of women outpaces that of men. The numbers of men in industry or services obviously depend on the country's degree of industrial development. Table 7.3 contains a sample of representative data for 1990 from all regions.

Discrepancies between men's and women's wages are revealed by data on earnings from manufacturing as reported by the UN for 2005. Table 7.4 presents 2005 figures for women's wages as a percentage of men's earnings in selected countries. And Table 7.5 lists women's share of administrative and managerial workers.

Not only are women's activities ignored or marginalized by national and international agencies that report economic participation, but their interests are also ignored or marginalized politically because of their marked underrepresentation in government either as elected officeholders or as appointed officials in decision-making capacities. The underrepresentation of women is universal in all existing national governments, although the degree varies considerably. Sweden and Norway have the highest percentage of women in elected parliaments, but even there women constitute barely 40 percent of elected representatives, not equal to their proportion in the population. Table 7.6 lists those countries where women constitute more than 20 percent of the members of elected parliaments as of 2004 (note that data reflect the percentage of women in a single house of parliament or in the lower house if there are two legislative chambers).

In the majority of countries of the world, less than 20 percent of elected representatives are women. Many countries, in fact, have less than 10 percent and a large number have even less than 5 percent. In Europe only the Ukraine, and in the Americas only Haiti and Belize, have less than 5 percent female representation; but in Africa, a majority of national parliaments have less than 10 percent women, while quite a number have less than 5 percent.

TABLE 7.3 Sectoral Employment for Men and Women, 1990

	Agriculture		Industry		Services	
Country	Women	Men	Women	Men	Women	Men
DEVELOPED REGIONS:						
Australia	3.9	6.7	13.6	35.3	82.5	58.0
Canada	2.5	4.1	13.0	34.8	84.6	61.1
Germany	4.1	3.9	24.0	48.3	71.9	47.8
Ireland	3.3	19.5	18.9	33.1	77.8	47.4
Italy	9.1	8.3	22.6	36.5	68.3	55.2
Japan	8.3	6.6	27.0	39.0	64.6	54.5
Lithuania	13.4	23.2	33.7	46.9	53.0	29.9
Russia	9.8	17.4	34.8	48.2	55.5	34.3
Sweden	2.6	6.0	14.4	43.7	83.0	50.3
Ukraine	16.2	23.6	33.5	45.8	50.3	30.6
United States	1.4	4.0	15.2	34.6	83.5	61.4
AFRICA:						
Algeria	57.2	17.8	7.2	37.7	35.6	44.5
Angola	85.5	65.0	1.5	13.7	12.9	21.3
Chad	91.0	77.1	0.8	6.9	8.2	16.0
Congo	69.0	33.3	3.6	23.1	27.4	43.6
Egypt	60.5	32.8	10.2	25.7	29.3	41.5
Gambia	91.7	74.0	2.7	11.5	5.6	14.5
Kenya	85.3	74.6	3.0	10.9	11.8	14.5
Lesotho	59.3	29.0	5.0	41.0	35.7	30.0
Libya	27.5	7.2	4.5	27.1	68.0	65.8
Malawi	95.5	78.0	1.2	8.6	3.4	13.4
Morocco	63.1	35.0	18.8	28.0	18.2	37.1
Mozambique	95.9	70.3	1.2	14.5	2.9	15.2
Namibia	53.5	46.1	7.6	20.7	38.9	33.2
Nigeria	44.0	42.5	3.3	8.9	52.7	48.7
South Africa	10.0	15.6	14.5	42.2	75.6	42.2
Tunisia	42.0	22.5	31.6	33.3	26.5	44.2
Tanzania	91.1	77.9	1.8	7.9	7.1	14.2
Zimbabwe	81.0	58.0	2.4	13.0	16.7	29.0
ASIA AND THE PACIFIC:						
Bangladesh	73.6	59.3	19.1	14.5	7.3	26.2
Cambodia	78.3	68.7	7.5	7.5	14.2	23.8
China	76.1	69.1	13.3	16.5	10.6	14.4
Hong Kong	0.7	1.0	33.0	39.1	66.3	60.0
India	74.3	59.3	14.8	16.6	10.9	24.1
Iraq	39.1	11.6	9.4	19.1	51.6	69.3
Israel	2.2	5.3	15.3	37.5	82.5	57.2

(continued)

TABLE 7.3   Continued

Country	Agriculture		Industry		Services	
	Women	Men	Women	Men	Women	Men
ASIA AND THE PACIFIC (*continued*):						
Japan	8.3	6.6	27.0	39.0	64.6	54.5
Korea	20.2	16.7	30.1	38.8	49.7	44.5
Macau	0.1	0.2	50.7	36.8	49.2	63.0
Malaysia	25.6	28.3	22.7	23.4	51.8	48.3
Pakistan	72.3	45.3	12.8	20.3	14.9	34.3
Philippines	30.8	54.4	13.6	16.3	55.6	29.3
Singapore	0.2	0.5	34.0	36.8	65.9	62.7
Sri Lanka	51.0	47.2	23.0	19.8	26.0	33.0
Syria	68.8	21.6	6.3	29.7	24.9	48.7
Turkey	82.5	38.3	6.8	24.1	10.7	37.6
Viet Nam	73.1	69.5	10.9	17.1	16.0	13.4
Papua New Guinea	88.8	72.5	2.8	9.1	8.4	18.4
LATIN AMERICA AND THE CARIBBEAN:						
Argentina	2.9	15.8	16.7	38.6	80.5	45.5
Bahamas	1.6	8.4	5.2	24.2	93.2	67.5
Chile	5.9	24.3	14.8	29.9	79.3	45.8
Cuba	8.4	23.7	21,2	35.6	70.5	40.8
El Salvador	7.0	49.8	18.8	21.6	74.2	28.6
Guatemala	15.9	63.6	23.2	15.7	61.0	20.7
Haiti	57.3	75.8	8.0	9.4	34.7	14.9
Jamaica	14.5	33.6	13.1	32.1	72.4	34.4
Mexico	11.6	34.8	19.9	25.4	68.5	39.9
Puerto Rico	0.4	6.4	21.6	29.0	78.0	64.6

These include Egypt, Liberia, Madagascar, Mauritania, and Niger. In Asia and the Middle East, nations with less than 5 percent elected female representation include Armenia, Bahrain, Bangladesh, Iran, Kuwait, Lebanon, Nepal, Turkey, United Arab Emirates, and Yemen. In the Pacific, a majority of island nations have less than 5 percent female representation in parliaments. These include Fiji, the Marshall Islands, Micronesia, Palau, Papua New Guinea Samoa, the Solomon Islands, Tonga, and Vanuatu. In Latin America, a handful of parliaments have more than 20 percent female representation, while most have between 10 and 20 percent. And in North America, only Canada has more than 20 percent female representation (21%), while in the United States only 14 percent of members of the House of Representatives are women (UN Department of Economic and Social Affairs, 2005).

TABLE 7.4   Women's Wages as a Percentage of Men's
Wages in Manufacturing, 2005

Country	Ratio of Women's Earnings to Men's
AFRICA:	
Botswana	52
Egypt	68
Kenya	123
THE AMERICAS:	
Mexico	70
Panama	93
Brazil	61
Colombia	65
Peru	55
ASIA:	
Bahrain	44
Hong Kong	64
Iran	80
Japan	60
Jordan	65
Myanmar (Burma)	112
Occupied Palestinian Territory	49
Philippines	80
South Korea	56
Turkey	97
EUROPE:	
Austria	60
Belgium	81
Denmark	87
France	78
Germany	74
Ireland	69
Netherlands	78
Norway	88
Portugal	64
Switzerland	133
United Kingdom	79
OCEANIA:	
Australia	89
New Zealand	80

TABLE 7.5 **Women's Share of Administrative and Managerial Occupations, 2005 (percentages)**

Country	Percentage of Women in Administrative and Managerial Occupations
AFRICA:	
Egypt	9
Ghana	34
South Africa	27
NORTH AMERICA:	
Bahamas	40
Canada	35
Costa Rica	29
Mexico	25
Puerto Rico	41
United States	46
SOUTH AMERICA:	
Argentina	25
Bolivia	36
Chile	24
Colombia	38
Peru	23
Venezuela	27
ASIA AND THE MIDDLE EAST:	
Bahrain	10
Bangladesh	8
Cambodia	14
Hong Kong	26
Iran	13
Iraq	15
Israel	29
Japan	10
Occupied Palestinian Territory	12
Oman	9
Pakistan	2
Philippines	58
South Korea	6
Turkey	6
EUROPE:	
Belgium	31
Denmark	26
Germany	36
Ireland	29

Italy	21
Poland	34
Russian Federation	39
Spain	30
Sweden	30
Ukraine	39
United Kingdom	33
PACIFIC:	
Australia	36
Marshall Islands	19
New Zealand	36
Tonga	19

TABLE 7.6   Countries with Women as More Than 20 Percent
of Elected Members of Parliament, 2004

Country	Percentage
EUROPE:	
Austria	34
Belarus	29
Belgium	35
Bulgaria	26
Denmark	38
Finland	38
Germany	32
Iceland	30
Latvia	21
Lithuania	21
Luxembourg	20
Netherlands	37
Norway	36
Poland	20
Spain	36
Sweden	45
Switzerland	25
AFRICA:	
Eritrea	22
Mozambique	30
Rwanda	49

(continued)

TABLE 7.6   Continued

Country	Percentage
AFRICA (*continued*):	
Seychelles	27
South Africa	33
Tanzania	21
Tunisia	23
Uganda	25
ASIA AND THE PACIFIC:	
Australia	25
China	20
Korea (Democratic Peoples Rep.)	20
Lao	23
New Zealand	28
Pakistan	22
Timor	26
Vietnam	27
LATIN AMERICA AND THE CARIBBEAN:	
Argentina	34
Bahamas	20
Costa Rica	35
Cuba	36
Grenada	27
Guyana	20
Mexico	23
Nicaragua	21
NORTH AMERICA:	
Canada	21

The scarcity of women as elected representatives is replicated in appointed ministerial and subministerial positions that confer decision-making capacities. The appointment of women to ministerial (ministers or the equivalent) or subministerial (deputy or assistant ministers) decision-making positions is most likely in developed regions, but in only a small number of countries do women occupy more than 20 percent of such positions (Australia, Austria, Finland, Ireland, Lichtenstein, Luxembourg, Macedonia, Netherlands, New Zealand, Norway, Sweden, and the United States). Of African nations, only in Seychelles do women constitute 20 percent of ministerial and subministerial positions. No country in the Middle East falls into this category, and in Asia and the Pacific, only the Philippines does so. Finally, Latin American and Caribbean nations in which women serve in more than 20 percent of appointed decision-making offices include Antigua,

Bahamas, Barbados, Colombia, Costa Rica, Dominica, El Salvador, Grenada, and Haiti (UN Division for the Advancement of Women, Worldwide Government Directory).

SUMMARY

A review of research and documentation regarding economic development indicates the critical role of the planning and implementation of programs to safeguard women's interests. Planning agencies need also to consider a society's foundations and the traditions in which modernization takes place. Unfortunately, development programs in agriculture tend to limit women's ability to participate in new technologies and landholding patterns and instead relegate women to subsistence farming, which becomes devalued in a cash- and income-oriented economy. In the past, women's centrality in household subsistence gained them the respect of their families, but as these roles have lost value, women have lost status relative to men, who have been monopolizing the occupations that earn income and prestige. In government statistics, women's vital economic contributions are often rendered invisible because subsistence work that does not directly earn income is ignored. As women's work becomes devalued, their status within their households and communities deteriorates.In traditionally male-dominated rural societies, women lose their rights to land and other productive resources and become increasingly dependent and restricted.

Women in the industrial sector rarely fare much better. They are recruited into low-paying, dead-end, or temporary jobs, especially in textiles and electronics, where they are incorporated as subordinate workers in a hierarchal organization that replicates the patriarchal structure of their families. According to some estimates, about 80 percent of workers in light manufacturing plants worldwide are young women between the ages of 13 and 25 (Moore, 1988, p. 100).

Although participation in paid employment has the potential to enhance the status of individual women and to protect the autonomy of women as a group, that potential may be realized only under two conditions. First, women must be able to obtain jobs that confer the same kinds of prestige as men receive. Gender segregation in the workplace generally relegates women to jobs with low social prestige, low financial compensation, and few opportunities for decision making, control, and advancement. Second, women's autonomy and prestige can be protected and advanced only where social values confer respect and rewards for their work. In male-dominated societies where women have no traditional protections and no rights to property, the effects of development will not be to their benefit but in fact may contribute to a deterioration in their status. As we have seen, some governments are sensitive to these issues and have passed legislation to protect women's rights, but legislation alone is not sufficient and has not yet led to fundamental changes in social attitudes.

REFERENCES

AMIN, SAMIR. 1974. *Modern Migrations in Western Africa.* Oxford: Oxford University Press.

ARIZPE, LOURDES. 1977. "Women in the informal labor sector: The case of Mexico City." *Signs: Journal of Women in Culture and Society,* 3 (1): 25–37.

BENERIA, LOURDES. 1982a. "Accounting for women's work." In *Women and Development: The Sexual Division of Labor in Rural Society* (ed. Lourdes Beneria). New York: Praeger, pp. 119–147.

———. 1982b. "Introduction." In *Women and Development: The Sexual Division of Labor in Rural Society* (ed. Lourdes Beneria). New York: Praeger, pp. xi–xxiii.

BENERIA, LOURDES, AND GITA SEN. 1986. "Accumulation, reproduction, and women's role in economic development: Boserup revisited." In *Women's Work: Development and the Division of Labor by Gender* (ed. Eleanor Leacock and Helen Safa). Cambridge: Bergin & Garvey, pp. 141–157.

BENGELSDORF, CAROLLEE. 1997. "[Re]considering Cuban women in a time of troubles." In *Daughters of Caliban: Caribbean women in the 20th century.* (ed. Lopez Springfield). Bloomington: Indiana University Press, pp. 229–255.

BOSERUP, ESTER. 1970. *Women's Role in Economic Development.* London: Allen & Unwin.

CHANEY, ELSA, AND MARIANNE SCHMINK. 1976. "Women and modernization: Access to tools." In *Sex and Class in Latin America* (ed. June Nash and Helen Safa). New York: Praeger, pp. 160–182.

COX, ELIZABETH. 1987. "Women in rural settlement schemes: Institutionalized gender bias and informal gender abuses." In *The Ethics of Development: Women as Unequal Partners in Development* (ed. Susan Stratigos and Philip Hughes). Port Moresby: University of Papua New Guinea, pp. 28–66.

CROLL, ELISABETH. 1986. "Rural production and reproduction: Socialist development experiences." In *Women's Work: Development and the Division of Labor by Gender* (ed. Eleanor Leacock and Helen Safa). Cambridge: Bergin & Garvey, pp. 224–252.

CUBA SOLIDARITY CAMPAIGN. 2004. "Charting Women's Progress Since 1959." www.cuba-solidarity.org/cubasi.

ENGELS, FRIEDRICH. 1972. *The Origins of the Family, Private Property, and the State.* New York: International. (Original work published 1884).

FERNANDEZ-KELLY, MARIA. 1983. "Mexican border industrialization, female labor force participation, and migration." In *Women, Men, and the International Division of Labor* (ed. June Nash and Maria Fernandez-Kelly). Albany: State University of New York Press, pp. 205–223.

FERNANDEZ-KELLY, MARIA. 1997. "Maquiladoras: The view from the inside." In *Gender in Cross-Cultural Perspective,* 2nd ed. (ed. Caroline Brettell and Carolyn Sargent). Upper Saddle River, NJ: Prentice Hall, pp. 525–537.

FUENTES, ANNETTE, AND BARBARA EHRENREICH. 1983. *Women in the Global Factory.* Cambridge, MA: South End Press.

GOVERNMENT OF CUBA. 2000. "Economic Results, Year 2000, Ministry of Economy and Planning." www.cubagov.cu.

GOVERNMENT OF TANZANIA. 2001. "Integrated LabourForce Survey, 2000/2001, Analytical Report." www.tanzania.go.tz.

HUMAN DEVELOPMENT REPORTS. 2005. "Russian Federation." www.hdr.undp.org/statistics/data/countries.

JELIN, ELIZABETH. 1986. "Migration and labor force participation of Latin American women: The domestic servants in the cities." *Signs: Journal of Women in Culture and Scoiety,* 3 (1): 129–141.

KRUKS, SONIA, AND BEN WISNER. 1989. "Ambiguous transformations: Women, politics, and production in Mozambique." In *Promissory Notes: Women in the Transition to Socialism* (ed. Sonia Kruks et al.). New York: Monthly Review Press, pp. 148–171.

KUNG, LYDIA. 1976. "Factory work and women in Taiwan: Changes in self image and status." *Signs: Journal of Women in Culture and Society,* 2 (1): 35–58.

LOCKWOOD, VICTORIA. 1997. "The impact of development on women: The interplay of material conditions and gender ideology." In *Gender in Cross Cultural Perspective,* 2nd ed. (ed. Caroline Brettell and Carolyn Sargent). Upper Saddle River, New Jersey: Prentice Hall, pp. 504–517.

MEIS, MARIA. 1982. "The dynamics of the sexual division of labor and integration of rural women into the world market." In *Women and Development: The Sexual Division of Labor in Rural Societies* (ed. Lourdes Beneria). New York: Praeger, pp. 1–27.

MOORE, HENRIETTA. 1988. *Feminism and Anthropology.* Minneapolis: University of Minnesota Press.

MULLINGS, LEITH. 1976. "Women and economic change in Africa." In *Women in Africa: Studies in Social and Economic Change* (ed. Nancy Hafkin and Edna Bay). Stanford, CA: Stanford University Press, pp. 239–264.

NAZZARI, MURIEL. 1989. "The women question" in Cuba: An analysis of material constraints on its resolution." In *Promissory Notes: Women in the Transition to Socialism* (ed. Sonia Kruks et al.). New York: Monthly Review Press, pp. 109–126.

ONG, AIHWA. 1987. *Spirits of Resistance and Capitalist Discipline: Factory Women in Malaysia*. Albany: State University of New York Press.

RODMAN, MARGARET. 1993. "Keeping options open: Copra and fish in rural Vanuatu." In *Contemporary Pacific Societies: Studies in Development and Change* (ed. Victoria Lockwood et al.). Upper Saddle River, NJ: Prentice Hall, pp. 171–184.

RUSSIAN FEDERATION. 2006. Population and Labour Market. www.gks.ru/scripts.

SEN, GITA. 1982. "Women workers and the Green Revolution." In *Women and Development: The Sexual Division of Labor in Rural Societies* (ed. Lourdes Beneria). New York: Praeger, pp. 29–64.

SEXTON, LORRAINE. 1993. "Pigs, pearlshells, and 'women's work': Collective response to change in highland Papua New Guinea." In *Contemporary Pacific Societies: Studies in Development and Change* (ed. Victoria Lockwood et al.). Upper Saddle River, NJ: Prentice Hall, pp. 117–134.

SUDARKASA, NIARA. 1986. "Women and migration in contemporary West Africa." *Signs: Journal of Women in Culture and Society*, 3 (1): 178–189.

UN DIVISION FOR THE ADVANCEMENT OF WOMEN. 2005.

UNITED NATIONS CONVENTION ON THE ELIMINATION OF ALL FORMS OF DISCRIMINATION AGAINST WOMEN. 1996. United Republic of Tanzania.

VASQUES DE MIRANDA, GLAURA. 1977. "Women's labor force participation in a developing society: The case of Brazil." *Signs: Journal of Women in Culture and Society*, 3 (1): 261–274.

WARREN, KAY, AND SUSAN BOURQUE. 1991. "Women, technology, and international development ideologies: Analyzing feminist voices." In *Gender at the Crossroads of Knowledge: Feminist Anthropology in the Postmodern Era* (ed. Micaela di Leonardo). Berkeley: University of California Press, pp. 278–311.

WATERS, ELIZABETH, AND ANASTASIA POSADSKAYA. 1995. "Democracy without women is no democracy: Women's struggles in post-communist Russia." In *The Challenge of Local Feminisms: Women's Movements in Global Perspective* (ed. Amrita Basu). Boulder, CO: Westview, pp. 351–373.

WONG, ALINE. 1986. "Planned development, social stratification, and the sexual division of labor in Singapore." In *Women's Work: Development and the Division of Labor by Gender* (ed. Eleanor Leacock and Helen Safa). Cambridge: Bergin & Garvey, pp. 207–223.

YEOMAN, LYN. 1987. "Universal primary education: Factors affecting the enrolment and retention of girls in Papua New Guinea community schools." In *The Ethics of Development: Women as Unequal Partners in Development* (ed. Susan Stratigos and Philip Hughes). Port Moresby: University of Papua New Guinea, pp. 108–155.

PART II

Ideological Constraints on Gender Constructs

Chapters in Part II examine some of the ways that ideology constrains the activities of men and women and the evaluation accorded to the genders. Roles are allocated consistent with societal beliefs about the nature of women and men and their inherent capabilities. These beliefs are often expressed directly through behavior and outright pronouncements. But they are also typically expressed through symbols enshrined in religious teachings that present supernatural origin and/or sanction for people's behavior. In addition, ideological constructs are conveyed in daily experience through language and communicative interactions.

Chapter 8 deals with interconnections among beliefs about gender and the body, about gender and biological sex, and about women's and men's natures, physiological endowments and processes, and abilities and worthiness. Attitudes toward the body and its functioning not only serve to differentiate between men and women but also lead to contrasting rights and chances for maintaining health and ensuring survival.

In Chapter 9, religious beliefs and practices are analyzed as they directly and indirectly express notions about the inherent worth of women and men. The roles male or female deities are assigned in the supernatural realm, and the rights of human men or women to participate as religious practitioners have an impact on social relations and cultural values ascribed to the genders.

Finally, Chapter 10 is concerned with topics of language, linguistic expression, and communicative behavior. Words used to describe women and men, the ways that their activities are talked about, and their rights to speak and to be heard all carry critical messages about their worthiness.

CHAPTER 8

Gender and the Body

Cultural constructs of gender are conveyed through beliefs and practices that prevail in diverse societal domains. In previous chapters, we emphasized interrelationships among productive modes, economic roles, and a society's concepts of women's and men's rights and responsibilities. In this chapter, we focus on how concepts of gender are interconnected with beliefs about the human body. We discuss the possibility, existing in many native societies of North America (among others), of a third gender category in addition to the typical distinctions between women and men. We also consider the impact of gender constructs on individual health and well-being. Examination of issues of gender and health reveals some of the ways that cultures transmit and reinforce ideological beliefs related to women's and men's worthiness. Among the relevant topics are attitudes prevailing in a culture regarding biological processes, differential allocation of foods to women and men, and people's rights to function in their society as health care practitioners.

Notions concerning physiological attributes are often metaphors for underlying attitudes about an individual's place in his or her society. The human body may symbolize concepts related to people's roles and responsibilities. In addition, the types and amounts of foods deemed appropriate for females and males may signal and reinforce basic cultural constructs of the worthiness of the genders. Differential medical intervention and treatment also have direct impacts on one's health and survival. Finally, because in most, if not all, cultures, the role of healers is well respected, women's and men's access to this specialty is an indication of their social valuation and a factor contributing to their prestige.

As part of a culture's construction of reality, all peoples have an awareness of human physiological processes. Whether their concepts are scientifically accurate or not, members of a given culture share beliefs about causes and dynamics of biological functions, physical changes in human bodies, and the ways individuals can control or influence somatic processes. Many ideas concerning physical functioning apply equally to men and women. However, some biological processes are specifically relevant to only one gender. Beliefs about these distinctive traits often reveal underlying cultural constructs related to attitudes toward women and men. In discussing these, and other, topics in this chapter, we offer examples of characteristic notions and behaviors as demonstrative, rather than exhaustive, instances of prevalent patterns.

A THIRD GENDER

In previous sections of this book, we dealt with economic, social, and political roles of people as they are culturally assigned to one of two genders—that is, as women or men. Although the division of humans into two gender categories is certainly the most common cultural pattern, other possibilities exist. There are (or were) many native cultures of North America that recognized a third gender category as well. Although third genders are also attested in societies in other parts of the world, because the most well-documented and consistent examples come from native North America, we discuss these data in detail.

Of utmost importance in understanding the native concept of a third gender is to separate the social being from the biological body. The third gender was decidedly a social concept. It included biological males and females who, for various reasons discussed later, assumed social roles other than (or sometimes in addition to) the roles usually associated with their sex. Their behavior and appearance combined features appropriate to women and men and also incorporated activities specifically assigned to them. The third gender was a distinct gender category. That is, although the social and ritual roles of members of the third gender at times approximated that of men and women, they are not best understood as examples of "gender crossing" or "gender mixing" as they are sometimes described (see Blackwood, 1984; Callender and Kochems, 1983). Third-gender status does not connote any particular relationship to men and women but rather simply denotes a third possibility, different from woman and man even though in some ways resembling them.

The third gender is given various names in each culture in which it existed. Except for the Navajo (Southwest), differences between female and male members of the third gender were noted in the terms used by native peoples. The third gender does not yet have an established terminology in the anthropological literature. The term *berdache* is often used for biological males; a comparable term for females is not widely cited, although *berdache* is sometimes applied to both males and females (Callender and Kochems, 1983). Evelyn Blackwood (1984) employs the label *cross-gender females*, but this terminology is unsatisfactory because it implies that females become like men rather than assume a third gender. Walter Williams (1986) introduced the term *amazon* to describe such females to avoid the implications of gender crossing and to note a "status specific to women that is not subservient to male definitions" (p. 234). *Amazon*, however, has not been adopted by others, perhaps because it may carry misleading connotations coming from Greek mythology that are totally unwarranted for Native American cultures. Finally, the label *Two-Spirit* is now encountered and has the advantage of incorporating an important feature of the third gender—namely, its power or spiritual component. Another benefit of the term *Two-Spirit* is its neutrality regarding biological sex. Given these considerations, we employ it here as the cover term for members of the third gender, although at times it will be necessary to distinguish between males and females because their roles were not identical, and some cultures did not provide third-gender status for both females and males.

According to documentary evidence reviewed by Charles Callender and Lee Kochems (1983), 113 native North American societies provided a third gender status as a possibility for their members. A lack of mention of third genders in other cultures does not necessarily mean they were absent, because their existence may not have been noted by Euro-American observers. In any case, third genders were well established in most regions of North America, especially from "California to the Mississippi Valley and upper Great Lakes, with scattered occurrences beyond it" (p. 444). They existed especially in California, the Great Basin, and parts of the Plains and Prairies, and they were less numerous in the Southwest and Northwest coast. Two-Spirits were least likely in the Arctic, Subarctic, and East, although they were not unknown in these areas. Callender and Kochems find no correlation between types of social or economic systems and the possibility of third genders except that perhaps their scarcity in the Arctic and Subarctic might be motivated by subsistence economies that relied on hunting, and therefore "the contribution of males was too valuable to promote their transformation" (p. 445). They also note, significantly, that among western Subarctic peoples, females were the most common Two-Spirits and that among the Kaska and Carrier, for example, only females could be Two-Spirits.

From historical and anthropological literature on the subject, it seems the number of male Two-Spirits was much higher than of females. However, as with treatment of other cultural features, absence or scarcity of accounts of female Two-Spirits may either be an accurate expression of fact or a reflection of females' invisibility to male observers. If accurate, it is possible that females were less likely than males to become Two-Spirits because social values stressed the importance of women's reproductive role and made females less likely to abandon customary gender expectations.

Each culture that provided a third gender category incorporated its specific definition of the roles appropriate to members. However, some tendencies have wide applicability. Two-Spirits generally were viewed as special people who fulfilled roles that conferred social prestige. They were respected for their practical skills and spiritual knowledge. They were everywhere understood to be a group distinct from women and men regardless of the fact that they resembled females and males biologically. That the Two-Spirit tradition is an excellent instantiation of the distinction between gender and biological sex is tellingly reflected by the Ingalik of Arctic Alaska, among whom female Two-Spirits took part in male ceremonies in the *kashim*, or "men's house," including sweat baths in which participants undressed and were ritually purified. In these instances, men "were said not to perceive the [Two-Spirits'] true sex" (Blackwood, 1984, p. 32). Men's behavior here is not surprising at all but rather underscores the fact that they reacted to Two-Spirits according to the social roles the third gender assumed, not the physical attributes of their bodies.

People became Two-Spirits as a result of either personal inclination or spiritual calling. In the first instance, a young girl or boy might from an early age take an interest in the occupations and demeanors usually displayed by members of the other sex. Parents noted their child's preferences and thereafter trained her or him in the subsistence skills appropriate to their child's chosen role. Among some groups such as the Kaska of Yukon Territory (Canada), parents who had no sons might choose one of their daughters to learn hunting skills so she could contribute directly to household subsistence as a son would.

The second mode of recruitment, and the more common, was to receive a spiritual calling through a vision or dream. This pattern is consistent with fundamental themes in Native American religions regarding the spiritual significance of dreams and the honor conferred on a person who has an especially powerful dream or vision. Dreaming to assume the third gender gave both spiritual and social validation to a male's or female's transformation, just as in some native cultures males achieved adult manhood through visions and in most native societies religious practitioners received spirit knowledge and healing powers through dreams. The parallel between third genders and religious experience is crucial because Two-Spirits were often thought to have extraordinary powers, as demonstrated by their ability to heal and to prophesy or foretell the future.

Many native peoples formally validated Two-Spirits' social role with rituals that publicly marked their special status. Among the Kaska, when a female Two-Spirit reached the age of 5, her parents tied a bear's dried ovaries to her belt to protect her from becoming pregnant (Blackwood, 1984). At puberty, female Two-Spirits of the Cocopa (Southwest) had their noses pierced like men did rather than having tatoos incised in their chins like women. Male Two-Spirits also received ritual and social validation. Among the Mohave (Southwest), for example, when a male Two-Spirit was about 10 years old, he participated in a public ceremony in which he was led into a circle surrounded by an audience and a singer. When the singer sang initiation songs, the Two-Spirit danced as women did and was proclaimed an *aylha* (Two-Spirit) after the fourth dance. He or she was then ritually bathed, was given a woman's skirt, and announced a new woman's name for him or herself (Williams, 1986).

Although the behavior of Two-Spirits differed in various societies, they typically performed economic duties usually appropriate to the opposite sex, sometimes in addition to those associated with their own biological sex. Female Two-Spirits were hunters, trappers, and occasionally warriors as well. Male Two-Spirits contributed their labor as farmers (where economies included horticulture) and were trained in domestic skills such as sewing, embroidery, and food preparation.

Where warfare was a significant activity, male Two-Spirits generally refrained from participation. However, in some societies, male Two-Spirits did join war parties, either as active fighters or as carriers of supplies (for example, Natchez and Timucua of the Southeast) (Callender and Kochems, 1983). Among the Cheyenne of the northern Plains, male Two-Spirits accompanied war expeditions, serving critical quasi-religious functions as healers of the wounded and guardians of scalps obtained in battle. They also had charge of scalp dances that followed victorious raids. Although female Two-Spirits did not always participate as warriors, they were not constrained from doing so, and some became famous for their military and tactical skills.

Two-Spirits are often described in the literature as unusually prosperous in comparison with other members of their community. They had economic advantages due to their ability to perform both women's and men's work and were thus able to maximize opportunities for production and resource exploitation. In some societies, Two-Spirits had sources of income not available to any other people because they performed quasi-ritual functions specifically assigned to them. For example, Teton Lakota (Plains) Two-Spirits bestowed secret, spiritually powerful names on children, receiving horses in payment for their services. In several California groups, Two-Spirits were responsible for burial and mourning rituals. In societies such as the Navajo, Cheyenne, and Omaha (among others), they functioned as go-betweens between men and women by resolving conflicts between spouses or arranging liaisons and marriages, usually receiving payment for their services (Williams, 1986).

One of the consistent features of the third-gender tradition was that members wore clothing and hairstyles associated with their chosen social role rather than with their biological sex. Male Two-Spirits adopted women's clothing, and female Two-Spirits dressed as men did. This pattern demonstrates that gender distinctions can be given symbolic as well as practical value. Differences in clothing are, after all, external artifices that serve the function of immediate categorization of people into culturally defined groups. In a literal as well as figurative sense, people wear the markings of the gender with which they are associated. In some cultures, Two-Spirits who performed both men's and women's occupations changed their clothing to fit the gender identity usually engaged in any given work. For instance, Western Mono (California) Two-Spirits wore men's clothing when hunting and women's dress when gathering; male Osage and Miami (Plains) Two-Spirits wore men's clothing when they joined war expeditions but dressed like women when they returned home (Callender and Kochems, 1983). Finally, to illustrate again the symbolic messages of clothing, gender, and sex, deceased male Zuni Two-Spirits were buried in women's dress and men's trousers.

The social and sexual lives of Two-Spirits were consistent with their gender roles. Their sexual activity and marriages usually involved relationships with members of the gender other than the one they resembled socially. That is, female Two-Spirits had sexual relations with and might marry women; males had sexual relations with and might marry men. In fact, Two-Spirits were often highly desired as mates because of their economic and productive skills and their spiritual knowledge and abilities. According to recorded accounts, they seemed not to have had any difficulty marrying and establishing successful households. The wives of female Two-Spirits sometimes had children fathered by men but claimed by the Two-Spirit husband in an expression of social fatherhood. In some societies, especially of the Plains and the Southwest, Two-Spirits might marry either men or women, although such practice was less common than the more restrictive pattern.

Two critically important points regarding sex and marriage need mention here. First, Two-Spirits never married other Two-Spirits. This fact underscores the notion that marriage is a cultural institution whose purpose is to unite dissimilar individuals in a joint economic and social unit (see the discussion of the functions of marriage in Chapter 1). Because Two-Spirits are similar as social gendered beings, they cannot marry each other. The second critical point is that native cultures did not view sexual relations between Two-Spirits and their mates as either *homosexual* or *heterosexual* in the sense those terms imply to Euro-Americans. That is, although intercourse between a female Two-Spirit and his or her wife is homosexual in the sense that it occurs between two people of the same biological sex, the Two-Spirit is not culturally defined as female but rather as a member of a distinct gender. Neither was the behavior considered heterosexual in the sense of imitating sexual relations between ordinary men and women. This is a complicated, but highly meaningful, symbolic transformation. It is gender, not biological sex, that is important. Significant also is the fact that when marriages or liaisons between Two-Spirits and their mates ended, the partner typically next married a person whose gender identity differed from theirs; that is, the ex-wife of a female Two-Spirit married a man, whereas the ex-husband of a male Two-Spirit married a woman.

Two-Spirits' sexual activity, like all of their behavior, was deemed to be specific to them as members of a distinct third gender. It differed from both homosexual and heterosexual relationships that occurred between women and men. In other words, Two-Spirits and sexuality are complex issues not appropriately subsumed under the headings of a Western worldview. For most Native Americans, sexual activity was a private matter. Both heterosexual and homosexual relationships were viewed as normal and might be engaged in without public scrutiny and comment, whether favorable or unfavorable.

Discussion of Native American Two-Spirits leads to the need to explain the existence of a third gender in their cultures (and, by contrast, may help explain its absence in most societies elsewhere). Third-gender status cannot be divorced from the context of gender itself and of relationships between women and men. In most (but not all) Native American cultures, equality between women and men was typical, particularly before contact with Europeans had transformed indigenous economic, political, and social systems. Although aboriginal economies were based on a gender division of labor, most duties could be performed by anyone given the convenience or necessity of doing so. Few if any ritual or social taboos prohibited people from engaging in a given task. Gender equality is a prerequisite for the respect and high status most often conferred on Two-Spirits: It meant that people, whether males or females, neither gave up nor acquired social prestige by abandoning roles usually associated with their sex and instead assuming others. This critical point was missed by Euro-American observers who could not understand why males chose not to identify as men, interpreting their choice as a decline in status. In contrast to Euro-American values, Native American males did not relinquish dominance by abandoning men's roles because such roles did not include rights to dominate. In fact, they often exchanged men's work for other occupations, both economic and ritual, that gave them social prestige as well as material benefits. Again in contrast to Euro-American values, female Two-Spirits were not violating social or religious proscriptions because none existed. Their high social status did not accrue from the fact that they did men's work but rather because they were Two-Spirits—that is, people of a respected third gender.

Both the availability of the Two-Spirit role and the prestige associated with it are evidence of the flexibility of Native American gender systems that, unlike the Euro-American model, were not threatened by individuals choosing to reject gender roles usually associated with their sex. In addition, and of great significance, the existence of Two-Spirits was not only permitted but also was given mythological sanction in many cultures. For example, Navajo myths tell of the important contributions of Two-Spirits to human culture. When the first people, First Man and First Woman, arrived in the third of five primordial worlds, they encountered a pair of twins, known as White Shell Girl and Turquoise Boy. The twins were the first Two-Spirits, called *nadle* in Navajo. They helped First Man and First Woman learn to farm and also taught skills of pottery making and basketry. These stories symbolically convey the idea that the knowledge and skills of Two-Spirits have helped humans and have contributed greatly to their cultural development. In keeping with the gender equality pervasive in Navajo culture, female and male Two-Spirits are called by the same term (*nadle*) and have perhaps the greatest amount of flexibility in their occupational, ritual, and social options. They can perform men's or women's roles whenever they wish (always dressing in the clothing styles associated with the role) and may have sexual relations with and marry either men or women.

By the late nineteenth and early twentieth centuries, the number of Two-Spirits in native societies had declined because of voluntary or forced adoption of Euro-American attitudes and practices that, among other things, insisted on only a two-category system of gender, denigrated males who dressed like or assumed women's roles, and sternly proclaimed homosexuality to be a violation of natural and divine laws. Although the reported decrease in numbers is probably accurate, Native Americans may also have become reluctant to talk to observers about behavior that they knew would be greeted with hostility and contempt. Agents of the U.S. and Canadian governments who supervised native reservations tried, with varying success, to force male Two-Spirits to wear men's clothing and cut their hair short after American fashion.

Combined pressure by secular and religious personnel took its toll on the Two-Spirit tradition as well as on the individuals who assumed a third gender status. In the words of a Lakota religious leader speaking of events that occurred in the 1920s:

> When the people began to be influenced by the missions and the boarding schools, a lot of them forgot the traditional ways and the traditional medicine. Then they began to look down on the *winkte* [Two-Spirits] and lose respect. Some [changed their ways] and put on men's clothing. But others, rather than change, went out and hanged themselves. (quoted in Williams, 1986, p. 182)

Female Two-Spirits were also pressured into abandoning their social and sacred roles. The circumstances preceding the death of the last reported Mohave Two-Spirit, Sahaykwisa, in the late nineteenth century, illustrate the changing attitudes of Mohaves, previously one of the most permissive cultures. Men ridiculed the Two-Spirit and his/her wife, claiming that she/he was an inadequate sexual partner because she/he was not anatomically male and tried to lure his/her wife away. When a second woman left her husband to live with Sahaykwisa, the husband raped the Two-Spirit, literally and symbolically exerting male dominance over a biological female. Sahaykwisa soon gave up her Two-Spirit role but was nevertheless murdered as a witch a few years later (Blackwood, 1984).

Still, despite decades of concerted social and ideological pressures, Two-Spirits continue to exist in some Native American societies, particularly among peoples in the Southwest and Plains who have resisted Euro-American assaults on their beliefs and traditional practices.

THE BODY AND ITS ROLE IN REPRODUCTION

The most obvious physical and social feature differentiating the genders is their role in reproduction. Because reproduction is an issue of personal and societal concern, beliefs and practices related to it are especially powerful in reflecting and reinforcing gender constructs.

Puberty

People's bodies are prepared for potential reproduction through physiological changes highlighted by puberty. These changes are more dramatically evidenced in girls than in boys. The onset of menarche is a sudden and obvious somatic change. In many cultures, it signals not only biological readiness to procreate but also social availability for marriage and assumption of adult status.

Attention to girls' puberty is often reflective of underlying themes regarding women and their roles in society. A wide continuum of reactions to menarche exists worldwide, from expressions of delight and pride to those of fear and shame. In some cultures, of course, contradictory attitudes may also obtain.

The Western Apache, a Native American people residing in present-day Arizona, emphasize themes of fertility and power associated with girls' puberty. The ritual occasioned by a girl's first menstruation not only affects the girl herself but is thought to benefit the entire community. According to Keith Basso (1970), "of all Western Apache ceremonials, that which is performed on the most elaborate scale and which affects directly the greatest number of people is the girls' puberty rite. . . . [It] differs from other ceremonials in . . . the amount and richness of its symbolism" (p. 53).

The name of the ritual, *nai'es*, or "preparing her," "getting her ready," signifies one of its focal themes. It readies the pubescent girl for adulthood and motherhood. Preparations for the ceremony commence immediately upon the girl's first menstruation, although the rite is not performed until summertime regardless of when menarche occurs. The girl's parents begin by selecting a ritualist to supervise the ceremony and a woman to serve as sponsor for their daughter. The only restriction on the choice of a sponsor is that she not belong to the girl's matri- or patrilineal clan. Once the woman agrees to be a sponsor, a lasting social bond is established between hers and the young girl and girl's parents. Reciprocal obligations to aid one another thus unite nonkin participants in a type of relationship usually reserved for relatives.

The ceremony itself is a public event presented by the girl's family but attended by everyone in the community. It begins shortly after sunrise, a time considered spiritually powerful. The rite consists of eight separately named phases, each highlighting a different theme or activity believed to endow the girl with spiritual and material benefits. In the first phase, the girl dances in a public dance ground to attract supernatural powers given by a deity known as Changing Woman, one of the most important Apache deities. Changing Woman is a symbol of fertility and benevolence because, according to origin myths, she had sexual intercourse with Sun and conceived a baby, known as Slayer of Monsters, who later rid the earth of evil. Apaches believe the girl is transformed during puberty rites into Changing Woman and acquires her qualities and powers.

In the second ritual phase, the pubescent girl kneels on the ground and acts out Changing Woman's impregnation by Sun. This phase stresses the theme of fertility and prepares the girl for motherhood. The powers given by Changing Woman make the young girl's body soft and pliable so that during the third ceremonial phase, the girl's sponsor massages her body to mold her into a strong and energetic woman.

The next two phases ensure that the young girl will live a long, healthy life. Through various actions, four different stages of life are represented: infancy, childhood, adulthood, and old age.

In the sixth phase, the practitioner who supervises the puberty rite pours a basket of corn kernels and sweets over the girl's head and body. This act symbolizes endowing the girl with material bounty, including good crops and wealth.

The penultimate phase is one of "blessing her." The young girl and her sponsor dance in place and are blessed individually by each person present at the ceremony. This interaction is beneficial not only for the girl but also for those who come to address her. Anyone who so desires may request aid from the powers of Changing Woman that now reside in the pubescent girl. Basso (1970) recorded several specific requests made at one rite, including the following:

> . . . to have a good crop of corn and beans.
> . . . to make my sick wife get better.
> . . . my cattle, to get fat for sale time.
> . . . to cure my daughter.
> . . . rain.
> . . . my son in Dallas learning to be a barber, not get into any trouble. (p. 68)

Finally, the ritual ends when the young girl shakes out the buckskin blanket on which she has been dancing and then throws it toward the east. She subsequently throws a blanket toward each of the other three cardinal directions. These acts symbolize the cycle of long life, health, and material bounty encapsulated in previous ritual phases. After the puberty ceremony is completed, spiritual powers of Changing Woman remain in the girl's body for four additional days, during which time she can cure illness or bring rain.

Reviewing the events and themes ritually enacted by Apache girls, it is clear that the occasion of puberty has significant meaning for the girls, their families, and the entire community. A pubescent girl receives spiritual strength, linking herself to one of the most powerful and beloved Apache deities. This strength ensures her a long, healthy, and prosperous life. Second, she and her family enlarge their social networks through establishment of life-long ties with her ritual sponsor. Third, all people present at the ceremony may ask to be blessed, with the young girl's spiritual aid. Finally, her powers, which continue for four additional days, may benefit the entire community by bringing the fertile potential of rainfall.

An Apache girl's coming of age, then, is an occasion embued with much positive value. Her health and longevity are celebrated, as are her gifts to society of motherhood and productive work.

In contrast to public rejoicing in a young girl's maturity, some cultures place restrictions on pubescent girls' activities. For instance, among the Tiwi of Melville Island in northern Australia, a girl is isolated during her first menstruation and is compelled to adhere to many taboos. Were she to break these taboos, various forms of harm would befall her and/or her husband. (Among the Tiwi, girls are married before they reach puberty.)

Tiwi girls undergo two distinct ritualized events following menarche. The first involves physical isolation from their communities and restrictions on their behavior. The second is a familial ceremony subsequent to the end of their first menstruation.

Immediately upon noticing menstrual blood, the young girl runs from camp into the bush. The words of one Tiwi girl describe a typical sequence of events:

> One day I think I'm woman. I little bit shamed. I go bush all alone. I sit down. Jenny follow me up. Look about. Find me. She say, "You *murinaleta?*" [pubescent girl]. I no say. Five times she say it. By and by I say "Yes." She cry, cry. Make me cry. She get *pandanus* and kill me on arms and back. She make tight rings on my arms, ala same *pukamani* [mourning]. Can't touch food or drink. Might be by and by swell up. (Goodale, 1971, p. 47)

The pubescent girl is followed into the bush by her mother, co-wives (if any), and several other female relatives. These women erect a shelter for the group where all will reside for the next five to ten days. Men avoid the area near a menstrual hut because contact with menstruation is considered harmful to their health.

While the girl remains in the bush camp, she must follow many ritual taboos. Taken as a whole, the taboos transmit messages of danger. Specifically, they include the following:

> She cannot dig yams, gather or cook any foods, or touch any foods directly with her hands. In order to eat, she must use a stick or have someone else place food in her mouth. If she were to ignore these taboos, her body would swell up.
> She cannot touch water to drink. Someone else must give her water from a container. If she touches water, she will get sick.
> She cannot scratch herself with her fingers but must instead use a stick. If she scratches herself, her arm will break.
> She cannot make a fire or she will get burned.
> She cannot break any sticks or her legs will break.
> She cannot look at any bodies of water such as rivers, lakes, etc. If she were to do so, spirits living in these areas would kill her.
> She cannot leave camp alone or talk in a normal voice but instead must whisper. If her husband were to see her or hear her voice, he would get sick or die. (Goodale, 1971, pp. 48–49)

When a young woman's first menstrual period ends, she is led from the bush camp by her female relatives to another camp for completion of puberty rituals. Her father and her husband and his brothers await there to participate in the ceremony. Puberty rituals involve a series of activities stressing relationships between the woman and her husband and brothers-in-law, each of whom is a potential mate in the event of a woman's husband's death. In addition, an important bond is created during puberty ceremonies between the woman and a man chosen by her father to be her son-in-law. This man will later be married to daughters the woman bears.

Most of the ritual actions performed contain sexual symbolism. For example, the pubescent girl's father places a spear between her legs and then presents it to her son-in-law, who calls the spear "wife" and "hugs it just like a wife." Later, the girl's husband and his brothers, who are potential husbands, line up and each strikes her with a feather ball. Afterward, she sits in front of a tree while her husband and brothers-in-law throw spears at the tree. Finally, the men dance around the seated girl, symbolically asserting their rights to her as a potential mate.

Significant in Tiwi girls' puberty ceremonies is the control exerted by men over women. As mentioned, except for the girl herself, all ritual actors are men— namely, the girl's father, husband, brothers-in-law, and son-in-law. All of these people are present because of alliances previously negotiated by men. That is, because men choose husbands for their granddaughters, a girl's father had been selected as a mate for her mother by the mother's own grandfather, the girl's husband had been chosen by her mother's father, and the girl's son-in-law is named by her own father. In other words, men form social bonds with other men through the use of their daughters and granddaughters as tokens. Puberty ceremonies function, in part, to consolidate these bonds and ritually validate them.

Although various taboos affect Tiwi girls during their first menstruation, restrictions are not maintained in later monthly periods. However, a menstruating woman should not have sexual intercourse, nor should she sleep near her husband. Instead, she sleeps on the opposite side of the fire in their hut. If she were to sleep with her husband, his eyes would weaken.

Whereas Tiwi practice limits taboos to the first menstrual period, some cultures insist on restrictions on all menstruating women. In India, for example, women are isolated during their periods and must refrain from participating in their usual domestic or public activities. They cannot touch food intended for others or objects used by others.

In contrast to obvious physiological manifestations occurring in girls at puberty, boys' maturity is not usually associated with a dramatic biological change. Nonetheless, boys' coming of age is socially significant and often marked in a culturally appropriate manner. In some societies, boys' adulthood is celebrated through collective rituals; in others, each boy has an individual experience.

Among the Kpelle, a chiefdom in Liberia, boys are initiated by groups into a men's secret society called *Poro*. Initiations occur sporadically, perhaps once every ten or fifteen years. They involve boys' separation from their communities to an isolated bush area for a period of four years. During this time, boys are instructed in knowledge and skills needed to function productively in Kpelle society. They are taught farming techniques, methods of house building, and craft specialties. They also learn various dances, songs, and traditional histories. Finally, they learn how to behave appropriately and how to act with elders and chiefs (Gibbs, 1965). Social messages are reinforced by beatings and physical and verbal harassment.

A number of physical changes are imposed on boys during their initiation period. These include circumcision and scarification. Scars formed from cuts made on a boy's back and chest are permanent, publicly viewed signals of adult status. Such scars are said to be teeth marks of a "Great Masked Figure" who embodies a mythic spirit believed to eat the boy at the beginning of the initiation process. According to Kpelle beliefs, a boy dies when he enters the initiation camp and is reborn when the Great Masked Figure disgorges him. He then receives a new name signifying his new status. A boy's childhood name is never used thereafter.

Kpelle initiation rites unite boys through the collective experience of enduring a difficult period of separation from their communities. Psychological and physical means of fostering solidarity are employed. First, because young, uninitiated boys hear stories of initiates being eaten by the Great Masked Figure, they must approach their seclusion and training with at least some alarm. Then, during the four years of instruction, they are treated harshly and given constant reminders of their junior status relative to elders and other authorities. Perhaps because of the hardships encountered, boys who endure these conditions collectively form strong emotional and social bonds with one another.

In other cultures, boys undergo individual rather than collective experiences following their sexual maturity. For example, among many native peoples of the North American Plains and northern woodlands, a boy is expected to pursue a personal quest for visions and spiritual powers. Although girls in some of these societies may also engage in the same practice as boys, greater social pressure is exerted on boys to seek visions.

After a boy decides to go on a vision quest, he retreats by himself to an isolated area where he typically remains for four days. During this time, he refrains from eating or sleeping and drinks as little water as possible. These acts of self-denial are preceded by short periods of fasting throughout childhood to train children to endure privation. Visions are sought by concentrating one's mind on spiritual matters and by praying to the spiritual world.

Among Native Americans who engage in these practices, visions are personal, individualized encounters. They come in many visual and auditory forms and impart specific symbolic messages to seekers. Although a visionary episode is a profoundly religious experience, it also signals a boy's (or girl's) ability to endure isolation and deprivation. Personal traits required of mature men and women who sometimes must live through physical and psychic hardships are thus developed and, in a sense, celebrated.

Reproduction

The passage of puberty readies women and men for the next stage of biological and social potential: parenthood. Cultures differ in their beliefs about the physiological contributions made by mothers and fathers in achieving conception and in developing a fetus. These beliefs often transmit covert messages about women's and men's character, abilities, or worthiness. They may therefore cohere with other ideological constructs related to gender.

In many cultures, people believe that substances or essences contributed by each parent affect different parts of the growing fetus. For example, as recorded in Jewish Talmudic writings:

> Three co-operators are concerned with the making of [people]: God, the father and the mother. The father furnishes the white sperm, from which come the bones and tendons, the nails, the brain and the whites of the eyes; the mother furnishes the red sperm, from which come the skin and flesh and blood and hair and the black of the eyes; God gives the life and soul, the shine of the face, the sight of the eyes, the hearing of the ears, the speech of the mouth, the lifting of the hands, the going of the feet, the understanding and insight. (Ashburn, 1947; quoted in Wood, 1979, p. 128)

According to this theory, parents make interdependent contributions to a child's structure, and sensory, motor, and intellectual functioning is stimulated by a supernatural being. Similar types of beliefs that distinguish among human structures and/or processes are quite common.

In some cultures, male dominance is expressed through metaphoric allusions to differentiated parental roles in procreation. For instance, the Western metaphor describing conception as resulting from implantation of a father's "seed" into a mother's womb conveys an image of male activity and female passive receptivity.

According to rural Malaysians, a fetus begins to grow as a liquid in its father's brain before being implanted in the mother's uterus. While the fetal substance remains in its father for forty days, it acquires rationality and emotions derived from men. The fetus eventually passes through its father's body and is ejected into its mother during intercourse. As it grows, it acquires emotions derived from women (Laderman, 1983). Malaysians' theories directly reflect their beliefs about differences in male and female temperament and intellect.

Throughout the world, countless beliefs are profferred that restrict mothers' (and, in some cases, fathers') activities during pregnancy. All of these taboos proscribe certain actions that, if performed, would bring harm to the baby and/or mother. The widespread, if not universal, occurrence of some beliefs of this sort raises questions concerning their function. Because pregnancy and birthing are risky to mothers and an infant's health and survival cannot be assured, the existence of numerous taboos may provide explanations for tragic outcomes. That is, if a baby is unhealthy or deformed, or if it is stillborn or dies young, blame can be placed on its mother or father for violation of any of a myriad of taboos. The burden typically weighs more heavily on women because restrictions, and therefore sources of potential fault, affect mothers more than fathers.

As an example, the following taboos should ideally be followed by Malaysian women during pregnancy (Laderman, 1983):

> She should not tie cloths around her throat or arm lest the umbilical cord get looped around the baby's throat.
> She should not bathe in the evening or her baby will be born with excessive amounts of amniotic fluid.
> She should refrain from ridiculing other people lest the baby develop the same qualities as those she mocks.

> She should not sleep during the day or evil spirits will attack her.
> She should avoid being startled lest her baby be irritable and frenetic. (pp. 91–93)

A Malaysian father-to-be must also comply with numerous restrictions:

> He should not shoot an animal in the eye or the baby will be born blind.
> He should not pull on the legs of an animal or the baby will have one leg shorter than the other.
> He should not sit on house steps blocking the entrance or his wife's birth canal will be blocked during delivery. (pp. 91–93)

Although, as Carol Laderman (1983) points out, Malaysians often ignore one or more pregnancy taboos, the fact that they do so can conveniently be used to explain unfortunate outcomes. But although taboos may have a positive function as explanatory devices, they also increase a parent's sense of responsibility for his or her child's well-being. Because warnings are more often addressed to mothers than to fathers, psychological burdens associated with pregnancy and birth are disproportionately experienced by women.

Another burden typically placed more on women than men is blame for a couple's inability to reproduce. Cultural reactions to a woman's real or imputed barrenness vary from sympathy or pity to ridicule and contempt. Patriarchal societies, such as India and China, that define women's value exclusively in terms of their ability to provide husbands with male heirs are particularly harsh in their attitudes and treatment of barren women. A woman's inability to conceive is considered legitimate grounds for divorce. Given that such a woman is publicly identified as barren, no other man will marry her. Social censure against barren women may be demonstrated in many contexts. For example, among rural villagers in northern India:

> A "barren" woman is a disgrace to the family; she is a bad omen, and she is treated accordingly. To some, she is even a "witch" who can cast evil spells, especially upon children. She can never attend the birth of a child or its celebration, and she is barred from participation in many other happy occasions. (Mamdani, 1972, p. 140)

Finally, given that unmarried women in patriarchal societies can expect no social or emotional support from relatives, suicide is a frequent recourse taken by sterile women. In polygynous societies, or where a man remarries, and none of the husband's wives bear children, barrenness is still blamed on the women or on "bad luck." That is, it may be thought that some evildoer is causing the women's barrenness in order to harm the husband and make him suffer. This interpretation could be supported also in cases where a divorced women remarries and bears children with her new husband.

In some societies, the misfortune of sterility is compounded by conceptualizing it as a punishment for a woman's prior misdeeds or evil thoughts.

Barrenness may be explained as supernatural retribution for adultery, violation of taboos, or disrespect for spiritual beings.

Birthing

Culturally prescribed practices related to birthing techniques differ widely. Among many peoples, the birthing event is attended exclusively by women. In some cases, a male ritualist may be called to intervene in a difficult delivery, particularly where such problems are attributed to supernatural forces and where men function as religious practitioners.

Review of changes in birthing practices in the United States reveals underlying ideological constructs regarding women's autonomy. From colonial days until well into the nineteenth century, most births were attended by midwives. Although medical doctors in Europe and America had campaigned vigorously since the Middle Ages against supposedly untrained health practitioners, their efforts to eliminate midwifery were largely unsuccessful until the nineteenth century (Ehrenreich and English, 1978). A brief look at their attempts to persecute midwives demonstrates some strategies of patriarchal control.

During the fifteenth and sixteenth centuries, physicians united with authorities of the Catholic Church in attacks on lay healers, accusing them of being witches. A great majority of these healers were women, knowledgeable in herbal treatments and skilled in massage and other noninvasive healing techniques. Included in their repertory was midwifery. Indeed, according to organizers of witch-hunts, "[t]he greatest injuries to the Faith as regards the heresy of witches are done by midwives; and this is made clearer than daylight itself by the confessions of some who were afterwards burned" (Kramer and Sprenger, 1487, p. 218).

Women who dared to assert their healing knowledge, expertise, and independence were accused as witches. Estimates have been made that as many as several million witches were killed in Europe from the fifteenth through eighteenth centuries; 85 percent of the victims were women (Ehrenreich and English, 1978).

Despite attacks against them, midwives still flourished in both Europe and the United States. Physicians tended to look down on midwifery, considering the birthing process unworthy of their skills. However, as physicians in the nineteenth century began to organize their profession and attempted to eliminate competition from unaffiliated practitioners, they eventually turned their attention to midwives. By the late nineteenth century, middle- and upper-class American mothers generally were attended in births by medical doctors, although working-class and poor women sought the services of midwives. According to Barbara Ehrenreich and Deirdre English (1978), doctors became interested in expanding their domain in birthing because they sought patients for scientific study. As medical technology became more complex and as observation and experimentation with live patients became "scientifically" desirable, doctors wanted to enlist poor women as patients in teaching hospitals. A physician, Charles Zeigler, writing in the *Journal of the American*

Medical Association, advised, "It is at present impossible to secure cases suffi-cient for the proper training in obstetrics, since 75 percent of the material otherwise available for clinical purposes is utilized in providing a livelihood for midwives" (quoted in Ehrenreich and English, 1978, p. 95).

Medical doctors characterized midwives as ignorant, incompetent, and dirty:

> They may wash their hands, but oh, what myriads of dirt lurk under the finger-nails. We might well add to other causes of pyosalpinx [infection] "dirty midwives." She is the most virulent bacteria of them all, and she is truly a micro-coccus of the most poisonous kind. (Ehrenreich and English, pp. 95–96)

During the nineteenth century, arguments for excluding women practi-tioners were advanced that derived from prevailing ideological constructs regarding cognitive and emotional differences between the genders. Thus, an obstetrician, writing in 1820, advised against using the services of midwives:

> They [women] have not that power of action, or that active power of mind, which is essential to the practice of a surgeon. They have less power of restrain-ing and governing the natural tendencies to sympathy and are more disposed to yield to the expression of acute sensibility. . . . [W]here they become the princi-pal agents, the feelings of sympathy are too powerful for the cool exercise of judgment. (quoted in Wertz and Wertz, 1990, p. 153)

As a result of campaigns spearheaded by physicians in the early twentieth century, many states enacted laws prohibiting midwives from practicing. But rather than improving survival rates for mothers and newborns, the elimina-tion of midwives was correlated with increases in maternal and infant mortality. For instance, comparison of figures for maternal deaths between 1914 and 1916 in Newark, New Jersey, where midwives practiced legally, and Boston, Massachusetts, where they were banned, indicates a clear advantage favoring midwifery. In Newark, the maternal mortality rate was 1.6 per thousand, whereas in Boston it stood at 6.5. Similarly, the infant mortality rate in Newark was 8.5; in Boston it was 37.4 (Kobrin, 1966).

According to Richard Wertz and Dorothy Wertz (1990):

> The exclusion of women from midwifery and obstetrics had profound effects upon practice. Most obviously, it gave obstetrics a sexist bias; maleness became a necessary attribute of safety, and femaleness became a condition in need of male medical con-trol. Within this skewed view of ability and need, doctors found it nearly impossible to gain an objective view of what nature could do and what art should do, for one was identified with being a woman and the other with being a man. (pp. 158–159)

Furthermore, Wertz and Wertz state, "Obstetrics acquired a basic distortion in its orientation toward nature, a confusion of the need to be masterful and even male with the need for intervention" (p. 159).

Derived from such a confusion, many current medical procedures in birthing are of questionable health benefit. First and foremost is the routine position of childbirth, compelling the mother to lie on her back. This position contrasts with normal practice in most cultures throughout the world. Women in other societies usually give birth while kneeling, sitting, or squatting. These positions facilitate births by allowing the forces of gravity to work. According to research reported by Doris Haire (1978), the dorsal position used in the United States directly interferes with normal childbearing by "adversely affecting the mother's blood pressure, cardiac return, and pulmonary ventilation; decreasing the normal intensity of contractions; inhibiting the mother's voluntary efforts to push her baby out spontaneously; and inhibiting spontaneous expulsion of the placenta" (p. 192). Then, to counteract physiological problems created by having the mother lie on her back, medical and technological intervention is required. Drugs are often used to stimulate labor and relieve pain.

The combination of dorsal position and drug therapy renders mothers passive and unable to control their bodily processes. Obstetricians (93 percent of whom are men) rather than mothers become the primary actors in the birthing event. Women are thus deprived of autonomy and personal choices. Comparing American and Malaysian birthing, the latter characterized by mothers' freedom to assume any comfortable position, to eat or drink as they choose, and to be attended by midwives who employ massage and ritual incantations, Laderman (1983) comments:

> Whether one takes the view that traditional Malay childbirth practices expose the mother and child to unnecessary risks, or sees them as procedures that allow a woman to take command during the most important hours of her life, the essential difference between childbirth in America and childbirth in Merchang [Malaysia] is clear: American women are delivered by obstetricians; Malay women give birth. (p. 173)

As part of recent actions by women to reclaim autonomy and control over their bodies, midwifery is making a small comeback. Although it is still employed by only a minority of American mothers, the number of trained midwives is increasing. Some midwives are registered nurses who are specially trained in midwifery. These practitioners, called *nurse-midwives*, differ from lay midwives who are not nurses but who are trained and licensed. The former may attend births either in hospitals or at mothers' homes, whereas the latter attend only home births. Midwifery practice continues to be differentiated from obstetrical procedures. Midwives' approach to birthing is basically noninterventionist, often allowing mothers to give birth in whatever position is comfortable for them and allowing natural processes to set timetables and treatments (Rothman, 1990). Midwives working in hospitals have to adhere to institutional regulations and therefore not promote alternative birthing positions.

Women's So-Called Reproductive Illnesses

Since at least the middle of the nineteenth century, medical science and both medical and lay discourse have described natural processes in women's bodies such as menstruation and menopause as illnesses. Such practice is a self-serving strategy on the part of physicians, who can increase their control over patients (particularly women) by defining normal events as disease states requiring medical care. However, of greater significance, if menstruation and menopause are illnesses, women become inherently and inescapably sick. These words convey numerous negative concepts. Rather than recognizing the naturalness, healthiness, and balance of physiological processes that women experience, the words connote their very opposites. As in other types of discourse about gender, the male model is taken as normal, whereas the female experience is viewed as aberrant and in need of supervision and correction.

In the late nineteenth and early twentieth-centuries, physicians (predominantly male) wrote at length about the deleterious effects of women's "sexual condition": "It is impossible to form a correct opinion of the mental and physical suffering frequently endured from her sexual condition, caused by her monthly periods, which it has pleased her Heavenly Father to attach to woman" (John Gunn, M. D., *Gunn's New Family Physician*, 1924, p. 120; quoted in Ehrenreich and English, 1978, pp. 110–111). Another physician, writing in 1871, described menstruation as "periods of ill health" during which time he advised women to rest and recover. Because women were said to be prone to both psychological and physical distress every month, it was deemed sensible, even ethical, to bar them from occupations in which control and concentration were needed, for example, from science and medicine. As one doctor wrote:

> One shudders to think of the conclusions arrived at by female bacteriologists or histologists at the period when their entire system, both physical and mental, is "unstrung," to say nothing of the terrible mistakes which a lady surgeon might make under similar conditions. (quoted in Ehrenreich and English, 1978, p. 112)

The misogynist implications of these opinions are obvious, and the class bias is also barely hidden. That is, women of the middle and upper classes were advised (and could afford) to pamper their bodies during their menstrual periods, but poor women had no such luxuries, working long hours in factories, fields, and homes. But, luckily, as Dr. Lucien Warner wrote in 1874: "The African Negress, who toils in the fields of the south, and Bridget, who washes, and scrubs and toils in our homes at the north, enjoy for the most part good health, with comparative immunity from uterine disease" (*A Popular Treatise on the Functions and Diseases of Woman*; quoted in Ehrenreich and English, 1978, p. 114).

In the late nineteenth century, physicians discovered another so-called truth about women—namely, that women's entire physical and mental well-being was determined by the condition of their reproductive organs, although doctors disagreed as to whether the uterus or the ovaries were paramount. But, in any case, women's health depended on the health of these vital organs. When a woman suffered from any psychological or physical malady, the ultimate problem was thought to lie in her reproductive system. Physicians then developed numerous techniques to correct the diseased or malfunctioning organ, such as applying leeches or heated iron instruments to the neck of the cervix, as well as performing more extreme surgeries such as clitoridectomy and ovariotomy. Clitoridectomy (removal of the clitoris) was deemed appropriate to "cure" masturbation and strong sexual desire. Although the operation was performed only in "extreme" cases, Ehrenreich and English (1978) report that as late as 1948, a 5-year-old girl in the United States was subjected to the procedure to cure her masturbation. Ovariotomy (removal of the ovaries) was, in contrast, performed frequently in the late nineteenth and early twentieth centuries as a cure for a wide range of psychological distresses, including depression, anxiety, fearfulness, feelings of persecution, and all sorts of "unruly behavior." After the operation, according to a doctor writing in 1893, "Patients are improved, some of them cured; . . . the moral sense of the patient is elevated, she becomes tractable, orderly, industrious, and cleanly" (quoted in Ehrenreich and English, 1978, p. 124). Perhaps the words of Dr. Mary Putnam Jacobi, writing in 1895, help explain the origin of many of women's ailments: "I think it is in the increased attention paid to women, and especially in their new function as lucrative patients, that we find explanation for much of the ill-health among women, freshly discovered today" (quoted in Ehrenreich and English, 1978, p. 115). As we shall see, Jacobi's words have meaning for the late twentieth century as well.

Although medical opinions and interventions of decades ago are obviously ludicrous (as well as mean-spirited, perhaps spiteful) and the suffering of their victims indeed appalling, modern medicine has refined the attack on women's normalcy and has found new explanations for women's supposed emotionality, again justifying negative attitudes about women's competence and ability to function in demanding, high-status occupations. Today, rather than implicate female reproductive organs, the culprit is deemed to be female hormones and their cyclic changes. In the 1980s, medical science, with the media in close attendance, gave birth to a new female ailment called premenstrual syndrome (PMS). PMS is supposedly a "psychoneuroendocrine disorder" affecting up to 90 percent of women, although only 10 percent are said to suffer severe symptoms. Some 5 percent are said to be so affected that their behavior is characterized as a psychiatric disorder (Davis, 1996). According to Dona Davis (1996), some 150 symptoms are said to derive from PMS, mostly concentrated around mood swings and feelings of being out of control. Citing medical opinions, Davis reports that PMS is blamed as a factor in "marital discord, social isolation, work inefficiency or absenteeism, accidents, and criminal activities including child battering, theft, and murder" (p. 58). Clearly, medicine and the media have found another way to brand women as overly emotional, unstable, and unpredictable. Both medical and popular discourse have found another reason to justify exclusion of women from high-status occupations that require clear thinking, decisive action, and control.

Despite studies that claim to demonstrate the pervasiveness of PMS, Davis (1996) summarizes numerous criticisms of their scientific validity and testing procedures and, indeed, the definition of PMS itself. There is disagreement in the scientific community about the time frame of PMS and its associated symptoms. In addition to poor research design, fuzzy definitions of PMS, and the confusion of this so-called disorder with somatic problems such as backache, headache, and abdominal cramping, as well as misinterpretation of patients' self-reports, a basic conceptual dilemma arises: If PMS is a hormonal disorder, it should be found in similar proportions among women in all societies. Only a few cross-cultural studies have been carried out, and none report the conclusion of universality so necessary to the basic premise of the existence of PMS. The largest study, conducted by the World Health Organization in the 1980s, found that whereas symptoms of physical discomfort (backache and abdominal pain) were roughly comparable in the fourteen nations tested, no such similarities were attested for the supposedly diagnostic mood swings and other psychological symptoms.

In one of the few anthropological studies to research the prevalence of PMS and associated attitudes, Maureen Fitzgerald (1990) questioned members of three communities of Samoans regarding their knowledge and experience of menstruation. The three groups, differing in their degree of adherence to traditional Samoan culture, included people living in traditional settings in rural western Samoa, people living in rapidly modernizing towns in American Samoa, and Samoan immigrants in Honolulu. Traditional Samoan women did not think of menstruation as an illness but rather as a natural biological process. Whatever discomfort they felt during their periods was considered normal and endurable. Of the three Samoan groups, traditional women, who had never heard of the illness entity called PMS, reported the fewest symptoms, and, in fact, when asked about their own premenstrual discomforts, they reported experiencing only somatic problems. Samoans living in Honolulu had full knowledge of PMS as a medical condition and reported having a wider range of symptoms, both emotional and physical. Fitzgerald concludes that the exposure to medical models that include the illness category of PMS has influenced women's perceptions of their own internal changes, making them more attentive to affective states and giving them "a new symptom or illness vocabulary" (p. 146).

Like research and conclusions concerning PMS, scientific study of symptoms associated with menopause suffers from numerous difficulties. Although the hormonal changes that result from the cessation of ovulation at menopause (that is, decreases in estrogen and increases in gonadotrophins) are relatively specific, the symptomatology is diffuse and poorly measured (Davis, 1996). Symptoms typically attributed to hormonal changes include somatic discomforts such as hot flashes and cold sweats as well psychological problems such as irritability, nervousness, fatigue, and depression. Recent large-scale studies have demonstrated, however, that the vast majority of women do not experience the emotional symptoms attributed to menopause, and only about half of women studied experienced any of the somatic discomforts once thought to be much more common.

In addition to the lack of clear-cut physical or psychological changes, the very concept of a socially marked stage of menopause is problematic when viewed from a cross-cultural perspective. In many societies, women's lives during their reproductive years are filled with multiple pregnancies and prolonged periods of lactation when they do not menstruate or do so only sporadically. According to Margaret Lock (1991), interviews with middle-aged Samburu women of northern Kenya revealed that they remembered having only about a dozen menstrual cycles in their lives. Lock suggests that because the biological cessation of menstruation rarely coincides with symptoms, most women in the world are only aware of "menopause in retrospect, after it is evident that they have not become pregnant for some considerable time" (p. 707).

Despite the proven absence of distressing symptoms for the majority of women, medical science has refused to allow menopause to die as an illness category. Focus has now shifted to the negative consequences of lowered estrogen levels as contributing factors to cardiovascular disease and osteoporosis. Once diagnosed, these problems are said to require medical intervention, usually in the form of hormone replacement therapy or other medication. The fact that osteoporosis and heart disease are not universally associated with menopause is ignored, as is the fact that diet and exercise play an important role in maintaining strong bones and a healthy cardiovascular system.

Several anthropological studies have investigated the differing experiences of women at menopause in diverse cultures. Lock's (1986) work with Japanese women is particularly revealing. Japanese women rarely experience the "hot flash" supposedly diagnostic of hormonal changes at menopause. In fact, only 19.6 percent reported such somatic symptoms, a figure that contrasts dramatically with reports given by 64.6 percent of women in Manitoba, Canada. Although Lock suggests that biological differences may exist between the two populations, of equal significance are the cultural differences in women's attitudes and expectations. As Lock (1991) states, "socialization into a particular culture exerts a strong influence on the recognition and labeling of somatic sensations" (p. 709). Significant, too, is the fact that despite a lack of symptoms, Japanese women are currently adopting negative attitudes toward menopause. These attitudes are now frequently disseminated in Japanese media from medical sources that themselves have adopted Western biomedical models of disease and behavior (Lock, 1989).

Rather than concluding that menopause and PMS are discrete disorders with well-defined causes and symptoms, anthropological studies, as well as careful review of scientific research, demonstrate that they are best viewed as culturally derived illness categories. As such, they are results of cultural negotiation in which people learn to notice and name their own internal physical and emotional states. While learning the names and attributes of illnesses, people shape their experience into the categories themselves. This process is not remarkable at all but one that is consistent with theories of meaning in anthropology and linguistics: People perceive and experience the world largely in terms of the named categories of meaning that their culture and language provide. However, the particular conditions examined here are not neutral in their connotations. PMS and so-called menopausal disorders are embedded in the context of gender and reveal attitudes toward women that are negative and trivializing. Women are simultaneously encouraged to experience discomfort and blamed for the very experience. Both "disorders" are said to be inescapable results of what Dr. John Gunn called women's "sexual condition" more than eighty years ago. And both conditions are said to have psychological symptoms that render women unlikely, perhaps unfit, to succeed in prestige occupations.

FEMALE GENITAL MUTILATION

Control of female sexuality is starkly manifested in the controversial practice of female genital mutilation (FGM) or female circumcision prevalent in twenty-eight countries in Africa and found in other regions as well. The practice consists of the removal of part or all of the genitals of prepubescent girls. The specific procedure varies but, it usually entails the removal of the clitoris. In some areas, particularly in southern Egypt, the Sudan, Somalia, Ethiopia, and Mali, it also includes the removal of all external genitalia and infibulation—the stitching closed—of the vaginal opening, leaving only a tiny opening for the passage of urine and menstrual blood. An estimated 80 million women living today have undergone some form of the procedure (Armstrong, 1991, p. 42). Although FGM is now sometimes performed in hospitals, it is usually performed by local midwives working with crude tools and without anesthesia on girls who are typically between 5 and 11 years old.

The two most common names by which the practice is known—*female genital mutilation* and *female circumcision*—reflect diverging attitudes toward it. Calling it female circumcision equates it with the widespread practice of male circumcision, which is also debated but more widely accepted. But as Sue Armstrong (1991) points out, the term *female circumcision* is ". . . misleading for it implies an operation similar to male circumcision—the removal of a piece of skin. The female operation nearly always involves the removal of healthy organs"(p. 42). The term *female genital mutilation*, on the other hand, was introduced by the UN Inter-African Committee (IAC) on Traditional Practices Affecting the Health of Women and Children, a group established to help end the practice. This term reflects "the cruel and radical operation so many young girls are forced to undergo" (p. 42).

FGM has a long history. Although its exact origin is unknown, it is believed to have arisen in North Africa, possibly in ancient Egypt or along the shores of the Red Sea many centuries B.C. (Sanderson, 1981: Sanderson and Sanderson, 1981, pp. 26–27). It is, in other words, an entrenched feature of the cultures in which it is found. It predates both Christianity and Islam and occurs among people of both faiths as well as among followers of traditional African religions. It is most common today, however, in predominantly Islamic regions of Africa. The most severe forms of FGM are found in Egypt, Sudan, Ethiopia, and Somalia. Some forms of excision occur in the Arabian Peninsula, and less severe procedures have been reported in Indonesia and Malaysia (p. 32).

It is important to note that although FGM predates the Islamic religion, it has since been incorporated into some forms of Islam and is given religious justification by local practitioners, although Islamic scholars disagree about whether the Koran mandates the practices. As Richard Winter (1989) notes:

> Although excision did not originate with Islam, it seems that the custom spread with Islamic culture. It is possible that excision was absorbed into Islamic culture where it already existed, and was then extended with Muslim advance. Some of those who imitated it, at a later date, could have considered it an Islamic practice. And then Islamic theologians may have sought and found some authority. (p. 57)

Whatever its origin and its relationship to religion, FGM is certainly associated with strongly patriarchal cultures—that is, cultures that stress the subordination of women to male authority. The practice exerts control over women's sexual pleasure and is consistent with men's fear of, and therefore wish to control, women's sexual behavior. Women who are subjected to the procedure have reduced sexual desire, both because of the loss of part of their sexual organs and because of their fear of the pain involved with intercourse. They therefore are unlikely to engage in premarital or extramarital sexual activity that evidently threaten the patriarchal social systems that male-dominated ideologies legitimate. In addition to the control exerted over women, infibulation is thought to increase a man's sexual pleasure while causing pain to his partner.

Because the practice is often shrouded in secrecy, few data have been systematically collected about the medical consequences of FGM. Risks for girls undergoing the procedure reportedly include pain, shock, loss of bladder and bowel control, and potentially fatal infections and hemorrhaging (Gruenbaum, 1993). Infibulation in particular can have serious, painful, long-term consequences. Defenders of the procedure, however, claim there is no reliable evidence that it increases a girl's risk of death or excessive rates of medical complication. Opponents claim that FGM reduces a woman's capacity for sexual pleasure and that infibulation makes first intercourse and childbirth painful.

FGM is defended by some people who practice it—women as well as men—on cultural grounds. Justifications involve beliefs about the dangers of female sexuality and the need to ensure virginity as a condition of marriage. Infibulation is said to help ensure a woman's premarital chastity and her sexual fidelity to her husband while increasing his sexual pleasure.

Some prominent African women, such as Fuambai Ahmadu, an anthropologist from Sierra Leone, defend the practice. On the basis of her research, Ahmadu (2000) views FGM as an emotionally positive validation of womanhood (pp. 304–305). In Ahmadu's interviews with circumcised African women, the women reported that the practice did not diminish their sexual drive, inhibit sexual activity, or prevent sexual satisfaction and that it did not adversely affect their health or birthing. The women supported the practice and looked forward to carrying on the tradition to initiate their younger female relatives into the pride of womanhood. Other native observers, such as Olavinka Koso-Thomas, a physician who is also from Sierra Leone, oppose the practice because of its brutality, its dangerous consequences, and its role in perpetuating the subordination of women.

A large-scale study conducted by members of the World Health Organization in 2001–2003 investigated birth outcomes of more than 28,000 women who had previously undergone FGM in six African countries. The study concluded that FGM raises the risk that a woman would die in childbirth by between 20 and 50 percent depending upon the severity of genital cutting (Rosenthal, 2006). FGM also raises the risk that the baby would die. Women who had undergone the most extensive degree of genital cutting were the most likely to die but even milder forms of FGM raised the risk of maternal and infant death. The medical researchers assume that their findings are underestimates of the actual toll because the study documented the effect on births that occurred in hospitals, noting that many African women give birth at home.

Some anthropologists, citing cultural relativism and the ideal of objectivity, refuse to support external organizations that exert pressure on African, Middle Eastern, and Indonesian governments to abolish FGM. While not condoning the procedure, they prefer to hope for change from within. Other anthropologists point out that the concept of cultural relativism may help us understand a culture on its own terms, but it can also help us understand how cultural beliefs reinforce inequalities by convincing people to accept as natural practices that may be harmful and demeaning. Consider, for example, that in American history some slaves strongly defended slavery prior to Emancipation. It may appear that women approve of genital mutilation because they say they do, and it is women as midwives who perform FGM and women as mothers who arrange it for their daughters. But if genital mutilation is a prerequisite for marriage, as it apparently is in some places, women may say they accept the practice because they believe they must.

Many anthropologists, together with health workers, women's rights advocates, and human rights organizations, oppose FGM and are actively working to end it. They have had some success. In 1995 a UN-sponsored Conference on the Status of Women declared FGM to be a violation of human rights. In 1996 the U.S. Board of Immigration Appeals granted political asylum to Fauziya Kassindja, a young woman from Togo who feared returning to her native country because she would be forced to undergo the procedure as a prelude to her arranged marriage. The Board of Appeals ruled that FGM is a form of persecution (U.S. grants asylum to woman fleeing genital mutilation rite, 1996, pp. A1, B2).

In response to campaigns against FGM by the World Health Organization (WHO) and UNICEF (the UN Children's Fund), a few African governments have outlawed FGM and others have taken steps to limit its severity and improve the conditions under which it is performed by licensing practitioners and restricting the operation to clitoridectomy (Armstrong, 1991 pp. 45–46). These initiatives, inadequately funded and only half-heartedly enforced, have so far done little to eradicate what many see as a dangerous and degrading practice. However, recent reports indicate that some women who specialize in the procedure have decided not to continue their work. For example, a grass-roots organization called Womankind Kenya has persuaded some influential practitioners to join their cause in opposing FGM. Among the arguments they use are teachings from the Koran that some imams interpret as opposing FGM (Lacey, 2004). When women with status and influence in their communities begin to oppose the practice, their opinions carry weight. Other organizations are training women practitioners of FGM in other work, such as selling or making soap, because they understand that it is difficult for poor women to give up a steady source of income.

Finally, however, the fact that it is women as midwives who perform genital mutilation procedures and women as mothers who arrange the procedures for their daughters demonstrates the power of social and religious ideology and the paralyzing self-negating effects of patriarchal discrimination. To say, as some apologists do, that these are "cultural" practices ignores the mechanisms of indoctrination that result in women's internalization of beliefs about their own worthlessness. It also ignores the pressures exerted on women to comply. According to Winter's (1989) research in northern Sudan, where an overwhelming majority of girls undergo the most extreme form of genital mutilation, major reasons given by men and women for subjecting their daughters to the procedure are men's reluctance to marry a woman who has not had FGM done and men's wish to obtain the greater sexual pleasure they claim as their right regardless of the pain caused to their wives. Evidently, women "accept this because they think sexual enjoyment is a masculine right only, and they must do everything possible to please and satisfy their husbands" (p. 156).

Hormones and Behavior

In the popular mind, men's aggressive behavior, self-assertiveness, and dominance stem from their levels of the male hormone testosterone. Similarly, women's reputed passivity comes from their lack of this hormone. These ideas are promulgated by scientific experts in the fields of biology, psychology, and sociobiological approaches in anthropology. Although it is true that men have higher levels of testosterone than women, is it also true that hormones predict and determine behavior?

Some researchers question the simplicity of the connection between biology and behavior. Although there are physiological differences between females and males, there are also similarities and overlaps. Males and females are not "binary opposites" (Fausto-Sterling, 1985, p. 121). To explain male aggression as simply derived from male hormones masks the complexity of physiological functioning. Context and situational needs trigger or constrain the secretion of hormones and their utilization by the body. In addition, people have several different types of hormonal systems that operate in interaction rather than in isolation.

Socialization is also a key factor in the expression of aggression and other personality or behavioral traits. Girls and boys may be treated differently, handled differently, and spoken to differently from the very beginning of life. Studies in child development indicate that in the United States, parents and other caregivers interact with boys and girls differently. These studies, of course, indicate general patterns within populations; they do not predict any particular interactions between parents and children. Although there is enormous variability in any society in regard to expected norms and behaviors, research indicates that parents interact more physically with boy babies than with girls (Culp et al., 1983). Boys are held, touched, and stimulated more, a pattern that helps them develop stronger muscles and motor behavior. Boys also are handled more roughly than girls. In addition, when boys fuss, parents pay more attention to them than they do to fussy girls. Through these modes of interaction, boys learn to seek attention because they get attention, and girls learn to satisfy their own needs (Ember, 1981). Fathers in particular tend to handle their sons more roughly than their daughters. And boys tend to be punished physically more than girls, especially by their fathers. This pattern may encourage aggressiveness in boys because physical punishment of boys by fathers could result in increased anger: Unable to turn their anger toward their fathers, boys might displace it in aggressive behavior toward peers.

Research on expressing aggression suggests cross-sex permissiveness on the part of parents; that is, fathers may permit more aggression from daughters, and mothers may permit more aggression from sons. Mothers' greater tolerance for aggression in their sons may increase boys' aggressive behavior. Because children spend more time with their mothers than with their fathers, a mother's influence is likely to be greater.

Studies also show that girls spend more time playing at home than do boys. Girls are therefore under more adult supervision and are more likely to take on household chores, including helping to care for younger siblings. Boys, in contrast, interact more with peers. These patterns also may affect aggression. A child is likely to defer to adults and nurture younger children, so girls are more likely to develop these personality and behavior characteristics because of their patterns of interaction at home, whereas boys develop more aggressive behavior because of their patterns of interaction both at home and with peers.

In both cases, certain human behaviors are likely to be encouraged and developed (aggression in boys, nurturance in girls) while other behaviors are inhibited (aggression in girls, and nurturance in boys). Patterns of treatment and interaction therefore help mold a child's personality to conform to cultural norms.

In a study that investigated the role of observers' expectations in their attitudes toward children's aggression, John Condry and Sharon Condry (1976) found that people reacted differently to a child's behavior depending on whether they thought the child was a boy or girl. The stimuli in the experiment consisted of videotapes of a baby reacting to a jack-in-the-box. The subjects, male and female college students, were asked to watch the video and comment on the child's behavior. The first time the toy pops out of the box, the child appears "startled." When the event is repeated, the baby becomes "quite agitated, and begins to cry even before the box opens for the third time" (Fausto-Sterling, 1985, p. 151). The subjects described the baby's behavior as "anger" if they were told that the baby was a boy but as "fear" if they thought the baby was a girl. As Fausto-Sterling comments, "the behavior, crying, took on the emotional significance of anger or fear depending only upon the observer's belief about the baby sex" (p. 151).

All of these studies together indicate great complexity in people's behavior and in their reactions to the actions and words of others. Simply focusing on physiological explanations misses the depth of the interactions of biology, psychology, and social contexts and expectations.

NUTRITION

In addition to cultural beliefs and practices regarding women's and men's physiological functioning, gender constructs are sometimes enacted through differential nutritional allocations for men and women. In some societies, cultural norms define gender-specific routines for eating and for foods to be eaten. For example, patterns permitting men to eat first, leaving women whatever remains, have been attested in diverse cultures (Rosenberg, 1980). Among such peoples, years of nutritional disparities in the amount and quality of food taken by men and women result in women suffering chronic malnutrition. According to Ellen Rosenberg (1980), women therefore "may be weaker, smaller, more lethargic, more disease prone, and shorter-lived than their husbands" (p. 198). Women's comparatively poor health status may then "contribute to and justify their inferior social status." Frederick Dunn (1968) concurs, stating that, at least among foraging peoples, women's life expectancy is generally lower than men's because of "male-female dietary disparities" (p. 224).

Where food restrictions are followed, they sometimes bar or limit women's intake of meat. This proscription seems to be particularly common among pastoral and farming peoples in Africa, including the Nuba, Karamojong, Dodos, Azande, Kikuyu, and Bemba (Rosenberg, 1980). Some researchers have argued that these cultures associate meat with men because men are typically responsible for hunting or herding animals. Denial of meat to women is thus symbolic of women's exclusion from these economic roles.

Among the Mbum Kpau, a farming and herding society in Chad, barring women from eating chicken and goats is a reflection of gender asymmetries in authority and social status rather than of gender differences in the division of labor (O'Laughlin, 1974). Both women and men herd animals and tend gardens, but a significant contrast between the genders lies in the control over resources and distribution of wealth. Men, especially senior men, dominate Mbum Kpau society through their rights to allocate land, control inheritance, and exchange bridewealth.

Although the Mbum Kpau do not consider chicken and goats important in daily nutrition, exclusive consumption of these "prestige" foods by men on ceremonial occasions is symbolic of "sexual differences and sexual ranking." Prohibition of chicken and goats to women is justified ideologically by warnings that violation of the taboo results in various reproductive failures, including pain during childbirth, maternal death, deformed or sickly children, and sterility. In a male-dominated society where a woman's worth is measured by her successful childbearing, such dangers carry added meaning.

Curiously, cultural attitudes about gender and food preferences in our own society converge somewhat with those just reviewed. American culture does not prohibit particular foods to any social category, but nonetheless a meal of meat and potatoes is a stereotypical preference of men, whereas women supposedly like to eat salads. These presumed differences cohere as well with prevailing standards of beauty that have the effect of encouraging women to eat salads and other foods low in calories to avoid gaining weight.

In many cultures throughout the world, various taboos on specific foods are commonly imposed on women during pregnancy and lactation. Again, restricted foods often include meat or other sources of protein. Cultures that practice these taboos usually phrase them as benefits to mother and child. For example, in India, Burma, and other countries in Southeast Asia, women are told to limit their food intake in order to assure a small fetus and easy birth; pregnant women in Vietnam refrain from eating meat or fish because these foods are believed to generate poisons in the fetus (Rosenberg, 1980).

In contrast, a few societies that normally restrict food to women encourage them to eat more when they are pregnant or nursing. In traditional rural China, for instance, mothers were allowed to eat an improved diet containing foods otherwise rarely eaten by women, including meat, chicken, and eggs. Vegetables, which comprised women's usual diet, were banned. The dietary reversal is evidently linked to traditional Chinese attitudes toward women. Because women have low social status, they are normally denied access to valued foods, but because women's worth derives from their reproductive roles, they are given these foods when they produce children.

Few studies have rigorously documented the nutritional impact of food taboos during pregnancy or lactation. In one such attempt, Laderman's (1983) research in rural Malaysia indicates that restrictions imposed on Malaysian women following birth do not seriously affect their health. Laderman measured protein, vitamin, and hemoglobin levels in women's blood at various stages of pregnancy and at the end of the period of postpartum food restrictions, which in Malaysia lasts forty days. Her sample consisted of fourteen women; some adhered to food taboos for the full forty days, others followed them for shorter periods, and a few ignored them entirely. Analyses revealed no significant changes in serum values over the time of study and no significant differences among the group of fourteen women tested, despite the variation in adherence to food taboos.

Although Laderman's research is suggestive, it cannot be generalized to other societies for several reasons. First, Malaysian women do not follow food restrictions during pregnancy but only in the postpartum period. Second, even if food is limited after childbirth, the duration of taboos is short (forty days). Without similar biochemical studies of other cultures, it is not possible to ascertain the effects on women's health of taboos that are imposed throughout pregnancy and throughout the period of lactation, which may last several years.

Indeed, in some societies, restrictions on the quantity and quality of food affect females at all ages and therefore presumably have a significant deleterious impact on their ability to survive. Girls and boys may be treated differently during infancy and childhood. For example, according to Ellen Rosenberg (1980), girls in Arab countries are typically nursed for one or one and a half years, whereas boys continue to be nursed for an additional year. She further cites studies of India, Bangladesh, and traditional China, where girls are routinely given less to eat than boys. As a result, mortality rates are comparatively higher for girls. Not coincidentally, all of these societies are nearly prototypical examples of patriarchal culture.

Studies of the nutritional status of women in India reveal serious deficits beginning in early childhood and continuing throughout life. Calorie requirements are not met because of preferential feeding of boys and men both in terms of quantity of food and in terms of quality of food containing protein and other essential nutrients. Socioeconomic status does not affect the differential between males and females. People of higher incomes have greater access to quality food but among all groups, the differences between the food intake of males and females remained marked. For example, a study that compared the food intake of "privileged" and "underprivileged" people revealed that in the privileged group, 24 percent of the females were malnourished while only 14 percent of males were malnourished, and in the underprivileged group, 74 percent of females were not adequately fed while 67 percent of males were malnourished (Capoor, 2000:3). These data in fact indicate that the difference between male and female food intake is greater among the privileged groups than among the underprivileged. Males, therefore, benefit more from increased resources.

Women in India are also disadvantaged through cultural taboos, prohibiting them from eating high protein and high quality foods such as milk and green leafy vegetables during menstruation, pregnancy, and lactation (ibid.:4). Foods that are restricted during pregnancy include green leafy vegetables, peanuts, bananas, butter, milk, citrus fruits, and meat. Cultural and religious beliefs persuade women that if they eat any of these foods, they will cause harm to the baby or have a difficult delivery. In addition, girls and women are encouraged to fast on several days of the week because of beliefs that if they do so, they are likely to have a good husband and give birth to sons.

Studies conducted in a fishing village called Joal in Senegal uncovered similar discrepancies in the nutritional status of women as compared to men. Women in the prime childbearing age range of 24–34 years were found to suffer the most from malnutrition (Sy, 2006). A majority, 61 percent, of women surveyed were found to be seriously anemic. Some of the consequent health risks include susceptibility to infection and higher rates of maternal and fetal death.

Finally, an international study sponsored by the UN Office of the High Commissioner for Human Rights (1995) noted the prevalence of food taboos and other restrictions on food intake for women in many countries in Africa and Asia. These taboos especially prohibit high calorie and high protein foods for pregnant women, with negative short-term and long-term consequences for the health and life chances of mother and child. The report also noted that girls are usually weaned earlier than boys, depriving them of the nutrients in mother's milk.

A study by Radheshyam Bairagi (1986) of the health status of children aged 1 to 4 in Bangladesh documents the harmful effects of differential nutrition on girls. As a context for the study, Bairagi notes that mortality rates in childhood at all ages except the neonatal period (0 to 29 days) are consistently higher for girls than for boys. Bairagi's research then focused on survivors of a severe famine that occurred in Bangladesh in 1974–1975. He studied 1,400 children at two-month intervals from April 1975 to December 1976, comparing three indices indicative of health status: weight for age, height for age, and weight for height. These indices are sensitive to factors of "food intake, incidence of disease, and health care use, which are expected to be interrelated. . . . For children in rural Bangladesh, food intake is likely to be the main component determining weight-for-age" (p. 308). On all measurements, girls fared worse than boys. Girls showed consistently higher signs of poor growth and malnutrition, clearly indicating that they were given less to eat. Although both boys and girls were harmed as a result of widespread famine, girls suffered more.

Another significant finding reported by Bairagi (1986) is that families of higher socioeconomic status discriminated against their daughters even more than families of low status did. That is, although children in more prosperous families were healthier than those in poor families, "male-female differences were consistently higher among children of high socioeconomic status" (p. 312). Bairagi therefore concluded the following:

> Although the present study lacked data with which to investigate why sex differentials in nutritional status were more marked among children of high socioeconomic status, this finding has important policy relevance. A simple improvement in the level of household resources is unlikely to decrease male-female differences in this population. Rather, a fundamental structural change in the role, status, and economic value of women in Bangladesh will be required.

> In the meantime, it is important that those responsible for the design of programs directed toward child health and survival carefully consider the sex bias in the allocation of food and in the use of health care facilities and intervention. (p. 314)

It is interesting and critical to note the paradox that although in many societies, girls and women receive less or lower-quality food than boys and men, it is generally women who prepare and allocate food to their families. The strength of culturally based gender ideologies exerts dominating influences that counter women's own personal interests and survival.

GENDER AND AGING

In most countries of the world, except where deaths from AIDS or from incessant warfare have led to rapid decline in the statistical life span, people are living longer. And in many countries, a majority of the elderly are women. There are no definitive answers as to why women tend to live longer than men, but it has been suggestioned that biological hormonal protections allow women to better process cholesterol and thus be protected from heart disease. Behavioral factors are also implicated, especially higher rates of mortality among men from accidents, homicide, suicide, and war (Feachem, Phillips, and Bulatao, 1992). Rates of alcoholism and smoking are also higher among men, leading to early deaths.

Although it is true that women tend to live longer, they may not be healthier overall than men. But women's medical problems may spur them to seek medical care earlier and more frequently than men. In the United States, at least, women are more likely to suffer from chronic ailments and to visit doctors and take medications (Cattell, 1996, p. 91). In the long run, medical-seeking behavior may prolong women's lives because life-threatening illnesses may be caught earlier, when they are still treatable. It is a paradox that although women make relatively more visits to doctors and take more medications than men, most scientific studies of health and illness prevalence as well as studies aimed at developing medical treatments focus on males rather than females (Hamilton, 1996).

Although it is true that women tend to live longer than men, women's later years are frequently endured in poverty and social isolation. Because women often outlive their husbands, they face many years of widowhood, bringing with it loneliness and a decline in income. Among people 65 and older, women outnumber men by a ratio of 3:2, but among the eldest groups, over age 85, women outnumber men by a ratio of 5:2 (U.S. Census Bureau, 2005). Elderly men are therefore more likely to be married and living with a spouse while elderly women are more likely to be widowed. Census Bureau data indicate that 75 percent of elderly men are married while only 41 percent of elderly women live with a spouse. And further data indicate that 8 out of every 10 noninstitutionalized elderly people living alone are women. The chances that an elderly woman lives alone increases with age. One of the consequences of these patterns is that elderly women are more likely to require assistance performing daily tasks, including dressing, washing, and shopping, and therefore to need to rely on nonfamily members for help.

As a result of living longer and living without a spouse, the majority of American elder women live in poverty. The poverty rate for elderly women in 1995 was 16 percent, nearly double the poverty rate for men, which was 9 percent. As with other age groups, poverty rates vary with race. African Americans had the highest poverty rate among the elderly (33 percent), Hispanics had a lower poverty rate (22 percent), and whites had a much lower rate (11 percent). Indeed, income scales reveal the same disparities: Elderly white men have annual incomes more than twice that of elderly African American and Hispanic women (U.S. Census Bureau, 2005). These facts mean that among the elderly, white men are more likely to maintain a comfortable standard of living while nonwhite women are most likely to see their living conditions worsen.

In addition, women's longevity means that they become frail and, often, unable to live independently. Widows eventually need to seek help outside their own households. Because of cultural emphases on the nuclear family and loosening of responsibilities to other relatives, including one's elder parents, elderly women often end their lives in nursing homes where social isolation and emotional trauma are compounded.

According to Social Security Administration research (Anzick and Weaver, 2001), the poverty rate for elderly women continued to be nearly twice the rate for men (11.8% compared with 6.9%). Poverty rates vary for women depending on their marital status. Elderly women currently married have the lowest rates of poverty, 4.3 percent, while rates for divorced women are the highest, 20.4 percent. Women who are widows experienced poverty at a rate of 15.9 percent while those who never married have a poverty rate of 18.9 percent. The highest rates for divorced women reflect the fact that they are responsible for supporting their children in the absence of a husband's income. The lower rate of poverty for widows presumably reflects inheritance left by their husbands. Since women average fewer years as paid employees compared to men, their retirement benefits, including both Social Security and private pensions, are significantly smaller.

HEALING AND HEALERS

Ju/'hoansi Healers

Health and illness are universal concerns; therefore, people everywhere develop beliefs about how to maintain health and how to prevent or treat illnesses. Although all individuals have some knowledge of treatments, in every society some people specialize in explaining, diagnosing, and curing sickness. Because healing is a domain of personal and social significance, access to medical knowledge and rights to function as medical practitioners are indicative of a society's constructs of people's abilities.

Some healers are trained through formal, institutionalized instruction; others obtain their knowledge through informal networks, apprenticeships, and observation. In cultures characterized by egalitarian gender relations, women and men have access to both types of roles, but in male-dominated cultures, men tend to monopolize positions as formal practitioners.

The Ju/'hoansi of Namibia and Botswana, whose culture we discussed in Chapter 2, provide a relevant example of an egalitarian society permitting all people to become healers. Ju/'hoansi healing is a specialty endowed with great social prestige. Men and women who serve as healers are among the most valued members of a community. As is common in most traditional societies, Ju/'hoansi curing is a ritual as well as medical event. Therefore, a healer's prestige derives, in part, from his or her access to spiritual knowledge and power.

Ju/'hoansi men and women can become respected members of a camp by excelling in the accumulation and use of healing powers. These powers are amassed through ritualized dancing during which a dancer activates spiritual energy, called *num*. Activation of *num* gradually leads an individual to enter a trance state, called *kia*. In this state, the dancer can use his or her *num* to heal (Katz, 1982). Healing generally involves a transmission of the healer's

Ju/'hoansi healers enter a trance to aid their patients.

energy to the patient. Healers' *num* generates profuse sweat that the practitioner then rubs onto his or her hands and imparts to the patient through a massage.

Women or men can receive and activate *num* and can heal. However, the proportion of men who do so is higher than that of women. Approximately half of all men succeed in becoming healers; one-third of all women accumulate *num* and enter the *kia* state, but only 10 percent learn to heal. Men's acquisition of *num* generally results from a long apprenticeship to an experienced healer, whereas women tend to receive *num* after only a few days of training.

Although either men or women can become powerful healers, in practice most, but not all, of the most powerful are men. Among both men and women, older healers are more successful in activating *num* and in healing. Their enhanced success results from the fact that each activation of *num* is cumulative, helping the seeker amass more spiritual energy. Therefore, the longer the span of years during which an individual seeks *num*, the greater is its potential accumulation. Although in theory men and women have equal opportunity to activate *num*, in practice a discrepancy between the genders is apparent. The Ju/'hoansi consider it unwise for a pregnant woman to seek *num* because the power of spiritual energy is dangerous to her fetus and potentially to herself as well. Lapses in participation due to pregnancies thus interfere with steady increases in women's healing abilities.

Some women do become powerful healers. In some cases, their abilities to enter into a trance and heal combine with other personal qualities to enable them to exert social and political leadership. Michael Katz (1982) describes one such prominent woman, Wa Na, whom he portrays as "an awesome person in her early eighties. . . . She is considered the most powerful healer in the entire Dobe area" (p. xix):

> Wa Na's political significance is also great. She is acknowledged as the "owner" of the Goshe waterhole, her father having come to it first among the !Kung [Ju/'hoansi]. With her extensive kinship ties, her social significance is just as central as her political position. Her great age, her political centrality, her extensive kinship ties, and her uniquely powerful num are all signs of importance, enhancing each other. (p. 222)

Ju/'hoansi healing dances are differentiated in terms of the roles men and women play. In dance events known as "giraffe dances," men are the more prominent dancers and healers. At these dances, women provide the singing that accompanies and encourages the dancers. Men receive *num*, enter into a trance, and heal. Women may also dance at giraffe dances but ordinarily are in the minority of dancers and generally do not heal. Dances known as "drum dances" reverse these central and supportive roles. That is, a man functions as the drummer while women dance, receive *num*, enter *kia*, and heal. Other men attend drum dances but only to encourage the dancers.

Although the purposes of giraffe and drum dances are similar and the ways that *num* is activated and used are identical, Katz (1982) notes that women's dancing and visible manifestation of *kia* is "more controlled and less dramatic" than those of men. "The subtle, vibrant shaking of the women's *kia*, though no less intense, contrasts to the shrieking and howling that is part of the men's *kia*" (pp. 165–166).

Ju/'hoansi healing dances, especially giraffe, are intensely sensual, a quality "evident in the rhythmic crescendos of singing, the kinesthesia of warm, sweating dancers, the release and abandon of *kia*, and the deep massage essential to helping another in *kia*" (p. 175). Katz (1982) concludes:

> A dynamic balance exists between men and women at the Giraffe dance. As in relations between [Ju/'hoansi] men and women generally, imperfections in the balance occur. But the basic respect of each sex for the other's contribution to the dance constantly re-establishes the balance. The Giraffe exists for healing, and both women and men release the Giraffe's healing energy. (pp. 175–176)

And the Ju/'hoansi themselves concur:

> Kinachau (a male dancer): "It is good for women to have *num*. If they heal, they can save you! It is the same with the men.
> Nai (a female singer): "The healing in the singing circle is the same as the healing of the dancers." (p. 176)

Sri Lankan Healers

In large, complex societies, many types of treatment modalities may coexist, employed by diverse categories of practitioners. Different specialties may be the forte of men or women. For example, an elaborate, differentiated system of health care prevails in Sri Lanka, combining medical, religious, and cosmological beliefs and practices. Among the options available for treatment of illnesses are doctors trained in Ayurvedic (Indian) medicine, Western-style medical doctors, Buddhist priests, and a host of traditional ritualists, exorcists, astrologers, and fortune-tellers (Nordstrom, 1989). Men tend to dominate the fields of Ayurvedic and Western medicine, although women have recently made inroads into these professions. Healers associated with institutionalized religious traditions such as Buddhist priests and exorcists also are usually men. Other Sinhalese practitioners, including lay ritualists and astrologers, are equally likely to be men or women.

In addition to these specialists, some people have a great deal of knowledge of home remedies consisting of herbal treatments, ritual procedures, and cosmological readings. Most of these healers are women. Their practices are based in their homes, treating patients as a part-time specialty. Whereas Ayurvedic and Western biomedical doctors or Buddhist priests receive training from formal institutions, local healers gain their expertise from informal avenues of observation and apprenticeship. Their interest in patients extends beyond the purely physical, and their consultations include gathering information about a patient's family, social life, and work situation.

The preponderance of Sinhalese men in formal medical and religious professions is due to the fact that educational institutions that train these practitioners have, at least until recently, discriminated against women. The preponderance of women as local healers is explained by the Sinhalese through appeal to a set of beliefs about healing powers. The Sinhalese believe that a healer's ability to cure derives in part from his or her acquired knowledge of remedies and treatments and in part from a "gift" or "touch." This gift comes not from the mystical realm but from an individual's compassion and kindness. According to Sinhalese constructs of gender, women are more likely than men to have these personal qualities. The fact that local healers do not charge regular fees for their services but, rather, accept goods in exchange for their treatments is taken as an indication of their basic desire to help others.

Health Practitioners in the United States

In modern industrial nations, men and women have equal legal rights to enter health care professions, but the genders are disproportionately represented in these occupations. Data from the United States, for example, reflect a clear pattern of gender segregation within the field of health care. Women account for 97 percent of registered nurses, 98 percent of practical nurses, 94 percent of dieticians, and 72 percent of medical technicians (Sapiro, 1986). In contrast, men dominate fields of professional medicine that have higher social status and are rewarded with higher income. Men make up 86 percent of medical doctors, 95 percent of dentists, and 74 percent of pharmacists.

Nursing has always been a ghetto for women. It has been identified as a woman's occupation from the inception of its history as an organized profession. As nursing developed in the nineteenth century, it was constructed as a supportive adjunct to medical doctors. The roles of doctor and nurse were hierarchically organized. In accordance with prevailing notions concerning men's and women's relationships, nurses were advised, "Never assert your opinions and wishes, but defer to his. This is truly a feminine piece of counsel, and I beg you to lay it to your heart" (*Hospital*, January 8, 1898; quoted in Gamarnikow, 1978, p. 111).

Florence Nightingale, largely responsible for the professionalization of nursing, similarly described a nurse's qualities in terms of those deemed natural for women in the context of nineteenth-century constructs of the cult of domesticity. According to Nightingale (1867), "To be a good nurse, one must be a good woman.... What makes a good woman is the better or higher or holier nature: quietness, gentleness, patience, endurance, forbearance" (quoted in Gamarnikow, 1978, p. 115).

In a reinforcement of images of nurses as nurturing, caring women, nursing was explicitly equated with mothering:

> In the bearing of a nurse toward her charge there must be something of the indulgence of a mother for her child. That is why women are better nurses than men. . . . It is astonishing what can be done with gentleness, especially when dispensed by a woman, and as the medical man is there, I think it would be well if the so-called firmness, when needed, were left to him. (*Hospital,* April 28, 1894; quoted in Gamarnikow, 1978, p. 110)

> Nursing is distinctly woman's work. . . . Women are peculiarly fitted for the onerous task of patiently and skillfully caring for the patient in faithful obedience to the physician's orders. Ability to care for the helpless is woman's distinctive nature. Nursing is mothering. (*Hospital,* July 8, 1905; quoted in Gamarnikow, 1978, p. 110)

These advisories and commentaries transmit overt messages of the appropriateness of nurturing roles of nurse/mother and the authority of doctor/father. Although such constructs are not explicitly stated today, the same underlying relationship remains. It is reflected both in professional hierarchies and in gender segregation typical of the fields.

Within the medical profession itself, gender segregation is reflected in the particular specialty chosen. Those specialties in which women physicians are clustered include general practice (12.1 percent), pediatrics (17.9 percent), and psychiatry (13.7 percent). Fields having the smallest percentages of women include cardiology (0.8 percent), orthopedics (0.2 percent), and most surgical specialties (Fox and Hesse-Biber, 1984). Specialties practiced by women are of relatively low status within the profession. They are also associated with women's supposed inclinations toward an interest in children, families, and emotions.

Women's Informal Healing Roles

In many societies, regardless of whether women serve as professional medical specialists, women, especially in their roles as mothers, are often the first to be consulted in cases of illness. Data from a wide range of cultures throughout the world confirm the fact that the overwhelming majority of ailments are treated initially or exclusively at home, primarily by mothers or other women in the household (Finerman, 1989). Detailed studies of responses to illness episodes in Ecuador, Mexico, Guatemala, Taiwan, Hong Kong, and the United States attest to this pattern. For example, Arthur Kleinman's (1980) research among Taiwanese families documents that 93 percent of ailments are "first treated at home, and 73 percent receive their only treatment there" (p. 68). Similarly, among rural Guatemalans, 73 percent of illness episodes are treated at home; only 27 percent of patients seek formal medical care (Woods and Graves, 1976).

Women's role as healers is often seen as an extension of their responsibilities as mothers. Transmitting knowledge of health care, preventing illness, and providing medical treatment are adjuncts to a woman's caregiving to children and spouses. In addition to expertise in herbal remedies, nutritional supervision, and informal medical treatments, women in the household provide emotional support to sufferers. For instance, Ruthbeth Finerman's (1989) study of health care among native Ecuadorans recorded people's belief that the "personalized care" given by women "helps individuals cope with stress, physical pain, and frustration over incapacitation, which are thought to hinder convalescence. The compassion and interest mothers convey toward sick family members are thought to encourage recovery" (p. 57).

Women's importance as familial and professional health care providers has been stressed by John Caldwell (1986) in a comparative study of health and mortality in poor countries throughout the world. Caldwell reviews statistics from ninety-nine Third World countries on infant mortality and life expectancy, measured against per capita gross national product (GNP). He arrives at a division between eleven "superior health achievers" and eleven "poor health achievers" (p. 174). Among superior achievers are Sri Lanka, China, India, Zaire, Kenya, and Costa Rica. Among the poor achievers are Saudi Arabia, Iran, Algeria, Iraq, Senegal, and Sierra Leone. Caldwell suggests several features distinguishing the most and least successful nations. These features all share a common theme: Superior achievers institute policies supportive of women's autonomy, whereas poor achievers generally restrict women's activities. First, of the eleven poor achievers, nine are predominately or wholly Muslim countries; the two others (namely, Sierra Leone and Ivory Coast) have large Muslim minorities. Conversely, of the eleven superior achievers, none are Muslim. This religious difference has significant bearing on women's autonomy both within society and in their own households because Islamic traditions severely restrict women's rights as independent actors and decision makers.

Second, superior and poor achievers are distinguished in terms of rates of literacy and schooling for girls. All of the most successful health achievers have relatively high rates of girls' school attendance. Sri Lanka, Burma, and the state of Kerala in southern India are especially noteworthy in educating girls on a par with boys. Conversely, poor health achievers have extremely low rates of girls' schooling, especially marked in Saudi Arabia, Iran, and Libya.

Third, low infant mortality rates and improved life expectancy are correlated with relatively high percentages of married women using family planning techniques, whereas absence of family planning practices characterizes poor health achievers.

Data collected in 1998 indicate that Caldwell's assessments are essentially still accurate. Countries that Caldwell listed as superior health achievers continue to improve by increasing life expectancy and decreasing infant mortality rates (World Bank, 2006). For example, between 1980 and 1998 life expectancy rose in Sri Lanka from 68 to 73 years and infant mortality fell from 34/1000 live births to 16/1000. In India, life expectancy rose from 54 to 63 years while infant mortality rates fell from 115/1000 to 70/1000. Costa Rican life expectancy rose from 73 to 77 years and infant mortality rates dropped slightly from a very good 19/1000 to 13/1000. Most of the countries that Caldwell ranked as poor health achievers have remained so despite the fact that some of them (Algeria, Iran, Iraq, and Saudi Arabia) have Gross National Products far higher than most of the other countries surveyed by Caldwell. Only Senegal has demonstrated significant improvements in health statistics. Life expectancy there has risen from 70 to 75 years while infant mortality rates have declined from 15/1000 to a very positive 5/1000 live births.

Caldwell (1986) has carefully studied the cultural contexts in which significant advances have been made in health status in three areas deemed to have had remarkable achievements, including Sri Lanka, the Indian state of Kerala, and Costa Rica. Among the "striking parallels" shared by these countries are "a substantial degree of female autonomy, a dedication to education, an open political system, a largely civilian society, a history of egalitarianism and radicalism" (p. 182). Of these, he states, "A marked degree of female autonomy is probably central to exceptional mortality declines" (p. 184).

In addition to longstanding and continuing problems of nutrition and health care, HIV/AIDS has exacerbated already dire circumstances in many poor countries, especially in Africa. In a study of the socioeconomic effects of the disease in five African countries (Malawi, Mozambique, Tanzania, Uganda, and Zambia), researchers documented the growing prevalence of HIV/AIDS infection and its consequences on individual, family, and community well-being (Isaksen, Songstad, and Spissoy, 2002). Since 1985, all of these countries have experienced a sharp decline in life expectancy, erasing gains that had been made in the two prior decades. The numbers of deaths from AIDS will also continue to grow. African women are particularly hard-hit, both because their rates of disease are especially high and because they shoulder the burdens of caring for sick and dying family members. In the five countries under study, women's rates of HIV prevalence were about double that of men:

	Females (15–24)	Males (15–24)
Malawi	16.04	8.00
Mozambique	16.11	8.97
Tanzania	9.27	5.28
Uganda	8.99	5.12
Zambia	18.68	9.32

SOURCE: Isaksen, Songstad, and Spissoy, 2002, p. 6.

In addition to the health factors and domestic responsibilities affecting women, in the five countries surveyed, women earn lower wages than men and because of cultural attitudes about gender, their health care needs are generally less attended to than those of male family members.

The economies of affected households and communities suffer from sharp declines in income due to the inability of sick people to work. Food supplies also decline both in the commercial sector, due to lack of workers, and in the domestic subsistence sector, due to the weakness and death of family members. HIV/AIDS is a disease syndrome that afflicts women and men in their prime productive years. Their loss therefore has especially negative impacts on their households. Government support for programs that might otherwise develop agricultural and industrial sectors sometimes are diverted to attempting some improvements in health care but since the countries under study are among the poorest in the world, few funds are available for any social expenditures. The economic and social consequences of HIV/AIDS are likely to worsen in future decades.

Women's autonomy has a variety of interrelated effects on health status. Because good health is, in part, an outcome of treatment, provision of medical services, particularly in rural areas, is essential. Those countries with superior health achievements employ relatively large numbers of women trained as nurses, midwives, and health educators. Such workers provide medical services to a rural population that has few other treatment options, given the paucity of doctors practicing in poor nations as a whole and especially in rural areas within their countries. Because women's vocational opportunities are obviously connected to their education, nations dedicated to equal schooling for girls create a context in which women can function as health professionals.

Women are entering the medical profession in increasing rates. Approximately half of medical school students are women but far fewer, about 25 percent, of practicing doctors are women. Women doctors continue to be concentrated in family and internal medicine, pediatrics, obstetrics/gynecology, and psychiatry but their numbers are growing in other specialties as well. Women residents account for more than 50 percent of primary care practitioners, 75 percent of obstetrician/gynecologist residents, and 66 percent of pediatrician residents (Schapiro, 2005). Specialties in which women are especially underrepresented are neurosurgery, cardiology, and orthopedics. Women account for only about 20 percent of practitioners in all surgical specialties (Dorschner, 2003).

Although women physicians are increasing their presence within the profession, they continue to suffer from earning differentials with their male counterparts. Depending on specialty, women average about 60–85 percent of the earnings of male doctors. Women physicians are more concerned than their male counterparts with issues around scheduling and workload, presumably because they have to spend more time fulfilling household and childcare responsibilities. And a survey of members of the American Medical Women's

Association indicated that about 90 percent of female physicians support some form of universal health coverage (ibid). The American Medical Association, a professional organization dominated by men, strongly opposes such plans.

Women's autonomy is further associated with a relatively high incidence of the use of family planning techniques. Because smaller family size is correlated with lower infant mortality rates, and thus with higher life expectancy, the use of contraception contributes to overall personal and national health achievement. Where women's status is independent of their childbearing roles, women limit the number of children they bear. Conversely, women in cultures that define their worthiness in terms of reproductive success attempt to bear as many children as possible. In countries dominated by Islamic traditions, religious sanctions combine with social imperatives to bar use of contraceptive techniques.

Finally, where women have rights to act independently, they tend to seek early medical treatment for their children. According to Caldwell (1986):

> Greater female autonomy renders it more likely that a mother will make her own decision that something must be done when she identifies a child as sick (it also seems to lead her to make that identification at an earlier time), that she will venture outside the home to seek help, that she will struggle for adequate treatment with doctors and nurses, and that she will understand the advice and take responsibility for carrying it out. (p. 202)

Although women's equality may be correlated with educational and occupational opportunities, it ultimately derives from underlying ideological constructs. That is, "female autonomy is greatest where both society and women themselves have little doubt about a woman's right to make decisions and to battle for her and her children's rights in the public arena" (Caldwell, 1986, p. 202).

Finally, Caldwell's research demonstrates that women's rights to function independently and autonomously affect not only themselves and their families but also collectively their nation's health status.

SUMMARY

Issues related to health and healing can reveal cultural constructs of gender in the differentiation of attitudes toward the body, physiological processes, and rights to survival. The definition of gender itself does not emerge simply from biological factors but rather is a concept that has different interpretations in different cultures. Among native peoples of North America, for example, a third gender was a social category distinct from woman and man. In all cultures, people share notions about physiological attributes of men and women. Practices and beliefs related to puberty, pregnancy, and childbirth are particular manifestations of the roles and behaviors expected of people. These beliefs encapsulate ideological concepts about the worthiness of women and men.

The survival chances of women and men may vary in societies where nutritional differences between the genders tend to occur. In societies where women are devalued, they may face nutritional restrictions and taboos. In addition, young girls may not receive adequate food, resulting in chronic malnutrition and an increased risk of poor health and early death.

Finally, the ability of men and women to function as healers and health care practitioners may be allocated according to gender. In societies where men are accorded higher status than women, they tend to monopolize prestigeful roles as healers. However, in most cultures, women provide health care to their family and to other members of their communities in informal contexts.

REFERENCES

AHMADU, FUAMBAI. 2000. "Female circumcision." In *Africa: Culture, Controversy, and Change* (ed. Bettina Shell-Duncan and Ylva Hernlund). London: Rienner.

ANZICK, MICHAEL, AND DAVID WEAVER. 2001. "Reducing poverty among elderly women." Washington DC: Social Security Administration, Office of Policy. Office of Research, Evaluation, and Statistics. ORES.

ARMSTRONG, SUE. 1991. "Female circumcision: Fighting a cruel tradition." *New Scientist*, 2: 42–47.

ASHBURN, PERCY. 1947. *The Ranks of Death: A Medical History of the Conquest of America* (ed. Frank Ashburn). New York: Coward-McCann.

BAIRAGI, RADHESHYAM. 1986. "Food crisis, nutrition, and female children in rural Bangladesh." *Population and Development Review*, 12: 307–315.

BASSO, KEITH. 1970. *The Cibecue Apache.* New York: Holt, Rinehart & Winston.

BLACKWOOD, EVELYN. 1984. "Sexuality and gender in certain Native American tribes: The case of cross-gender females." *Signs: Journal of Women in Culture and Society*, 10: 27–42.

CALDWELL, JOHN. 1986. "Routes to low mortality in poor countries." *Population and Development Review*, 12: 171–220.

CALLENDER, CHARLES, AND LEE KOCHEMS. 1983. "The North American berdache." *Current Anthropology*, 24: 443–470.

CAPOOR, INDU. 2000, November 30. "Women and Nutrition: Victims or Decision Makers." Paper presented at a symposium on "Nutrition and Development," Basell, Switzerland.

CATTELL, MARIA. 1996. "Gender, aging, and health: A comparative approach." In *Gender and Health: An International Perspective* (ed. Carolyn Sargent and Caroline Brettell). Upper Saddle River, NJ: Prentice Hall, pp. 87–122.

CONDRY, JOHN, AND SHARON CONDRY. 1976. "Sex differences: A study in the eye of the beholder." *Child Development*, 47: 817.

CULP, R. E. et al. 1983. "A comparison of observational and reported adult-infant interactions: Effects of perceived sex." *Sex Roles*, 9: 475–479.

DAVIS, DONA. 1996. "The cultural construction of the premenstrual and menopause syndromes." In *Gender and Health: An International Perspective* (ed. Carolyn Sargent and Caroline Brettell). Upper Saddle River, NJ: Prentice Hall, pp. 57–86.

DORSCHNER, JOHN. 2003, March 25. "Growing number of female doctors changing medical profession." *The Standard Times.*

DUNN, FREDERICK. 1968. "Epidemiological factors: Health and disease in hunters and gatherers." In *Man the Hunter* (ed. Richard Lee and Irven DeVore). Chicago: Aldine-Atherton, pp. 221–228.

EHRENREICH, BARBARA, AND DEIRDRE ENGLISH. 1978. *For Her Own Good: 150 Years of the Experts' Advice to Women.* New York: Doubleday Anchor.

EMBER, Carol. 1981. "A cross-cultural perspective on sex differences." In *Handbook of Cross-Cultural Human Development* (ed. Ruth Munroe, Robert Munroe, and Beatrice Whiting). New York: Garland, pp. 531–580.

FAUSTO-STERLING, ANNE. 1985. *Myths of Gender: Biological Theories about Women and Men.* New York: Basic Books.

FEACHEM, RICHARD, MARGARET PHILLIPS, AND RODOLFO BULATAO. 1992. "Introducing adult health." In *The Health of Adults in the Developing World* (ed. Richard Feachem et al.). New York: Oxford University Press, pp. 1–22.

FINERMAN, RUTHBETH. 1989. "The forgotten healers: Women as family hearers in an Andean Indian community." In *Women as Healers: Cross-Cultural Perspectives* (ed. Carol McClain). New Brunswick, NJ: Rutgers University Press, pp. 24–41.

FITZGERALD, MAUREEN. 1990. "The interplay of culture and symptoms: Menstrual symptoms among Samoans." *Medical Anthropology*, 12: 145–167.

FOX, MARY, AND SHARLENE HESSE-BIBER. 1984. *Women at Work.* Palo Alto, CA: Mayfield.

GAMARNIKOW, EVA. 1978. "Sexual division of labour: The case of nursing." In *Feminism and Materialism* (ed. Annette Kuhn and Annmarie Wolpe). London: Routledge & Kegan Paul, pp. 220–244.

GIBBS, JAMES. 1965. "The Kpelle of Liberia." In *Peoples of Africa* (ed. James Gibbs). New York: Holt, Rinehart & Winston, pp. 197–240.

GOODALE, JANE. 1971. *Tiwi Wives: A Study of the Women of Melville Island, North Australia.* American Ethnological Society Monograph no. 51. Seattle: University of Washington Press.

GRUENBAUM, ELLEN. 1993. "The movement against clitoridectomy and infibulation in Sudan: Public health policy and the women's movement." In *Gender in Cross-Cultural Perspective* (ed. Caroline Brettell and Carolyn Sargent). Upper Saddle River, NJ: Prentice Hall, pp. 411–422.

HAIRE, DORIS. 1978. "The cultural warping of childbirth." In *The Cultural Crisis of Modern Medicine* (ed. J. Ehrenreich). New York: Monthly Review Press, pp. 185–200.

HAMILTON, JEAN. 1996. "Women and health policy: On the inclusion of females in clinical trials." In *Gender and Health: An International Perspective* (ed. Carolyn Sargent and Caroline Brettell). Upper Saddle River, NJ: Prentice Hall, pp. 292–325.

ISAKSEN, JAN, NILS SONGSTAD, AND ARILD SPISSOY. 2002. "Socioeconomic effects of HIV/AIDS in African countries." Bergen: Milchelsen Institute.

KATZ, MICHAEL. 1982. *Boiling Energy: Community Healing among the Kalahari !Kung.* Cambridge, MA: Harvard University Press.

KLEINMAN, ARTHUR. 1980. *Patients and Healers in the Context of Culture.* Berkeley: University of California Press.

KOBRIN, FRANCES. 1966. "The American midwife controversy: A crisis in professionalization." *Bulletin of the History of Medicine*, 4: 350–363.

KRAMER, HEINREICH, AND JACOB SPRENGER. 1487. *Malleus Maleficarum: The Hammer of the Witches* (trans. M. Summer; ed. P. Hughes). London: Folio Society.

LACEY, MARK. 2004, June 14. "Genital cutting shows signs of losing favor in Africa." *New York Times*, pp. A1, B2.

LADERMAN, CAROL. 1983. *Wives and Midwives: Childbirth and Nutrition in Rural Malaysia.* Berkeley: University of California Press.

LOCK, MARGARET. 1986. "Ambiguities of aging: Japanese experience and perceptions of menopause." *Culture, Medicine, and Psychiatry*, 10: 23–46.

———. 1989. "Castigations of a selfish housewife: National identity and menopausal rhetoric in Japan." *Kroeber Anthropological Society Papers*, 69–70: 1–13.

———. 1991. "Life-cycle transitions." *Encyclopedia of Human Biology*, 4: 697–710.

MAMDANI, MAHMOOD. 1972. *The Myth of Population Control: Family, Caste, and Class in an Indian Village.* New York: Monthly Review Press.

NORDSTROM, CAROLYN. 1989. "It's all in a name: Local-level female healers in Sri Lanka." In *Women as Healers: Cross-Cultural Perspectives* (ed. Carol McClain). New Brunswick, NJ: Rutgers University Press, pp. 42–57.

O'LAUGHLIN, BRIDGET. 1974. "Mediation of contradiction: Why Mbum women do not eat chicken." In *Woman, Culture and Society* (ed. Michelle Rosaldo and Louise Lamphere). Stanford, CA: Stanford University Press, pp. 301–318.

ROSENBERG, ELLEN. 1980. "Demographic effects of sex in differential nutrition." In *Nutritional Anthropology* (ed. Norge Jerome et al.). Pleasantville, NY: Redgrave, pp. 181–203.

ROSENTHAL, ELIZABETH. 2006, June 2. "Genital cutting raises by 50% likelihood mothers or their newborns will die, study finds." *The New York Times.*

ROTHMAN, BARBARA. 1990. "Midwives in transition: The structure of a clinical revolution." In *The Sociology of Health and Illness: Critical Perspectives*, 3rd ed. (ed. Peter Conrad and Rochelle Kern). New York: St. Martin's, pp. 339–347.

SANDERSON, LILIAN. 1981. *Against the Mutilation of Women.* London: Ithaca Press.

SANDERSON, LILLIAN, and NEVILLE SANDERSON. 1981. *Education, Religion and Politics in Southern Sudan 1899–1964.* London: Ithaca.

SAPIRO, VIRGINIA. 1986. *Women in American Society.* Palo Alto, CA: Mayfield.

SCHAPIRO, RENIE. 2005, September 18. "More women entering and changing medical profession." *Milwaukee Journal Sentinel.*

SY, SENABOU MARIE. 2006. "Nutritional, food security, hygiene, and sanitation conditions in the fishing community of Joal, Senegal." FAO Corporate Document Repository. www.fao.org/DOCREP.

UN Office of the High Commissioner for Human Rights. 1995. "Fact Sheet No. 23, Harmful Traditional Practices Affecting the Health of Women and Children." www.unhchr.ch.

"U.S. grants asylum to woman fleeing genital mutilation rite." 1996, June 14. *New York Times,* pp. A1, B2.

WERTZ, RICHARD, AND DOROTHY WERTZ. 1990. "Notes on the decline of midwives and the rise of medical obstetricians." In *The Sociology of Health and Illness: Critical Perspectives,* 3rd ed. (ed. Peter Conrad and Rochelle Kern). New York: St. Martin's, pp. 148–160.

WILLIAMS, WALTER. 1986. *The Spirit and the Flesh: Sexual Diversity in American Indian Culture.* Boston: Beacon.

WINTER, RICHARD. 1989. "Girls' circumcision in the Sudan." In *Kinship, Social Change and Evolution* (ed. Andre Gingrich et al.). Vienna Contributions to Ethnology and Anthropology, no. 5. Horn Wien: Berger, pp. 155–160.

WOOD, CORINNE. 1979. *Human Sickness and Health: A Biocultural View.* Palo Alto, CA: Mayfield.

WOODS, CLYDE, AND THEODORE GRAVES. 1976. "The process of medical change in a highland Guatemalan town." In *Medical Anthropology* (ed. Francis Grollig and Harold Haley). The Hague: Mouton.

Working Paper Series, number 87.

World Bank. 2006. Map of the World. www.worldbank.org/depweb/datanot.html

CHAPTER 9

Gender and Religion

Ideological constructs are powerfully incorporated into religious beliefs and practices. Consequently, through enactment of ritual and recitation of religious narratives, ideological foundations of a culture are transmitted and reinforced. Indeed, because people often have unquestioning adherence to their religion, religion is among the domains that most influence their construction of reality and society.

Notions about origins of the world, creation of human beings, and establishment of order in the universe are among the concepts enshrined in religious belief. Order in society is of fundamental concern as well and is therefore also addressed in religious doctrine. Because attributes and relationships of women and men are basic features of social life, religions offer people explanations for and justifications of prevailing cultural constructs of gender.

The analysis of interconnections between religion and gender are complicated by the fact that beliefs are not necessarily expressed directly. That is, stories of mythic origins, tales of human or animal protagonists, and admonitions rendered by spiritual beings may be transmitted through language that is metaphoric rather than explicit. Religion, then, expresses beliefs through symbols. By examining religious narratives and ritual practice, we can attempt to understand these symbols and to learn how people conceive of themselves and how they organize their lives.

CREATION AND CREATORS

To begin at the beginning, stories of creation encapsulate cultural explanations for environmental and human existence. Significant in these stories is the identity of creators. Creators may be female, male, androgynous, animal, or a supernatural force. In some cases, of course, more than one agent may be depicted. Peggy Sanday (1981) has suggested that the gender of creator(s) in a given culture is strongly correlated with the status of men and women in that group. Sanday claims that societies characterized by basically egalitarian gender relations tend to conceive of their creators as female or as a female-male pair, whereas male-dominated societies tend to think of their creators as either male or animal. Creation stories not only identify creators but also depict methods used to create. According to Sanday, there is a strong correlation between a creator's gender and the mode of creation:

> There are two primary modes for creating people—from the creator's body, as in sexual union, birth, and self-propagation; or from other than the body, as in making people magically out of clay, transforming people from plants or animals, or chiseling people from wood. With a few exceptions, female and couple agents create from the body. Male, animal, and supreme being creators create from other than the body. (p. 58)

Sanday (1981) characterizes creation from the body as an "inner orientation" and creation from other than the body as an "outer orientation." She discerns an association among the gender of creators, the types of orientation symbolized through creation stories in a given culture, and that culture's primary mode of subsistence. Female creators and inner orientations are prevalent in foraging societies that depend more on plant foods than on large animals. In contrast, male creators and outer orientations are typical of foraging societies dependent on large animals, particularly if plant sources are relatively unimportant. Peoples whose economies are based on horticulture, especially those with relatively simple technologies, tend to depict either female or couple creators. Peoples practicing intensive agriculture are evidently evenly divided between those having stories of male creators and those with female or couple creators. Finally, if a group's subsistence is based equally on plant and animal resources, both inner and outer orientations are depicted.

Following is a creation story told by residents of the Pacific island of Bali. Balinese culture has been characterized by Clifford Geertz (1973) as a "'unisex' society, a fact both its customs and its symbolism clearly express" (pp. 417–418). Productive and domestic roles are performed by either men or women; kinship systems and inheritance patterns are bilateral; religious practitioners may be of either gender; even styles of clothing and ornamentation are unisexual. The Balinese also conceive of their mythic origins in terms that unify the genders:

> The gods concentrated to make human beings and produced two couples; one yellow in color: Ketok Pita and Djenar; another red: Abang and Barak. From the yellow couple was born a boy, Nyoh Gading, "Yellow Coconut," and a girl named Kuning. The second couple had also two children, a boy named Tanah Barak, "Red Earth," and a girl Lewek. Yellow Coconut married Lewek; Red Earth married Kuning; and their descendants did the same until the population of Bali was created. (Covarrubias, 1938; cited in Sanday, 1981, p. 17)

Egalitarian Balinese concepts of mythic human origins create a social world of unity and balance between women and men. In contrast, stories told by the

Mundurucu (mun-du-ru-KU), a horticultural and hunting society in the Amazon region of Brazil, reflect and reinforce gender separation and male dominance. Mundurucu men and women are intensely segregated in all areas of economic, political, and social life. Men dominate community political and religious domains as well as their own households (Murphy and Murphy, 1973). Men are endowed with social prestige and power, values denied to women. Reflective of the social order, mythological men create; women play no active roles. Mundurucu origins are depicted as follows:

> Caru-Sacaebe appeared on the earth along with the first men. He was responsible for the appearance of the larger game and for teaching men how to hunt. He had neither father nor mother, but he had a son. Caru-Sacaebe became angry with the hunters who refused several times to grant him a request for fowl, and he retaliated by changing everyone into wild pigs. Then Caru-Sacaebe left with his companion. On arriving at a certain place, he stamped his foot on the ground, and from the large fissure that resulted he drew one pair of Mundurucu, one of white people, one of Indians, and one of Blacks. All but the Mundurucu couple set off to populate other lands. Caru-Sacaebe laid out a field and sowed it, and thus began the practice of agriculture. He taught people to build ovens and to make manioc flour. (Tocantins, 1877/1959; quoted in Sanday, 1981, pp. 37–38)

In addition to recounting origins of humans, creation stories often explain origins of plants, animals, and other natural entities and forces. For example, the Mundurucu narrative just cited credits Caru-Sacaebe not only with creating humans but also with introducing all essentials of Mundurucu subsistence; that is, he teaches people to hunt and to farm. He is even responsible for providing women with the means to prepare food and to cook. According to the Mundurucu worldview, as symbolized in their mythology and enacted in their lives, women perform no socially creative roles.

The Iroquois (see the discussion in chapter 2) have quite a different tale to tell. Traditions of the Iroquois, a native horticultural society in northeastern North America, depict both female and male creators. Several mythic figures are responsible for originating various aspects of the universe. Narratives tell that life on earth was motivated by creative actions of female beings, later to be modified by other female as well as male beings. According to traditional myths, creation took place as follows:

> At first there was no earth, only sky above and water below. In the Sky-World lived a woman who was pregnant. One day, while searching near roots of a large tree for medicines for her husband, she fell through a hole in the sky and descended toward the waters below. Animals in the sea saw her falling and decided to make a soft place for her to land. They dove beneath the water and took up some mud which they placed on a turtle's back. The woman landed unharmed and the turtle's back, covered with mud, gradually expanded to become the earth.
> The woman soon gave birth to a daughter. This daughter later became pregnant and gave birth to twin sons. One son was born in the normal manner but

the second was born through his mother's armpit, killing her in the process. The woman's mother buried her and out of her body grew plants of corn, beans, and squash.

The twin boys grew up and created various animals, wild fruits, trees, and mountains. (compiled from narrative accounts; Bonvillain, n.d.)

Just as Iroquoian women were responsible for supplying their families with produce of corn, beans, and squash, a mythic woman is responsible, through the generative potential of her own body, for originating these life-sustaining crops, known today by the Iroquois as "Our Life Supporters." Men also have creative roles, portrayed by the twins' activities. The mythic world of distinct but complementary actions performed by men and women mirrors the daily Iroquoian world of different but equal interdependent roles and responsibilities.

In some cultures, legends recount a reversal of women's and men's religious power in the mythic past. This theme is attested among several peoples in tropical South America, aboriginal Australia, and areas of Africa. Although widely divergent in place, the stories follow a similar line. It is typically recounted that in the past, ritual paraphernalia, often sacred trumpets or horns of some kind, were owned and played in secret by women. Men eventually seized control of the ritual instruments, through either stealth or struggle, and have since denied women access to them. Women (and children) are presently not supposed to overhear sounds made by sacred horns or to understand songs sung by men in secret rituals associated with the instruments.

Cultures that relate accounts of reversals of women's and men's ritual roles tend to be marked by male dominance and strict segregation of the genders. Present-day social rights and unequal power relations between the genders are thus justified by appeals to events in the mythic past. The message conveyed is that women had their chance but lost out because of men's superior abilities.

MENSTRUAL TABOOS

Separation of the genders is sometimes symbolized through avoidance of contact with women during their menstrual periods. Such beliefs are quite common, although they may take very different forms. In some societies, menstruating women perform their usual duties but refrain from contact with men's hunting gear or ritual paraphernalia. Some beliefs ordain that menstruating women should not prepare food given to men. In other societies, women are secluded in separate rooms in a house or separate huts during their periods. They must cease all their normal activities and rigorously adhere to a variety of taboos. Contact with menstrual blood can endanger other women, men, children, and/or bring harm to an entire community.

Although menstrual taboos clearly affirm a difference between the genders, their existence per se may not be correlated with gender inequality.

To test for correlations between menstrual restrictions and gender relations, Peggy Sanday (1981) considered five different types of taboos: (1) ban on sexual intercourse, (2) restrictions on activities and contact with other people, (3) taboos against contact with men's ritual equipment or weaponry, (4) taboos on cooking or handling food, and (5) total seclusion in a special hut. Sanday's statistical analysis of 156 societies indicates that the number of menstrual taboos is approximately the same among cultures she characterizes as egalitarian and those with male dominance. Eight societies (or 7 percent) in the sample have no beliefs regarding menstrual avoidances; at the other extreme, nineteen groups (17 percent) have all five types of restrictions.

Sanday's (1981) finding of a lack of correlation between menstrual taboos and dynamics of gender relations must be taken as tentative, however, because her analysis counts taboos numerically but does not examine their content. Therefore, one wonders, for instance, whether taboos in egalitarian or male-dominated societies are more or less restrictive. Another possible variable is whether consequences of violating taboos differ in societies where women and men are considered equal or unequal.

A further issue that can be raised in discussing menstrual restrictions is their culturally accepted motivation. Do people restrict menstruating women's activities or avoid contact with them because the women are considered powerful or polluting? Most ethnographic descriptions of menstrual taboos state or imply the latter, but one should be wary of accepting such statements without further analysis. Biases of anthropologists (or other observers) need to be considered. Although most people in Western cultures do not practice menstrual taboos, some do feel that menstruation (and perhaps by extension, menstruating women) is in some way "unclean." Western observers may then interpret other peoples' behavior, and even their words, in accordance with their own prejudices.

An additional interpretive problem arises regarding the frequent mention that menstrual blood is considered to be "dangerous." Danger can be related to power as well as to contamination. For instance, for comparative evidence from another religious domain, consider the belief common in Polynesia that physical contact between a chief and a commoner is dangerous to the latter and can result in his or her illness or death. Here the danger is believed to derive from a chief's *mana*, or spiritual power. A commoner is thought to be spiritually weak and therefore vulnerable to injury from the superior power amassed by chiefs. Similarly, many peoples believe that contact with ritual gear, sacred medicines, or supernatural beings is dangerous for those who are not spiritually prepared. These examples indicate that the concept of danger may derive from inherent power as well as from fears of pollution. They should provide a caution against an automatic reading of beliefs about the "danger" of menstrual blood.

Direct evidence of the misreading of menstrual rituals comes from Thomas Buckley's (1993) analysis of beliefs and practices of the Yurok, a native people whose aboriginal lands were in northwestern California. During menstruation, Yurok women retired to huts apart from their main dwellings, ate foods that were prepared separately from the family's fare, used a special stick to scratch themselves, and did not have contact with men. Buckley provides two interpretations of these practices. One, the "received" male view (Buckley's phrase), speaks of the polluting and contaminating effects of contact from a menstruating woman on men: men's food, hunting gear, and spiritual strength and success. The other, obtained from Buckley's contemporary female consultant, stresses the power associated with women's bodies that is heightened and made spiritually strong during menstruation. According to the Yurok woman, menstruation was a time "to find out the purpose of your life, to accumulate spiritual energy, . . . to go into yourself and make yourself stronger." She explained the purpose of using a scratching stick as a means of making every physical activity and sensation conscious: "You should feel all of your body exactly as it is, and pay attention" (p. 135). She equated menstrual huts with men's sweathouses where men went to pray and gain spiritual power.

Buckley's insights about the full meaning of menstruation are supported in a most telling discovery of field notes left by Alfred Kroeber, one of the major authorities on native peoples of California. Kroeber's notes include interviews conducted in 1902 with an elderly female consultant whose statements about menstruation have essentially the same positive meanings as those of the modern Yurok woman. But the critical point is that Kroeber never published these accounts. In his writings, he only mentions the male perception of menstruation as polluting and dangerous, describing menstrual shelters as "a hut used by Yurok women in their periodic *illnesses*" (p. 135; emphasis added). Buckley properly cautions against reading "received ethnographies" that have "double male biases (that is, in the descriptions of male anthropologists based on the testimony of primarily male consultants)" (p. 136).

Although on the surface menstrual restrictions emphasize a fundamental difference between women and men, in some societies they may reflect an attempt to equate the genders symbolically. As we have seen in examining gender roles in foraging and farming cultures, women's and men's productive activities are often differentiated and typically assign men the task of hunting. In addition, of course, women's reproductive roles are distinct. Menstrual taboos may function to balance the genders through manipulation of symbols of blood. Women's menstrual blood comes from their bodies as a signal and symbol of their procreative potential. Women's blood, then, enables women as childbearers to bring forth life and ensure the survival of their communities. In contrast, men as hunters are required to shed blood of other beings. This blood, although resulting from death, also supports life by supplying food for people's sustenance. Because blood shed by men has dual meanings of death and life, a symbolic reversal may be made to link women's life-giving blood with death or danger. This reversal, and subsequent equation of the genders, is accomplished by attributing danger to menstruating women.

In sum, then, menstrual taboos cannot be interpreted without reference to specific interrelated features of given cultures. Such taboos do not have a universal function but rather have culturally situated meanings. Among some peoples, they may symbolize awesome procreative powers of women, signaling women's contribution as givers of life. Among others, menstrual restrictions may function to segregate the genders, symbolizing men's culturally motivated need to dissociate themselves from contact with women to maintain their power.

It is tempting to speculate that positive interpretations of menstruation are more likely to be found in cultures where women and men are considered equal, whereas negative views are more consistent with ideologies of male dominance. This assumption seems logical, but it needs cross-cultural testing for verification. Although large-scale studies have not been conducted to address the issue, some correlations seem to obtain. For instance, evidence from patriarchal cultures supports an association between male dominance and negative attitudes toward menstruation. In fact, beliefs in some patriarchal societies make explicit a strongly hostile attitude toward women's bodies. For instance, doctrines of Hinduism prevalent in India and of the three major religions originating in the Near East (Judaism, Christianity, and Islam) share an underlying theme of danger to men of contamination from women and especially from women's sexuality.

PURITY, POLLUTION, AND SEXUALITY

Hinduism

Important concerns in Hinduism are issues of purity and the danger of pollution. These concerns are enshrined not simply in the religious domain but throughout the social order established in India. The Indian caste system, segmenting the populace into a rigid hierarchical order, is justified through concepts of purity and contamination. Castes are social groupings that are hereditary and endogamous. A child is born into a given caste and retains that identity for life. For most Indians, caste membership determines marriage options, occupation, residence area within a village, and even styles of dress and features of language such as pronunciation and choice of vocabulary. The hundreds of Indian castes are grouped into four major segments ordered hierarchically: *brahman* (priests), *kshatriya* (warriors), *vaisya* (artisans and merchants), and *sudra* (peasants). The caste system itself is symbolized as a human body, each caste associated with its place of origin from the universal cosmic essence: brahman are the mouth or head, kshatriya are the arms, vaisya are the legs, and sudra are the feet (Koller, 1982). Just as each part of the body has its place and function, each caste must remain in its proper order and perform its legitimate functions. Symbolism of caste thus justifies occupational **segmentation**:

> The brahmans are priests and teachers, for with the mouth one recites and chants; the kshatriyas rule and protect, for with the arms one defends and administers; the vaisyas produce and trade goods, for the legs enable one to tend cattle, till fields, and transport goods; the sudras serve the other three classes just as the feet serve the rest of the body. (p. 70)

Differences in prestige and power of each caste are also justified by notions of ritual purity. Brahmans are considered the purest; sudras have least purity and in fact have the potential to pollute members of higher castes. One's purity is always in danger of being degraded by contact with polluting agents—namely, people, animals, foods, or objects that are impure. This system of belief explains the necessity of social barriers between members of different castes, and, of course, it justifies and consolidates the power of elites.

Social order and religion are interrelated also through the principle of *dharma*, entailing an individual's obligations, duties, and responsibilities. Dharma is "in its broadest sense . . . whatever it is right to do" (Koller, 1982, p. 62). One's aim in life is to fulfill dharma—that is, to do what is right. What is right to do is determined, in part, by who one is. People in each caste have their specific duties and must fulfill them to live right. Fulfilling dharma results in accumulation of spiritual merits that in turn eventually leads to escape from the cycle of reincarnation linking death and rebirth. Escape from the cycle allows one to leave the suffering imposed by bodily form and merge with cosmic existence.

In India's complex system of social place and of religiously sanctioned relationships and obligations, gender is a significant factor. As we discussed in Chapter 5, India is a patriarchal society where women are subordinated to men in every societal domain. Daughters live under the authority of their fathers, wives are subservient to their husbands, and widows are dependent on their sons or brothers. A woman's dharma, or essential duty, is to serve her husband. She must prepare food, attend to the upkeep of their house, fulfill other domestic tasks, and, most important, provide her husband with sons. In demeanor, she must be obedient and deferential to her elders and to all men.

Religious concepts of dharma, of doing what is right, support constructs of gender inequality. Through religion, social constructs are rendered timeless and unalterable. As in all societies, a social order that is said to have sacred origins cannot be resisted or questioned without shaking the foundations of religious belief.

A dilemma posed for Hindu men is that although they depend on women to perform necessary work entailed in social and biological reproduction, contact with women's bodies is potentially contaminating to a man. Menstrual blood is considered to be one of the most polluting substances. Therefore, women are strictly secluded during their menstrual periods. Menstruating women must remain in a separate porch or room in the house and refrain from handling food, clothing, or any objects that other members of their household might come into contact with. They are even contaminating to their own children, although a nursing mother can continue to feed her baby because mother's milk is considered a purifying substance. The potential for pollution, then, is counteracted by the purifying force of mother's milk.

Women's bodies must also be controlled by strictures on their sexuality. Chastity is essential for girls prior to marriage; wives' fidelity to husbands is one of their major duties (dharma). Once again, social obligations are

Hindu religious festivals reinforce the beliefs and social order of India's rigidly patriarchal society.

enshrined in religious doctrine, and therefore wrongdoers are threatened with supernatural punishment.

Hindu Deities

Although Hindu belief symbolizes dangers derived from women's sexuality, it also presents a positive, protective, and life-sustaining image of women through goddesses that themselves frequently incorporate the two aspects of women into one being. Most Hindu deities, whether female or male, are thought of as composites of many different attributes or aspects. In one form, they may be kind and helpful; in another, they are cruel and vengeful. For example, the "Hindu Great Goddess . . . takes many forms, both benign and malevolent" (Preston, 1985, p. 10). Each form has her own name and attributes:

> As Saraswati she is the symbol of learning and culture. In her manifestation as Laksmi she represents good fortune, wealth and luxury. When she is Kali or Durga people both fear and respect her. In this aspect she is capable of great vengeance against those who would cross her. As Sitala the goddess she is able to either cause or cure diseases, particularly smallpox and cholera. (p. 10)

Of special significance is an association in Hinduism between the dual aspects of goddesses and their marital status. Goddesses in their benevolent, nurturing manifestations are depicted as faithful wives. In contrast, dangerous, vengeful goddesses are unmarried. This distinction implies that only when women's sexuality is controlled by men, as in marriage, are they benevolent. When they are independent and control their own sexual behavior, they are dangerous.

Hindu male deities are also complex, each having various manifestations and attributes. However, personalities of male deities are not related to their marital status. A message for humans, then, is that marriage does not affect men's behavior to the extent it affects women.

Marriage for deities, though, contrasts with marriage for humans. Although they may be married, each god and goddess has his or her own sphere of activity and functions independently. A goddess in her married aspect may be a faithful wife, but she is not subservient. She wields authority in her domain just as her husband controls his own actions.

The independence of Hindu goddesses is, of course, a radical departure from culturally sanctioned behavior of living women. Deities, then, are not representations of people even though they have anthropomorphic form and attributes of human personalities. Instead, gods and goddesses are symbols of universal cosmic essence. As married couples, they represent the dual nature of existence, male and female, stressed in Hindu belief.

Judaism

Hinduism is far from unique among religions associated with patriarchal cultures in its imposition of restrictions on women. Judaism also contains themes of purity and pollution and of dangers to men posed by contact with women. Menstruating women are considered ritually unclean and contaminating. Although they need not be secluded, they should not touch a man lest he become ritually impure as well. At the end of each menstrual period, a woman must take a purifying bath, or *mikva*, to cleanse herself and return to normal life.

Negative attitudes toward women condensed in Judaic doctrine are enacted in separation of the genders in synagogues. Men must protect themselves from sexual temptation by women. Negative attitudes are further made explicit in Orthodox men's morning prayers, containing the phrase, "Praised are you, O Lord our God, King of the Universe, who has not created me a woman." The Talmud, a collection of teachings of early Jewish philosophers, reflects dangers believed to stem from women's sexual impulses. According to the writings of Flavius Josephus, for example, women are "overcome by a spirit of fornication" that they cannot themselves control (Carmody, 1987, p. 193). Men therefore must exert control over women, not only to save women from destruction but to save society as well. Josephus also warned of threats posed by women because they "plot in their hearts against men." He did not speculate as to why women might plot against men.

Islam

Islamic doctrine developed, in part, from prior teachings derived from both Judaism and Christianity. It continues—and, in fact, intensifies—gender inequality. Subordination of women in Islamic culture is severe. Patriarchal control must be exerted against women to mute their sexual desires and counteract dangers to men posed by contamination from women.

The custom of *purdah*, or seclusion of women, is basic to Islamic practice. Ideally a woman should be secluded in her home, and particularly in separate quarters within the house, away from contact with men. If she appears in public, she must be veiled so as not to display any part of her body. Menstruating women are especially dangerous to men, who must therefore avoid any contact, tactile or visual, with them. While religious texts, especially the Koran, are sometimes ambiguous, they are usually interpreted "as clear mandates and have [been] legislated as such. . . . Phrases and verses that might be seen as favoring [veiling, seclusion of women, clitoridectomy] have often been interpreted as making them mandatory" (Molyneux, 1989, p. 200). Moreover, "there can be little doubt that the ideological ensemble that articulates women's inferiority in many Muslim societies *claims* a religious derivation and on the basis of this derivation establishes its legitimacy" (Molyneux, 1989, pp. 200–201; emphasis in original).

In Islamic belief, a theme often stressed is the danger to men derived from women's impurity. Only chaste women are pure; once they have had sexual intercourse, women lose their ability to control their sexual impulses, and order must be imposed by men. A woman's sexual fidelity is assured only if she is a virgin or if she is strictly secluded.

The Islamic version of Paradise contains an example of this emphasis on sexual purity. In Paradise, a man has a wife and seventy concubines, called *hur*. The *hur*, unlike real women, never menstruate and are perpetual virgins. In this realm of fantasy, even after a man has intercourse with a *hur*, her virginity returns.

Christianity

Christian doctrine, too, has, at various times in its history, been greatly concerned with notions of danger derived from women's sexuality. Although strict seclusion and physical separation of the genders is not part of Christian belief, visions of women as inherently evil, lustful, and destructive are encoded in numerous teachings. The sin associated with Eve is one of Christianity's dominating themes. As Tertullian, an early Christian philosopher, explicated:

> You [Eve] are the Devil's gateway. You are the unsealer of that forbidden tree. You are the first deserter of the divine law. You are she who persuaded him whom the Devil was not valiant enough to attack. You destroyed so easily God's image, man. On account of your desert, that is death, even the Son of God had to die. (quoted in Ruether, 1983, p. 168)

As punishment for Eve's sin of disobedience to God, she (and thereafter all women) must obey her husband. This edict is stated directly by God: "I will increase your labor and your pain, and in labor you shall bear children. You shall be eager for your husband, and he shall be your master" (Gen. 3:16). New Testament teachings continue the theme: "Wives, be subject to your husbands as to the Lord; for the man is the head of the woman, just as Christ also is the head of the Church . . . but just as the church is subject to Christ, so must women be to their husbands in everything" (Eph. 5:22–24). Finally, according to the Judeo-Christian creation story, 1 Corinthians (11:8–10) states, "For man did not originally spring from woman, but woman was made out of man; and man was not created for woman's sake, but woman for the sake of man."

Fears of women's sexuality directly contributed to the wave of witch-hunts in Europe and colonial America beginning in the fifteenth century and lasting into the eighteenth. As we noted in Chapter 8, several million people (85 percent of whom were women) were accused and executed as witches (Ehrenreich and English, 1978). One of the dominant beliefs about witches was that they indulged in wild sexual orgies. They were also accused of having intercourse with the devil. Images of witches were, in a sense, exaggerations of the sexuality, destructiveness, and disobedience symbolized by Eve.

Somewhat balancing the image of Eve is the Christian figure of Mary, the mother of Jesus Christ. Whereas Eve is selfish and uncontrolled, Mary is benevolent and nurturing. Significantly, she conceived Jesus without "sin"—that is, as a virgin. Although on the surface Mary may symbolize positive attributes of women and thus balance negative attributes of Eve, Mary is an unattainable ideal. She therefore cannot serve as a realistic embodiment of womanhood; rather, she is a standard against which all living women fall short. Women are the daughters of Eve, not of Mary.

Religion and Homosexuality

It should not be surprising that some of the religions that express fears of women's sexual desire also preach against homosexuality. The two prejudices are connected in their contradiction of the accepted model of sexuality as a coupling of a dominant male and a passive female. Just as religious texts express misogynist attitudes, homophobic prejudice is also easily discernible. Biblical passages condemn homosexual relations as violating divine laws, claiming that the sexual and social bond between a man and a woman is the only acceptable human pairing. For example, in a listing of vices, the Old Testament states, "Thou shalt not lie with mankind as with womankind: it is abomination" (Lev. 18:22). (Note, significantly, that the text is addressed to men.) Moreover, the penalty for homosexual relations is severe: "They shall surely be put to death; their blood shall be upon them" (Lev. 20:13). The New Testament repeats the condemnation of homosexuality, adding, "Those [evidently men] who lie with men will not inherit the Kingdom of God" (1 Cor. 6:9). Romans 1:24–32 elaborates on and criticizes the "impurities" and "unnatural" acts committed by men who have sex with men and similarly describes as "unnatural" sexual relations between women. Perpetrators are said to "deserve to die."

The attitude that sexual relations have only one proper purpose—namely, procreation—leads to homosexuality being deemed "unnatural" because conception and reproduction are obviously impossible outcomes. Because of the "unnaturalness" of homosexuality, society protects itself against homosexuals (who are by definition "unnatural" or "abnormal") by using the legal apparatus of the state to enforce adherence to "natural" laws or at least to punish those who violate them. Punishment of homosexual acts in some nations dominated by Judeo-Christian ideology consists even today of prison sentences (although in Israel, homosexual activity is no longer illegal). As recently as 1986, the U.S. Supreme Court, deciding in the case of *Bowers v. Hardwick*, upheld states' right to make private sexual relations (that is, sodomy) between consenting adult homosexuals a crime punishable by imprisonment. The Supreme Court majority ruled that the constitutional right to privacy is not relevant, and the due process clause of the Fourteenth Amendment does not grant homosexuals any "fundamental right to engage in acts of consensual sodomy" despite the objections of dissenting justices, who noted that Georgia's statute against sodomy is not uniformly applied because it is never invoked against consenting heterosexual couples (married or unmarried). In many Islamic countries, homosexual acts are met with more severe retribution, mimicking the opinions expressed in Leviticus and Romans that "they shall surely be put to death."

The reasoning espoused by Judeo-Christian-Islamic traditions and laws is based on a premise that is far from universal. Why does sexual activity have no legitimate purpose other than procreation? Differences between attitudes expressed by the trinity of Judaism, Christianity, and Islam and those reflected by Hindu social and religious practice turn precisely on this point. In Hindu society, homosexuality is regarded as one of the possible expressions of human desire. Hindu mythic stories portray both heterosexual and homosexual experience as natural and joyful, and Hindu mythic characters engage in sex for their personal pleasure. Hinduism's "sex-positive" (Nanda, 1990) mythology actually contradicts condemnation of homosexuality set down when Hindu moral laws were codified in the second century B.C., but, in fact, Indian society has always accepted homosexual activity as a human possibility. Contradictions also coexist between the mythological portrayal of the pleasure of sex and official Hindu fears of the contaminating effects of women on men. Perhaps contrasting messages about sexuality derive from the fact that official Hindu moral laws did not completely overwhelm local folk beliefs symbolized by the activities of deities and other mythic personages.

In fact, homosexual or transsexual behavior is depicted in numerous episodes in Hindu mythology. The pantheon of deities includes some who are sexually ambiguous, combining aspects of maleness and femaleness, or who transform themselves from one gender to the other. The god Vishnu, for example, transforms himself into a beautiful woman called Mohini so he can take back sacred nectar that had been stolen by demons. Samba, the son of Krishna (an incarnation of Vishnu), is a homosexual and transvestite, often dressing as a pregnant woman. Hindu deities and myths such as these are currently cited as the models for male homosexuals and transvestites who adopt a role as *hijras*, people thought of as "neither man nor woman." Although *hijras* are sometimes feared and ridiculed, they also are considered sacred, combining and mediating between female and male aspects believed to exist in all humans. Especially in North India, they perform important ritual functions, reciting blessings at homes after the birth of sons and ceremonially bestowing fertility at weddings.

In contrast to Judaism, Christianity, and Islam, which formally condemn homosexuality, and Hinduism, which tolerates and accepts it, the religious beliefs of the Etoro, a horticultural society in New Guinea, insist on male homosexual activity to ensure physical growth as well as to enhance physical and spiritual strength. Etoro attitudes concerning homosexuality cannot be divorced from their attitudes about heterosexuality, and both systems of sexuality are contextualized within their beliefs about spiritual essences and the ways in which these essences are either strengthened or weakened. According to Etoro religious notions, people have two forms of spirit within them: one, called *ausulubo*, is a kind of spirit double that resides within a person's body; the second, called *hame*, is formless but functions as the "animating principle and vital energy of human existence" (Kelly, 1976, p. 39). Because a person's energy and vitality derive from his or her *hame*, it is necessary to nurture and protect it so it will grow in strength and power. In fact, it must be strengthened because at birth only a small amount of *hame* is placed in a child, not enough to protect it for a long, healthy life. As people mature, they must try to augment their store of *hame* or life force. They must also protect it from potential sources of depletion.

Hame is principally diminished by one of two methods: witchcraft and sexual intercourse. Etoro witchcraft involves theft of a victim's *hame* through magical means. Sexual intercourse depletes a man's *hame* because, although *hame* resides in all parts of the body, it is thought to especially accumulate in semen. Therefore, men must guard expenditure of semen so as not to weaken their vitality and their resistance to disease and witchcraft.

Given these assumptions, many ritual taboos, mostly having to do with farming and trading cycles, prohibit heterosexual intercourse on what Kelly (1976) estimates to amount to some 205 to 260 days per year. But protection against depletion is not enough; because the Etoro also believe that boys lack the *hame*-containing semen in their youth, they can only acquire *hame* only by receiving semen from adult men. Boys are inseminated by orally consuming a man's semen after manipulating his penis to the point of ejaculation.

In contrast to men, women are thought (at least by men) to have a limited amount of *hame*, thus explaining their relative weakness compared to men. Of special note, Kelly reports that he was unable to obtain information concerning women's beliefs and activities because "a male anthropologist [cannot] develop an informant relationship with a female" (p. 47). However, although Etoro men claim that "only the women know what the women do," they believe that women engage in some form of homosexual activity through which adult women may transmit menstrual blood to young girls to initiate their reproductive capacity.

According to Kelly, Etoro men do not fear contact with women, having no concerns about contamination from menstrual blood or any other ill effects of association common elsewhere in New Guinea. It is heterosexual intercourse, not women as such, that is avoided because of its role in depleting a man's *hame*, and homosexual activity is practiced precisely because of its role in the acquisition and strengthening of a male's *hame*. Perhaps, though, we should not be too quick to accept Kelly's assessment that Etoro men do not fear contact with women. Even if it is true that they do not fear contamination, their particular beliefs about the weakening effects of sexual intercourse with women must be a symbolic transformation of a more general fear of women. (Women may have comparable fears of men that were not documented, given Kelly's inability to consult them.)

In any case, although the religious proscriptions and prescriptions of the beliefs of Jews, Christians, and Muslims are obviously vastly different from those of the Etoro, an identical process is involved in their development. Religious reasoning is everywhere logical given acceptance of a starting premise that in these (as well as many other) instances is seriously flawed. Whether a religion prohibits homosexuality because it is deemed to violate so-called natural laws of human desire or whether it insists on homosexuality because that practice is deemed to be the means of acquiring physical and spiritual strength, the result is that religious beliefs mold people's attitudes and behaviors by transmitting notions that are said (and believed) to be of divine origin.

THE IDENTITY OF GOD

The polytheistic spirit world of Hinduism is vastly different from the monotheistic vision of Judaism, Christianity, and Islam. In these three religions, there is only one god, and that god is depicted as male. Although there may be female mythic figures, such as Eve, Mary, and numerous women in biblical narratives, they do not have the same standing as the male god. God is the creator, all-knowing and all-powerful. No female is endowed with such attributes. The Christian figure of Jesus Christ presents somewhat of an enigma. Although he is definitely male, he has certain qualities that distinguish him markedly from Old Testament male heroes. Jesus is gentle, benevolent, nurturing, nonviolent, and emotional. He is introspective, even to the point of occasionally doubting himself. Additionally, of course, he sacrifices his own life for the good of others.

Controversy has arisen in the last several decades over the nature of Jesus and in fact of the identity and attributes of the supreme deity. According to some historians, portrayal of God as solely male is an alteration of original concepts about the deity. This argument is supported by a set of early Christian documents discovered in 1945 in a cave in northern Egypt. The documents consist of teachings, commentaries, and debates among theologians. They are Coptic translations dating from approximately A.D. 350 to 400. The time of their writing is a source of disagreement among modern scholars, but most suggest that the texts were probably set down by A.D. 150 (Pagels, 1981).

Some of the documents refer to God as a dyad with male and female attributes. For instance, the Apocryphon of John relates an interaction between Christ's disciple John and a vision of God. God says to John, "I am the one who is with you always. I am the Father; I am the Mother; I am the Son" (1.31–2.9; quoted in Pagels, 1981, p. 61). Another text quotes the Creator's words: "Let us make humanity . . . according to the image of God Father and Mother" (p. 67).

Among the documents are accounts of Jesus' life, providing some historians with examples of Jesus' positive attitudes toward women. He is regarded by some as having advocated equality of the genders. Statements advocating equality are also contained in the Bible. Galatians 3:28, for example, refers to the equality of the followers of Jesus, saying that "there is neither Jew nor Greek, there is neither bond nor free, there is neither male nor female: for you are all one in Christ Jesus." Similarly, possibility of direct religious experience and spiritual authority is given to both women and men, as in Acts 2:17: "I will pour out my Spirit upon all flesh, and your sons and your daughters shall prophesy."

In addition, early Christian texts support a contention that Mary Magdalene was one of Christ's disciples and, in fact, that she was preferred by him. The Gospel of Philip recounts rivalries between Jesus' male disciples and Mary Magdalene and states:

> The companion of the Savior is Mary Magdalene. But Christ loved her more than all the disciples. The rest of the disciples were offended. They said to him, "Why do you love her more than all of us?" The Savior answered and said to them, "Why do I not love you as I love her?" (63.32–64.5; quoted in Pagels, 1981, p. 77).

In Pistis Sophia ("Faith Wisdom"), when Mary relates to Jesus her hesitation to speak in the presence of the disciple Peter because of his dislike of her, Jesus responds that any man or woman who is inspired by the Spirit has the right to speak (Pagels, 1981). "Wisdom" itself was earlier identified with the Holy Spirit and formed part of the Christian Holy Trinity. Significantly, Wisdom (Sophia) was traditionally personified as female.

The Christian believers who presumably wrote the documents discovered in Egypt were condemned as heretics by church authorities in the second century A.D. They were especially condemned because they allowed women to participate actively in religious debates and rituals. For instance, Tertullian, an influential theologian in the formative years of consolidation of the Catholic Church, claimed, "These heretical women—how audacious they are! They have no modesty; they are bold enough to teach, to engage in argument, to enact exorcisms, to undertake cures, and, it may be, even to baptize!" (quoted in Pagels, 1981, p. 71).

Obliteration of positive images of women may have been a result of actions by Christian theologians as a means to consolidate their power within the church. If so, it may have been motivated as a reassertion of patriarchal control that Jesus' vision of an egalitarian society attempted to subvert.

WOMEN'S SPIRITUALITY

Some women within the religious community have begun to look for specifically female forms of worship and spirituality. They celebrate the religious concept of the Goddess, not viewed as a particular deity but rather as the embodiment or symbol of "the divine within women and all that is female in the universe" (Budapest, 1979, p. 272). The Goddess is a source of spiritual energy and knowledge, one that celebrates women's physical and spiritual selves. Worship or celebration of the Goddess is also an affirmation of women's connectedness to nature through the rhythms and cycles of their bodies and their life-creative potential.

The forces of life and nature that are now honored through the Goddess symbol were in fact features of ancient and traditional religions throughout the world. Riane Eisler (1987) has written concerning the interconnected historical denigration of women and female deities:

> It had to be established that the old powers that ruled the universe—as symbolized by the life-giving Chalice—had been replaced by newer and more powerful deities in whose hands the Blade was now supreme. And to this end, not only her earthly representative—woman—but the Goddess herself had to be pulled down from her exalted place. (p. 92)

It is to reaffirm and renew female powers both within all humans (women and men) and within the divine that the "women's spirituality movement" is principally addressed.

Others within the movement practice rituals of witchcraft based on continuities with the past as well as introduction of new ceremonies. Resurrecting the archaic form of the word for "witch," *wicce*, meaning "wise ones," followers of feminist witchcraft stress the ancient role of witches as sources of prophesy and healing. That is, wise women had divinely inspired knowledge that they used for positive goals in their lives and in the lives of community members. Modern practitioners similarly view their roles as life sustaining and fulfilling.

SPIRIT POSSESSION

Although cultural edicts transmitted through religious belief and inculcated in socialization processes convince most women to abide by the values and practices dominant in their societies, some women make use of options available in their religions to assert their autonomy. For instance, many religions provide alternatives to "normal" behavior in the form of beliefs in spirit possession. People possessed by spirits are, by definition, under the control of supernatural beings and therefore not responsible for their own actions or words. Relief from actual control by others in daily life may be a benefit derived from spirit possession.

For example, Stanley and Ruth Freed's (1967) study of a North Indian woman's experience as a victim of possession indicates that the ordeal can have positive social and emotional outcomes. The young woman, Daya, aged 15, was newly married and living in her husband's extended family household. She was subordinate in the household, under the authority of her mother-in-law and elder male affines. Daya had little emotional support from her husband and was also isolated from her natal family. In this social and emotional context, Daya was possessed by a ghost, manifested by feelings of intense cold, fainting spells, and verbal incoherence. Treatment by a local ritualist was mandated, and eventually the ghost was exorcised with promises of food and monetary offerings.

During her ordeal, Daya became the focus of household activity. No longer inconspicuous and dominated, her wants and needs were attended to. In a nonconscious way, she utilized features of local belief systems to carve out some respite for herself from household demands on her labor and from the sexual demands of her husband, who frightened her.

In some societies, spirit possession is associated with a closely integrated group experience. Among Muslims in northern Ethiopia, people believed to be possessed by *zar* spirits must join a *zar* society as part of their ritual treatment and cure. Possession is manifested by convulsive seizures and emotional apathy. A successful cure results in placating the *zar*, who thereafter remains dormant in its victim. Participation by all *zar* victims in annual collective rituals is necessary to maintain the cure (Messing, 1967).

Most targets of *zar* possession are married women. As is typical of Muslim communities, married women are intensely subordinated and isolated in their households, rarely even leaving their family compounds. They have little autonomy and are barred from assuming any valued public roles. Women who are possessed by *zar* spirits manage to escape their isolation and become the center of attention. In addition, because they must be initiated into the *zar* society and attend its rituals, their wishes to associate with others outside their households cannot be denied.

Membership in *zar* societies is lifelong and serves to establish important affectional bonds for women. According to Simon Messing (1967), "The *zar* cult functions as a form of group therapy. Chronic patients become devotees who form a close-knit social group in which they find security and recognition" (p. 292). Not only are individual needs fulfilled, but a sense of solidarity with others is also achieved.

Elizabeth Colson's (1969) study of the Tonga, traditionally a horticultural society in Zambia, compares the frequency of spirit possession in two Tongan groups differentiated by their economies and gender roles.

"Plateau Tonga" engage in farming, marketing, and cash cropping. Both women and men contribute productively, and both are able to maintain a degree of economic independence. Gender relations are generally egalitarian. In contrast, among "Valley Tonga," men are employed as laborers in local and distant towns, whereas women remain at home, dependent on money earned exclusively by men. Women's economic dependence on their husbands is used to justify their subordination and lack of social worth. Significantly, beliefs in spirit possession and participation in spirit cults is strong among Valley Tongan women, whereas it is weak among Plateau women. According to Colson, membership in spirit cults provides Valley Tongan women with a "subculture" that allows expression of their individuality.

Data from India, Ethiopia, and Zambia indicate a fairly common pattern of belief systems that, although they may be subsidiary within a culture's religion as a whole, do provide people with a means of counteracting normative expectations. Not surprisingly, this option is frequently chosen by women. I. M. Lewis (1971, 1986) contends that women may use beliefs and practices related to spirit possession as a form of protest against the subordinate position ordained for women in male-dominated societies. As support for his argument, Lewis reviews studies of such diverse peoples as Tungus in northern Siberia, Inuit of Arctic Canada, Manus of New Guinea, Haitians, Burmese, Zulus, Ethiopians, and Somalis. He also notes that beliefs in spirit possession have spread in Africa in tandem with the spread of Islam. As women's activities have been restricted and as their social status has declined, they have increasingly found relief through spirit possession and its social and personal aftermath.

> [Through spirit possession,] women and other depressed categories exert mystical pressures on their superiors in circumstances of deprivation and frustration when few other sanctions are available to them. . . . [Spirit possession can be] a means both of obliquely airing their grievances and of gaining some satisfaction. (Lewis, 1986, pp. 34, 39)

A study by Aihwa Ong (1987) of young women industrial workers in Malaysia provides evidence of a use of beliefs in spirit possession to counteract an oppressive work situation. Ong documents several episodes among employees of an electronics plant that began when a worker was possessed by a ghost in the factory. The initial incident spread to claims by other workers of similar experiences, eventually leading to mass evacuation of the plant by the entire workforce. Employees refused to return to the factory until it was ritually purified by an exorcist. Ong concludes that the women employed religious beliefs common among rural Malaysians to voice their protests against regimentation of work in the factory. As young women in a patriarchal culture, they used one of the few means at their disposal to resist authority and assert some degree of independence.

RITUALISTS

Asian Shaman

Research in Korea and Japan documents the preponderance of women both as targets of spirit possession and as ritualists dealing with possession. For instance, Kokan Sasaki (1984) notes that in Japan, "women are considered more easily possessed or influenced by the supernatural than are men" (p. 81). Episodes of possession are usually antedated by prior emotional stress resulting from any of numerous factors, including death in one's family, divorce, sudden economic failures, and prolonged illness. Sasaki infers that the experience of emotional outburst and attendant nurturing responses by others to victims of spirit possession are means of "dissolving personal frustration and maintaining social order" (p. 80). Women are more vulnerable than men because of Japanese beliefs that women are "more easily susceptible to symptoms of mental and physical abnormalities" in response to personal and familial crises (p. 82).

Because victims of spirit possession often become ritualists as part of their cure, women predominate as certain types of religious specialists in several Asian countries. They typically become shamans, whose duties are to conduct rites for spirits, to intervene between spirits and humans, and to diagnose and cure ailments, especially those caused by harmful spirits or angry ancestors.

For example, most Korean shaman, or *mansin*, are women. Their clients are also predominantly women who seek intercession with spirits, relief from illnesses suffered by household members, and supernatural protection during pregnancy and birthing (Kendall, 1984).

In a detailed study of Korean *mansin*, Youngsook Kim Harvey (1979) offers insights into personal and social meanings of their roles as ritualists in a patriarchal society. *Mansin* usually begin their careers as victims of spirit possession. Indeed, being possessed is interpreted as a call from the supernatural, signaling a spirit's wish that the target become a shaman. Acceptance of the role ordained by spirits is part of one's cure. A woman who becomes a mansin cannot be held responsible for her choice of role because the calling has come directly from the supernatural. As Harvey notes, women are able to alter their individual roles and positions in their households with full supernatural sanction. For instance, spirits are believed to be jealous of their victims' relationships with family members, especially with their husbands, and want to establish exclusive bonds between spirit and victim. A woman can therefore justify disinterest in or refusal to fulfill domestic tasks and/or to avoid sexual activity with her husband by claiming she is following dictates of spirit beings.

Harvey (1979) discerns several personal attributes shared by the six *mansin* she studied in depth. These include intelligence, imagination, self-reliance, sensitivity to covert cues of others, and strategic interpersonal skills. Of equal significance, prior to experiencing episodes of spirit possession, each *mansin* had endured "severe conflicts between their individual sense of self and the definition of the domestic role they had to accept and enact" (p. 236). Through the experience and consequences of spirit possession,

> [Korean women can] make the transition from being helpless housewives trapped in the impasse of a double bind to being shamans who transcend the natural (culturally defined) limits of being a woman, who have a system of social support independent of their domestic role, who have economic autonomy, and who have clear professional identities in the larger society. (p. 237)

A *mansin*'s family members may resent the new roles she assumes, but they are constrained from interference by a web of cultural beliefs related to the etiology and outcome of spirit possession. Because spirits are thought to possess individuals who have been made vulnerable due to stress or suffering caused by others, a victim's family is obliquely blamed for causing the episodes. The family therefore cannot legitimately object to her subsequent behavior and in fact must comply with her wishes to avoid further disaster.

> [Constellations of Korean beliefs about spirit possession thus provide a] mechanism whereby the oppressed can turn the table on the oppressors with the latter's cooperation and support while the shaman role provides a mechanism for maintaining it or, failing that, of permitting the shaman a viable means of escaping from the family situation. The most remarkable feature of these strategies is that they are face-saving, blame-free pathways out of impasses, which leave no individual burdened with guilt. (Harvey, 1979, p. 239)

Specialization of Men's and Women's Ritual Roles

In many societies, ritual roles are allocated differentially to women and men. Such a division of labor in religious domains may reflect divisions of labor by gender in other societal activities. It may also express and reinforce cultural notions of the distinctiveness and separation of men and women.

In band and tribal cultures, duties of ritualists frequently include healing because these peoples typically believe that illness can be caused by supernatural beings and forces. Practitioners therefore often merge curing and ritual acts. Different techniques or contrasting spheres of expertise may be allotted to men or women healers. For instance, among Inuit of the North American Arctic, women tend to heal by administering medicinal and massage treatments in conjunction with the use of prayers and protective charms. Men, however, specialize in healing through spirit mediums. Male shamans are experts in conducting intensely dramatic public rites in which they send their spirit helpers to do battle with witches and malevolent supernatural beings responsible for a patient's illness. During a community ritual, a shaman enters a trance state and vocalizes the calls of his spirit helpers as well as responses of a multitude of supernatural beings.

One could, perhaps, note certain parallels between Inuit ritual performance and subsistence activities. Just as Inuit men fulfill publicly prominent roles, risking their lives hunting in a dangerous environment, shaman enact public rituals highlighted by dramatic encounters with malevolent beings in which the shaman's life is believed to be in jeopardy. Similarly, just as productive work of Inuit women is more private and individualized, their healing roles are performed in domestic and personal contexts.

In some cultures, associations between religious roles and dynamics of gender relations may be quite explicit. Among the Yanomamo (see the discussion in chapter 3), for example, women are barred from assuming duties as ritualists just as they are denied access to any other socially valued roles. In contrast, the balanced and interdependent equality of the genders legitimated in Iroquois society is reflected in the allocation of religious specialties. Iroquois communal ceremonies are planned and organized by a group of fifty "Keepers of the Faith," evenly divided between women and men. Although differentiation of Iroquoian ritual tasks prevails in some spheres, many ritual roles, such as healing and fortune-telling, may be performed by men and women.

In complex, stratified societies, especially where official religions support the power of elites, men tend to monopolize roles within religious organizations. Hierarchical relations in the society as a whole are usually replicated in religious structures and are dominated by men. Women may occupy subsidiary positions and perform adjunctive or supportive functions. Catholic nuns, Greek or Roman virgin priestesses, and African oracles and diviners are examples of women who enter religious service but are relegated to secondary roles. However, even in patriarchal cultures where men control official religious positions, women often fulfill ritual functions in their local communities and particularly in their households. In some cases, familial ceremonies may be allocated according to gender consistent with domestic divisions of activity. For instance, in traditional Korean households, men perform rituals dedicated to ancestors. These duties cohere with principles of patrilineal descent, linking a man to his ancestors. A man conducts rites for his parents and grandparents in his home and at graves of the deceased (Lee, 1984).

Korean women also have ritual responsibilities, but their duties revolve around ceremonial care of a multitude of spirits believed to reside in and protect one's house and its occupants. In addition to a House Master god who is situated in a central area of the house, each section has its specific protector. These deities include a Fire God, located in the kitchen; a House Site God, residing in the yard; a Storage God; a Toilet God; and a Gate God. Women perform rites to honor these numerous deities, thanking them for their protection and requesting continued aid.

In Western societies, some women are presently attempting to be accepted as religious practitioners within the organized structure of their religions. Protestant and Jewish women have made small inroads into the once exclusively male domains of ministers and rabbis. Women have been ordained in a few Protestant denominations since the middle of the nineteenth century. Their numbers, however, remain relatively small, as noted in Table 9.1.

TABLE 9.1 Women Clergy in the United States, 1981

Denomination	First Ordination of Women	Percentage of Women Clergy
United Church of Christ	1853	7.8
American Baptist Churches	100+ years ago	1.8
Disciples of Christ	1888	4.8
United Presbyterian	1956	4.5
United Methodist	1956	3.6
Presbyterian, U.S.A.	1964	3.3
Lutheran Church in America	1970	2.6
American Lutheran Church	1970	1.3
Episcopal Church	1977	3.4

SOURCE: Virginia Sapiro, *Women in American Society* (Palo Alto, CA: Mayfield, 1986), p. 187.

Ordination of women in Judaism commenced in 1972 among Reform Jews. Since then, Conservative women rabbis have also been ordained. Among Orthodox Jews and Catholics, women continue to be barred from the clergy.

Several studies document the effects on congregations of the presence of women religious practitioners. For instance, a Congregational minister made the following observation:

> By their very presence in ministry, women open up questions of vulnerability for those in the congregation. The unexpected, the unanticipated opens up queries not previously addressed with the same intensity. Seeing women in a role that has been traditionally viewed as male raises questions about many assumptions, attitudes, and presuppositions upon which people have built their lives and sometimes their faith. (Gill, 1985; quoted in Briggs, 1987, p. 415)

These professional observations are echoed by Jewish congregants, as reported by Rabbi Laura Geller:

> Rabbi, I [a middle-aged woman] can't tell you how different I felt about services because you are a woman. For the first time in my life I felt as though I could learn those prayers, I could study Torah, I could lead this service.... Knowing that made me feel much more involved in the service—much more involved with Judaism. Also, it made me think about God in a different way. (Geller, 1983; quoted in Sapiro, 1986, p. 189)

Despite positive sentiments on the part of some clergy and their congregants, resistance to ordaining women remains strong, particularly in more conservative sects. Although strong antifeminist biases obviously exist in Western religions, some women founded important religious movements and sects within Christianity in the eighteenth and nineteenth centuries. For example, the Seventh-Day Adventist Church was founded by Ellen White; the Shaker religion (a group closely associated with the Quakers in its origin) was established by Ann Lee; and the Church of Christ, Scientist, was founded by Mary Baker Eddy. Although these groups were all established and initially led by charismatic women, only the Shakers questioned the basic Christian tenet of gender inequality. And even they accepted prevailing views of the legitimacy of an economic division of labor that associated women with domestic tasks and nurturing roles.

In total, according to the US Bureau of Labor Statistics reporting for 2004, 15 percent of all currently employed clergy were women (US Bureau of Labor Statistics, Table 11). The number of women varies considerably in different denominations. Conservative Christian groups such as the Southern Baptists and the Eastern Orthodox Church do not ordain women. Some Protestant groups allow women to serve in some pastoral roles but do not ordain them as ministers. In other groups, the number of women ministers has grown considerably in the last several decades. For example, the number of women ordained as clergy in the American Baptist Church grew from 157 to 712; in the Episcopal Churches of the USA from 94 to 1394, and in the United Methodist Church from 319 to 3003 (Religious Tolerance.org, 2006). And women constitute more than 50 percent of the 853 pastors serving in the Unitarian Universalist Church (Dodd, 2000).

THE LANGUAGE OF RELIGION

In addition to attempts by women to gain acceptance as specialists, some women and men have addressed the significant issue of religious language. The ways deities are described and the wordings employed in religious teachings contribute to creating gender constructs that perpetuate inequality between men and women. Recent revisions of the Bible and other religious tracts have altered some basic images. For example, in 1983 the National Council of Churches published its *Inclusive Lectionary*, advocating substitutions of gender-neutral words for traditional male terminology. Among recommendations were changing "son of God" to "child of God" and "Lord" to "Sovereign," as well as including reference to God as "Our Father and Mother." Such alterations have been adopted by some denominations, although controversy and objections continue.

Not only does the language of religion cast and foster distinctions between the genders, but everyday language and communicative behavior similarly reflect and reinforce constructs of gender that tend to emphasize men as primary or normative and women as secondary or deviant. In Chapter 10, we turn our attention to this critical area of concern.

SUMMARY

Gender constructs prevalent in a culture are often directly and powerfully expressed through religious beliefs and practices. Myths of creation and the identity and actions of creators reveal and reinforce a people's accepted notions of the proper place of women and men in society. Expectations of an individual's behavior and evaluations of his or her worthiness are also implied or directly stated in religious teachings.

In societies where gender equality prevails, male and female supernatural beings have similar roles. In societies where men dominate women, male creators and male spirits monopolize important roles in the supernatural realm and in relations with humans.

Religious teachings concerning pollution and sexuality also reflect and reinforce societal attitudes toward women and men. In societies characterized by male dominance, women are often thought to be ritually impure and contaminating. Women's sexuality is considered dangerous and must be controlled by men.

Attitudes toward the worthiness of the genders are manifested in the ability of women and men to function as ritual practitioners. In societies where women are denied access to roles accorded high prestige, they are usually barred from formal roles as ritualists. However, they may perform rituals associated with their households. In some cultures where women are socially and politically dominated by men, they are allowed religious and emotional expression through spirit possession.

In sum, in societies where women and men have similar opportunities for religious participation and where religious beliefs and symbols express the worthiness of all people, both men and women can find empowerment and validation through their religions. In contrast, where women are denied access to ritual functions and where myths and practices express their unworthiness, religion can be an instrument of patriarchal control.

REFERENCES

BONVILLAIN, NANCY. n.d. Mohawk fieldnotes, Akwesasne (St. Regis) Reserve, 1969–1991.

BRIGGS, SHEILA. 1987. "Women and religion." In *Analyzing Gender* (ed. Beth Hess and Myra Marx Ferree). Newbury Park, CA: Sage, pp. 408–441.

BUCKLEY, THOMAS. 1993. "Menstruation and the power of Yurok women." In *Gender in Cross-Cultural Perspective* (ed. Caroline Brettell and Carolyn Sargent). Upper Saddle River, NJ: Prentice Hall, pp. 133–148.

BUDAPEST, Z. E. 1979. "Self blessing ritual." In *Womanspirit Rising: A Feminist Reader in Religion* (ed. Carol Christ and Judith Plaskow). San Francisco: Harper & Row, pp. 269–272.

CARMODY, DENISE. 1987. "Judaism." In *Women in World Religions* (ed. Arvind Sharma). Albany: State University of New York Press, pp. 183–207.

COLSON, ELIZABETH. 1969. "Spirit possession among the Tonga of Zambia." In *Spirit Mediumship and Society in Africa* (ed. J. Beattie and J. Middleton). London: Routledge & Kegan Paul, pp. 69–103.

COVARRUBIAS, MIGUEL. 1938. *Island of Bali.* New York: Knopf.

DODD, D. AILEEN. 2000. "Women Clergy Changing Face of Unitarian Church." Miami Herald, February 15, 2000.

EHRENREICH, BARBARA, and DEIRDRE ENGLISH. 1978. *For Her Own Good: 150 Years of the Experts' Advice to Women.* New York: Doubleday Anchor.

EISLER, RIANE. 1987. *The Chalice and the Blade: Our History, Our Future.* San Francisco: Harper & Row.

FREED, STANLEY, and RUTH FREED. 1967. "Spirit possession as illness in a North Indian village." In *Magic, Witchcraft and Curing* (ed. John Middleton). Garden City, NY: Natural History Press, pp. 295–320.

GEERTZ, CLIFFORD. 1973. *The Interpretation of Cultures.* New York: Basic Books.

GELLER, LAURA. 1983. "Reactions to a woman rabbi." In *On Being a Jewish Feminist* (ed. Susannah Heschel). New York: Schocken, pp. 210–213.

GILL, B. 1985. "A ministry of presence." In *Women Ministers: How Women Are Redefining Traditional Roles* (ed. Judith Weidman). San Francisco: Harper & Row.

HARVEY, YOUNGSOOK KIM. 1979. *Six Korean Women: The Socialization of Shamans.* St. Paul, MN: West.

KELLY, RAYMOND. 1976. "Witchcraft and sexual relations: An exploration in the social and semantic implications of the structure of belief." In *Man and Woman in the New Guinea Highlands* (ed. Paula Brown and G. Buchbinder). Washington D.C.: American Anthropological Association, Special Publication no. 8, pp. 36–53.

KENDALL, LAUREL. 1984. "Korean shaminism: Women's rites and a Chinese comparison." In *Religion and the Family in East Asia* (ed. George DeVos and Takao Sofue). Berkeley: University of California Press, pp. 57–74.

KOLLER, JOHN. 1982. *The Indian Way.* New York: Macmillan.

LEE, KWANG KYU. 1984. "Family and religion in traditional and contemporary Korea." In *Religion and the Family in East Asia* (ed. George DeVos and Takao Sofue). Berkeley: University of California Press, pp. 185–200.

LEWIS, I. M. 1971. *Ecstatic Religion.* New York: Penguin.

———. 1986. *Religion in Context: Cults and Charisma.* New York: Cambridge University Press.

MESSING, SIMON. 1967. "Group therapy and social status in the Zar cult of Ethiopia." In *Magic, Witchcraft and Curing* (ed. John Middleton) Garden City, NY: Natural History Press, pp. 285–294.

MOLYNEUX, MAXINE. 1989. "Legal reform and socialist revolution in South Yemen: Women and the family." In *Promissory Notes: Women in the Transition to Socialism* (ed. Sonia Kruks et al.). New York: Monthly Review Press, pp. 193–214.

MURPHY, YOLANDA, and ROBERT MURPHY. 1973. *Women of the Forest.* New York: Columbia University Press.

NANDA, SERENA. 1990. *Neither Man nor Woman: The Hijras of India.* Belmont, CA: Wadsworth.

ONG, AIHWA. 1987. *Spirits of Resistance and Capitalist Discipline: Factory Women in Malaysia.* Albany: State University of New York Press.

PAGELS, ELAINE. 1981. *The Gnostic Gospels.* New York: Vintage.

PRESTON, JAMES. 1985. *Cult of the Goddess: Social and Religious Change in a Hindu Temple.* Prospect Heights, IL: Waveland.

Religious Tolerance.org. 2006. "Female Clergy in Eastern Orthodox Churches, Protestant Denominations, and Other Religions." www.religioustolerance.org/femclrg4.htm.

RUETHER, ROSEMARY. 1983. *Sexism and God-Talk: Toward a Feminist Theology.* Boston: Beacon.

SANDAY, PEGGY. 1981. *Female Power and Male Dominance: On the Origins of Sexual Inequality.* New York: Cambridge University Press.

SAPIRO, VIRGINIA. 1986. *Women in American Society.* Palo Alto, CA: Mayfield.

SASAKI, KOKAN. 1984. "Spirit possession as an indigenous religion in Japan and Okinawa." In *Religion and the Family in East Asia* (ed. George DeVos and Takao Sofue). Berkeley: University of California Press, pp. 75–84.

TOCANTINS, ANTONIO. 1959. *Studies on the Mundurucu Tribe* (trans. A. Brunel). New Haven, CT: HRAF Press. (Original work published 1877)

U.S. BUREAU OF LABOR STATISTICS. 2006. Table and then. Employed persons by detailed occupation and sex.

CHAPTER 10

Gender and Language

Concepts of gender are used by societies to transform female and male human beings into social participants as women and men, assigning them roles and according them cultural value. As we have seen, this process involves expectations and evaluations of behavior, entailing societal attitudes about women's and men's proper work roles and their participation in family and community life. Gender constructs also delineate modes of demeanor considered proper for women and men, assigning each a range of appropriate styles of communicative behavior. In this chapter, we will review research concerning the ways that men and women speak and interact.

It is probably a universal fact that all cultures contain differences in how men and women communicate because in all cultures, the genders are socially distinguished. Wherever societal distinctions are made among community members, linguistic and stylistic variations arise to reflect and reinforce existing segmentation. However, difference itself is neutral; it is the contrast in how behavior is evaluated that is socially significant.

It is useful to distinguish between languages with gender-exclusive patterns, in which women and men always use linguistic alternatives appropriate to their own gender, and languages having patterns of gender preference, in which men and women exhibit different statistical frequencies in their use of socially marked linguistic forms. We will begin by reviewing data of the first type of language and then proceed to the second. We will conclude the chapter with an examination of words and constructions in a number of languages that demonstrate the ways that languages encode and transmit cultural attitudes about women and men.

GENDER-EXCLUSIVE PATTERNS

The earliest known documentation of exclusive gender differences in speech are seventeenth-century reports of native Carib people living on islands of the Lesser Antilles. Early European statements claimed that Carib men and women spoke different languages. This is clearly impossible since, if they did, husbands and wives, parents and children, would not have been able to communicate. It turns out, however, that there were a number of vocabulary differences in the speech of the two genders. Some of these denoted kinship relations, such as "my father" was *youmaan* in men's speech and *noukouchili* in women's speech (Jespersen, 1922, p. 238). This pattern is not unusual; many languages have distinct kinship terms used by male or female speakers. Another category of gender-related words referred to some body parts, possibly in recognition of physical differences between women and men. The remaining words denoted the following: friend, enemy, joy, work, war, house, garden, bed, poison, tree, sun, moon, sea, and earth (Jespersen, 1922, p. 238, citing Rochefort, *Histoire naturelle et morale des Iles Antilles*, 1665).

More reliable documentation of gender-exclusive linguistic patterns has been generated by research beginning in the early twentieth century. Such studies detail pronunciation differences applying to particular sounds. In Chukchee, a language spoken by native people in Siberia, some words are distinguished by men's use of consonants *č* and *r* and women's use of *š*. For example, for the construction meaning "by a buck," men say *čumnata*, whereas women say *šumnata* (Bogoras, 1922, p. 665).

According to Waldemar Bogoras (1922), women and men employ each other's pronunciations when they quote a statement made by the other gender in storytelling or personal narrative. However, he states, "In ordinary conversation, the pronunciation of men is considered as unbecoming a woman" (p. 665). This comment indicates that Chukchees gave social evaluations to gender-appropriate behavior, although we should be wary of taking the statement at face value because Bogoras did not specify his sources or context for the remark. Of perhaps equal interest, Bogoras revealed his own bias regarding gender patterns when he noted in discussing consonant replacements that "the sounds *č* and *r* are quite frequent; so that the speech of women, with its ever-recurring *š*, sounds quite peculiar, and is not easily understood by an inexperienced ear" (p. 665). This kind of statement, taking male behavior as the norm and interpreting female behavior as deviant or "peculiar," is not at all unusual in (male) discussions of gender differences.

Studies of several Native American languages have documented gender distinctions. For example, in Yana, a language spoken in California, complex differences in pronunciation and formation of words obtain between women's and men's speech (Sapir, 1929). Most Yana words have male and female forms, derived through various procedures. If the male form of a word is basic, then females reduce or eliminate the final syllable; if the female form is basic, then males add a final syllable. The system is quite complex, and rules vary depending on the length and type of word. As an illustration, men add the syllable *-na* to monosyllabic nouns used by women; for example, *ya* (person) becomes *yana*.

According to Edward Sapir (1929), male forms of speech are used by men when talking to other men. Female speech is used by women talking to either women or men and by men to women. Women, however, use male words when quoting a male speaker. Noting that "male" speech is an exclusive marker of male interaction, Sapir attempts to explain Yana linguistic differences in sociocultural terms—certainly a laudable goal, but one wonders whether his explanation reveals an American bias rather than a Yana perspective: "Possibly the reduced female forms constitute a conventionalized symbolism of the less considered or ceremonious status of women in the community. Men, in dealing with men, speak fully and deliberately; where women are concerned, one prefers a clipped style of utterance!" (p. 212).

Gender differences have been documented in some Native American languages spoken in the southeastern United States (Haas, 1944). For example, in Koasati, contrasts of pronunciation in male and female speech affected various classes of words depending on the structure of the word. Koasati men and women used each other's speech when quoting a speaker or formerly when correcting a child's speech to reinforce gender-appropriate styles. Women's speech, however, was evidently on the decline by midcentury: Haas (1944) notes that "only middle-aged and elderly women use the women's form, while younger women are now using the form characteristic of men's speech" (p. 146). Even so, one of Haas's male informants said that he thought women's speech to be "better" than men's. Since Haas did not pursue this issue in her writing, it is impossible to know precisely what the speaker meant by his remark.

The disappearance of female forms of speech in favor of male forms has been documented in other Native American languages, including Hitchiti (Southeast), Biloxi (Midwest), and Gros Ventre (northern Plains) (see Flannery, 1946; Gatschet, 1884; Haas, 1944). This process of replacement, more than the linguistic differences themselves, indicates gender stratification. While gender-specific styles demonstrate social differentiation, they do not necessarily imply a hierarchical relationship between women and men. But when one style is consistently replaced by the other, status and value distinctions between men and women can be assumed. Such distinctions have increased in many native cultures along with other aspects of assimilation to Euro-American society. Gender segmentation certainly existed in earlier aboriginal native cultures, but it seems to have stressed complementary roles more often than unequal status relations.

Although differences in pronunciation have been studied in relatively few languages, it is reasonable to assume that such patterns exist or existed elsewhere. Gender-exclusive usages may have gone unnoticed by linguists, particularly if they dealt only with either male or female speakers. Moreover, processes of change, similar to those documented in Native America, may well have obscured or eliminated gender differentiation previously encoded in other languages.

Hints about the possibility of ideological struggle in gender-exclusive styles are provided by Chiquita, spoken by native people in Bolivia. In women's speech, all nouns are treated in identical fashion, but in men's speech, nouns are divided into two classes that are marked grammatically. One class consists of nouns referring to men and supernatural beings; the other consists of all other nouns (reported in Bodine, 1975a). Men's speech therefore links the category of "male" to that of supernatural beings. This style is employed by men only when speaking to other men; women never use it, and it is never used in speech to them. Ann Bodine (1975a) speculates that "Chiquita men have tried to use language to symbolically elevate themselves, but . . . Chiquita women have refused to go along with it" (p. 144). This assessment is consistent with the fact that social conflicts are often revealed in linguistic forms and styles. Struggle over ideological issues is frequently exhibited in and through language. Use of a particular form can demonstrate a social attitude just as refusal to use that form can signify a rejection of implied cultural meaning.

All the examples documenting differences in pronunciation and vocabulary are actually rather restricted when viewed in terms of each linguistic system as a whole. They involve either a small number of sounds or a handful of words. They do not alter the fundamental character of a language. Nevertheless, gender-exclusive forms have great social significance, reflecting and reinforcing cultural constructs of gender dichotomy.

LINGUISTIC AND STYLISTIC PREFERENCES

Most languages do not have exclusive forms used by men and women but instead show differences in the frequencies with which women and men employ particular alternatives of pronunciation and grammar. These are stylistic choices made on the basis of cultural norms that assign as appropriate certain kinds of communicative behavior to men and women. We will begin discussion of language usage with data from English and then examine research from several other languages.

Gender Differences in English

Pronunciation.   Except for some regional variations, speakers of English make use of the same inventory of sounds, but there are differences in the frequencies with which men and women use particular consonants and vowels. In general, women tend to employ sounds that are socially perceived as "standard" or "prestige" forms, whereas men are more likely to use "nonstandard" pronunciations. We should note two additional factors producing linguistic variation, those of class and contextual or situational style. That is, members of higher classes tend to use standard sounds, whereas lower-class speakers employ nonstandard forms. Also, in formal contexts, most speakers regularly shift to standard pronunciations. Studies reveal that many sounds in English are sensitive to these characteristics. For example, gender-related patterns have been found in pronunciation of *-ing*, the progressive suffix on verbs. Relevant variants are *-ɪŋ* ("-ing") and *-ɪn* ("-in"), as in *rʌnɪŋ* (running) or *rʌnɪn* (runnin). In a study of speakers in Norwich, England, members of the higher class (both men and women) tended to use standard *-ɪŋ*, whereas lower-class speakers used *-ɪn* (Trudgill, 1972). In formal contexts, most speakers regularly shift to standard pronunciations. Within class and context, women employ standard features at greater frequencies than do men. Women exhibit marked style shifting, significantly increasing their use of *-ɪŋ* as contexts become more formal (Trudgill, 1972, p. 182).

Gender differences in Norwich were particularly significant for the highest and lowest social groups. Middle-class women used standard pronunciation all the time, whereas middle-class men used nonstandard pronunciations in casual speech about one-third of the time. At the lower end of class segmentation, men used nonstandard *-ɪn* completely in all contexts except the "most formal style," whereas women in the lowest group began to shift to standard *-ɪŋ* in "formal style."

Gender-appropriate patterns of pronunciation are learned quite early in life, as demonstrated by a study of children in a small New England town (Fischer, 1958). The children ranged in age from 3 to 10 years. Context was relevant: Children tended to employ standard *-ɪŋ* more when responding to formal questionnaires than when in casual play. However, in all contexts, girls used standard pronunciations more often than did boys.

Studies of the variable of "postvocalic /-r/" has been analyzed in several American dialects in relation to gender differences. The term *postvocalic /-r/* refers to the pronunciation or omission of the consonant /-r/ following a vowel in the same word (for example, *car; card*). Gender has been revealed as related to the use of postvocalic /-r/ among white speakers in North Carolina: Levine and Crockett (1967) presented subjects with two kinds of lists to be read aloud. One list was made up of sentences containing words with the targeted /-r/ feature. The second was composed of words to be spoken in isolation. Men's and women's sentence readings did not differ, but women showed a marked increase in pronouncing /-r/ in word lists. It is this "net increase" to isolated words that is of most significance, reflecting women's greater sensitivity to prestige norms by their increased use of the prestige variable in a context where more attention is given to speech.

An additional study demonstrated that African American speakers follow the same patterns as do whites. Investigations of black English in Detroit indicate that gender has an impact on variables of pronunciation, again given class and contextual parameters (Wolfram, 1969). In this speech community, women use more of the prestige postvocalic /-r/ than do men. Similar gender-differentiated pronunciations are attested among Detroit speakers for other phonological variables as well, including deletion of standard *th* at the ends of words (for example, *tooth*) or between vowels (*nothing*) or its replacement with the consonant *t*.

These studies support the contention that variants of pronunciation act, in part, as markers of gender. Whether the research has been conducted among children, among speakers of American or British regional dialects, or among African Americans or whites, the conclusions are identical: Females exhibit greater use of standard and prestige prounciations than do males of similar age or social or racial groups. In studies that take account of context, females demonstrate quicker and sharper stylistic shifting toward prestige norms in increasingly formal styles. One explanation for these patterns is that women are more conscious of prestige norms and strive to use them because they are critically judged by their social self-presentation. They are socialized to behave in ways considered polite and refined. Aware of strong social sanction if they do not conform, women use linguistic style as one manifestation of their "proper" behavior. Women's use of careful pronunciations reflects their insecurity in a hierarchical system of gender differentiation in which they are culturally relegated to second place.

Peter Trudgill (1972) has developed another explanation of gender differences that is compatible with the one just offerred. He introduced the concept of "covert prestige" to account for the fact that men exhibit less standard pronunciations and less style shifting toward the standard. Although standard language is given overt social prestige, shown by comments about one's own or another's speech, a competing norm gives "covert prestige" to male behavior that rejects the standard. In other words, men and women are acting in accordance with different norms. An important indication of this is found in self-reports about one's own speech. Trudgill's subjects were given self-evaluation tests, asking them to specify which of two sounds they used, each set paired for standard and nonstandard pronunciations. Results of these tests demonstrate a tendency for women to claim greater use of standard pronunciations, whereas men tend to claim greater use of the nonstandard than actually realized in their speech. While women claim to produce pronunciations having overt prestige, men model their behavior purposely, although nonconsciously, toward nonstandard forms having covert prestige.

Trudgill (1972) also notes an interesting link between masculinity and working-class behavior, exhibited by patterns of male self-reports. Nonstandard pronunciations that men often claim to use are stereotypical traits of working-class speech. In a significant finding, no differences are shown in men's self-reports when disaggregated for class so that middle-class men are just as likely to claim nonstandard speech as are working-class men.

This observation raises additional questions about sociocultural models of gender. Perhaps an explanation lies in the complexities of gender dichotomization. Given that women are socialized to behave with propriety and politeness (reflected by "middle-class" careful speech), and given a system of gender stratification in which men are privileged and men who act like women are strongly criticized, men consciously or unconsciously strive toward speech norms that reject styles associated with women. Because women model their behavior on "middle-class" styles, then, men covertly prefer "working-class" speech. Therefore, both women and men choose linguistic styles to reflect gender identity.

Intonation. Intonational patterns are crucial components in differentiating how people sound. Intonation is not linked to one particular segment of speech but rather is a constellation of rhythm, volume, and voice pitch that overlays utterances. It is heard by listeners as relative changes in these "prosodic" features rather than as absolute qualities.

Some intriguing research has investigated differences in female/male intonational patterns and has discovered cues people use in evaluating others' speech. In general, women use more dynamic intonational contours than men. They employ a wider range of pitches within their repertory and a more rapid and marked shift in volume and velocity. Sally McConnell-Ginet (1983) notes that dynamic patterns are interpreted as indicating emotionality and natural impulses, whereas usage of narrow intonational ranges is taken as evidence of control and restraint (pp. 76–77). This is primarily a cultural evaluation of speech behavior, although it may have physiological correlates since internal emotion has an impact on respiration and on muscular tension or relaxation that may be manifested, in part, in intonational dynamism. By employing more monotonic styles, men are perceived as being in control of their emotions, whereas women are seen as more expressive. "Masculine speech melodies can be heard as metaphors for control and feminine speech melodies as uncontrolled" (p. 82).

Intonational patterns may also serve pragmatic functions. McConnell-Ginet (1983) suggests that women's frequent changes in pitch and volume

> may serve the important function of attracting and holding the listener's attention. Women may need this device more than men because of their relative powerlessness and their frequent contact with young children who are not yet socialized to attend reliably to verbal signals. (p. 83)

Studies of intonational patterns suggest that women and men employ sentence contours in distinctive ways in some linguistic or interactional contexts. For instance, women may employ rising pitch at the end of declarative statements, whereas men use a steady or lowering pitch. The rising-pitch variant is interpreted as a questioning contour, which, according to some linguists such as Robin Lakoff (1975, p. 17), leads to women's self-presentation as hesitant, uncertain, and nonassertive. Other linguists, including McConnell-Ginet (1983) and Pamela Fishman (1983), focus on pragmatic functions of rising-pitch or questioning contours. They suggest that because addressees usually respond to questions, women attempt to secure a reaction from listeners by using rising-pitch rhythms.

Grammatical Variants. Although research dealing with gender differences in pronunciation consistently demonstrates similar trends, studies of gender-related grammatical alternatives are often problematic. Part of the problem may be the small samples selected in research projects. Another factor is more difficult to address: Grammatical options may be chosen depending not only on speaker's gender but also on the addressee, context, and speaker's intentions and goals. Because speaking is an activity that achieves personal and interpersonal goals, motivations for stylistic choice are difficult to disentangle. It is not sufficient to count examples of occurrences of a particular grammatical feature; rather, it is necessary to place that feature in overall contexts of discourse. Attention to situational context and the speaker's purpose therefore may reveal actual meanings of grammatical variation. With these cautions in mind, we can turn to examining some of the relevant research and debates dealing with gender and grammar.

Gender differences have been found in the usage of nonstandard grammatical constructions by adolescent girls and boys in a working-class district of Reading, England (Cheshire, 1982, pp. 153–154). Eleven linguistic features were targeted, among them, use of present tense -s with plural subjects ("We goes shopping on Saturdays); multiple negation ("I'm *not* going *nowhere*"); *what*, replacing *who, whom, which*, and *that* ("Are you the boy *what's* just come?"); and use of *ain't* instead of *haven't* or *isn't.*

In the Reading community, boys consistently employed nonstandard grammatical constructions at higher frequencies than did girls (p. 163). The Reading data are compatible with studies of pronunciation discussed earlier that similarly demonstrate a strong association between gender and style: females use more standard and prestige features, whereas males prefer nonstandard forms.

Lakoff (1975) points out, from anecdotal evidence, that a number of grammatical patterns appear in women's speech more frequently than in men's. Of the sentence constructions she discusses, the one receiving the most subsequent attention is the "tag-question." Tag-questions are sentences in which a speaker makes a declarative statement and adds on a "tag" in the form of a question about their assertion, as in "Jane came home, didn't she?" or "It's cold in here, isn't it?" Lakoff states that women use tag-questions as a signal of their reluctance to make direct assertions. They "can avoid committing [themselves] and thereby avoid coming into conflict with the addressee" (pp. 16–17). Although such deferential style can be favorably evaluated, it can also be perceived as indicating the speaker's uncertainty and lack of definite opinions.

Some studies (for example, Dubois and Crouch, 1975) of actual behavior demonstrate no clear gender preferences for the use of tag-questions, but others indicate the critical necessity of considering context and speakers' goals on linguistic choice. Gender differences in the employment of tag-questions may be related to their diverse interactional functions. A useful distinction is between "modal" and "affective" tags (Holmes, 1984, p. 53). *Modals* request information from the addressee or request that the latter confirm a statement about which the speaker is unsure. Janet Holmes (1984) calls these "speaker-oriented" because they function to supplement the speaker's knowledge, as in "She's coming around noon, isn't she?" *Affective* tags are "addressee-oriented," indicating the speaker's interest in or concern for addressees. One class of affective tags functions as "softeners" to mitigate or soften the force of a command or criticism: "Open the oven door for me, could you?" or "You're driving rather fast, aren't you?" A second class of affective tags is termed "facilitative" and indicates the speaker's desire to engage the addressee in continuing conversation: "Still working hard at your office, are you?" or "The hen's brown, isn't it?" (p. 55). These tags are essentially mechanisms to establish turns of conversation between interlocutors. They invite an addressee to build on a topic offerred by current speaker; thus, they "facilitate" conversation.

After differentiating among the functions of tags, Holmes (1984) discovered gender-related patterns in their usage (p. 54). Men more often use tags for "speaker-oriented" goals, to obtain or confirm information for themselves, whereas women more often use tags for "addressee-oriented" goals, particularly as strategies to engage addressees in talk. (Recall a similar possible function of women's use of rising or questioning intonational contours.)

By taking account of interactional meaning, Holmes's research demonstrates the inadequacy of simply tabulating occurrences of form without attending to functions of discourse. Another study of tags pointed out their use in asymmetrical status interactions (Cameron, McAlinden, and O'Leary, 1988). Deborah Cameron and her colleagues (1988) recorded television and radio talk-show and classroom programs and noted differences in "powerful" (such as medical expert, teacher, program host) and "powerless" roles (client, student, program guests). Sampling included a balance between women and men in each asymmetrical role. Although they found that women used more tags than men, the numbers were not significant (61 and 55, respectively). However, role "power" seemed to function as a determinant in the kind of tag employed. Using Holmes's terminology for classifying tags, Cameron and colleagues found that "powerful" participants employed "affective" tags, whereas "powerless" speakers preferred "modal" tags (p. 89).

Although status asymmetry is an operative factor in use of tags, gender also is significant. Cameron and her colleagues do not discuss gender differences in the asymmetrical roles, but an examination of their data demonstrates support for Holmes's (1984) findings; that is, powerful men are more likely than powerful women to employ modal tags (18 percent versus 5 percent), and, contrastingly, powerful women are more likely than powerful men to use affective tags (80 percent versus 52 percent).

Several studies have noted women's tendency to use more "hedge words" in discourse than men do. *Hedges* are words or expressions that covertly comment on assertions in one's statements: "*Perhaps* we *could try* fixing it"; "I've been *sort of wondering whether* I should go"; or "*Well*, I *guess* it's *approximately* four feet high." These constructions mark a speaker's uncertainty about the validity of his or her statement. By using hedge words, the speaker creates an impression of indecisiveness and lack of clarity. Because females are socialized to defer to others and avoid conflict, they choose to state opinions interspersed with hedges to minimize confrontation with an addressee who may hold a different view. In addition, making assertions in a tentative style allows speakers to modify or retract statements if they are challenged. But women who conform to social and communicative etiquette by avoiding a display of self-assertion are then often criticized for imprecision and uncertainty.

Hedges also function to "express the speaker's attitude to the addressee, i.e. to signal affective meaning"—for example, "*Well,* I *think* George is a *bit er perhaps* foolish" (Holmes, 1984, p. 48). This statement was made by a woman commenting on the behavior of her friend's husband. By hedging the assertion that George is foolish, the speaker demonstrated concern for the addressee instead of making a blunt criticism.

Using hedges as part of a politeness strategy is invoked not simply by gender but also by status and context. Note the following excerpt from an interviewer's questioning of the prime minister of New Zealand: "I *had the feeling* that with all the talk about the future that *perhaps* some of the Ministers were not talking *quite so strongly* in an election year context and I *wondered whether perhaps* you were surprised that . . . " (quoted in Holmes, 1984, p. 49).

To test the relative weight of gender, status, and context on stylistic choice, Faye Crosby and Linda Nyquist (1977) measured usage by women and men of what they call the "female register" (p. 314), based on Lakoff's (1975) characterization of women's speech. As they point out, the female register can be used by either women or men:

> The distinguishing feature of the female register is not that it is used exclusively by women but rather that it embodies the female role in our society. The female register is both expressive (e.g. polite rather than direct and informative) and non-assertive. Both of these attributes are central aspects of the stereotyped feminine role in our culture. (p. 314)

Traits included hedges, tag questions, intensifiers (*so*) and politeness formulas (*please, thank you*). Crosby and Nyquist discovered that among people familiar with each other, women more often produced speech conforming to the female register. However, in dyadic relations involving people of different status, subordinate men and women were likely to use the female register. Subordinates (and women in general) are expected to behave politely and show deference to higher-status people. Females learn deferential styles as part of their socialization and employ them in most interactions. Through these processes linking style, gender, and status, cultural models of personal and gender images are reinforced and justified.

Conversational Style.   Much of the research investigating options women and men use when participating in talk reveals pragmatic alternatives in conversational turns taken by speakers, in the introduction and control of topics, and in mechanisms of signaling active listenership. Studies tend to demonstrate that women are especially sensitive to their coparticipants' interests, or *face,* to use Brown and Levinson's (1987) term.

One cultural stereotype of the genders is that women are more talkative than men. However, an experiment aimed at measuring verbosity (amount of talk) demonstrated the opposite pattern. Male and female college students were presented with three pictures by Albrecht Dürer, a fifteenth-century Flemish artist, and were asked to describe the drawings as thoroughly as possible, taking as much time as they liked (Swacker, 1975). Results showed striking gender differences. The mean time for all three pictures was 13.0 minutes for males and only 3.17 for females (Swacker, 1975, p. 80). Choosing only the second description, men's speaking length averaged 333.41 seconds, whereas women's averaged 96.0 seconds. Verbosity differed significantly, but rather than confirming the stereotype of talkative women, male speakers talked more. In the face of evidence about men's verbosity, Cheris Kramer (1975) suggests that because females are socialized to defer to their coconversationalists, "perhaps a 'talkative' woman is one who does talk as much as a man" (p. 47).

In actual (rather than experimental) settings, men also tend to be more talkative than women. Observation of conversation in university faculty meetings revealed that the speaking turns of male teachers were from 1G to nearly 4 times longer than those of females (Edelsky, 1981, p. 415). Greater formality of topic and presentation style of meetings was correlated with lengthening men's contributions and shortening those of women. In more relaxed, give-and-take exchanges, women's and men's turns were equalized.

Context and content are determinants of patterns of talk. In some encounters, men are more silent than women, particularly in regard to discussion of emotions. Jack Sattel (1983) contends that men's tendency toward emotional inexpressiveness or unwillingness to talk about affect either with women or with other men stems from their desire to maintain and assert power. "Keeping cool, keeping distant as others challenge you or make demands upon you, is a strategy for keeping the upper hand" (p. 120). It functions as part of competitive displays of dominance since "to not say anything is to say something very important indeed: that the battle is to be fought by [his] rules and when [he] chooses to fight" (p. 122). This tactic is particularly effective when used in interactions with women because of women's tendencies for emotional self-disclosure.

Two important studies by Candace West and Don Zimmerman (1983; Zimmerman and West, 1975) investigated conversation between two speakers, focusing on instances of one speaker's turn limited or interrupted by a coparticipant. An *interruption* is an instance of one speaker beginning his or her turn before the current speaker has concluded. An interruption differs significantly from an *overlap*, which is simultaneous speech at or near the end of the current speaker's turn. Both in casual conversations between people who knew each other and in experimental situations involving college students who were previously unacquainted, Zimmerman and West (1975) found a marked difference in patterns of overlap and interruption in same-sex and cross-sex conversations. In the former, overlaps and interruptions were evenly distributed, each speaker contributing approximately the same number, but

TABLE 10.1   **Patterns of Conversation**

INTERRUPTIONS AND OVERLAPS IN TWENTY SAME-SEX CONVERSATIONS

	1st Speaker	2nd Speaker	Total
Interruptions	43% (3)	57% (4)	100% (7)
Overlaps	55% (12)	45% (10)	100% (22)

INTERRUPTIONS AND OVERLAPS IN ELEVEN CROSS-SEX CONVERSATIONS

	Males	Females	Total
Interruptions	96% (46)	4% (2)	100% (48)
Overlaps	100% (9)	———	100% (9)

SOURCE: Don Zimmerman and Candace West, 1975, p. 115–116.

in cross-sex conversations, almost all errors and intrusions were initiated by men. Table 10.1 presents data obtained in the first study (1975, pp. 115, 116).

In addition to marked gender differences in cross-sex conversations, another significant fact displayed in Table 10.1 is that in same-sex interactions, most conversational errors are overlaps (minor mistakes of timing), whereas in interactions between men and women, most intrusions are interruptions (violations of current speakers' turns). Exercise of power by male participants therefore seems to be an operative principle in many cross-sex encounters. Because they frequently lead to changes in topics establishing the interests of the interrupter, interruptions function as tactics to exert control over topics of conversation.

In research designed to test hypotheses concerning relative influences of gender and occupational status on the frequency of interruption, Nicola Woods (1988) tape-recorded triadic interactions in work settings involving male and female supervisors and subordinates. She discovered that gender is the most important determinant of behavior, although relative status is also significant:

> Essentially, while the power base of occupational status did influence the way that both men and women organised conversation, nevertheless even when women held high-status occupational positions male subordinates still organised the interaction in a way that allowed them to dominate the floor. (p. 149)

Powerful people (high-status and male) were more likely to interrupt coparticipants successfully and least likely to be interrupted in their turns. Moreover, when men intruded on other speakers, they were usually successful in gaining the floor (data indicate 17 out of 20 attempts), whereas women interrupters were not as likely to succeed (only 11 of 21 attempts) (p. 151). Men interrupt other speakers' turns even when the men are subordinates, particularly when subordinate to a higher-status woman. Women are the most likely targets of successful interruptions even when they are in higher-status

Women's and men's posture send different gender signals. Men typically sit with arms and legs apart; women try to take up as little space as possible.

positions. When the double factors of low status and female gender co-occur, women are especially likely to be interrupted.

In studies of talk between couples, Pamela Fishman (1983) collected 52 hours of tape recordings made in the homes of three white middle-class couples (with their approval and ability to censor material if they wished). Fishman's data reveal a "variety of strategies to insure, encourage and subvert conversation" (p. 93). On the whole, women do more of the interactional work, attempting to gain their partners' attention and responding to their partners' talk. Women tended to employ the following devices: "attention beginnings" ("This is interesting"), used twice as often by women as by men; "asking questions," used about two and a half times more often by women; and "asking 'D'ya know what?'" used by women twice as much as by men (pp. 94–95). In addition, Fishman discovered that although women suggested nearly twice as many topics as men, they were successful in establishing only about one-third of the accepted topics (p. 97). Men's topics were almost always accepted, whereas women had a failure ratio of nearly 2:1.

Gender Differences in Japanese

Japanese society is stratified in terms of class, gender, and age. Class status is marked by deference shown to people of wealth and high position in occupational hierarchies, men are accorded greater social status relative to women, and seniority both within households and communities bestows prestige on elders. Many aspects of the Japanese language encode these status differences between interlocutors. As in other complex societies, factors of region, class, and age, as well as gender, affect speakers' choice of linguistic features. According to Scott Clark, a researcher of Japanese language and culture, an important distinction in Japanese is that of a speaker's position relative to addressee and his or her attitude toward him- or herself and the addressee (1996, personal communication). Words and sentence constructions can be altered to reflect respect toward the addressee. Women tend to employ these markers with greater frequency than do men. In addition, Japanese speakers make use of some gender-exclusive linguistic distinctions. Other linguistic features are differentiated as frequencies in preferences for stylistic alternatives. Linguistic devices reflective of gender occur in pronunciation, construction of words and sentences, and vocabulary (Shibamoto, 1987, p. 27).

Gender styles are also exhibited in intonational patterns. As in the speech of American women, Japanese women's intonation is more dynamic than men's, manifested by sharper changes in pitch and stress. Japanese women also tend to use rising intonational contours at ends of sentences.

While friends greet each other warmly, strangers use a more formal handshake.

In addition to distinctions in pronunciation, Japanese men and women tend to employ different words for some objects, activities, or ideas. The differences are indicators of politeness; that is, women tend to use words marked for a greater degree of politeness, whereas men tend to employ less polite forms. Some examples are as follows (Shibamoto, 1987, p. 28):

Less Polite Forms	More Polite Forms	
Hara	*onaka*	(stomach)
Mizu	*ohiya*	(water)
Umai	*oisii*	(delicious)
Kuu	*taberu*	(eat)

The prefixes {o-} (as in the preceding list), {go-}, and {omi-} can be attached to any noun to render the speaking style more polite or refined. They can be used by either gender but occur in women's speech with much greater frequency. Relative status of speakers in any dyadic interaction is also significant. Both men and women use polite forms to superiors. However, because women are socially defined as inferior in status in many intergender interactions, they tend to use polite forms with greater frequency than do men (Clark, personal communication, 1996).

Additional linguistic evidence of underlying cultural images of gender in Japanese society is the distinctive use of words at the ends of sentences to mark speakers' attitudes. Common words or particles in women's speech indicate "femininity" {wa}, "childishness" {no}, and "uncertainty" {-te}. In contrast, words most often used by men are "emphatics" {ze}, {zo} (Shibamoto, 1987, pp. 33–34). Gender styles in usage can thus be compared to patterns of vocabulary or grammatical choices in English. As we have seen, Anglo-American women tend to mark their speech with indicators of mitigation and uncertainty (hedges, tags), whereas men tend to use more direct ("emphatic"?) constructions.

With an understanding of the possibilities of gender distinctions in Japanese, Janet Shibamoto (1987) conducted a study of casual conversations among friends to determine their actual usage. Self-recruited groups of three were observed and recorded. On the basis of these recordings, Shibamoto found that women consistently employed the polite features at much higher rates than did men, providing strong evidence of gender styles.

Gender Differences in Javanese

The language spoken in Java, an island in the Indonesian chain, is characterized by complex indicators of politeness and deference that occur in both women's and men's speech, but their use by each gender differs significantly. Of equal importance, gender-related usage is evaluated differently by men and women, raising a critical issue concerning the ability of groups of people to define their own or another's behavior.

Javanese culture contains conflicting notions of gender status. An egalitarian ideology stresses women's and men's autonomy. Women participate in work inside and outside the home, with primary responsibilities for managing household income and for hosting social gatherings. An important nationwide reflection of one attitude toward gender is the fact that girls and boys are equally educated. However, other societal norms restrict women's actual participation in public life; women do not usually fill roles of political or religious leadership, although they can occasionally function in place of their husbands (Smith-Hefner, 1988, pp. 538–539). Javanese culture, then, gives some support for gender equality, but in practice stratification exists in certain areas of life.

The Javanese language has two "speech levels," chosen by speakers to reflect their relationship with addressees. One is a familiar style called *ngoko* used with intimates and people of lower status, and the other is a formal style called *kromo* for speech to people who are unfamiliar, older, or of higher social status. In addition to this basic distinction, Javanese has some 250 to 300 markers indicating various degrees of respectful attitudes. One class "elevates the addressee" in relation to the speaker, and the second class "humbles the speaker" in relation to the addressee (Smith-Hefner, 1988, p. 540).

In Javanese, gender hierarchy is reflected in choices of vocabulary, differential use of speech levels and respect markers, and the interactional significance attached to such usage. One manifestation of hierarchical relationships between women and men is the pattern of address terms used by wives and husbands that indicates the lower status of wives. In Javanese households, a husband generally calls his wife by her first name, a nickname, or the kinship term *khik*, which means "younger sibling." In contrast, wives address their husbands with the kin term *mas*, "older brother" (Smith-Hefner, 1988, p. 541). Although Javanese husbands usually are older than their wives, this asymmetrical encoding of seniority is employed even by couples of similar ages who had addressed each other as equals before marriage, demonstrating that the marital relationship is symbolized as hierarchical. Additionally, wives are expected to speak to their husbands with styles replete with polite markers, whereas husbands use plainer, familiar forms of speech to their wives.

Nancy Smith-Hefner (1988) describes a significant contrast in evaluations of women's speech styles given by the two genders. Javanese men interpret women's style as an indication of their lower status within the family, whereas women assert that their speech reflects politeness and refinement. Smith-Hefner remarks, "It is very possible for speakers to interpret their own speech behavior in a given speech interaction as statusful, while the other interlocutor regards it as deferential" (pp. 540–541).

Women may speak in a polite and refined manner because of their roles in socializing children to speak in culturally appropriate styles reflecting a child's junior and subordinate status. Children must learn to use respectful speech to their elders and superiors, including fathers and older siblings. Mothers instruct children by using the desired respectful speech, and children model their own language after that of their mother (Smith-Hefner,

1988, pp. 542–543). Furthermore, since their activities take place predominantly within their households, women are not likely to develop a wide range of speech styles.

Demonstrations of politeness can be manifestations of several underlying cultural premises and therefore can have ambiguous meanings. Both Javanese men and women use polite speech, but they do so in different contexts. While women employ polite styles at home, men use elaborate polite speech in public roles as officials or ceremonial leaders. Their use of polite and respectful language can be coercive in a social system that compels people to act in a deferential manner toward their superiors. If a higher-status person speaks politely to someone of lower rank, the latter, in recognition of his or her actual lowly position, must use language that is even more respectful. "If social inferiors were to respond to a higher status interlocutor in a lower speech level than that with which they were addressed, they would be claiming in effect to be of a higher status than their interlocutor" (Smith-Hefner, 1988, p. 549). Such behavior would demean one's own position by causing an affront to one's superior.

Javanese language and culture, then, demonstrate a complex connection between politeness and gender. In many cultures, where polite speech is most typical of women (such as Anglo-American societies and Japan), it is interpreted as a signal of deference and lower status. However, in other societies (Java), polite speech is manipulated by men to convey messages of power and superiority.

Gender Differences in Malagasy

Malagasy is a Malayo-Polynesian language spoken in Madagascar, a large island in the Indian Ocean off the eastern coast of Africa. Studies of Malagasy speech usage reveal similarities to and differences from the Javanese example. Like Javanese, Malagasy has two types of speaking styles. One style is called *resaka*, an "everyday" or familiar form, and the other is *kabary*, a "ceremonial" or ritualized form. *Resaka* is used in daily interactions, discussions, and informal talk; *kabary* is used in rituals and formal secular situations such as expressing thanks to a host or sympathy to mourners (Keenan, 1974, p. 126). Interrelated with the two speech styles are cultural norms that emphasize values of behaving and speaking in nonconfrontational and nonargumentative manners in most social interactions. Manifestations of reserve and dignity of speech are positively perceived by both men and women, whereas direct and emotionally expressive language is disvalued.

Indirect speech is favored in everyday behavior, masking potentially unpleasant interactions. Forms of indirection are typical of everyday *resaka* speech, but *kabary* is characterized by even more elaborate use of mitigated means for issuing commands, making requests, and transmitting unpleasant news.

Gender segmentation becomes relevant in expectations of and approval/disapproval given to men's and women's behavior. In Malagasy culture, only men cultivate and use *kabary* speech. They employ mitigated speech, instructive proverbs, and other forms of polite allusion and innuendo.

In contrast, Malagasy women typically employ styles of everyday language that violate cultural norms of nonconfrontation. Women argue in public, criticize others' behavior, and express anger and disapproval. Although these strategies are socially denigrated, women's freedom to engage openly in conflict is sometimes exploited by men who encourage women to speak for them. When disputes arise or a man experiences an affront, his wife makes public accusations and criticisms on his behalf. All the while, the husband remains silent and seemingly aloof (Keenan, 1974, pp. 137–138). Elinor Keenan summarizes Malagasy gender-related behavior as follows:

> Women use one kind of power and men another. Women. . . discuss in detail the shameful behavior of others in daily gossip and speak openly of those who *mangala-baraka*, steal honor away from the family. They are associated with direct criticism and haggling in markets. They are able to put others on the spot, to confront others with possibly offensive information where men cannot or prefer not. Women tend to be direct and open in manner. Men tend to conduct themselves with discretion and subtlety. Women dominate situations where directness is called for. Men, on the other hand, dominate situations where indirectness is desirable. (p. 139)

Gender Differences in Kuna

A complex pattern of gender-differentiated communicative behavior exists among the Kuna, a native people of San Blas, Panama. Kuna society is basically egalitarian both in its social and political structure and in relationships between women and men. In theory, leadership roles in political and ritual activities can be held by either men or women, although in practice, female leaders are rare. Kuna people conceptualize economic and social responsibilities of women and men as distinct yet complementary and harmonious. Men are expected to supply their families with food obtained from farming and hunting; women perform domestic labor, including food preparation, child care, and other household duties. In addition, women's artistry in making *molas* (appliquéd cloth blouses) for market sale is highly prized and praised. These products are important not only in economic terms but also as valued symbols of Kuna ethnicity (Sherzer, 1987, pp. 95, 101). The traditional complementarity of gender roles is expressed in an excerpt from a ritual narrative:

> Rattlesnake says to his wife:
> "For you I will go hunting.
> For you I will kill an animal."
> Rattlesnake's wife responds:
> "You are going hunting for me.
> You will kill an animal for me.
> I will prepare your beverage for you." (Sherzer, 1987, p. 108)

Distinctions between women's and men's communicative behavior are manifested in speech genres associated with each. Some of these genres occur in public or ceremonial contexts; others take place in private, familial settings.

Each is typified by linguistic and topical characteristics that distinguish it from everyday speech. Men's genres include political oratory and ritual incantations. Two types of speaking occur at political gatherings: extemporaneous speeches and debates of community leaders and the formalized chanting of chiefs. These roles are nearly always held by men. Curing chants are performed by (usually) male specialists who gather medicines and administer them in rituals (Sherzer, 1987, pp. 102–103).

There is some overlap between women's and men's speaking roles. Women hold public political gatherings, too, mostly concerned with issues related to *mola* cooperatives. At these meetings, women make speeches, engage in debates, and express their opinions. Ritual speech is also performed by some women who recite curing chants taught to them by spirits in their dreams. But women's distinctive genres are lullabies and "tuneful weeping" chanted to dying and deceased relatives. These genres are similar in their focus on individual, family happenings (Sherzer, 1987, pp. 102–105).

According to Joel Sherzer (1987), the egalitarian and complementary division of labor in Kuna society is reflected in the division of speech genres generally performed by women or men. Although the genres are different, no single linguistic style is considered appropriate only to men or women. Each gender has occasion to employ elaborate, rhetorical styles replete with metaphor and symbolic allusions. Each also uses chanting and rhythmic patterns or tunes in certain contexts. Finally, both men and women speak directly and confidently when voicing their opinions (pp. 110–111).

In Kuna society, women and men are expected to perform different but complementary economic and social duties, and they are versed in different but complementary speech genres. Gifted speakers, whether they be women or men, are equally praised.

Communicative behavior of Kuna people contrasts with that of the Malagasy or Javanese. Whereas the latter sharply differentiate between men's and women's stylistic traits, the former make no absolute dichotomization of linguistic style. In addition, unlike the Malagasy and Javanese, the Kuna do not render more or less favorable evaluations to the speech of women or men. Both are highly regarded. It is tempting to conclude that attitudes toward speech and gender are related to the social structure of these societies. Hierarchical organization of status and gender relations among the Malagasy and Javanese is reflected in negative evaluations of women's speech and/or denial of women's access to status-enhancing styles that instead are reserved only for men. In contrast, the egalitarian social system of the Kuna is reflected in positive evaluations and prestige accorded to skilled verbal performers of both genders.

GENDER IMAGES IN LANGUAGES

Language is a vehicle for expressing cultural constructs or models, in part through the way people, activities, and ideas are named. Variations obviously abound in the linguistic forms where these images are encoded and in their cultural implications. In societies with entrenched gender stratification where women and their behavior are disvalued, inequalities in linguistic images comprise one manifestation of the denigration of women. By continual usage of words and expressions that demean females, speakers unconsciously (or consciously) reproduce and reinforce negative stereotypes. These stereotypes become internalized symbols for both genders, resulting in male attitudes toward females as "deviant" and female acceptance of negative self-assessments.

English

The English language encodes gender distinctions by labeling and talking about people. English creates a context for the interaction of genders with the term *opposite sex*. Certainly the sexes are different, but in what sense are they "opposite"? The word itself connotes a polarity, denying possibilities of overlap or congruence. It also implies conflict and antagonism.

Words that refer to human beings are often paired for female and male exemplars, but in ordinary usage, males precede and females appear in linguistic "second place." Some instances of this common ordering are *male and female, man and woman, he or she,* and *husband and wife.* Such pairing denotes the primary status of males because the order of linguistic components is generally of cognitive importance; that is, more salient elements usually occur earlier in sentences. Two counterexamples to the male + female ordering are *ladies and gentlemen* and *bride and groom.* The first is typically used in public formal situations in which polite speech is preferred; perhaps its use is akin to chivalrous behavior that often masks underlying power. The second, *bride and groom,* is also a conventionalized expression relevant in a formal ceremonial context. Note, however, that after the wedding, the couple is transformed from *bride and groom* to *husband and wife.* Variation in the usual ordering occurs in kin term pairs; for example, *mother and father* is as likely as *father and mother.* Perhaps this flexibility reflects individual choice based on attitudes toward relatives; it may also indicate social stereotypes of closer emotional bonds between children and their mothers.

The English language provides evidence of gender hierarchy in marital relationships, first in the traditional, although disappearing, formula "I now pronounce you man and wife," in which the male is labeled by his humanness but the female is defined in relation to her husband. Second, our culture decrees that women give up their "maiden" names at marriage and assume their husband's last name. A wife can be referred to by her husband's full name (first + last) with the preposed address term *Mrs.*—for example, "Mrs. John Smith." The couple can then be called "the Smiths" or even "the John Smiths," depriving the wife of her own identity. Finally, couples are frequently described by use of husband's name + "his wife," as in "John Smith and his wife." In such usages, the wife appears almost as a possession or appendage without an autonomous existence. A contrasting construction, "Jane Jones and her husband," has marked meaning and would typically occur only if special attention is given to "Jane Jones" for particular contextual or affective purposes.

Another symbolic reflection of females' subsidiary status is the possibility of deriving girls' names from male sources. "Feminine" endings *-a, -ette, -ine, -y* (or *-ie*) are thus added to male names (such as Roberta, Bernadette, Geraldine, or Stephanie). Any male name can idiosyncratically be converted into a girl's name by this procedure. The only boy's name obtained from a female source is Marion, which occurs rarely in contemporary American society but in any case has a special derivation, originating from the religious symbol of Mary.

In a further reflection of the semantics of gender, "feminine" suffixes *-ette* (or *-et*) and *-y* (or *-ie*) can function as diminutives (markers of smallness)—for example, *booklet* and *itsy-bitsy*. Diminutives carry related meanings of endearment, reflected in nicknames and affectionate or youthful versions of personal names, such as Cathy and Tommy. Although both girls and boys are addressed with these forms as children, males tend to outgrow their diminutive names (except among kin), whereas females often retain them throughout life.

The interaction of age and gender is also differentially marked for males and females in the terms *boy, girl, man,* and *woman*. Boys typically become men at roughly the age of adulthood, although exact demarcation of the change is often vague. But girls can remain girls long after they become adults. While it is true that this usage is unacceptable today among many people, it is still frequently employed. Comparable use of the word *boy* to refer to an adult man is restricted to certain regional varieties, as in the American South. These examples demonstrate that although the words *girl* and *boy* have definitions that might appear to be distinguished solely on the basis of gender, they actually have uses and implications that are quite different in recognition or denial of adult status.

Some sets of words for males and females illustrate another process of inequality in images of gender. Consider the following pairs: *lord/lady, sir/dame, master/mistress, king/queen, bachelor/spinster, governor/governess*. In each of these, there is one level of meaning that equates the paired individuals. But a critical process has affected females in a consistent manner. That process is often referred to as *semantic derogation*—that is, changes in meaning by which negative attributes become attached to senses of words. Semantic derogation of words for women has historically resulted in secondary meanings that typically demean or trivialize women and their activities or that emphasize their sexuality. The words *mistress* and *dame* exemplify words taking on sexual connotations, while *governess* is a trivialization. *Queen* also has a sexual semantic, although it is applied to men, rather than women, in a derogatory fashion. *Spinster* implies negation of sexuality, so that a spinster is not an "unmarried woman" in the same way that a *bachelor* is an "unmarried man." A *bachelor* is a man who is desirable as a potential husband, whereas a *spinster* is an undesirable mate. Because of this negative implication, the expression *bachelor girl* (or even *bachelorette*) has evolved.

The word *lady* has special complexities. In one of its uses, it retains polite, respectful implications of its origin. However, it also occurs in casual contexts as a label for a woman whose name is unknown to a speaker: "Hey, lady, move your car!" Perhaps its most interesting function is as a euphemism for "woman." The word *woman* needs a euphemistic replacement because it, too, has acquired sexual connotations. Compare the following (adapted from Lakoff, 1975, p. 26): "She's only twelve, but she already acts like a woman" and "She's only twelve, but she already acts like a lady." These sentences highlight two cultural images of females promulgated by our society: the first suggests her sexuality; the second encodes the polite and "proper" behavior expected of her.

The pair *woman/man* also deserves attention. *Woman* refers specifically and only to females, whereas *man* is used not only for males but for *people* in general, as in "mankind." Furthermore, *man* appears as a verb meaning "operate" or "control": "We need someone to man the elevator." The semantics of adjectives and adverbs based on *woman* and *man* demonstrate significant contrasts. Compare the following entries from the *Random House Dictionary of the English Language* (1987) for a succinct rendering of cultural symbols:

> MANLY, MANFUL, MANNISH mean having the traits that a culture regards as especially characteristic or ideally appropriate to adult men. MANLY is usually a term of approval, suggesting traits admired by society, such as determination, decisiveness and steadiness. MANFUL also a term of approval, stresses courage, strength and fortitude. MANNISH is most often used derogatorally in reference to traits, manners and accouterments of a woman that are thought to be more appropriate or typical of a man (e.g. a mannish abruptness in her speech). (p. 1170)
>
> WOMANLY, WOMANLIKE, WOMANISH mean having traits that a culture regards as especially characteristic or ideally appropriate to adult women. WOMANLY is usually a term of approval, suggesting the display of traits admired by society, such as self-possession, modesty, motherliness and calm competence. WOMANLIKE may be a neutral synonym or it may suggest mild disapproval. WOMANISH is usually disparaging, applied to a woman it suggests traits not generally socially approved. Applied to a man, it suggests traits culturally deemed inappropriate for men and to be found in women (e.g. a womanish shrillness in his speech). (p. 2185)

In addition, many English words are based on roots or compounds with *man, master,* or other male-oriented sources—for example, *bachelor's degree, bedfellow, brotherhood, forefather, fraternize, freshman, manpower, masterful, mastermind, patronize,* and *statesmanship* (Nilsen, 1977, p. 36).

As Muriel Schulz (1975) points out, many words associated with females that began with innocuous or even positive connotations have undergone processes of derogation, most often with sexual implications. For example, *hussy* is derived from Old English *huswife* (housewife), originally meaning "female head of household." It gradually came to mean "a rustic or rude woman" and finally "a lewd, brazen woman or a prostitute." The words *nymph* and *nymphet* were first endearments referring to "beautiful young girls or women" and then became euphemisms for prostitutes, finally meaning "a sexually precocious girl; a loose young woman." Semantic narrowing and derogation also affected the word *whore*, originally a polite term for "a lover of either sex." It then narrowed its referent only to women and degenerated in meaning as a label for prostitutes (Schulz, 1975, pp. 66–69).

Terms in black English similarly encode derogatory or trivialized meanings for females. In black English slang, most words for women emphasize physical characteristics, including variations in skin color (*redbone, spotlight, high yaller, pinky*) or apply animal terms to females (*fox, filly, butterfly*) (Scott, 1974, p. 220).

Generic He *and* Man.   One of the most frequently debated examples of linguistic favoritism toward males is the use of so-called *generic he* and *man* to refer to people without regard to gender. In some contexts, the masculine pronoun has a singular referent ("A child learns his reading skills in the first grade"), but in others it has underlying nonsingular semantic referents ("Everyone should take his coat"). Grammarians' insistence on *he* to denote indefinite person or people in general in sentences such as these dates to the eighteenth century (Bodine, 1975b). Prior to that time, the pronoun *they* and its variations were used for singular or plural indefinites and generics, as attested in writing and presumably in speaking. In a discussion of English pronouns, George McKnight (1928) collected quotations from no less than William Shakespeare's *Much Ado about Nothing*: "God send every one their heart's desire" and "Each leaning on their elbows and their hips." Later authors continued to use *they* forms, including Jane Austen in *Mansfield Park*: "Nobody put themselves out of the way" and "Each had their favorite" (pp. 197, 528). Although people are taught in school to use *he* in formal speech and especially in writing, even casual observation shows that speakers employ *they* in ordinary conversation. Finally, in addition to overlooking semantics and failing to hear actual speech, the grammarian approach ignores the existence of a linguistic context in which only the pronoun *they* can occur. In tag-questions, when the subject of a statement is a generic or indefinite person, the underlying replacement pronoun surfacing in the tag is clearly *they*: "Everyone left the room, didn't they?" Even when an indefinite noun refers to a single individual, its pronoun representation is *they*: "Somebody left the room, didn't they?"

Experimental tests of people's reaction to sentences with generic *he* or *his* consistently support the contention that *he* or *his* is never gender-neutral but contains some of its basic masculine sense. Underlying notions of gender associated with generic pronouns have been ascertained in several experiments conducted by Donald MacKay (1983). One study presented male and female college students at the University of California at Los Angeles with sentences containing pronouns such as "When a botanist is in the field, he is usually working." Test sentences were mixed, so that some referred to stereotypically "male-related" antecedents (engineer, doctor), others to "female-related" antecedents (model, secretary), and others to "neutral" referents (student, musician). Subjects were asked to decide quickly whether sentences could refer to females. Results revealed that 95 percent of respondents (10 women and 10 men) judged that the sentences could not refer to females. Male and female subjects had similar reactions. Whether sentences had gender-stereotyped or neutral antecedents had no impact on rates of exclusion of females (p. 41).

In a related experiment, MacKay (1983) presented subjects with sentences identical to those in the first test except that pronoun referents were omitted, such as "A botanist who is in the field is usually working." Results were strikingly different: 43 percent of the subjects (as compared to 95 percent in the prior study) responded that the sentences could not refer to females. Moreover, identity of antecedents became significant. Subjects thought that 68 percent of sentences with male antecedents, 42 percent with neutral antecedents, and 19 percent with female antecedents could not refer to females. Finally, sex of subject also affected judgments: men were more likely than women to restrict sentences to male referents. MacKay concludes, "These findings suggest that adding prescriptive *he* dramatically increases the exclusion of females and washes out effects of subject sex and nature of the antecedent" (p. 42).

Supposedly neutral interpretations of *man* face similar problems. This word has an interesting history, beginning in Old English to mean "a human being" with no gender association. Separate unambiguous words existed to denote females, *wif,* and males, *wer* or *carl. Man* could combine with these to refer specifically to adults of their respective genders: *wifman* and *werman* or *carlman. Wifman* eventually became *woman,* and male designators were replaced by the semantic narrowing of *man* to refer to males (Miller and Swift, 1977, p. 25). Experimental studies have revealed that even when *man* is used in generic contexts, male images surface. In one experiment, Joseph Schneider and Sally Hacker (1973) asked college students to select and submit illustrations for an introductory sociology textbook. Each of two groups was presented with alternative titles for chapters, one phrased as "Urban Man," "Political Man," or "Social Man" and the second as "Urban Life," "Political Behavior," or "Society." In the first group, 64 percent of respondents chose only photographs of males, whereas half of those in the second group chose male-only illustrations (p. 14). The likelihood of including women in photographs varied for different titles. The only one in which women appeared in a majority of illustrations was "Social Man," in which case a male was typically shown surrounded by females in contexts of social or leisure activities. The title "Urban Man" elicited nearly equal representation, "males only" in 55 percent of illustrations. For "Political Man," "Industrial Man," and "Economic Man" chapters, women appeared in a small minority of photographs (p. 16). On the basis of their study, Schneider and Hacker assert that uses of *man* as a label "may serve to 'filter-out' women, largely by suggesting imagery appropriate only or primarily to men" (p. 12).

In response to concerns over the symbolic preference for males expressed covertly and overtly by words such as *man, he,* and *his,* advocates of gender equality in language have suggested replacing these words with genuinely neutral forms such as *person, people,* and *she or he, his or her.* A curious development has occurred in the case of *-person* when used in compounds such as *spokesperson* and *chairperson.* In common usage, there is currently a tendency to restrict *-person* nouns to females, retaining *-man* for males. *Spokesperson* therefore has replaced *spokeswoman* but not *spokesman.* A similar failure to get the point of an advocated change concerns address designations of *Ms./Miss/Mrs.* The title *Ms.* was introduced to eliminate labeling women according to their marital status. Although intended as a replacement for both *Miss* and *Mrs.,* it has come to be employed (if at all) to refer to unmarried women.

Data uncovered in analyses of English linguistic forms indicate a pervasive, covert ascription of positive and normative qualities to males and negative or secondary ones to females. Continual repetition of English words and expressions, as both speakers and hearers, reinforces cultural evaluations that enhance males' status and disvalue females. These judgments do not originate in the language but arise linguistically to express, supplement, and justify entrenched cultural constructs.

French

French contains a singular pronoun, *on,* that is not marked for gender. It occurs in sentences with indefinite or generic subjects, such as "Ici *on* parle français" ("*One, they, people* speak French here").

Since French possessive pronouns (comparable to *his* and *her*) agree in grammatical gender with possessed nouns rather than sex of possessors, the English problem of using the masculine form *his* or the neutral *his or her* or *their* does not arise. However, even though French signals neutrality in singular pronouns, bias in favor of males surfaces in plurals. Whereas English has one plural third-person pronoun not marked for gender (*they*), French has two, distinguishing female and male aggregates—*elles* and *ils,* respectively. Inequality is demonstrated when reference is made to mixed-sex groups: *elles* is used only if all members are female; *ils* occurs for all-male or male-female groups. Therefore, the presence of even one male is enough to tip the semantic balance toward the masculine pronoun.

German

The German language classifies nouns as masculine, feminine, or neuter and marks articles, adjectives, and verbs to agree with the gender of nouns. Whereas grammatically feminine nouns for persons refer only to females, some masculine nouns can be used for either males or females. The masculine nouns *der Burgen* (citizen), *der Wahler* (voter), and *der Kunde* (customer) may have male or female referents (Hellinger, 1989, p. 275).

Feminine subjects can co-occur with masculine nouns, but masculine subjects never co-occur with feminine nouns (Hellinger, 1989). For example, one can say, "He/She is a second Einstein" (*Er/Sie ist ein zweiter Einstein*), but one cannot say, "He is a second Marie Curie" (*Er ist eine zweite Marie Curie*).

Some masculine nouns can be transformed by feminizing suffixes to refer to females, such as *der Lehrer* ("the teacher") and *die Lehrerin* ("the woman teacher") (Hellinger, 1989, p. 276). The words without suffixes symbolize men as neutral or expected exemplars, whereas the feminine words symbolize women as derivative or unusual.

Finally, in the few cases in which feminine nouns are used for men, they take on derogatory meanings. The words *die Memme, die Tucke*, and *die Tunte*, all meaning "coward," are used as insults in referring to homosexuals (Hellinger, 1989, p. 275).

Spanish

In some pairs of words having male/female counterparts, the Spanish language encodes sexual semantics for females. Compare the following words and their meanings (Hellinger 1989, pp. 277, 284–285):

Masculine	Feminine
un reo, "a criminal"	*una rea*, "an impoverished prostitute"
el inocente, "an innocent person"	*la inocente*, "a virgin"
un doncel, "a young nobleman"	*una doncella*, "a virgin"

In addition, when feminine suffixes are added to some masculine occupational terms, the derived word does not refer to a woman of that profession but rather to a wife, such as *el medico* (doctor) but *la medica* (doctor's wife) (Hellinger, 1989, p. 285).

Both the German and Spanish examples demonstrate a similar theme: men are neutral, generic, or usual persons, whereas women are derived, secondary, or restricted.

Russian

Analysis of the semantics of male/female kinship terms in Russian also demonstrates a restricted representation of females. Roots occurring in kin terms can be extended to name other people or entities, but different patterns obtain for female and male forms. Associated derivatives from female roots generally refer to domesticity and/or sexuality, whereas those derived from male bases have wider "semantic space," referring to activities or qualities of a more social character (Wobst, 1981, pp. 42–43). In addition, female words tend to acquire negative connotations, most strongly so when applied to men, whereas male terms are positive even when applied to women. For example, roots for "grandmother," *bab-*, and "grandfather," *dyed-*, can both be extended to nonkin (note that in reference to one's grandmother, the root word *baba* is never used; rather, it always appears with a diminutive suffix in *babushka*). Words derived from *bab-* have meanings including "old woman," "wife" (in slang), and scornfully "stout or loutish woman." Words with *dyed-*, on the other hand, are "ancestors" or "village elders" (Wobst, 1981, pp. 36–38).

The mother/father pair, *mat-/otyets-*, also is extended. Words with *mat-* include "maternity" and "motherhood" in positive tone, but others can be applied to males as terms of abuse. Words derived from *otyets* mean "protector, benefactor, leader, founder, and ancestors" (Wobst, 1981, pp. 38–39).

Finally, the roots for sister, *syestr-*, and brother, *brat-*, demonstrate now-familiar patterns. *Syestr-* has limited use, appearing only as a kin term and in restricted contexts as a female friend. In contrast, *brat-* has rich connotations, including "companionship, friendship, someone who loves people as brothers" (note comparable forms in English, "brotherhood," "brotherly love"). In addition, the root *brat-* can combine with a feminine suffix and be used to refer to females with positive affect, as in expressions for "a sister who is a friend" or a greeting to any woman (Wobst, 1981, p. 39).

Japanese

In Japanese, gender hierarchy within the family is revealed by forms of address employed between spouses and by words used to refer to one's spouse. Husbands typically address their wives by either of two second-person pronouns: *omae* or *kimi*. *Omae* is the pronoun generally used by status superiors to addressees of lower status; *kimi* is used to subordinates or intimates but not to superiors (Lee, 1976, p. 993). A wife's choice of second-person pronoun in addressing her husband differs from the one she receives. A wife generally employs the pronoun *anata* that is used by lower-status people to higher-status addressees (pp. 996–997). The differential usage of second-person pronouns therefore carries symbolic messages of status. A woman addresses her husband with pronouns that indicate her lower status, whereas a man uses a familiar, plain form of address and a pronoun indicating his higher position. Pronouns used by men and women to their spouses are also employed to other interlocutors. Men choose pronouns depending on status relationships: *omae* to inferiors, *kimi* to inferiors or equals, and *anata* to superiors. Women generally address all interlocutors with *anata*, thus symbolizing women's social subordination (Shibamoto, 1987, p. 29).

In addition to pronominal choices, Motoko Lee (1976) states that Japanese men frequently address their wives by their first name alone; in contrast, if a wife addresses her husband by his first name, she adds the honorific suffix *-san*. Husbands may occasionally add *-san* to their wife's name as a marker of emphatic politeness, but such usage by a male speaker is not common (Clark, personal communication, 1996). Clark notes, however, that Japanese spouses rarely address their mates with first names but rather employ the kinship terms *otoosan* ("father"; said by wife to husband) and *okaasan* ("mother"; said by husband to wife). Although in formal contexts, the use of parental kin terms and status-differentiated pronouns can signal distance and dominance/subordination, in other contexts, pronominal choices used by Japanese husbands and wives may indicate intimacy.

In Japanese society, bowing is a nonverbal sign of respect.

Japanese patterns for reference about one's spouse indicate gender differentiation, as do patterns of address. For referring to his wife, a man has a number of options (Lee, 1976):

> *kanai* (derived from *ka* "home, family, house" + *nai* "inside"); *tuma* (also meaning "garnishing vegetable served with raw fish; side plank supporting the main part of a roof"); *nyoboo* ("assistant, secondary person"); *gusai* ("stupid wife"); *uti no yatu* (derived from *uti* "my home" + *no* "of" + *yatu* "fellow"). (pp. 993–995)

According to Lee (1976), these words and expressions connote a secondary person, restricted to the home or participating in a subsidiary capacity. *Gusai*, "stupid wife," is employed pragmatically to humble a speaker when conversing with someone of higher status. Its use is not meant to insult the speaker's wife but rather to honor the addressee by demeaning a person (wife) associated with the speaker (p. 995). The last expression, *uti no yatu*, is an impolite or informal reference to a person of lower status.

Japanese wives can refer to husbands with the expression *uti no hito*, literally "person of my house." This phrase carries polite meaning, used by a lower-status speaker to label a superior. Wives also refer to their husbands as *shujin*, "master." Finally, Lee (1976) reports two humorous words used by women: *teishu*, "master of my house," and *yakoroku*, "my lodger." She states that these words have sarcastic implications but does not specify the contexts of their use (p. 998). Clark (personal communication, 1996) notes that a

Japanese woman may refer to her retired husband as *nureochiba*, meaning "wet, sodden leaves," a term that implies that the husband gets in the way and is difficult to move.

Taken as a group, the differentiated pronouns, nouns, and expressions used by Japanese wives and husbands clearly demonstrate gender stratification, directly symbolizing the subordinate status of women but also expressing spousal hierarchy and antagonism.

Mohawk

Mohawk is a language spoken by people belonging to the Mohawk Nation, one of the original five nations of the Iroquois Confederacy (see chapter 3 for a discussion of Iroquoian culture). In contrast to European practices restricting feminine referents, the Mohawk language elaborates feminine semantics. In Mohawk, there are three pronouns for third-person singular subjects, occurring as prefixes in verbs. One prefix, {la-}, is used exclusively for males (human and animal); another, {ka-}, denotes female animals, some female humans, and all inanimate objects; and a third, {ye-}, refers to some female humans and all indefinite or generalized persons (Bonvillain 1973, pp. 85–87), as in "he's planting it," "she's planting it," and "she, someone is planting it."

Pronouns for human females are semantically complex. Speakers can use either {ka-} or {ye-}; choice is dependent on context, attitude, and the relationship to the addressee. Most people employ {ye-} in reference to older women, relatives, and/or any woman toward whom the speaker has a feeling of respect or admiration. {Ka-} is used more often as either a form neutral for attitude or actually negative in affect.

Mohawk speakers use these pronouns somewhat idiosyncratically because there are no absolute grammatical rules governing their realization. Alternatives are selected for pragmatic and contextual reasons. This seems not to have always been the case. Samples of Mohawk spoken in the early twentieth century indicate a different, presumably traditional, pattern in which the semantics of feminine pronouns entail a focus on female reproductive capacities. The pronoun {ye-} was evidently used in reference to both young girls and older women, while {ka-} was selected for women in their child-bearing years. The Mohawk language, then, directly symbolized the distinctiveness of women's reproduction. Remembering that the significance of linguistic form can be understood in specific contexts of culture, Mohawk emphasis on reproduction as denoted by the pronouns was a positive reflection of women's status.

As discussed in Chapter 3, the Mohawk kinship system is based on matrilineal clans (that is, descent is traced through women). In addition to their prominence in kinship groups, women had important economic roles in traditional Mohawk culture. They were food producers, providing their families with basic crops of corn, beans, and squash. These crops are symbolized as females, referred to as "The Three Sisters" or "Our Life Supporters." In Mohawk mythology, they are derived from the body of a female mythic personage. Given religious and economic concerns with fertility of the land, kinship groups and the Mohawk Nation itself, special note of women's child-bearing role reflected the acknowledged contributions of women to society.

Pragmatic meanings of {ye-} and {ka-} have changed, the former now employed to mark respect or positive feeling toward a female, probably as a result of its traditional use for elder women. Although some of the meanings of feminine pronouns have shifted, the linguistic attention to females and the use of {ye-} to mark indefinite or generic person can be interpreted as continuing a valued symbolization of women in Mohawk culture.

Summary

Although contrasts in the communicative behavior of men and women occur in many societies, the degree of difference and the specific linguistic patterns that display gender distinctions vary cross-culturally. In some languages, rules of gender-exclusive forms prevail. These rules clearly mark and symbolize the separation of women and men. However, a more common pattern is that of preferences for linguistic alternatives, demonstrated through frequencies in use of a range of stylistic variants, including sounds, words, or grammatical constructions.

The existence of differences in men's and women's speech in many languages calls for explanations based on the social roles of women and men and the extent of hierarchy in their relationships. In societies where men have more prestige and rights than women, language and style are used to underscore male privilege. In societies where gender equality exists, communicative behavior and meanings accord value and worth to both genders. Language is thus revealed as a partner in generating cultural models of females and males. It encapsulates images of their "proper" status and behavior by both reflecting in form and reinforcing through use a culture's entrenched symbols of gender.

References

BODINE, ANN. 1975a. "Androcentrism in prescriptive grammar." *Language in Society*, 4: 129–146.
———. 1975b. "Sex differentiation in language." In *Language and Sex* (ed. Barrie Thorne and Nancy Henley). Rowley, MA: Newbury House, pp. 130–151.
BOGORAS, WALDEMAR. 1922. "Chukchee." In *Handbook of American Indian Languages*. Washington D.C.: Bureau of American Ethnology, Bulletin no. 40, part 2, pp. 631–903.
BONVILLAIN, NANCY. 1973. *A Grammar of Akwesasne Mohawk*. Ottawa: National Museum of Canada, Mercury Series no. 8.
BROWN, PENELOPE, and STEPHEN LEVINSON. 1987. *Politeness: Some Universals in Language Usage*. New York: Cambridge University Press.
CAMERON, DEBORAH, F. MCALINDEN, AND K. O'LEARY. 1988. "Lakoff in context: The social and linguistic functions of tag questions." In *Women in their Speech Communities* (ed. Jennifer Coates and Deborah Cameron) London: Longman, pp. 74–93.
CHESHIRE, JENNY. 1982. "Linguistic variation and social function." In *Sociolinguistic Variation in Speech Communities* (ed. Suzanne Romaine). London: Arnold, pp. 153–166.
CROSBY, FAYE, AND LINDA NYQUIST. 1977 "The female register: An empirical study of Lakoff's hypotheses." *Language in Society*, 6: 313–322.

DUBOIS, BETTY LOU, AND ISABEL CROUCH. 1975. "The question of tag-questions in women's speech: They don't really use more of them, do they?" *Language in Society*, 4: 289–294.

EDELSKY, CAROL. 1981. "Who's got the floor?" *Language in Society*, 10: 383–421.

FISCHER, JOHN. 1958. "Social influences on the choice of a linguistic variant." *Word*, 14: 47–56.

FISHMAN, PAMELA. 1983. "Interaction: The work women do." In *Language, Gender and Society* (ed. Barrie Thorne, Nancy Henley, and Cheris Kramarae). Rowley, MA: Newbury House, pp. 89–101.

FLANNERY, REGINA. 1946. "Men's and women's speech in Gros Ventre." *International Journal of American Linguistics*, 12: 133–135.

GATSCHET, ALBERT. 1884. *A Migration Legend of the Creek Indians.* Philadelphia: Brinton.

HAAS, MARY. 1944. "Men's and women's speech in Koasati." *Language*, 20: 142–149.

HELLINGER, MARLIS. 1989. "Revising the patriarchal paradigm: Language change and feminist language policies." In *Language, Power, and Ideology* (ed. Ruth Wodak). Philadelphia: Benjamins, pp. 273–288.

HOLMES, JANET. 1984. "Hedging your bets and sitting on the fence: Some evidence for hedges as support structures." *Te Reo*, 27: 47–62.

JESPERSEN, OTTO. 1922. *Language: Its Nature, Development and Origins.* London: Allen & Unwin.

KEENAN, ELINOR OCHS. 1974. "Norm-makers and norm-breakers: Uses of speech by men and women in a Malagasy community." In *Explorations in the Ethnography of Speaking* (ed. Richard Bauman and Joel Sherzer) New York: Cambridge University Press, pp. 125–143.

KRAMER, CHERIS. 1975. "Women's speech: Separate but unequal." In *Language and Sex* (ed. Barrie Thorne and Nancy Henley). Rowley, MA: Newbury House, pp. 43–56.

LAKOFF, ROBIN. 1975. *Language and Woman's Place.* New York: Harper & Row.

LEE, MOTOKO. 1976. "The married woman's status and role in Japanese: An exploratory sociolinguistic study." *Signs: Journal of Women in Culture and Society*, 1: 991–999.

LEVINE, LEWIS, AND HARRY CROCKETT. 1967. "Speech variation in a Piedmont community: Postvocalic *r*." In *Explorations in Sociolinguistics* (ed. Stanley Lieberson). Bloomington: Indiana University Press, pp. 76–98.

MACKAY, DONALD. 1983. "Prescriptive grammar and the pronoun problem." In *Language, Gender and Society* (ed. Barrie Thorne, Nancy Henley, and Cheris Kramarae). Rowley, MA: Newbury House, pp. 38–53.

MCCONNELL-GINET, SALLY. 1983. "Intonation in a man's world." In *Language, Gender and Society* (ed. Barrie Thorne, Nancy Henley, and Cheris Kramarae). Rowley, MA: Newbury House, pp. 69–88.

MCKNIGHT, GEORGE. 1928. *Modern English in the Making.* New York: Appleton.

MILLER, CASEY, AND KATE SWIFT. 1977. *Words and Women.* New York: Anchor.

NILSEN, ALLEEN. 1977. "Sexism as shown in the English language." In *Sexism and Language* (ed. Alleen Nilsen et al.). Urbana, IL: National Council of Teachers of English, pp. 27–42.

Random House Dictionary of the English Language (2nd ed.). 1987. New York: Random House.

SAPIR, EDWARD. 1929. "Male and female forms of speech in Yana." Reprinted in *Selected Writings of Edward Sapir*, 1949 (ed. David Mandelbaum). Berkeley: University of California Press, pp. 206–212.

SATTEL, JACK. 1983. "Men, inexpressiveness and power." In *Language, Gender and Society* (ed. Barrie Thorne, Nancy Henley, and Cheris Kramarae). Rowley, MA: Newbury House, pp. 118–124.

SCHNEIDER, JOSEPH. AND SALLY HACKER. 1973. "Sex role imagery and use of the generic 'Man' in introductory texts: A case in the sociology of sociology." *American Sociologist*. 8: 12–18.

SCHULZ, MURIEL. 1975. "The semantic derogation of women." In *Language and Sex: Difference and Dominance* (ed. Barrie Thorne and Nancy Henley). Rowley, MA: Newbury House, pp. 64–75.

SCOTT, PATRICIA B. 1974. "The English language and Black womanhood: A low blow at self-esteem." *Journal of Afro-American Issues*, 2: 218–224.

SHERZER, JOEL. 1987. "A diversity of voices: Men's and women's speech in ethnographic perspective." In *Language, Gender and Sex in Comparative Perspective* (ed. Susan Philips, Susan Steele, and Christine Tanz). New York: Cambridge University Press, pp. 95–120.

SHIBAMOTO, JANET. 1987. "The womanly woman: Manipulation of stereotypical and non-stereotypical features of Japanese women's speech." In *Language, Gender and Sex in Comparative Perspective* (ed. Susan Philips, Susan Steele, and Christine Tanz). New York: Cambridge University Press, pp. 26–49.

SMITH-HEFNER, NANCY. 1988. "Women and politeness: The Javanese example." *Language in Society*, 17: 535–554.

SWACKER, MARJORIE. 1975. "The sex of the speaker as a sociolinguistic variable." In *Language and Sex: Difference and Dominance* (ed. Barrie Thorne and Nancy Henley). Rowley, MA: Newbury House, pp. 76–83.

TRUDGILL, PETER. 1972. "Sex, covert prestige and linguistic change in the urban British English of Norwich." *Language in Society*, 1: 179–195.

WEST, CANDACE, AND DON ZIMMERMAN. 1983. "Small insults: A study of interruptions in cross-sex conversations between unacquainted persons." In *Language, Gender and Society* (ed. Barrie Thorne, Nancy Henley, and Cheris Kramarae). Rowley, MA: Newbury House, pp. 103–118.

WOBST, SUSAN. 1981. "Male and female reference in semantic space in Russian." *Russian Language Journal*, 35(121–122): 35–44.

WOLFRAM, WALT. 1969. *A Sociolinguistic Description of Detroit Negro Speech*. Washington D.C.: Center for Applied Linguistics.

WOODS, NICOLA. 1988. "Talking shop: Sex and status as determinants of floor apportionment in a work setting." In *Women in Their Speech Communities* (ed. Jennifer Coates and Deborah Cameron). London: Longman, pp. 141–157.

ZIMMERMAN, DON, AND CANDACE WEST. 1975. "Sex roles, interruptions and silences in conversation." In *Language and Sex: Difference and Dominance* (ed. Barrie Thorne and Nancy Henley). Rowley, MA: Newbury House, pp. 105–129.

CHAPTER 11

Epilogue

M odels of gender entail the range of activities deemed appropriate for women and men. They entail the beliefs and attitudes people have about men's and women's abilities and inherent worthiness. The cross-cultural survey of different types of societies presented in this book allows us to ascertain tendencies in the development and maintenance of different gender models.

In analyzing gender models and behaviors, we have stressed two fundamental features of culture. First, we noted the importance of structural relations derived from economic modes of production and from systems of political integration. These material conditions of life have great consequences for the ways that women and men participate in their households and communities.

Second, we have emphasized the significance of ideological constructs in supporting and legitimating behaviors that are manifested in economic, political, and social contexts. The intersection between structural roles embedded in material conditions and ideological constructs is extremely complex. Beliefs about the world and people's place within it arise from material relations but then serve to reinforce and justify those very relations. Ideology, therefore, is a principal means of integrating diverse aspects of culture and of mediating every individual's participation in his or her society.

The potential for gender equality is perhaps greatest in foraging societies, where women and men have relatively equal access to subsistence resources and have control of their own productive activities. However, other factors may intervene to subvert the equality of women and men. For instance, strong reliance on animal sources for food may favor the development of male dominance because men are typically assigned the work of hunting. Competition with other peoples over resources, combined with threats of warfare, may also undermine women's status and justify male dominance.

Data from the Ju/'hoansi and the Inuit/Inupiat demonstrate contrasting adaptations of foraging peoples and the interrelationship between these adaptations and gender models. Among the traditional Ju/'hoansi, women and men enjoy autonomous control over resources. Although their economic tasks are differentiated, both contribute to household subsistence and plan and direct their own activities. In contrast, Inuit/Inupiat men are the principal subsistence workers in their communities. Relying heavily on hunting large animals in a dangerous environment, men are able to translate their economic importance into social worthiness. Men's social valuation is reflected in rights to dominate their wives and daughters. Men's dominance is not total but is tempered by egalitarian ethics validating some degree of autonomous functioning of both women and men.

In horticultural and pastoral societies, the potential for gender equality also exists and is, in fact, manifested in many such cultures. However, intervening factors may affect the balanced relations between men and women. Control over resources emerges again as a salient feature in determining the rights and valuations accorded to the genders. In societies such as the Iroquois, where women exerted major control over production and distribution of resources, their social and political equality with men was assured. Women's status was supported and reinforced by social and religious ideologies stressing their productive and reproductive value. In contrast, among the Yanomamo, men's control over every aspect of economic production is combined with their political monopoly and their social supremacy. These structural features are reflected in men's aggressive dominance over women. The economic, political, and social relations of men's dominance and women's subordination are justified by religious symbols and teachings.

Other factors affecting the quality of relations between men and women include the need to assert control over a large population base and the need to establish cohesive and integrative mechanisms to ensure community stability. Because horticultural and pastoral societies vary in their size, this factor may or may not be significant in any given group. In small communities, societal integration is relatively informal and requires little intervention or management. But in larger communities, such management emerges as a necessity. In these cases, men have usually assumed responsibilities to direct and control official political roles. Yet data concerning the Iroquois demonstrate that women may exert public influence in complex political systems when they have high social status derived from their economic roles and legitimated by ideological constructs.

Data from many West African societies, such as the Igbo, provide additional evidence of the importance of control over economic production in creating social rights. Although Igbo men assert authority in political organization and men's dominance is idealized and justified through religious ideology, Igbo women are able to counter men's prerogatives because of their control over household and market economies. Women's roles as traders in village and regional markets give them the ability to act independently in their own households and communities. Women who engage in trade are thus able to free themselves from social and ideological constraints that generally legitimate men's authority.

In societies that develop complex mechanisms of political control leading to hierarchial structural relations among segmented sectors of the population, the potential for gender equality is diminished. In these cultures, men usually assume most roles in directing economic production and distribution, as well as in managing the mechanisms of political integration. Chiefdoms and states are characterized by systems of social stratification that often imply or make use of inequalities between men and women. This tendency is usually greater in states than in chiefdoms because states typically entail a greater degree of hierarchical ordering and a greater need to control large populations.

Men's dominance in chiefdoms and states is often further enhanced by the necessity of protecting communities against external warfare and of waging war against other peoples in competition over resources and over territory. Examination of the development of a chiefdom into a state in the Tongan Islands provides insights into the ways that increasing social and political stratification creates, intensifies, and exploits inequalities between women and men. As Tongan men assumed greater control over their kin groups and their communities, women's rights were subverted. The ideological value accorded to women's work and to their productive goods was concomitantly undermined.

The interconnection between hierarchial ordering and gender inequality is illustrated in many agricultural states throughout the world. India and China are two examples of societies characterized by stratification in social and political functioning and by intense male dominance reflected in men's control over their wives and children. Women's unworthiness is given ideological justification through entrenched philosophical and religious teachings.

Analysis of the development of industrial production in the United States indicates that preexisting inequalities between women and men can be exploited to further the economic and political control asserted by men on the basis of both gender and class. Capitalist production did not create gender inequality but, rather, used it to exploit women's labor in the creation of profit. Gender inequality was, and is, then used to foster competition between male and female workers. This competition relegates women to secondary roles in the economy. It affects relations in the household as well. Women's subsidiary economic roles are used to justify men's social dominance.

Although gender roles and relations in any given culture can be analyzed synchronically, it is crucial to understand the forces of change that transform people's behavior and their concepts of themselves and others. The possibility of change always exists and is, indeed, what makes culture a dynamic rather than static system. Gender relations can become more or less equal or hierarchical depending on the specific context and operative forces experienced by each group.

European colonization has had a tremendous impact on the gender roles and constructs of indigenous peoples in many areas of the world. For example, as native peoples of North America became enmeshed in trade with

Europeans, fundamental transformations of their economic systems led to concomitant shifts in the previous equality between women and men. European traders preferred to deal with native men and thus ignored and subverted the economic contributions of native women. The productive value and control over economic decisions traditionally exerted by Haida and Tlingit women was diminished. Among cultures of the Plains, men's control over buffalo hunting increased in importance as trade relations with Europeans and Americans became the focus of Plains economies. At the same time, women became subsidiary workers under the direction and management of their fathers and husbands. As this process deepened, women's autonomy was restricted and their social status was devalued.

European missionaries also had a direct and indirect influence on transforming gender relations in indigenous societies. French Jesuits working in northeastern North America among the Montagnais, Naskapi, and Huron were determined to mold relations between native husbands and wives in accordance with European principles of patriarchal domination and women's submission. In Tonga, British Wesleyan missionaries pursued the same goals and produced similar results. Native peoples gradually adopted European values that created or intensified men's prerogatives in their households and communities.

Finally, European colonization affected indigenous political systems by legitimating native men's authority and by diminishing the public political roles previously enjoyed by women. Among the Iroquois, women's voice in selecting chiefs and in contributing to public discussion was muted or silenced. In many African societies, women chiefs were bypassed in favor of male competitors. And in Tonga, as male leaders assumed greater political power and amassed greater wealth, the advice and influence wielded by their sisters were ignored. A sister's authority in her brother's family was eventually legally suppressed.

Despite the weighty evidence of change from egalitarian to hierarchical gender relations, other possibilities exist. Tendencies toward gender equality can, and have, emerged in modern contexts. Governmental intervention in India and China, for instance, has led to recognition of the injustices suffered by women in these intensely patriarchical and hierarchical societies. Although actual social equality between women and men does not yet exist in either nation, moves in that direction have been undertaken and have had varying degrees of success.

In the United States, the productive contributions of women in wage work have led to some shifts in familial relations and in public perceptions of women's rights. Calls for equal treatment in the workplace have been linked with calls for equal social status in the community and the household. In developing nations of the world, possibilities exist for the emancipation of women from patriarchal family structures by their emergence into public economic and political life. In many countries in both the developed and developing world, some women and men are trying to promote social, economic, and political strategies that will create conditions and relations of equality between the genders for the benefit of all people.

A critical factor in impeding social change, however, derives from ideological constructs concerning gender models. Traditional beliefs about the proper place of women and men and about their inherent abilities and interests may slow the pace of social, economic, and political change. Although these beliefs do not present insurmountable barriers to change, it is important to understand their impact. In India and China, for example, millennia of religious and philosophical teachings have guided people to think of men as superior and women as inferior. Men's prerogatives include not only the right to their own autonomy but also the right to control and dominate their wives and children. These concepts, enshrined in religious symbols and messages, change very slowly despite economic and political transformations giving women greater access to public roles.

In the United States, religious and secular constructs are also used to justify the continuation of male dominance in the household and public arenas, again despite the real economic contributions of women to their families and communities.

The relations between ideology and behavior are extremely complex. Although ideological systems develop in response to structural conditions, changes in these structural conditions usually occur much more rapidly than do changes in the ideological constructs validating them. People's beliefs may continue despite changes in the contexts that produced them. Therefore, people sometimes have difficulty accepting a new social order and new social concepts.

Additional difficulties in changing ideological constructs derive from the fact that they are often embedded in two powerful systems. First, religious teachings set forth a social world that is given supernatural origin and/or sanction. Believers are extremely reluctant to accept transformations of such beliefs because doing so would implicitly or explicitly question basic concepts of their religion.

Second, ideological constructs are embedded in and expressed through daily interactions. Individuals usually experience their own behavior as normal and natural rather than as motivated and mediated by cultural constraints. They are therefore largely unaware of the underlying rationales influencing their actions and responses. Language plays a part in this process by transmitting cultural symbols and values on a nonconscious level. These symbols then become experienced as inherent features of human consciousness. The fact that consciousness itself is socially derived is not recognized.

Analyses of gender roles and constructs in societies throughout the world demonstrate the diversity of possibilities of human life. People are not forever bound by traditional beliefs and practices. They can accept changes in their actions, and they can adopt new ideological concepts relevant to their own experience. Just as we can uncover and understand the transformative dynamics that have occurred in the past, we can also witness and appreciate changes occurring in the present. And we can look to the future for further consequences of ongoing processes.

Glossary

Affinal bonds Kinship relationships based on marriage.

Affines Relatives by marriage (in-iaws).

Agriculture Economic mode using intensive farming techniques; agriculturalists expend a great deal of labor and/or technology in food production.

Autonomy Ability to act independently, make decisions for oneself.

Avunculocal residence Pattern of residence whereby boys go to live with one of their mother's brothers; occurs in some, but not all, matrilineal societies.

Band Small, loosely organized group of people; bands are politically autonomous and have minimal leadership; most bands have economies based on foraging.

Bilateral kinship System of descent that recognizes relationship to both the mother's and father's kin.

Caste System of social stratification that assigns people to a grouping (caste) at birth; castes are hierarchically ordered; members of a given caste are usually not able to alter their status and generally marry within their group.

Chiefdom Society characterized by an established system of leadership and inheritance of political office; the leader or "chief" represents his or her kin group and locality; the chief has a role in organizing production and redistribution of goods; some form of social stratification or ranking separates social groups.

Clan Named groups having some corporate interests; a group of people who believe they are related; clan members cannot trace actual relationship to all members; clans are usually exogamous.

Endogamy Marriage pattern in which members of a group or locality marry within the group or locality.

Ethnocentrism Attitudes that one's own cultural practices and beliefs are superior to those of other societies.

Exogamy Marriage pattern that prohibits marriage between members of a group or locality.

Extended family Family unit consisting of three or more generations.

Foraging Economic mode based on obtaining foods from naturally occurring resources; foraging usually includes hunting, fishing, and gathering of plants.

Gender constructs/gender models Cultural beliefs about gender, including appropriate roles of women and men, relationships between women and men, and social values accorded to women and men.

Gender equality System in which both women and men have access to equal rights, prestige, autonomy, and social value; women and men may have different roles, but both are considered worthy.

Gender inequality System characterized by the denial of autonomy, rights, and prestige to one group of people based solely on their gender.

Hierarchy System of social inequality in which some individuals or groups have greater power, prestige, and wealth than others.

Horticulture Economic mode using relatively simple farming techniques; labor and technology are not intensively utilized.

Ideology Cultural beliefs about the world and people; cultural values and symbols.

Indigenous people Group of people who are native to a country or territory and who have been colonized or overwhelmed by an intruding group.

Lineage Group of people who can trace actual descent from a common ancestor.

Male dominance Ability of men to control women's behavior; attitudes of male superiority and denial of women's worthiness.

Matriarchy Social system in which women have exclusive control over power and wealth in the society.

Matrilineal descent Kinship system in which relationships are traced through women; children belong to their mother's kin group.

Matrilocal residence Pattern of postmarital residence whereby a couple lives with the wife's kin.

Monogamy Pattern of marriage in which one man and one woman are married to each other.

Norms Patterns of socially acceptable behavior and beliefs shared by members of a community.

Nuclear family Family unit consisting of parents and their children.

Parallel descent Kinship system in which women trace descent through women, and men trace descent through men.

Pastoralism Economic mode based on keeping herds or flocks of animals.

Patriarchy Social system in which men have exclusive control over power and wealth in the society.

Patrilineal descent Kinship system in which relationships are traced through men; children belong to their father's kin group.

Patrilocal residence Pattern of postmarital residence whereby a couple lives with the husband's natal household.

Polity Community that is united by a system of political organization having leadership positions and mechanisms for decision making and social control.

Polyandry Marriage pattern in which a woman marries more than one man.

Polygyny Marriage pattern in which a man marries more than one woman.

Primogeniture Pattern of inheritance whereby the eldest child inherits from his or her parents.

Rank Classification in which people do not have equal rights, prestige, value, or access to resources and opportunities.

Rites of passage Rituals that mark individual's stage in the cycle of life, including birth, puberty, marriage, and death.

Segmentation Social process of separating a community into groups based on various criteria, such as class, gender, ethnicity, and race.

State Society characterized by a high degree of organization, centralization of political authority, defined political officers and administrators, a police and/or military force, bureaucracy, tribute or taxation, control over boundaries, laws, and formalized social controls.

Stratification Social system in which people do not have equal rights, prestige, value, and access to resources and opportunities.

Subsistence Means by which people obtain their food (foraging, horticulture, agriculture).

Taboo Rule of behavior that prohibits specific actions; if someone violates a taboo, he or she risks a specific supernatural punishment.

Tribe Society that unites (with varying degrees of cohesion) local communities within a recognized named group; tribes have some recognized leaders, but these people do not hold formal political office; social and/or political unity may be limited to the level of villages or may combine villages into networks of decision making and cooperation.

Usufruct rights Rights of individuals to use the land and other resources held in common by their kinship group (by their family, lineage, or clan).

Uxorilocal residence Postmarital residence rule whereby the couple lives with the wife's kin.

Virilocal residence Postmarital residence rule whereby the couple lives with the husband's kin.

Photo Credits

Photos: Page 30: Lee/Anthro-Photo File; page 37: Lawrence Migdale/Lawrence Migdale/Pix; page 72: Grames/Bilderberg/Peter Arnold, Inc.; page 84: F. G. Speck/ National Museum of the American Indian/Smithsonian Institution; page 103: United Nations; page 165: Novastock/The Stock Connection; page 173: Mark Avery/AP Wide World Photos; page 178: Scala/Art Resource, N.Y.; page 180: Library of Congress; page 289: Marjory Shostale/Anthro-Photo File; page 289: Irven DeVore/Anthro Photo File; page 309: Alan Oddie/PhotoEdit Inc.; page 339: Innervisions; page 340: Michael S. Yamashita/Corbis/Bettmann; page 354: Holos/Getty Images.

Index